The Purposeful Graduate

The Purposeful
GRADUATE

Why Colleges Must Talk to Students about Vocation

Tim Clydesdale

The University of Chicago Press

Chicago and London

Tim Clydesdale is professor of sociology at the College of New Jersey. He is the author of *The First Year Out: Understanding American Teens after High School.*

The University of Chicago Press, Chicago 60637
The University of Chicago Press, Ltd., London
© 2015 by The University of Chicago
All rights reserved. Published 2015.
Printed in the United States of America

24 23 22 21 20 19 18 17 16 15   1 2 3 4 5

ISBN-13: 978-0-226-23634-6 (cloth)
ISBN-13: 978-0-226-23648-3 (e-book)
DOI: 10.7208/chicago/9780226236483.001.0001

Library of Congress Cataloging-in-Publication Data

Clydesdale, Timothy T. (Timothy Thomas), 1965– author.
  The purposeful graduate : why colleges must talk to students about vocation /
Tim Clydesdale.
     pages cm
  Includes bibliographical references and index.
ISBN 978-0-226-23634-6 (cloth : alk. paper) — ISBN 978-0-226-23648-3 (e-book)
1. Career education—United States. 2. Religious education—United States.
3. College students—Recruiting—United States. I. Title.
  LC1037.5.C594 2015
  370.113—dc23

                                                          2014033596

To the late Ivan J. Fahs
Professor, mentor, and friend

CONTENTS

ACKNOWLEDGMENTS

This book would not exist had it not been for the cooperation, support, and encouragement of hundreds of individuals. My first thanks go to the students, alumni, faculty, staff, and administrators who graciously agreed to interviews, survey participation, or conversations that helped me better understand this eighty-eight-campus, eight-year, and $225 million initiative of the Lilly Endowment Inc. I especially thank the campus project directors and their indefatigable assistants who hosted me so graciously. I cannot identify these individuals, and simply hope that they know that their kind cooperation not only made this evaluation possible but made it a rewarding and pleasant undertaking as well.

I am equally indebted to my evaluation staff—transcriptionists extraordinaire Karen Myers and Laura Hoseley; invaluable research assistants Anna Bradshaw, Virginia Grisham, Matthew Keating, Ashley Toms, and Matthew Warren; talented interviewers Lenore Johnson, Janet Kennedy, Chuck Stokes, and Jon Woodring; and the always helpful staff of ResearchTalk: Ray Maietta and Jeff Petruzzelli. Of inestimable assistance were two former students whom I am pleased to call my colleagues and friends—Keith Brown and Patricia Tevington. Keith is now assistant professor of sociology at Saint Joseph's University in Philadelphia, but he graciously accepted a coethnographer role while completing his sociology dissertation. Keith did more than collect data, however; he offered suggestions, shared critiques, and conveyed hunches that were invaluable. Patricia is now a PhD student in sociology at the University of Pennsylvania, but as an undergraduate research assistant, then as my postbaccalaureate project manager and research associate, she was a one-woman data-collecting superhero—locating research participants around the globe, overseeing an enormous qualitative textbase, and merging nine campus surveys into a single, easy-to-use SPSS database. Most recently, Patricia has been a godsend as a close reader and critic of this book; she has saved me from a host of errors, and done this exceptional work despite the heavy load of her own studies and research program. The University of Pennsylvania is fortunate to have Patricia as a PhD student; she will prove herself to be an extraordinary scholar and educator.

Backing up this evaluation staff have been two dozen dedicated student assistants. I learned much from them and because of them. Special thanks go to Lindsey Aloia, Susan Cosgrove, Joanna DeLeon, Mena Gawargi, Frank Janks, Jen Slavin, Justin Tompkins, my entire 2006 SOC404 qualitative methods tutorial, and three dedicated transcribers: Bridgette McGuire, Deb Mitra, and Amanda Tobin.

I received gracious support from the entire staff of the Lilly Endowment Inc., and particularly Chris Coble, Gayle Doucey, and Craig Dykstra. I am also grateful to the wider endowment circle of Kathleen Cahalan, Kim Maphis Early, Rebecca Eberhart, Della Stanley Green, Jim Lewis, Elizabeth Lynn, Diane Millis, Susie Quern Pratt, Shirley Roels, Melissa Wiginton, and Karla Van Zee. These scholars and practitioners helped me understand essential components of this initiative, of its history, and of its wider impact.

At my own institution, the College of New Jersey, I acknowledge the multitasking grant-accounting wunderkind Amy LoPrinzi, without whom I would still be digging out from under a mountain of paperwork. Other staff and administrators also went beyond the call of duty to assist me: Carol Bresnahan, Steve Briggs, Barbara Cape, Deborah Compte, Emily Weiss Dodd,

Terry Epperson, Matthew Golden, Chris Larthey, John Marcy, Diane Minger, Ceil O'Callaghan, Beth Paul, Lloyd Ricketts, Benjamin Rifkin, Angela Sgroi, and Intervarsity staffer Laura Vellenga. I am particularly thankful to department chairs Rachel Adler and Diane Bates, whose own workload increased because of my half-time assignment to this project. And I am grateful for the support of local colleagues: David Blake, Elizabeth Borland, Jody Brodsky, Daniel Crofts, the late Alan Dawley, Hilary DelPrete, Karen Dubrule, Lynn Gazley, David Holleran, Regina Kenen, Rebecca Li, Michael Robertson, Nino Scarpati, and Miriam Shakow.

Collegiality knows no boundaries, and I gratefully acknowledge the support of Rebecca Burwell, Ron Burwell, Cheryl Crawford, William Damon, Katie Day, Andrew Delbanco, Melinda Denton, Robert Dixon, David Evans, Kathleen Garces-Foley, the late Dean Hoge, Richard Hope, Paul Kennedy, James Lang, Albert Lee, Kathleen Mahoney, Elizabeth Marquardt, Gerardo Marti, Michael Mason, Matt McAlack, Derek Melleby, Sharon Miller, Douglas Mitchell, Ken Myers, William Pannapacker, Sharon Dalos Parks, Allison Payne, Lisa Pearce, Anthony Pogorelc, Mark Regnerus, John Schmalzbauer, Andrew Singleton, Christian Smith, Molly Sutphen, David Voas, Ruth Webber, Betty Weiler, Robert Wuthnow, and James Youniss. I particularly thank William Sullivan, whose brilliant work in *Habits of the Heart* helped draw me to sociology some twenty-five years ago, and whom I am now pleased to call a colleague. Bill read and offered cogent critiques of every chapter in this book, and I am grateful for his suggestions and encouragement. And I gratefully acknowledge the support and encouragement of my editor, Elizabeth Branch Dyson; without her sustained efforts, this book would not have ever reached readers like you.

Many friends offered support and good-natured ribbing as I slowly made my way through this project. I am thankful for the support of Jules and Virginia Grisham, Jeff and Rachel MacKay, Brian and JoAnn Smith, and Steve and Tricia Wittekind. To have one good friend is to be rich indeed; to have eight is beyond calculation.

My father did not live to see this book published, but he did hold my first book in his hands, and he imparted the work ethic that helped me write that book, this one, and any more that will come. My mother remains an ardent supporter, but will love me even if I never write another thing—moms are great that way. Larry and Betty Suydam, beloved in-laws, have been generous and understanding, taking my children out on adventures so that I could continue to write, and patiently listening to me talk about this project day after day, year after year.

Writing this from a home office in a house with excellent acoustics made me appreciate the engineers who designed my noise-canceling headphones, and appreciate even more my family who endured too many mornings being quieter than they preferred, and too many other days out of the house so that I could write without interruption. Eight years is a long time in the lives of children; I went from counting their years with single digits to double digits, and from hearing the squeals of children to the lower pitches and house-shaking thuds of teenagers. It has been my special privilege to watch Jonah and Grace discover diverse interests these past eight years, and my prayer is that they will discern a clear sense of their own calling. As for their mother, Dawn, my dearest friend and companion, words cannot express the debt of gratitude I feel for her patient endurance and constant encouragement. Loving me is not an easy calling (ask the friends above), but Dawn has been unwaveringly faithful and patient. More than the hundreds of thousands of evaluation dollars from the Lilly Endowment, more than the thousands who participated in this evaluation project, more than the scores who supported me and the dozens who directly assisted me, this book exists because of her generosity and love. I shall be grateful to her and for her the rest of my days.

To hear hundreds speak so vulnerably about their own exploration of calling and purpose inevitably leads to one's own reflection about these matters. And perhaps because I am a sociologist, or simply because I am human, those reflections led me to consider the significant relationships and pivotal individuals who inspired recalibration of my own life trajectory. Several of those pivotal individuals were my educators: men and women of extraordinary skill and intelligence who chose to invest their time and talent not in personal gain but in nurturing the talents of the next generation. I would not be the person I am today had it not been for their timely challenges and warm support. There is one educator, however, who had a singular influence on me. He identified my skills in social research before I recognized them, encouraged my scholarly writing, helped me discern a passion for social justice, and embodied all three. I often referred to him as a second father, as his influence formed me as a scholar, educator, and citizen, and continues to do so. True education is inevitably formative, a lesson clearly demonstrated to me during this project, but that Ivan understood in the very core of his being. I dedicate this book in loving memory of Professor Ivan J. Fahs; may his passionate scholarship, pursuit of justice, and resolute faith endure for generations.

PREFACE

We are in sore need of some good news in American higher education. Evidence continues to pour in that college students are not only "academically adrift," but that even after graduating from college as "aspiring adults," they are "adrift" and oftentimes "lost in transition." The traditional goals of adulthood, such as beginning a career and finding a long-term partner, to say nothing of attaining financial independence or creating successful households, now consume the better part of one's twenties—if they are accomplished at all.[1] And while those in higher education can protest that global competition and macrocultural change deserve the lion's share of blame for drifting young adults, our voices are smothered by charts showing tuition increases at twice the rate of inflation and drowned out by video clips decrying the price of college, with President (and former law professor) Barack Obama's 2014 State of the Union complaint about tuition prices and student debt among the most prominent. It feels as if we in higher education got yanked out of our comfortable library chairs and thrown into a public boxing ring, where a grinning heavyweight champion unleashed his signature left jab and right cross sequence across our unshielded faces. Staggering against the ropes, our appeals to the referee denied, we *have* to find a new strategy—and fast. Is there anything from that self-defense class we took decades ago during our first semester of college that we can still use? I believe there is. There is a maneuver once part of many collegians' education that, updated and redeployed, can interrupt our challenger's blows and sway audience members to our side, buying us crucial time while we bring the rest of our game up to the level of our competition.

Or, to describe it sociologically rather than analogically, it is apparent that American higher education confronts significant macroinstitutional pressures, brought on by global economic shifts that have kept graduates' median incomes flat, and by macrocultural changes that have diversified and extended paths to adulthood. In theory, these pressures have little bearing on higher education. But because the comfortable and secure career paths once readily available to college graduates have grown elusive, America's public and its many populist pundits—incapable of transcending individually reductionist analysis—blame higher education for overpriced and inadequate training of students. That many American college graduates do lack basic academic skills, and that tuition has outpaced inflation, is cited as proof of higher education's failure. What this analysis ignores, however, is that comfortable and secure jobs would be elusive *even if* college tuition were halved and *even if* every college graduate posted proficient verbal, quantitative, and analytical scores; the era of global competition will not end no matter how skilled America's college graduates become, nor will graduates' extended exploration of lifestyle options cease with a new tide of widespread career opportunities. American colleges and universities must be responsibly administered, and their graduates must possess broad academic proficiencies; I do not dispute these assertions in the slightest. But there is an equally important task that institutions of higher education, if they wish to maintain their autonomy and core structure, *must* undertake: intentional and systematic assistance to students in identifying talents, clarifying values, and developing the grit that will sustain them on the long path to productive, global citizenship.

Colleges and universities have come to embrace a supply-side model of student learning and development that is marginally effective at best: that is, they supply an intellectually vibrant environment offering a variety of academic pathways, on the assumption that admitted students will be able and eager to make the most of this learning environment. This widespread assumption has made an—well, we know how the rest of that saying goes. Colleges and universities must counterbalance this supply-side model with demand-creating initiatives, and they need to do so before they lose consciousness under the champion boxer's blows.

To be sure, a portion of students nationwide arrives eager to make the most of the rich learning environment we call college. There is certainly no shortage of capable and eager applicants for PhD study or university careers, for instance.[2] But for the vast majority of the nation's undergraduates, college is a four- to six-year hazing they call "meeting degree requirements," endured because graduates presumably obtain comfortable and secure incomes. With the hollowness of that presumption now growing apparent, those institutions most vulnerable to consumers' cost-benefit analyses (i.e., private, nonelite colleges and universities) have left no option unexplored in their effort to fill seats—discounting prices, increasing part-time instructor usage and full-time instructor teaching loads, expanding online courses and professional majors, even offering incentives sadly reminiscent of car and appliance dealers (e.g., 20 percent price cuts, free housing for new students, four-year graduation guarantees).[3] Public institutions, meanwhile, confront their own challenges, as legislatures and governors back them into corners by reducing funding, blocking tuition increases, demanding enrollment increases, and specifying graduation rates. The pressure on higher education to prioritize workforce preparation has never been greater, and combined with the tepid accomplishments of its supply-side model of student development and learning, can leave even the most intrepid proponent of the idea of *higher* (i.e., liberal and transformative) education despondent.

What, then, is this good news for higher education that I offer? It is this: when colleges and universities meaningfully engage their organizational histories to launch sustained conversations with students about questions of purpose, the result is a rise in overall campus engagement and recalibration of postcollege trajectories that set graduates on journeys of significance and impact. Fostering academically capable, socially responsible, and resilient college graduates is neither a Herculean nor costly undertaking, and such graduates, in broad numbers, not only embody the accomplishment of higher education's core mission but also supply its only indisputable response to the maelstrom of higher education critics and regulatory intrusion. They are our best hope for disrupting the left jab (rising costs) and right cross (weak student skills) of our champion opponent, because they represent a line of broadly skilled, thoughtfully engaged, and purposeful college graduates marching through the middle of the boxing ring — with some being the champion's own kin. Most encouraging of all, this undertaking does not require acquisition of an alien skill, for "sustained conversations about questions of purpose" is but a method of nurturing examined living, which educators since Socrates have considered their core purpose. The method's novelty lies only in its systematic and ecumenical implementation in a campus setting; that is, in its intentional and programmatic character, and in its religious inclusivity.

To call on purpose is not to ask colleges and universities to go beyond their core mission; it is to ask that they *intentionally and systematically* implement their already-existing pledge — to produce purposeful, globally engaged citizens and to do so with broader inclusivity than they may ever have done before. Nor do colleges and universities have to reinvent the wheel, as this volume will describe a few of the many creative ways that institutions tapped their histories to launch inviting conversations with students about questions of purpose, show how these conversations in turn improved campus engagement and recalibrated student participants' postcollege trajectories, offer recommendations for implementation, and suggest resources for further investigation. Purposeful and resilient graduates will thwart our opponents' blows better than any defense of liberal education or new scholarly discovery, supplying precious time for us to restructure — on our own — our institutions for the globally competitive and diversifying era now at hand.

I am therefore optimistic about the potential that campus-based programs for the exploration of purpose hold at this moment. Much time and many resources have been devoted to developing supportive tools, texts, and media, and these are now widely available and readily adaptable. Many educators have also acquired experience and skill in engaging students in thoughtful conversations about questions of purpose, meaning, calling, or vocation (using the term most suited to their contexts). And many campuses have reaped the rewards of this exploration in the form of improved morale, reenergized educators, and thriving cocurricular life. The tools, the know-how, and the models for exploring questions of life purpose in a collegiate context now exist in variety and plentitude.

It will nonetheless require some effort and money to launch these campus programs. But I liken the effort to planting a garden with the ready advantages of a quality garden supply store and a friendly neighborhood gardening club. The first step, building consensus among campus members about the type of garden desired, is the hardest, and there are no shortcuts. No single garden will appeal to everyone, nor will most withstand an accountant's cost-benefit analysis, so it is critical to obtain broad agreement about the purposes and design of the intended garden. After that, tilling and planting can occur in quick succession. The important thing is that no one is surprised when tulips and tomatoes, rather than roses and rhubarb, begin to grow.

Gardens possess a multimillennia history because they have broad appeal, succeed in virtually any location that sustains ongoing human life, and supply both nourishment and refreshment. I recommend campus-based programming for exploration of purpose, therefore, because I have observed firsthand that these programs contribute to more mission-effective campuses, and present evidence regarding their broad appeal, organizational adaptability, and ability to supply nourishment and refreshment. Anyone who works with college students or recent college graduates will find much in this volume that will help them better understand the lives and experiences of today's college students, and much that will make their interactions with recent college graduates more effective and meaningful. Similarly, anyone who is concerned about the state of American higher education and curious about what is happening behind the gates of US colleges and universities will encounter evidence and analysis that will substantially improve their ability to make sense of higher education's challenges and promises at the start of the twenty-first century.

Slow Conversations, Broad Conversations

I was in graduate school when I first heard a scholar describe her research and its publication in book form as "part of a conversation." How on earth, I thought, could a book be remotely like a conversation? A book is a static object, wholly disembodied from its author. But I have since learned that she was absolutely right. It is a slow conversation, to be sure, but thoughtful conversations usually are. It begins with invited lectures, interviews, and blog posts, and the subsequent posing of good questions. It continues with published reviews and references in lectures and essays. And it comes full circle when other scholars engage one's writing in publications of their own. I was pleased to watch this conversation unfold following the publication of my first book, and I hope to engage it again with the publication of this book. It is a delight to see one's claims seriously considered, and I look forward to engaging conversations as readers honor me with their close readings and hard questions.

It is in that conversational spirit, then, that I situate this book in the context of four recent and duly prominent studies of American higher education. The first of these is Andrew Delbanco's *College: What It Was, Is, and Should Be*, published in 2012 by Princeton University Press; the second is Richard Arum and Josipa Roksa's *Academically Adrift: Limited Learning on College Campuses*, published in 2010 by the University of Chicago Press; the third is Richard Keeling and Richard Hersh's *We're Losing Our Minds: Rethinking American Higher Education*, published in 2011 by Palgrave Macmillan; and the fourth is Alexander W. Astin, Helen S. Astin, and Jennifer A. Lindholm's *Cultivating the Spirit: How College Can Enhance Students' Inner Lives*, published in 2010 by Jossey-Bass. Those who have read and been challenged by these works will find many connections between them and this book, and much of interest as well.

Delbanco's volume has generated the most uniformly positive praise, as he describes the travails, triumphs, and enduring purposes of liberal arts education, particularly as represented in the traditional liberal arts college. His volume stands in a long tradition of eloquent defenses of the liberal arts, and it has become my new favorite for its succinctly elegant exposition. It could not serve any more effectively as an introduction to this book. Delbanco defends a liberal arts education because it represents the ideal space for young adults to debate within and without about what comprises a meaningful life, and to find out that self-advancement and service to others are not irreconcilable: "A college should not be a haven from worldly contention, but a place where young people fight out among and within themselves contending ideas of the meaningful life, and where they discover that self-interest need not be at odds with concern for one another." Nothing less than democracy, Delbanco concludes, "depends on it."[4] Stirring rhetoric for all who affirm education's liberating potential, and bound to fire up the faithful. But where should those passionate about the liberal arts invest their energies? Let me suggest that they read on, and consider the track record of meaning exploration programs evaluated herein.

Arum and Roksa's volume, by contrast, set off a firestorm. Its damning report of limited (and often no) learning after three full-time semesters of collegiate education illuminated the dangerously compromised foundation on which the edifice of American undergraduate education now rests. Responses were politicized and criticism was vociferous, but critics have been gradually swamped by the flood of replicating evidence. What passes for undergraduate education on the majority of American campuses today is a national embarrassment. Will bachelor's degrees become like high school diplomas—required for admission to the next level of education, but otherwise worth no more than the paper they are written on? Or might we yet be able to shore up the foundations of our nation's undergraduate programs? I am agnostic about the first question, but optimistic that individual campuses, with the right leadership and grassroots commitment to campus mission, can restore a transformative undergraduate education, especially if they partner that restoration with the purpose exploration programming described herein.

Prominent education administrators and scholars Richard Keeling and Richard Hirsch, building upon Arum and Roksa's findings along with corroborating evidence from the Wabash National Study of Liberal Arts Education and the 2005 Futures Project, outline the radical changes necessary to return higher learning to higher education. "At the heart of the matter is the need to change institutional culture. Making learning the first priority will require radical, not incremental, changes in concepts, policies, and practices throughout the academic world" (*We're Losing Our Minds*, 3). True higher learning is transformative, developmentally keyed, best understood as an apprenticeship, and requires as much intentionality about learning *outside* of classrooms as within them. Only through higher learning will students "have enough knowledge of self and others to be whole, moral persons who have authentic relationships and exercise solid civic commitments in a complex, diverse society" (ibid., 12). Unbeknownst to Keeling and Hirsch, several variations of their prescription have been successfully field-tested on four score and eight campuses, as readers will see in the pages that follow.

Astin, Astin, and Lindholm's volume, *Cultivating the Spirit*, conveys nationally representative findings from a decadelong project by the University of California–Los Angeles's Higher Education Research Institute. It demonstrates the various, positive contributions that spiritual development and engagement have made to student experiences and college outcomes. Those students who grew spiritually and religiously during their college years had higher grades, more self-confidence, higher well-being, wider campus engagement, and higher overall satisfaction with their college experience. Moreover, these positive effects occurred on campuses that had only the usual array of religious and spiritual life programming. What would happen if campuses combined these demonstrated results with Keeling and Hirsch's call for institutional change, becoming intentional about engaging undergraduates in conversations about purpose and vocation? That is precisely what this book investigates, and why I situate this volume as continuing the important conversation about American higher education that the above authors have so powerfully begun.

Campus conversations about purpose do not, of course, require engagement of theology or spirituality. Two scholars report positive results from nonreligious examination of meaning and purpose by college students,[5] and I encountered many individuals during this project who held positive and resolutely nonreligious perspectives on meaning and purpose. But religion, spirituality, and theology should not be viewed as electrified and deadly third rails of American higher education. As Keeling and Hersh argue, and Astin, Astin, and Lindholm demonstrate, powerful learning and positive outcomes result when the academic, social, and spiritual comingle. Campuses *can* spawn creative, intellectually engaged, and pluralistically respectful conversations and exploration of purpose and vocation, including these concepts' theological underpinnings, because campus citizens can learn how to tell meaning-making stories that convey particularistic origins and lessons without disrespecting other origins and lessons. It is not that hard to learn, in fact. It takes a few examples, an inviting context, some useful terms, and citizens of goodwill. Particularism is not the enemy of inclusion per se; its restriction, however, surely is.

I invite the reader, therefore, to grant me a hearing—to consider the results I convey; to discuss matters of purpose, meaning, calling, and vocation with the young adults in his or her own life; and to share with me and others the results of those conversations. These matters are too important not to be engaged, debated, or evaluated. My wine shop has a sign that reads "Life Is Too Short to Drink Bad Wine." True indeed. It is also too short for young adults to devote themselves to the default purposes of popular culture or nostalgic traditions. The examined life remains the only life worth living. Thankfully, there are examining lenses of wide variety, and it matters little which lens one chooses to begin; it matters only that one begins. It is my hope that this book, and the lenses it describes, will ultimately aid young adults in their most important examination.

1

Purposeful Paths

Too Little, Too Late

It was an iffy spring day: overcast, damp, showers possible. These certainly were not the conditions that Princeton University seniors had hoped for as they assembled in front of Nassau Hall for graduation. And yet, the weather on that June day matched the national moment—with banks "too big to fail" propped up by federal funds and interest-free loans from Federal Reserve Chairman Ben Bernanke, President Obama leading not just the free world but also General Motors, and a global economy wobbling and near collapse. As Princeton's then president, Shirley Tilghman was by tradition its commencement speaker as well. I did not envy her task that day. Already, a $4 billion loss from the university's endowment had forced her to make deep budget cuts, push early retirements, and issue the first layoffs in the university's storied history. What could she possibly say to these graduates as they entered the most dismal labor market since the Great Depression?

Tilghman's message was to make lemonade of out lemons. Well, that is not *exactly* how she put it. She worded it more eloquently: "Let me suggest there has never been a more opportune time to be a seeker after purpose and meaning."[1] Tilghman acknowledged that "the complexity of global challenges," like replacing a carbon-based global economy with green technologies or violent hatred with tolerance, was "enormous." Yet Princeton's graduates could "become leaders" and "change the world for the better" if they help "to find solutions to these challenges." In other words, we grown-ups have so messed things up that our only hope is for you kids to fix it, but take heart—doing so will give you a deep sense of meaning and purpose. The irony is that Tilghman was right. We grown-ups *have* made a royal mess, and anyone who makes progress on a pressing global problem often finds a profound sense of meaning and purpose in that endeavor. But a ten-minute lesson about seeking meaning and purpose, delivered at the eleventh hour and fiftieth minute of a student's undergraduate experience, was about as useful as finding a hundred parts and no assembly instructions inside my bouncing eight-year-old's bicycle box on Christmas morning. Such a lesson, if it is to be learned, must be introduced before prospective students apply and developed throughout their years of higher education; it ought not be relegated to a university's final oration.

President Tilghman's challenge was, nonetheless, apt. I do not critique her message, only its timing. Encouraging young adults to seek after meaning and purpose is as relevant during boom years as it is during busts. And it is as important to embed in its curriculum, cocurricular programs, and everyday organizational culture as it is to articulate during convocations. This book, in short, is an account of what happens when colleges and universities infuse undergraduate education with exploration of meaning and purpose. Such exploration was once foundational to liberal arts education. That baby got tossed out with a lot of dirty bathwater, however.[2] Ever since, thoughtful critics have pleaded with contemporary universities to resist marketplace pressures, return to the big questions of life, and recapture the historic role that universities have played in society.[3] This book continues in that tradition, yet contributes uniquely to it, for it is an empirical study—of an initiative implemented in eighty-eight colleges and universities that invited students, faculty, staff, and administrators to incorporate questions of meaning and purpose into the undergraduate experience.

This initiative, launched by the Lilly Endowment Inc., invited church-affiliated colleges and universities to develop programming that would foster campus conversations about questions of meaning and purpose, and in particular their religious underpinnings, which is the theology of vocation. The endowment posed three questions in its request for proposals, asking campuses how they might foster students' exploration of the idea of vocation, support preclergy students specifically, and strengthen student mentorship by faculty and staff. The endowment directed applicants to draw from their own campus's tradition and practices in answering these questions, inviting proposals for $50,000 planning grants followed by $2 million implementation grants. More than four hundred church-affiliated colleges and universities applied, designing programs that fit with their institutional cultures and theological traditions. This initiative was thus comprised of willing, often enthusiastic, applicant-designed programs, developed by conservative-to-liberal campuses with proud-to-nominal church affiliations. It was not comprised of reluctant, begrudged efforts by campuses at the behest of meddling bishops or denominational boards. It further represents one of the largest curricular and cocurricular undertakings in American higher education history, and is applicable to campuses of various affiliations or none. This initiative, in short, embodies what happens when campuses intentionally and creatively engage students in conversations about purpose and meaning, a conversation of interest to anyone who embraces Socrates's notion of the examined life.

The participating colleges and universities were a surprisingly diverse lot—from internationally acclaimed research universities to small liberal arts colleges surrounded by cornfields—possessing prominent to neglected church affiliations (see appendix 1). What they had in common was the desire to engage students with questions of purpose and meaning long before graduation day—when reflection on these ideas could positively impact the choices students made and the futures they planned. Not all students nor all eighty-eight campuses had deeply meaningful or lasting experiences through this initiative. Some were untouched and others unfazed. Yet for a remarkable number of students, as well as faculty and staff, these conversations about purpose became, like Max Weber's analogy of ideas as train switchmen altering history's path, profoundly consequential in their lives. Moreover, quite a few participating institutions reclaimed the intentional exploration of purpose and meaning as core to their educational missions. Ideas, in other words, still have consequences. This book tells a story about the consequences of systematically inviting and supporting reflection about life's purpose on dozens of college and university campuses, and among thousands of students, faculty, and staff.

A few examples will help illustrate the shorter- and longer-term impacts that purposeful reflection can have. I begin with stories of three students who attended colleges that participated in this initiative and who took advantage of the available exploration programming. To add contrast, I pair each with another young adult whose life followed a similar trajectory save for exploration programming. As we journey alongside these young adults, I address important questions about self-selection, about programmatic supply versus individual demand, and about the nature of purpose exploration that it should engage young adults at the start of the twenty-first century. I then conclude the chapter with a clear statement of this book's goals, its organizing structure, and its claim about the necessity of engaging the whole student at this critical moment in American higher education.

Melody and Katie

Melody Thompson and Katie Lombardi have a lot in common.* Born just nine months apart in the mid-1980s to college-educated and progressive parents, they were reared with younger siblings in well-appointed suburban homes and attended generously supported suburban schools. They grew up taking dance lessons, playing recreational soccer, spending summers at themed day camps, earning money babysitting, and participating in a variety of school clubs and volunteer organizations. And like one out of two American teens today, they attended church nearly every week with their families:[4] Melody's family attended a Presbyterian congregation that hosted a soup kitchen and was active in the sanctuary movement, and Katie's family attended a Catholic parish whose Honduran priest was keen on liberation theology and nuclear disarmament. Not that Melody or Katie were particularly devout. They occupied, rather, the middle ground of semireligious American teens: those who see religion as a "nice thing" but also as something to keep on the periphery of one's life.[5] Their peers were a bit surprised, then, when Melody and Katie

*All participant and place names are pseudonyms.

chose colleges affiliated with their denominations. But sizable merit scholarships combined with overnight visits that revealed nice buildings, lots of campus fun, and nothing "too religious" left Melody and Katie eager to attend.

Melody enrolled at Presbyter College, a small liberal arts college of twelve hundred students located three hours' drive from her home, while Katie enrolled at Olde Augustinian University, a medium-sized institution of five thousand students located near a large US city and about ninety minutes' drive from her home. Both young women began with a major in the humanities, added a second major to augment their preparation for the workplace, and posted good grades as they followed their life goals of graduating, obtaining a fulfilling job and good income, marrying and having children, and enjoying a variety of leisure and voluntary activities. Katie, for example, hoped to marry "by twenty-five," work until she had children, and then stay home "because I do want to be there for my kids." Katie even shifted her career focus to journalism, after her summer job made it clear that a career in law would not comport readily with her vision of motherhood. Melody voiced similar goals of balancing marriage, family, and career: she did not "envision having a job that makes a significant amount of money, just enough to take care of my family and be able to send my kids to college." Enough to support her love of traveling and maybe a bit more, Melody admitted embarrassedly, to cover the costs of being "really into clothes." Melody need not have felt embarrassed. She had plenty of company, as goals like hers and Katie's are common among traditional-age college students in America, and even laudable compared to the self-destructive behaviors of too many young adults.

Observed across a room, one would see that Melody and Katie had two other commonalities: both were popular among their peers, and neither lacked for suitors. It was tempting, in fact, to conclude that their chief differences were hair and eye color—Melody was a blonde with blue eyes, Katie a brunette with brown eyes. Had I not listened to each young woman talk about her life and experiences for an hour and a half during their final semesters of college, and again one year after they graduated from college, I might have drawn such a conclusion. But important differences between Melody and Katie became apparent during our first interview, and grew large by the time I reinterviewed them. At the root of these differences was Melody's merit scholarship to Presbyter College. More than a welcomed credit on her tuition invoices, this scholarship inserted Melody into a strategically de-

signed program of purpose exploration that included coursework, cocurricular events, service, and internship experiences. Known as the Purpose Scholars program, it selected six bright, prospective leaders from each entering
class, assigned them to a faculty mentor, and required their involvement with
the diverse activities of the college's Purpose Exploration Center.

Melody thus found herself at the heart of a well-funded campus program
that awarded minigrants to faculty to develop and offer courses that infused
exploration of purpose into classes like writing, literature, education, social
change, public policy, and art; sponsored impressive alternative spring-break
service programs; ran a social justice lecture series that featured speakers
like poet Maya Angelou and Father Gustavo Gutierrez; organized an annual
nonprofit and volunteer service career fair; and offered summer intern placements that included stipends so even students on financial aid could participate in them. In four years' time, Melody went from nibbling at these
programs and their underlying ideals to devouring them, coming to see her
original goals of comfortable suburban family life as insular if not selfish,
and reorienting her entire future to the pursuit of international human rights
and sustainable Third World development. She explained, "Since I've come
to college, my worldview has developed significantly; I've seen pieces of the
world that I never knew existed, and those situations have prompted me to
want to become involved in correcting some of the flaws that have come
about because of globalization and a lot of US policy and some European
policy, too." Consequently, Melody said that her new "awareness of the world
has led me to want to work in human rights." She was no longer content to
"live just for myself and my own personal comfort," but desired "a profession
that embodies my values . . . [yet] incorporates the family piece into my vocation." (While her college's Purpose Center did not lead with the term *vocation*, it did not shy from it either, since it occupies a prominent place in the
history of Presbyterian theology. Within a couple of years of matriculation,
Purpose Scholars used theological terminology frequently in their everyday
conversations.)

By contrast, Katie's scholarship required timely completion of degree requirements and an overall grade average of B or better. That was no problem;
Katie met her grade obligation every semester and made steady progress on
her course requirements, including Olde Augustinian's religion requirement.

None of her courses generated much enthusiasm, however, nor altered her thinking very much. Not that Katie objected. Being efficient with her studies left Katie plenty of time to spend with one, then another boyfriend, and with her sorority sisters. Thus, the mainstream goals with which Katie had entered the university remained intact throughout her four years of study, and she recounted them easily: "I want to have a good career, and I want to have a family, but ultimately, I just want to be happy — 'cause you see so many people who, you know, have this great job, and this great status, but they're not happy, so, that's really all. I just want to be happy. Whatever it takes to get there, you know?" Katie, like most Americans, viewed college as an instrumental means to a practical end. Her college years thus served their purpose — she earned her degree and had fun in the process.

Melody and Katie graduated from college within a few days of each other, but they could not have been further apart on the educational idealism-realism continuum. During their graduation ceremony, Melody and Katie each heard speeches relaying heartfelt entreaties to apply their knowledge and skills to serve humanity. The speech reminded Melody of professors who had mentored her and reinforced the reasons she would join an international development project the following week; it made Katie regret that she'd skipped breakfast and ponder where to get lunch. Melody was that idealistic graduate who swells the heart of professors like me; Katie was that sensible graduate whose career plans would secure her a comfortable future. But this book would not be worth reading and the initiative it evaluates not worth considering if its only product were idealistic graduates. Idealism for its own sake is maladaptive in this far from ideal world. Melody knew this world's failings well, however. More important, Melody appreciated the complexities and repeated setbacks involved in attempting to repair a minuscule part of it. Melody possessed a *grounded* idealism; she revised her formerly mainstream perspective, recalibrated her life trajectory, enacted decisions to effect that trajectory, and anticipated both setbacks and a slow path. On graduation day, her observable differences from Katie were theoretical. But during the days that followed, Melody set off on a trajectory that, one year later, located her in a very different place from Katie, and on a course that would separate her further still.

Melody spent the summer after her graduation in the heat and crude conditions of a relief compound in Uganda. This was Melody's second time in Uganda; the first visit occurred as part of a course on political change taught by a professor at Presbyter College. Uganda became a life-changing experience for Melody, not only because it confirmed her interest in international human rights, but also because it was there that she met and fell in love with Peder, a handsome Danish relief worker. By the summer's end, in fact, she and Peder announced their engagement. While I can only imagine Melody's parents' shock at this decision, Melody proved she was no dizzy bride-to-be. Even before she returned from Uganda, Melody lined up full-time work as an office manager for a battered women's shelter, and had a stack of mail from graduate programs in international relations awaiting her at home. Her maturity in these matters resolved her parents' concerns about Melody's future education and career, Peder's visit that fall revealed him to be a compassionate and thoughtful man, and soon all were immersed in wedding preparations.

Then the other shoe dropped: Melody was pregnant! And her adamancy about keeping the baby sorely tested her parents' progressivism. But Melody held firm, rescheduled her wedding from June to Valentine's Day, poured herself into her work, and submitted graduate school applications. Winter soon set in, as did morning sickness, so Melody's world narrowed to work, rest, and wedding preparations. Then, in late January, a wonderfully thick envelope arrived from Top Ivy University, offering Melody a full scholarship for a master's degree in international policy. She, Peder, and her parents were overjoyed. It was the "best wedding present" Melody could have, and deepened the celebration that Valentine Day's as her parents walked her down the aisle and Melody was married by the same minister who had baptized her. After a weekend honeymoon in the city, Melody and Peder settled into her aunt's vacation house, that June she gave birth to a healthy baby girl, and when we caught up with her in August, all three were settling into a graduate student apartment at Top Ivy.

I was struck by the sheer number of major events in Melody's life since graduation—three months doing relief work in Uganda, finding and working a full-time job, getting engaged, planning a wedding, getting married, having a baby, and moving twice. Few young adults experience more than two such events in their first year after college, and most focus a lot of effort on managing those. Melody compressed several years' worth of life events into one, yet was nonplussed as she described this year to us. Melody spoke of the deep commitment to social change that she and her husband shared: "The way we live our life, the places we want to work, and the things we want to do are really tied to an idea of what we want to do in the world and things we see that need to be changed or developed." She also explained how "the biggest change was the baby," and how it "really impacted" her relationship with Peder, as they had anticipated no children for the first few years of their marriage. Consequently, they had to work through "this idea of having a baby and getting married," and it required them to take "the same ideas about the world and what we want to do . . . [and] support each other." And though Melody had yet to attend her first graduate class, she was already thinking over her next move: "We are interested in maybe going to the Middle East; that's where a lot of students in this program are going right now, and my husband could find work there. But it's also hard with our daughter and our family and stuff. It's hard [to plan, but] we both would like to go abroad for a while." In short, Melody managed a host of anticipated and unanticipated life events, and did so with maturity, resilience, and intentionality.

And what about Katie? At her father's bidding, Katie spent the summer after her graduation relaxing beside her parents' pool and going out with friends. Katie's father wanted her to enjoy the summer, since it was her last break before "entering the rat race," as his own fast-paced executive career rarely afforded him a week of downtime. Katie thus launched her job search in the fall, seeking work as an investigative reporter for print or television news, and if not that, related work in print or television journalism. After a month scanning help-wanted ads, a couple of dozen unanswered e-mails to local news stations, and phone calls that never got past the receptionist, Katie abandoned her job search and accepted a sales trainee position at her dad's insurance company. Complicating matters, Katie's mother had a lupus flare-up, so Katie stepped up to care for the house and prepare meals for her parents and younger siblings. For several months that fall, Katie worked the two shifts that many career women do: a paid position at the office and an unpaid position at home.[6]

Though working at an insurance company was not Katie's ideal job nor her desired career field, Katie's efficiency and ability to learn, honed during sixteen years of formal schooling, helped her excel. In fact, she was soon promoted to a junior sales management position, giving her a good salary and additional opportunities to move up, but little time to do much of anything else — until she ran into Rob at a friend's Christmas party. He was an old high school acquaintance, on leave from the navy for three weeks following an assignment in the Middle East. Katie and Rob began an intense romance, and when Rob returned to his base across the country, Katie was forlorn. So six weeks later, she requested a transfer to the company's office nearest Rob's navy base, received it, and moved two thousand miles away and into Rob's apartment, leaving her mother and family to get along without her. How did Katie come to make this decision? Her answer made it clear that as important as Katie's family was, her family came second to her personal happiness and individual desires: "I really started to feel like my family was depending on me . . . but I had to sit and look at it from the perspective that it is *my* life, I have to live my life, I have to do what makes me happy." In short, Katie found both work and love, but paid a high price: her career hopes and family ideals.

I tell Melody's and Katie's stories not to praise the former or shame the latter. I tell their stories because they share intelligence, diligence, interpersonal skills, and advantaged backgrounds. I tell their stories because neither was particularly devout or altruistic when she began college. I tell their stories because what most differentiates these two young women were the many opportunities to explore questions of purpose that Melody enjoyed at Presbyter College but that Katie lacked at Olde Augustinian University. Had Katie's scholarship at Olde Augustinian inserted her into a suite of reflection programs and experiences, and Melody's scholarship required but a minimum grade point average, their stories could have easily flipped. Katie's story could have been marked by maturity, intentionality and resilience, and Melody's by circumstance and reactivity. I say this with the confidence that comes from carefully reviewing panel interviews with 125 college graduates: 60 graduates of purpose exploration campuses like Melody's and 65 graduates of nonparticipating campuses like Katie's (along with a host of other evidence; see chapter 2 and appendix 2). Melody chose to accept Presbyter College's Purpose Scholarship, and her self-selection was undoubtedly important. Absent that scholarship program, however, Melody's choice would not have existed. Few of us would choose to reject a $10 million inheritance from a rich aunt — but few of us confront that decision; rich aunts are in decidedly scarce supply.

Self-Selection, Program Supply

Melody's and Katie's stories were two of hundreds that I heard while evalu-ating the effects of the Lilly Endowment's nearly quarter-billion-dollar in-vestment in purpose exploration programs on eighty-eight college campuses across the United States. Not all of the stories revealed differences as strik-ing as Katie's and Melody's do — but to my surprise, many of them did. I was initially dubious that such programs would have more than a passing influ-ence on their participants, and skeptical of administrators' claims that they had "impacted the entire campus." And I found some support for these early doubts among a few programs. But among a solid majority of programs, fully three-quarters of the twenty-six campuses I studied, I observed sizable indi-vidual effects not just among students like Melody, but among faculty and staff participants, too. Moreover, on one-quarter of campuses, I saw evidence of program impacts that went deeper and wider than any had even hoped, and that have sustained themselves more than five years after grant funds were consumed. I write, then, about the impact that conversations regarding purpose or vocation can have on young adults like Melody, on professors and university staff occupying early to late adulthood, and on colleges and uni-versities as a whole. I write about organically designed and organizationally savvy programs that took rarefied ideas and injected them into institutional cultures in ways that engaged and intrigued individuals of every sort.

Grant me an analogy. Imagine eighty-eight children selected from four hundred applicants to attend a summer baseball camp. Some of these chil-dren had years of Little League playing experience, some had only a passing knowledge of the game, with the majority falling in between. Imagine further that the camp featured no professional players nor a single baseball coach on its staff, just a few kindhearted folk who encouraged each child to contrib-ute all that he or she could to the camp experience, to learn everything pos-sible from one another as well as from the camp library, and to most of all enjoy playing baseball. At the end of the summer, aside from few homesick children, the campers all reported having a great time and said they learned how to play baseball better. A nice outcome, gained a bit unconventionally, but otherwise unexceptional. A dozen years later, however, sixty-six of these children had become varsity collegiate baseball players, and twenty-two of the sixty-six had been signed by professional baseball teams. Now this camp experience becomes extraordinary. There's not a sports camp director, base-ball coach, or Little League parent anywhere in the country who would not want to know what happened at that summer camp and why.

To relay what happened at that remarkable camp, and analyze why it achieved the outcomes it did, is my goal. To accomplish that, I must begin with the matter of self-selection. Was there something special about the four hundred institutions that applied for purpose exploration funding, or distinc-tive about the eighty-eight institutions that received these awards? All four hundred institutions were church-affiliated and regionally accredited colleges and universities, and submitted well-written and properly organized propos-als. But it would be a stretch to say the busy foundation officers who reviewed proposals for this initiative knew the hidden characteristics that would make programs successful. I also studied twenty-six of these eighty-eight campuses, attended gatherings of representatives from all eighty-eight, and can confirm that the largest differences lie not between selected campuses and American campuses in general, but within the eighty-eight selected campuses them-selves. At the first gathering of the eighty-eight program directors, I was told, in fact, that directors from some elite schools were aghast to see the affilia-tions of their tablemates ("I had never heard of half of these schools!" one recalled). The novelty of this initiative helped program directors move past initial reservations, and most came to respect the thoughtful commitment to this effort they widely encountered among the diverse campus represen-tatives.

That there were more differences within these eighty-eight campus par-ticipants than between these campuses and American colleges in general thus redirects the question of selection. Was there something distinctive about the *individual* students, faculty, and staff who chose to attend or work at such campuses? Here the role of selection grows more important. We know that *elite* four-year colleges and universities attract better-prepared and often more affluent students. And we know that elite colleges and universities also pay their faculty and staff more than other campuses, attracting employees with the best credentials and résumés.[7] Since *some* of the eighty-eight campuses that participated in this initiative were elite, we can list factors that might pre-dispose individuals on these campuses toward participation in exploration programs: more affluent students expect institutions to serve their needs, and that likely includes their existential questions; better-prepared students may find philosophical conversations more intriguing; faculty or staff with strong records of student mentoring may seek employment at campuses with the broadest resources and most rewards for doing so; and students, faculty, or staff who personally affiliate with a particular denomination may disproportionately seek admission or employment with their denomination's colleges and universities (see also appendix 2).

Most of the eighty-eight institutions that participated in this initiative, however, cannot be enumerated among the nation's elite campuses. Most faced a different challenge: recruiting students and employees in competition with well-resourced elite campuses and state-subsidized public campuses. Some portion of students and employees would assign a high value to these campuses' religious affiliations, and thus be favorably predisposed to conversations about purpose and vocation. But on most of the eighty-eight campuses that participated in this initiative, the majority of students and employees were not affiliated with the campuses' sponsoring denomination. This made campus religious affiliations a recruitment liability—in addition to the liabilities of higher costs, fewer resources, and lower salaries. And since external rankings, largely determined by entering students' test scores and faculty publications, have become the ubiquitous yardstick of higher education, these campuses generally enrolled students with average academic preparations and representative economic origins, to be educated by a comparatively underpaid and underresourced faculty and staff.[8] In sum, a minority of students and employees on most participating campuses, who were able to overcome the time constraints posed by fewer individual and campus resources, may have been predisposed toward engagement with purpose exploration programming.

Knowing that some members of religiously affiliated campuses may be more likely to participate in exploration programming tells us little, however. To start, no amount of individual interest in such exploration can create programs ex nihilo. Olde Augustinian University did not provide Katie, her classmates, or its employees with the option to participate in such exploration programs, nor did eight hundred other religiously affiliated colleges in the United States. Programmatic opportunities must first exist in order for individuals to choose to participate in them. Second, proportionately few church-affiliated colleges require students and employees to affirm a particular faith; three-quarters of eighty-eight funded campuses welcomed individuals from all religious persuasions, including "none." While purpose exploration programs did attract many devout participants, they also drew a goodly share of nonreligious, non-Christian, and nominally religious participants. Third, interest in questions of purpose or vocation is dynamic. Individuals who refused to go near an exploration program at one moment might queue for it at another, and vice versa. Fourth, quality offerings, exciting opportunities, incentives, and positive word of mouth can draw a wide audience, who, once sold on a program, become its best advertisement. As those in the marketing industry know well, a good product can generate its own demand. After all, who wanted an iPod (or i-anything) before such a product existed?

The iPod's success would have been impossible, of course, had the necessary infrastructure not been in place and had consumers not become dissatisfied with dominant modes of music delivery. That is, personal computers had to become household fixtures, high-speed Internet connections had to become widely available and reasonably affordable, and music tastes had to so differentiate that current radio stations no longer satisfied the majority of listeners. In a similar way, these eighty-eight institutions as well as their campus populations found themselves structurally amenable to purpose exploration programming. Increased competition had left college leaders eager to identify and market their institution's distinct characteristics, college deans in a tug-of-war with disciplines over faculty priorities, and student life officers challenged by retention rates. More broadly, with the collapse of cultural authority embedded in American popular norms, questions of purpose and meaning must be resolved by everyone. A liberal arts education once constructively engaged such matters, but today largely focuses on deconstructing traditional sources of authority, offering in its place little more than world-weary conversation at Café Ennui. So at the start of a new millennium, when this purpose exploration initiative was launched, institutional leaders were willing to try anything—even designing a suite of purpose exploration programs for students, faculty, and staff. To their surprise, their efforts succeeded.

That this initiative prioritized college students, who enjoy wide freedom to engage ideas and calibrate future trajectories, and secondarily targeted their faculty and staff mentors, who enjoy considerable autonomy to define their work's foci, was critical to its impact. Melody, for example, was structurally well situated to engage new ideas and consider actions that would move her in new directions. Melody's progressive parents, moreover, endorsed her global interests. Some students are not as structurally free or philosophically open as Melody was, however. Could exploration programming benefit those with fewer structural freedoms or firm philosophical commitments? I was dubious, and again I was wrong. So I share two examples. The first is about a young man as religiously zealous as they come, the second about a young woman confronting the pressures common to first-generational college students from recently immigrated families. Despite the former's ability to quote Bible verses from memory and the latter's drive to succeed, purpose exploration still made a world of difference.

Jeff and Rosa

Jeff Johnson and Rosa Rios both knew from an early age that they wanted to be doctors, but beyond this their childhood similarities were few. Jeff was the child of two physicians, highly regarded specialists in a midsized city famous for its hospitals, and both paternal and maternal grandfathers were physicians as well. Rosa was the child of undocumented migrant Mexican farmworkers and had no permanent home until age twelve, when her parents moved into a trailer park not far from the Mexican border. Jeff attended an elite prep school; Rosa graduated from her border town's low-performing public schools. But Jeff did not feel terribly at home in the privileged and amoral environment of his prep school, which he attributes to his devout, born-again Christian faith — a faith passed on by his parents and grandparents. And Rosa found that her minority ethnicity, combined with her ambition, placed her at the margins of peer acceptance. So they each chose colleges that would be a better fit and had solid premed programs, with Jeff enrolling at evangelical Pullman College and Rosa at Hispanic-serving (and Roman Catholic) Mexicana College. It was there that they encountered exploration programs designed to foster theological self-reflection and global engagement, and the result was substantial.

To be sure, Jeff's upbringing had long exposed him to the idea of "following God's will," and Rosa loved her parish priest for the many good deeds he performed in her community. But neither had the sustained engagement with the idea and practice of vocation that Pullman or Mexicana Colleges infused into their work with students. Because of Pullman's evangelical identity, most students arrived ready to use "their gifts and talents" in the service of God, and Jeff was no exception. Pullman's exploration programs therefore paid less attention to identifying student abilities, and more to pushing students beyond dominant American individualism and consumerism to see the enormity and complexity of global needs. Mexicana College's ethnic identity, by contrast, meant its exploration program had to overcome the generally tacit Catholicism of its Hispanic students to personally engage students with their "baptismal calling" to serve Christ and the world. It therefore redesigned its first-semester academic program to include a significant exposure to the history and ministries of the religious order that established the college's Hispanic-serving mission, and refocused its campus volunteer opportunities to increase student involvement in local, regional, and international Catholic ministries.

Both Jeff and Rosa, despite the heavy demands of their premed programs, made it a priority to participate in their campus's exploration programs. Jeff joined a spiritual mentorship group with six other male students and a faculty mentor, while Rosa opted for weekly meals and conversations with the sisters who lived in an adjacent convent. Both participated in local and international service projects, rising to leadership positions in these campus activities, and Jeff received an undergraduate summer fellowship to assist a biology professor with research. The effects of their participation were profound, even as they might be difficult to discern from a distance, since both Jeff and Rosa kept to their premed paths and long-term career goals—with Jeff still planning to become a medical missionary, and Rosa still planning to work in a medical clinic back in her border town, where she intended to provide undocumented and uninsured patients with the same level of care that insured patients enjoyed.

Jeff explained that his participation in exploration programs led him to pair his commitment to medical missions with a commitment to medical research. Rosa explained that her participation steeled her resolve to attend medical school despite academic challenges and financial setbacks. Jeff wanted to become an evangelical version of Paul Farmer, the famous Harvard physician-anthropologist who founded Partners in Health to (initially) combat tuberculosis in Haiti, and who also publishes first-order research in both infectious disease and medical anthropology.[9] Rosa strategically delayed preparation for the Medical College Admission Test (MCAT) until she completed her college degree, because she knew her grades would suffer if she combined MCAT preparation with her senior-year classes. It was not a happy choice, but Rosa explained, "As you get older and you experience certain things, you have to learn how to sacrifice. . . . For example, I wanted to go to med school right after college. That didn't happen." Jeff recognized that his decision to become a medical missionary had high opportunity costs: "Becoming a doctor and then going into the mission field is like throwing away ridiculous amounts of money, but I guess I just know that that's what I've been called to, and I've been fortunate to be around professors who have done the same thing." Similarly, Rosa recognized that her decision to postpone MCAT preparation would prolong her path to medical school, but this decision did not undermine her determination. Rosa told us that her life had "a certain purpose . . . that going to medical school and becoming a doctor is really what I'm meant to do, so that guides me."

We caught up with Jeff and Rosa about fifteen months after they graduated from college, and learned that much had unfolded in the interim. Jeff was about to begin his second year of medical school at his state's flagship university, Rosa was employed at a community health center and about to begin her MCAT preparation course, and both had married their college sweethearts. Jeff told us he got married at the end of his first year of medical school, that he and his bride had an "eight-week honeymoon" in Sri Lanka doing medical missions work, and that they had just moved their belongings into the basement of an old home where they were enjoying settling in before Jeff's second year of medical school began. Rosa explained how she spent months seeking employment before finding a job at a community health center, how that long search and loss of income had delayed her enrollment in an MCAT preparation course for a second year, and how, once employed, she chose to devote her salary to paying for her (modest) wedding expenses and the cost of renting an apartment with her husband.

While others might be bitter about the long job search, financial stress, wedding costs, and delayed medical school applications—Rosa voiced contentment and optimism: she was enjoying life as a newlywed, pleased with her apartment's location "ten minutes away" from her parents and younger siblings, happy to be working in the health field, and eager to begin her MCAT review course in a couple of weeks. Similarly, while many medical students gripe about having no time for a social life, and few twenty-two-year-old children of upper-middle-class professionals would abide an unregistered basement apartment in an inner-city neighborhood, Jeff offered no complaint, and was strikingly reflective:

> I think there are a lot of paradoxes in the Christian faith that can sometimes seem hard to apply to how, at least, we in America have set up life: very busy, very loud, very on-the-go. And I think I'm kind of learning how, within that, to develop important principles in the Christian faith of silence and contemplation, social activism with a cause, but yet not making that such a busy process.

Jeff sounded more like a Benedictine monk than a medical student scrambling to set up an apartment with his new wife before the start of his second year of medical school. What struck me about Jeff and Rosa, and about Melody and the vast majority of other participants in campus exploration programs, was the breadth of their perspective on life after college, and their resilience despite setbacks. What characterized Jeff, Rosa, and Melody was *grounded idealism*—not a maladaptive wishfulness that collapsed when the challenges of attaining adulthood in a competitive global economy grew apparent, but a resilience and a persistence that combined broad contentment with their present lives with ongoing progress toward a life that would positively impact others. By contrast, peers with similar social origins and collegiate backgrounds, but without opportunities to explore ideas of purpose and vocation, did not articulate perspectives nearly as broad nor demonstrate nearly the degree of resilience as those who had examined these ideas while in college.

Michael Thompson and Leah Domingo, for example, attended colleges that did not have purpose exploration programs. Michael, like Jeff, was the son and grandson of physicians, and a third-generation evangelical Christian. Like Rosa, Leah was the American-born child of first-generation immigrants to the United States (from the Philippines, in Leah's case), and spent her first decade in RustBelt City's public housing before her parents received a "Section 8" (a housing assistance voucher with fewer geographic restrictions) and moved to a suburban apartment. Until ninth grade, Michael and Leah planned to become physicians. In high school, however, Michael had a change of heart—prompted by a series of conversations with his father. Medicine, he told Michael, "was not worth it" anymore. Insurance companies second-guess every decision and pay a fraction of one's fee. Patients believed the Internet sooner than the physician who had treated them their whole life. And Michael knew all too well his dad's opinion of lawyers and malpractice insurance. Business, he told Michael, was the only profession left where hard work was still rewarded. Michael listened, switched his career focus to business and finance, and never considered medicine again. Leah, by contrast, never discussed her career plans with her parents, only endured the "embarrassment" of her mother's bold announcements to family and friends that Leah was "going to be a doctor."

Leah chose to attend Costly Private University (CPU), which had a national reputation for quality and enrolled an affluent and liberal-leaning student body. This made Leah an ethnic and social class minority at her university. But CPU was located adjacent to a major and racially diverse US city, and made a concerted effort to support students of color, so Leah felt accepted at CPU and found important cultural connections in the city. Michael opted to attend a small college associated with his church's denomination, of which his father and mother were also alums, earning good grades and becoming active in its business careers club. Academically, Leah struggled during her first year at CPU. Science "wasn't for me," she told us; she discovered a passion for photography, and photojournalism in particular. So midway through her second semester, Leah took copies of student newspapers that featured her photos, and used them to obtain her parents' blessing on switching to a major in photojournalism. From that point forward, Leah's grades improved significantly, and she immersed herself in urban life—shopping, visiting cafés, and dancing in the city's many nightclubs.

When we caught up with Leah and Michael some fifteen months after they graduated from college, they were both proud to be living in apartments on their own. This accomplishment strained Leah's relationship with her parents, who, being "very traditional" and Catholic, expected Leah to remain a virgin and marry as soon as she graduated. It was "too late" for virginity, Leah told us with a laugh, and she would take the city "any day" over "praying the Rosary" at home. To minimize conflict, Leah avoided going home and reduced communication with her parents. But Leah worried she might be forced to move home for financial reasons, as she could not find work in photojournalism, and was even rejected for clerical positions at two newspapers. Desperate, she accepted temporary work as a secretary in a financial firm. Leah blamed her alma mater for insufficiently preparing for the job market: "I will honestly say that I didn't expect the job search to be so hard: it was really difficult and it cost a lot of money, and I feel like they don't quite prepare you for that in college." More important, Leah gave no indication of pursuing photography in the near or distant future; her exclusive focus was on hoping her temporary position would become permanent so she could stay in the city and "get benefits."

For Michael, his career was following the path he had anticipated while in college. He landed a well-paid position in finance with a major bank, and was highly satisfied with his work despite its demanding hours. Michael told us that his favorite part of the job was how "you get to travel the world and see different things or you take clients out to dinner, you go on these big extravagant dinners." Aside from work, however, Michael had little time for anything else. He remained as committed as ever to getting married, having children, and becoming an active member of an evangelical church. But he broke up with his girlfriend because he "didn't have time" for a relationship and had not even attended church in several months. "Most of my decision making involves where am I trying to go professionally," Michael said a bit embarrassedly.

In many ways, Michael and Leah were doing well. They were financially independent, even though Leah was living paycheck to paycheck, and working to solidify their career paths. Graduating a couple of years prior to the global financial crisis of 2008 certainly worked to their advantage; still, they were doing better at launching their adult lives than many twenty-two-year-olds. I convey their stories not to cast aspersions, but to contrast their stories with those of peers who took advantage of special opportunities to explore ideas of purpose and vocation. Jeff and Rosa used exploration programs to thoughtfully calibrate their life trajectories during their college years, which in turn helped them to maintain their overall paths despite challenges. Had Michael and Leah enjoyed similar opportunities to examine and calibrate their life trajectories while in college, I suspect they also would have voiced longer-term perspectives and deeper satisfaction with their postcollege lives as Jeff and Rosa did. Educators since Socrates have valued the examined life; what these stories demonstrate is the efficaciousness of campus-based exploration programs for that examination process.

An Appealing Conversation

That Rosa, Jeff, and Melody's peers, as well as professors and staff professionals, made broad use of exploration programs may leave some readers surprised. Why, of all things, would exploration programming emphasizing theologies of vocation draw in so many? I suggest the following:

First, while living in this postmodern world offers many advantages, a major disadvantage is the fact that it assigns individuals the task of navigating life's purpose amid ever-churning seas of meaning. Theologies of vocation offer navigational charts, weaving long-established (meta-) narratives of divine purpose together with compelling reasons for proactive engagement with the world.[10] As pragmatic as America's students may be, the desire to positively engage with others persists: two out of three college juniors nationally endorsed as a life goal "reducing pain and suffering in the world," a majority hoped "to improve their understanding of other countries and cultures,"[11] and all 125 of this project's in-depth interviewees agreed that they wanted their lives "to make a difference." The majority of college students seek a meaningful life, and most are willing to hear any narrative of purpose that is genuinely conveyed.

Second, too many academics and intellectuals project their own secularity onto campus populations, unaware that one out of two American college juniors consider "integrating spirituality in my life" to be "very important" if not "essential," that two out five assign equal importance to "seeking to follow religious teachings" in daily life, that three out of four young adults nationally identify as religious, and that two out of three identify as Christian.[12] This ignorance of student religious and spiritual life is ironic, since four out of five faculty self-identify as spiritual to "some" or "a great extent," two out of three identify as religious, and a solid majority pray or meditate regularly.[13] In short, campus populations are rife with religious and spiritual engagement, so programs that invite this population to consider their own giftedness and contribution to humanity appeal not only to their American egos but also to their broad spiritual interests.

Third, an *exploration* of purpose and theologies of vocation is wholly different from an indoctrination about the same, as the former invites intelligent participants into conversations with one another about texts and concepts marked by cognitive sophistication. Theologies of vocation ably challenge professors and staff to their own game of intellectual discourse, impress students with their scholarly rigor, while raising questions that strike at the heart of what readers are doing with their lives, what they hope to do with them, and why. I witnessed it myself: professors, staff, or students gathered in a room, nudged to create a trusting and open atmosphere, with a reflective question introduced. Someone would answer it honestly, that honesty would draw in others, and in less than twenty minutes, a rich conversation was flowing about purpose, meaning, fulfillment, and making a difference.

Fourth, even as we observe steady increases in American religious diversity and in religiously unaffiliated Americans, there persists this reality: two out of three Americans identify as Christian. Christianity, I tell students in my American religion course, is the elephant on the seesaw of American religious life. The elephant, to be sure, is losing weight and suffers from multiple personality syndrome, while the variety and size of creatures arrayed on the seesaw's high side grows. Nevertheless, it will be *decades* before that elephant feels herself lifting off the ground. That means Christian narratives of purpose and vocation represent reasonable departure points for exploratory conversation, especially when the colleges and universities hosting these conversations go out of their way to affirm the religious and spiritual heterogeneity of their campus populations (which they did quite consistently).

Max Weber, the pioneering German sociologist, recognized that human sociability is essential to human life, and that human sociability results, necessarily, in the creation and inhabitation of normative systems of meaning. In other words, human life and human society are impossible without meaning. This inserts each of us into an irresolvable conundrum, since all systems of meaning stand on metaphysical assumptions that cannot be proved and merit critique. While despair is a valid response, it is neither a popular nor a healthy one. Positive engagement with the world thus requires counterbalancing deconstructive critique with a humble recognition of human limitations. The latter is rare in academic circles, but it is a significant component of theological discourse. Contemporary theology, especially of the sort that was popular in the campus exploration programs we studied, is strikingly humble about human limitations and forthright about the challenge of certainty. It is also nuanced in its understanding of the world we share. Thus, it sparked deep conversations, and assisted participants in constructing a working framework for positive and engaged living in a globalized and postmodern world.

Evaluated, Analyzed, and Recommended

There is much I intend to relay in this book. A road map is therefore in order, and a clear statement of my goals — which are three. First, this book is an *evaluation* of the Programs for the Theological Exploration of Vocation (PTEV) initiative of the Lilly Endowment, based on study of programs at twenty-six different colleges and universities, interviews with 284 students and 274 faculty and staff, comparison interviews with 65 students not attending PTEV-affiliated campuses, and a survey of 2,111 program participants nationwide. Relaying the results of this evaluation is foundational, so I spend much time doing so. But it is my second and third goals that give this book transferable value for readers who educate students in or out of classrooms, who oversee faculty or manage staff, who lead schools or universities, or who care about young adults and higher education. The book's second goal, then, is a *sociological analysis* of why the majority of these programs worked when and where they did, given the organizational pressures within higher education and wider cultural factors at play. And the third goal, given the findings and analysis, is a *recommendation* that a space for, and means of, purpose exploration be developed and systematically implemented at colleges and universities of every sort.

I make this recommendation unabashedly, but I do not make it uncritically. There are many ways to stumble in such an endeavor, the chief of which is to view purpose exploration like modular IKEA furniture that one selects according to personal preferences and assembles in hours. Rather, developing exploration programs requires honest conversation among a wide pool of stakeholders, occurs over many weeks and months, is rooted in the organization's history and culture, and is keyed to its specific needs. While I offer strategic recommendations (chapter 6) and append resources to help those engaging in this process on their own campuses (appendix 5), I offer these as conversation starters, not blueprints. A more apt analogy for implementing exploration programming is to designing and planting a garden. It takes time, effort, and resources to have a successful garden. Though some have little appreciation for gardens, many more are nourished by time spent therein, and find their time away enriched as well. I recommend this garden as a worthy investment, but emphasize that it requires an organic process of design and a commitment to ongoing maintenance.

In the next chapter, I shift perspective, beginning with the story of one faculty participant on one campus, widening to the initiative in general, locating this initiative within the broader context of American higher education since the turn of the millennium, before returning to my involvement and the specifics of this evaluation. In chapter 3, I examine purpose exploration programs as stimuli, visiting four specific programs that had substantial and lasting impacts on their campuses, then addressing general matters of design and implementation. In chapters 4 and 5, I present the heart of the evidence — describing the nature and analyzing the impact of purpose exploration on students, faculty, and staff. In chapter 6, I take a strategic and organizational perspective, analyzing successful and unsuccessful programmatic strategies, situating exploration programs within organizational and larger ecologies, and offering recommendations for effective and lasting engagement with questions of purpose among students, faculty, and staff. In chapter 7, I embed this initiative's impact within the macroinstitutional challenges facing American higher education, summarize the initiative's "levers of engagement," and draw out implications for campus-to-global citizenship, for effective launching of young adults, and for college and university organizations as sites of healthy, formative communities. To close the book, I include appendixes that list schools that participated in the PTEV initiative; describe my evaluation methods; detail the interview and survey questions; summarize in tabular form the twenty-six campuses studied; and supply text, film, and programmatic resources for exploration programming.

Reelevating Higher Education

As I write this, in the spring of 2014, the US and global economies have wobbled to their feet — but it is uncertain whether they will fall yet again or regain a solid footing. Either way, the effects on American higher education have been palpable. Private universities with endowments larger than the gross national product of half the world's countries cut staff and slashed budgets, while public university systems once the envy of the world raised tuition by 30 percent, shuttered departments, and stranded thousands of students without seats in required courses. Could there be a worse time to recommend purpose exploration programming? Certainly not, if such programming is hastily developed, poorly implemented, badly managed, and expensive. The decline of public support starkly reveals our waning ability to convince publics about higher education's purposes, while the corresponding flood of organizational immediacies so distracts us that even we lose sight of the purposes that drew us to higher education in the first place.

More than a few university leaders have recognized this loss of purpose, and responded with eloquent pleas about the centrality of higher education to a well-lived life and to an engaged citizenry.[14] "Higher education is, and is supposed to be, qualitatively different from the forms of education that came before it," argue higher education scholars and former college administrators Richard Keeling and Richard Hersh. "We expect colleges to change students' hearts and minds and somehow build them into whole, more mature persons."[15] But what passes for higher education today bears little resemblance to higher education of earlier eras. Earlier eras delivered a higher education marked by a coherent theme of creating a meaningful and engaged life, which lauded public service and contributing to the greater good. Today, valid epistemological questions render normative claims suspicious, save for those promoting tolerance and diversity, and these are readily missed by students choosing the least demanding classes from a menu of thousands. In short, contemporary higher education no longer engages the heart.[16] (It barely engages the mind, as so many have documented.)[17] What this volume contributes is not another verse to this sad song, however. It writes instead of hearts young and old, and of *every* persuasion, who encounter on their campuses practices of reflection, conversation, and mutual support, who find strength in these practices, and who use them to launch (and relaunch) lives of service.

Truth be told, we understand little about what inspires people to action or what sustains them in spite of setbacks. I suspect that is because we academics have little understanding of how the human heart operates and serious doubts, despite centuries of inspired music, art, literature, and poetry, about its existence. I do not share these doubts, but I do think hearts can be fed or starved, and consequently heard clearly or silenced. For many educators, higher education fed minds and hearts, and inspired lifelong academic journeys. But unaware of how atypical these experiences were compared to their peers, many academics view higher education with rose-colored glasses. For the vast majority of today's students, higher education does not engage the heart, and improved pedagogy or new curricular designs, while important, are not the answer; they supply improvements of degree only. We need differences of kind, and that requires exploring new ways (and recovering old ways) that lie beyond conventional notions of higher education. Hence, we arrive at intentional, contextually suited, campus-based programming for exploration of purpose and vocation.

What separates Melody, Jeff, and Rosa from Katie, Michael, and Leah are vibrant, engaged, and future-oriented hearts gripped by a robust sense of life purpose and an unrelenting desire to contribute to others. The same was true of faculty and staff participants, as subsequent chapters demonstrate. Purpose exploration programs are not, of course, the deus ex machina of higher education's woes. It took American higher education a long time to arrive at its present state, and it will take us a long time to restructure effectively. Still, the more we have students like Melody, Jeff, and Rosa populating our campuses, the more we become the engaged and contributing community we promise to be, the more readily we can put purposeful graduates before a skeptical public and dubious legislatures, and the more we recover the passion that drew us to higher education in the first place. Please journey with me as I relay what can happen on campuses when genuine learning and passionate purposes unite.

2

Contexts

From Silo to Citizen

Vzzzt . . . vzzzt . . . vzzzt. Shelly Brown turned to identify the sound. It was coming from the camera of a student photographer, who was capturing stop-motion images of the Ignatius University (IU) varsity women's crew practice on Mallory Lake. "That will make a nice photograph," Shelly thought, as the scene evoked nineteenth-century paintings by Thomas Eakins, yet reflected the present, too, with its subject being the women's crew team. Had Shelly not been pressed for time, she might have paused longer to enjoy this picturesque moment. But Shelly, or more precisely *Assistant Professor of Education* Shelly Brown, as she enjoyed reminding herself, needed to get to her three-hour Educating the Whole Student seminar with nine other faculty and ten professional staff members. The seminar, sponsored by the Campus Center for Engagement, provided faculty with a one-course teaching reduction in exchange for their participation—to read, think, and talk about "their role in the education of students." Applying, Shelly told me, was a "no-brainer." For a one-course reduction, this busy third-year faculty member "would've swept the quad" every Tuesday afternoon. The incentive was compliments, as the reader might have guessed, of a purpose exploration grant to the Campus Center for Engagement at Ignatius University.

Shelly heard of the seminar from a senior member of her department, who spoke highly of his own participation, and nominated Shelly for inclusion. His nomination, combined with Shelly's application, was successful— and shortly thereafter Shelly received a letter with the seminar's time and location, along with a list of its participants. Shelly did not recognize most of the names, save for Father John, an affable priest whom Shelly had met during her new-faculty orientation three years ago, who was the university's vice president for mission and one of two seminar leaders. Happy to be selected, Shelly confirmed that her chairperson had adjusted her teaching schedule, noted the seminar's meeting dates on her fall calendar, and largely forgot about it until the seminar began eight months later.

At the seminar's first meeting, Father John and the other leader, Gregory, stood just inside the door of the Campus Center's conference room to welcome participants. They greeted Shelly warmly, making small talk that indicated familiarity with her application as well as her position at the university. Gregory, the director of the Campus Center, then pointed her toward an attractively set refreshment table, where earlier arrivals were politely choosing cookies, fruit, and beverages. Shelly poured some iced tea as she introduced herself to the others—an associate professor of electrical engineering, a director of a residence hall, and a lieutenant from the campus police. The four then carried their refreshments and conversation to the conference table as others arrived.

Placed neatly at each chair was a glossy folder imprinted with the Campus Center for Engagement's logo and a matching pen, and in the center of the table sat two stacks—twenty copy-center-bound packets of seminar readings, and twenty copies of *The Autobiography of St. Ignatius Loyola.* The latter caught Shelly's eye. Although she was not a religious person herself, Shelly's three years at the university had accustomed her to the accoutrements of Catholicism—the crucifix in each classroom, the prominent chapel, the invocations and benedictions at every ceremony, even Christmas trees that appeared unapologetically each December. But the books, clearly meant for the seminar participants, combined with the seminar's coleadership by Father John, crossed a new boundary. Shelly grew wary.

Father John's opening remarks addressed Shelly's concerns head-on. "We're not here to make Catholics out of you," he said plainly, then continued, "But this is a Catholic university, founded by the Society of Jesus [i.e., Jesuits], and committed to educating the whole person." The seminar was therefore "designed to be an opportunity for honest conversation around some engaging readings, both classic and contemporary, that speak to the heart of our purpose as educators." Reading Ignatius of Loyola, Father John explained, would be the simplest and most direct way to understand who Jesuits are and why they have a particular interest in education.

That sounded reasonable enough to Shelly: "I could handle reading it as history. Besides, I was a bit embarrassed that I didn't know the first thing about the guy." Following these opening remarks, Father John and Gregory asked each participant to share a little bit about their "vocational journeys" and how these had brought them to their current work. The seminar leaders went first. They briefly spoke of their upbringings and the early forces that had shaped them, shared more about their college and graduate school experiences, described their work trajectories, and then closed with a little about their current activities both at and beyond Ignatius University. They were warm descriptions, with a touch of humor and self-disclosure, but nothing too personal or inappropriate for the setting.

After a brief pause, one participant volunteered her story, then another, and so on. The stories focused on career matters, yet interwove these with life in general, telling of partnerships begun and ended, of children born and parents aging, of alcoholism and depression, of physical ailments and spiritual seeking. The mood in the room grew warmer with each story; there were nods of agreement, moments of shared laughter, and knowing looks born of common heartaches. The first session's three hours were nearly consumed, in fact, by the telling of these twenty-two stories, with only a few moments left to distribute reading materials and highlight key dates on the seminar schedule. Still, there was no rush for the door when the seminar ended. Participants chatted with one another based on the commonalities discovered—as alumni of various schools, as parents of teenagers, as residents of the same suburb. "It was a really nice group of people, and every one of them took their work at the university seriously," Shelly explained. "I thought, 'Maybe this would be a good experience after all.'"

Shelly was right. The ten-week seminar covered a wide range of topics, from the philosophy of the university and the practice of Ignatian discernment to the psychology of young adult development and the results of IU student surveys, and included both thoughtful readings and guest presentations. Perhaps most important, the tenor of open and honest communication established during that first session carried forward in each subsequent session, and that, combined with engaging texts and discussion, made the seminar one of the week's highlights for Shelly. Indeed, even a beautiful fall day on a picturesque campus could not distract Shelly from attending.

We asked Shelly if the seminar brought about any new perspectives or plans for her work or her life in general. "New? I wouldn't say new. But I would say that it reinforced why I became a professor in the first place, why I will always be about more than my research, and why I put a priority on my teaching and working with students." It also did something else important. "It was great to get to know some twenty other people at [Ignatius], both faculty and staff, who share the same commitment to educating students as I do, and to know that [Ignatius University], whatever its other flaws, is committed to that, too." Such words, and the commitments they signify, are worth their weight in gold—and more than a few deans and college presidents would pay handsomely to replicate them on their own campuses.

But was Shelly's experience representative? It was, in fact. An associate professor of economics told us that the seminar was "really helping the rest of the university, who are not Jesuits, to understand the Ignatian philosophy. That's had a tremendous, positive impact." A professor of journalism gave it an even stronger endorsement:

> I'm not Catholic, I'm not Christian, I'm Jewish—and it [the seminar] was actually one of the most welcoming experiences I've had here. Not all of my experiences have been as welcoming, to be perfectly honest, but that [seminar] has been incredibly welcoming, and I felt very much dignified and validated, [and] affirmed for my perspective and my background. I've become friendly with a number of the Jesuits, and it's been really been a great experience; I'd say it's really been transformative, because it really helped me to internalize the Jesuit ideology in a way that fit for me.

Staff participants were equally enthusiastic. Joan, clinical placement director for nursing, participated in a two-week summer version of the seminar. Her enthusiasm was unbridled:

> I participated in the faculty/staff seminar in the summer of 2001, in an intensive ten-day experience, and it rocked my world! Truly, it was very enriching. I didn't know what to expect. I didn't go in with any expectations really, and it proved to be . . . all these [i.e., six] years later, the most valuable thing I've done at [IU]. It made me feel connected with the bigger picture at [Ignatius University], I met some outstanding folks whom I ordinarily would not have had the chance to connect with, and we explored deep and important issues around student development and vocational discernment and what gives you joy.

Another midlevel administrator, "buried in *adminis-trivia*" for several years, longed to "do something more meaningful." He was grateful to the seminar for helping him identify that and begin a process to put that change in place. Indeed, 72 percent of 230 seminar participants I surveyed at IU rated the seminar as "excellent," with 42 percent of the 230 agreeing and 53 percent strongly agreeing that the seminar "deepened their appreciation for the mission" of Ignatius University.[1]

What this seminar generated was a safe, honest, and stimulating context in which professors like Shelly Brown, staff members like Joan from nursing, and senior administrators like Father John could affirm their valuing of students as whole persons; appreciate IU as the organization it was: imperfect yet with noble aspirations; and find affirmation of their own humanity. Context may not—as the saying goes—be everything. But understanding one's various contexts and situating these contexts within wider organizational settings is an important human skill. It is also an essential step in accomplishing this book's goals. I therefore use this chapter to unfold the contexts of campus-based exploration of purpose and vocation—starting with employees like Shelly Brown, moving to the campus programs that engaged her and others, then broadening to the initiative and its origins. I then switch gears, laying out my involvement with this initiative as its external evaluator, outlining the design of this evaluation, and then drawing out the evaluation's implications for scholars and educational practitioners alike.

Organizational Realities in Higher Education

An important feature of IU's Educating the Whole Student seminar was its equal inclusion of faculty and staff, and equal treatment of both. Shelly Brown emphasized this, as did Joan, who appreciated the "level playing field" of the seminar. Too often, Joan noted, the "hierarchy" of "academia, or scholars" and "the others, the staff" dominates employee interaction. In the seminar room, "everyone took off their labels . . . and you could share an opinion with a really recognized, brilliant scholar and not feel that you were stumbling over yourself." Such conversations, and the social connections they engender, help bridge the divide between faculty and staff. Having spent time on over fifty campuses nationwide, I can attest to a significant divide between faculty and staff on all but the tiniest campuses. Faculty self-segregate and frequently ignore the student experience beyond academics, while staff drown in bureaucratic minutiae and often dismiss the relentless pressure to publish, obtain grants, and mentor students. Faculty are right that teaching and learning occupy the center of an educational institution, but it is staff who keep the institution running twenty-four hours a day and know its students most intimately. Just as physicians and nurses rely on each other to care for patients effectively, so faculty and staff need each other to educate students effectively. When arrogance and resentment drive a wedge between these necessary partners, it is patients and students who suffer. The more a college can bridge its faculty and staff divide, the better it can deliver the education it promises.

There is an important caveat to Shelly's story. Proportionately few tenure-track faculty members received nominations for the seminar, and fewer still participated. IU is a top-tier research university, and its junior professors must produce first-order scholarship, teach core required courses in their departments, and mentor students. IU's deans, chairs, and senior faculty thus, as Shelly put it, sought to "protect" junior faculty from "demands" like the Educating the Whole Student seminar. Shelly refused their protections:

> Once I got here, I realized that there's so much more to [Ignatius University] and so much that I could experience and grow and develop. But I felt the pressure of the tenure clock, and the constant [frustration of] people sheltering you when you don't want to be. Some people don't want to be sheltered, you know? They don't want that. Don't put me into this silo—I don't want to be there.

So when this [seminar] opportunity presented itself, I thought it was a way to explore . . . where I would go, who I am, how I could connect and become more of a university citizen, versus . . . just being a departmental one.

Shelly's presence, and her junior colleagues' absence, reveals a contradiction at the center of Ignatius University: junior faculty must earn, via publishing, grants, and tenure, the right to reflect upon their whole personhood.

This contradiction is important, and I return to it in chapter 6. At the same time, I have yet to discover a formal organization that is not hypocritical in some way, and yet to encounter a research university that did not impose similarly high expectations on its junior faculty and graduate students. These realities, in fact, make the broad embrace of this seminar and its related programs by so many members of the IU community quite remarkable. How did that happen? The answer is threefold. It involves the intellectually engaging and generative nature of theological exploration of purpose. It involves a shared, institutionally specific language and style of communicating meaning-making narratives. And it involves program design that is organic, strategically focused, responsive to feedback, and savvy in its choice of leaders.

Those unfamiliar with theological writing and scholarship, which can include the majority of the devout, are often surprised by how sophisticated this field is; how long and diverse is its history; how interwoven it is with philosophy, ethics, linguistics, and literary analysis; and how generative it can be to one's own thinking. Because theology seeks to answer core questions of human existence, draws from powerful narratives, and links these with contemporary contexts, it can assist readers in constructing a framework for engaged living in a globalized and postmodern world. Popular entreaties to live meaningfully—from eulogies to advice columns to chain e-mails—are, of course, legion. But popular entreaties, though they evoke sentiment, lack nuance, depth, and appreciation for the complexities of contemporary life. Theology possesses a diverse array of primary texts as well as scholarly efforts that challenge the brightest of minds and engage central questions in life.

Shelly found herself intrigued as she read Ignatius of Loyola's journey from faith to doubt to faith again, and moved by his pioneering commitment to holistic education. Shelly's fellow seminar participants found themselves similarly engaged by the seminar's texts and conversations, acquiring during the sessions an Ignatian-rooted vocabulary for talking about purpose as well as a manner of telling meaning-making stories that respected both the stories' particularism and the audience's diversity. This engagement of theology's depth and discovery of its contemporary relevance, combined with a shared vocabulary and style of storytelling that were equally respectful of particularism and diversity, were central to the success of the purpose exploration program at IU (and at other colleges and universities; see chapters 3–5). They supplied the substantive core that organic program design and savvy organizational leadership then maximized.

Launching Ignatius University's Campus Center for Engagement

History and culture are important, and when it comes to discernment of life purpose, Jesuits possess both in abundance. Discernment is who Jesuits are and what Jesuits do. Thus, asking Jesuits to participate in a program to encourage purpose exploration is like asking fish to participate in a learn-to-swim program. This advantage explains why Jesuit university exploration programs, more than those of any other college or university participating in this initiative, were first and strongest out of the starting gate.

Imagine the Lilly Endowment's announcement of this initiative arriving in Ignatius University's office of the president. The president, a *Jesuit*, immediately routes the letter to his *Jesuit* vice president of mission, who in turn invites other *Jesuit* employees along with some Catholic-friendly faculty and staff to plan the university's response. Already this invitation has accumulated invaluable organizational support, and the planning group has yet to convene. And when it did convene, these Jesuits knew the first thing they had to do was find a vocabulary amenable to college students. "I spent about a year working with a group to think about what we wanted to do here at [IU] with respect to 'theological exploration of vocation,'" said the dean of residential life. "I'll always remember that phrase — and how we *all* said we are *going to work on that* so it appeals to more people." The word *vocation* has several meanings, but to most lay Catholics it signifies those who have taken religious vows. In other words, a vocation is what a priest or nun has, not a layperson. As much as Jesuits might like to see more pursue vowed religious life, they knew they had to avoid the term *vocation* — as well as its theological cousin, *calling* — as either term would scare off their audience before any message could be delivered.

This IU planning group identified five tasks at its initial meeting. First, they needed to select terminology that would appeal to the whole university community. Second, they needed to create programs that would draw undergraduates into reflection and exploration of purpose. Third and fourth, they needed to nurture conversation among faculty and staff about how to better mentor undergraduates and create a pathway for undergraduates interested in ministry to explore the same—as these were specifically identified in the Lilly Endowment's invitation. And fifth, they needed to present these ideas in a compelling grant application.

For the first task, the planning group was aided by a popular professor of theology who helped them identify the two core dimensions of purpose exploration—self-knowledge and self-transcendence. In other words, thoughtful consideration of two sets of questions: (1) what skills and talents do I possess and enjoy using; and (2) what are the needs of the local, regional, national, and global communities in which I live? For the second task, the planning group drew from Catholicism's tradition of spiritual retreats to create a *non*religious retreat for undergraduates (save for an optional, concluding Mass), led by a rotating pool of staff and faculty. For the third task, the planning group found the faculty and staff seminar described above to be a straightforward choice, as was creating a set of church ministry internships for the fourth task. For the fifth task, the planning group was fortunate to have among its members a junior professor who knew the Lilly Endowment's religion division well, having just received a sizable grant from that division, and who consequently led the group's writing effort.

So far, so good. The IU planning group, with its mix of Jesuits and non-Jesuits, faculty and staff, scholars and practitioners, got along well and shared enthusiasm for the work they sought to do. This garden society, to return to my analogy from the first chapter, had identified good seeds, selected a nice patch of fertile soil, and soon obtained $2 million worth of sunshine in which to till soil and plant seeds. They needed only a full-time gardener—a program director to implement, troubleshoot, adapt, and oversee the programs. They found their candidate within the planning group's own ranks—Steve Wright, an assistant dean of students with a background in management. His hiring brought them several advantages: Steve understood and embraced the vision for the program, as he had helped to create it; he knew IU's organizational structure and student culture from his years working at IU; and while he respected Catholicism, Steve was a lifelong Lutheran who brought an outsider's perspective to the program. Moreover, Steve was not a wannabe professor[2]—he preferred working in student life, yet possessed a master's degree in philosophy, which gave him confidence when interacting with faculty. Finally, Steve had experience in business management, which imparted entrepreneurial savvy and an understanding of the importance of marketing and product development. In short, Steve was the perfect hire for this position.

To launch the Campus Center for Engagement, Steve knew he had to make a good first impression and build positive word of mouth. So he began with the center's biggest program: its student retreat. Steve recruited a marketing team, who drew from IU's prominence in NCAA Division 1 Basketball to name the program "Rebound," commissioned the design of an attractive logo, and put into effect an advertising plan. That plan included Steve reaching out to IU's basketball coach, who in turn recruited an IU alum turned superstar to videotape an appeal for Rebound that was then broadcast on student center video monitors and before IU home basketball games. Consequently, the Rebound program had a full bus for its first Rebound retreat, and thanks to solid programming by the Rebound retreat team along with eagerness to improve based on participant feedback, it has enjoyed enthusiastic word of mouth ever since.

As of the date of this writing, more than two thousand IU students have chosen to participate in one of more than fifty Rebound retreats, making it one of the most successful student programs in the university's history. Rebound's appeal is both extrinsic and intrinsic. Extrinsically, the retreat takes place at one of two mountain locations, costs no money (students' fifty-dollar deposits are refunded when they board the bus), occurs on seven weekends each year—making scheduling easy, and serves as a gateway for other appealing Campus Center programs (like service trips and paid internships). Such factors undeniably contribute to the retreat's popularity, yet I find them insufficient to explain Rebound's rapid growth and the unrelenting demand for the program. The larger factors are intrinsic: Rebound leaders have learned how to draw students into thinking about questions that matter to them, questions of self-knowledge and self-transcendence.

For some students, attending Rebound was prompted by academic major and career decisions. Suzanna, a chemistry major from Arkansas, told us:

> I was questioning my major, questioning my vocational goals, and everything like that. And [Rebound] gave me the tools and opportunity to really sit with the questions and to really work through them . . . to just give me some sort of guidance. . . . The peace of mind that I got from [Rebound] was just monumental to me.

Suzanna opted to stay on her original path, and tapped tutoring services to help her successfully repeat a difficult class. Other students used Rebound to make more significant changes:

> I had this, like, *revelation* on [Rebound], and I'm sure that not everyone has that, but I [found the] courage to kind of take that step back and realize the path that I was on wasn't the path that I wanted to be on. And I owe that completely to [Rebound]. I completely give it credit.

Another student, Nicolo, told us the "laid-back" Jesuit "system of looking at your life outside of yourself" was "incredibly useful" in "thinking about a meaningful life as opposed to just making money." Nicolo's perception of Jesuits as laid-back was not accidental. Rebound intentionally downplayed its Jesuit and Catholic roots, so that "*anybody* can do [Rebound]," as a nonreligious attendee told us. Of course, there are students who attended Rebound, as one student said, "because it was free." Yet, Rebound's positive atmosphere and structure would draw even free riders in, and many of these students would report gaining "a lot more out of the weekend" than they "ever expected." What Rebound offered was an intense yet malleable experience of engaging meaning that appealed to young adults facing decisions and calibrating life trajectories, which they could then interpret through religious or nonreligious frameworks as they saw fit.

Underscoring the intensity of the Rebound experience was its engineering of a three-day, multigenerational protocommunity. It did this by recruiting faculty and staff who had participated in the seminar described above to serve as Rebound cofacilitators. Thus, each Rebound retreat included a half dozen faculty and staff cofacilitators who, *along with their spouses or children,* attended the weekend activities, dined with the students, and shared their "vocational stories" during strategic points in the program. This produced a win-win situation for all parties: faculty and staff enjoyed sharing their stories with students, and students appreciated these IU employees as whole persons with families and recreational interests. One faculty member enthused that Rebound participants "get to see us as more than just a teaching machine or a grading machine." Another explained how her experience talking with students at Rebound "helped me immensely in how I respond to certain teaching moments as they arise, such as . . . in the aftermath of [the deadly rampage at] Virginia Tech."

Students who attended Rebound were likewise enthusiastic: "To listen to the faculty stories, that was probably my favorite part because . . . the lead faculty person, he's a successful professor here, but it took him, like, a twenty-year journey to get here, you know? And just understanding that that was OK, and . . . almost optimal in a way, to have that whole journey to get to where you need to go." Another remarked how the faculty and staff presence at the retreat "motivates students to take advantage of faculty and administrators" after students return, because he realized for the first time "that a lot of faculty here *want* to talk to undergrads and work with undergrads." This protocommunity, combined with Steve Wright's ongoing adjustments based on participants' feedback, helped to make Rebound the signature program of the Campus Center for Engagement.

The Campus Center was, of course, comprised of more than just the Rebound retreat and the faculty/staff seminar. There were internships in church ministry that provided stipends to site supervisors and interns alike, as well as weeklong service trips to communities devastated by Hurricane Katrina, follow-up lunch conversations for alumni of these internships or service projects, courses with discernment themes, and seminars in various residence halls for Rebound alumni. There were also further opportunities for faculty and staff who participated in the Educating the Whole Student seminar, from lunchtime gatherings to follow-up seminars to curricular and programmatic development minigrants. Last there were campus-wide events, such as lectures by education guru Parker Palmer, concerts by folk singer Carrie Newcomer, and information fairs devoted to nonprofit careers and longer-term volunteer opportunities.

Not every Campus Center program was successful. Efforts by the Campus Center to engage graduate students, for example, foundered. Graduate students were largely ignored in the initial design of the Campus Center, and aside from its own graduate assistants, few graduate students took advantage of the center's programs. Campus Center programs also attracted proportionately fewer male undergraduates than female — a common pattern among religious and spiritual life organizations but nonetheless notable. Internal center reports indicated that its student blog attracted few readers, and its Rebound-like retreats for area high school students facilitated little reflection among adolescent attendees. Both efforts were discontinued, decisions attributable to Steve Wright's entrepreneurialism as well as the Lilly Endowment's encouragement of experimentation and evaluation. Thus, Steve and his staff embraced creativity and experimentation, but expected new programs to flourish in order to continue, and zealously collected feedback to inform their decisions.

It might seem ironic that an office charged with fostering exploration and reflection would possess a marketplace orientation to its work. But that orientation was critical to the Campus Center's broad success. The Campus Center built upon IU's strengths, such as its "laid-back" Jesuit tradition and often-voiced commitment to student formation; accepted its hypocrisies, such as its prioritization of research that discouraged participation by junior faculty and graduate students; and worked in tandem with its student culture, such as its celebrated sports teams and trendy urban locale. What Steve Wright and his oversight board understood was that Ignatius University was not a monolith but rather a confederation that included an ambitious research university, an NCAA Division 1 sports powerhouse, an upwardly mobile "work hard, play hard" student body, and a Catholic school in the Jesuit tradition. And what the Campus Center nurtured was a pluralistic-embracing revival of the latter, which in turn united some of the best elements across the IU confederation.

I would be remiss to end this story of the Campus Center without highlighting several factors critical to its achievements. First, participation in center programs was always voluntary. I could not determine if this was an intentional decision or just a taken-for-granted assumption given IU's religious heterogeneity. Either way, it made for good policy. Exploration programs on other campuses sometimes included compulsory program components, like mandatory convocations or freshman seminars, which could generate resentment. The Campus Center avoided this entirely. Second, the program often featured a participation incentive. Faculty initially received a one-course teaching buyout for participation in the faculty/staff seminar, and later a cash stipend as staff participants did.[3] For students, an out-of-town weekend at an attractive mountain retreat center functioned in much the same way—along with the real cost of students' fifty-dollar deposits if they did not board the retreat bus. Such inducements, besides drawing in participants, helped to diversify participants as well.

A crucial third factor was the Rebound retreat's restriction to sophomores, juniors, and seniors, to avoid competing with a long-standing freshman retreat offered by IU. For a number of cultural, organizational, and developmental reasons that I elucidated in my first book, this timing was invaluable to Rebound's success. One IU junior, a participant in both retreats, put it this way:

> At least in my experience, the reason that [the freshman retreat] is so different than [Rebound] is because [younger] people haven't yet figured out who they are. There's a lot of growing up that happens in the first year and a half or so of college. So I think the time you start to get ... involved with [Rebound] is when I started to really realize what I wanted to be involved in. So it was a lot easier for me to be receptive to the whole [Campus Center] thing. ... Younger people aren't ready yet, because there's so much of figuring out their major and being away from home and living on their own and finding new friends ... that takes up so much of your thought process and your experience for that first chunk of time.

A fourth factor underlying the Campus Center's success was the clear and consistent support of IU's president—which was mostly for the center's raison d'être, but was underscored by a powerful extrinsic force: the pope himself. In 1990, Pope John Paul II issued an encyclical, *Ex corde ecclesiae*, challenging Catholic universities to preserve their Catholic identity and strengthen ties to their bishops. This encyclical set off a flurry of activity within Catholic higher education in the United States, a description of which lies beyond this book's scope. Suffice it to say here that the encyclical did much to reinforce the IU administration's support for the Campus Center for Engagement.

All four of these factors, combined with organic program design and organizationally savvy program leadership, contributed to the Campus Center for Engagement's success at Ignatius University. While some programmatically oriented readers might be tempted to stop reading and launch equivalent endeavors, that would be a mistake. Without the thoughtful contextualization—that is, without the organic process from which the Campus Center's program design emerged—transplanting will likely fail. Palm trees may grow beautifully on Florida campuses, but that does not mean Minnesota colleges should plant them. Successful programs are not possible without thorough, consensus-building origins and strategic engagement of their organizational, structural, and cultural contexts.

Gelatin Capsules and Philanthropic Initiatives

To move this story forward, some background is necessary. Readers should know how it was that the Lilly Endowment sought to invest in college students' exploration of purpose and vocation, and how it was that I came to be this initiative's national evaluator. The origins of this initiative, and my involvement in it, are not hard to recount, but they are best recounted historically. At the core of this undertaking one finds a charitable foundation, chartered to support American Christianity, confident that churches benefit from vocationally attuned clergy and laity, positioned to distribute nearly a quarter-billion dollars to foster exploration of purpose and vocation on eighty-eight religiously affiliated college campuses, committed to an external and objective evaluation, and eager to have a higher education audience and an interested public hear what happens when campuses explore questions of purpose and vocation creatively and intentionally.

So why invest in campus exploration of purpose and vocation? The answer begins with gelatin capsules and cherry-flavored liquid medicine. Here's how: In 1876, former Union army colonel turned pharmacist Eli Lilly founded a pharmaceutical business under his own name, where his innovations of gelatin capsules and fruit-flavored medicines brought him quick success. Remember Lilly's then competition—imprecisely mixed medicines prepared by local pharmacists of unknown training, and cure-all elixirs hawked by traveling salesmen. By contrast, the medicines that Lilly manufactured cost less, tasted better, and worked as described. So Eli Lilly made a rightful fortune in just fourteen years, after which he turned over management of his company to his son, Josiah K. (Sr.), so he could devote his remaining years to philanthropic interests like children's health and developing resources for the "deserving poor."

Josiah K. Lilly Sr. continued both his father's tradition of pharmaceutical innovation, successfully navigating the company through the economically turbulent 1890s, and his father's philanthropy. In 1937, Josiah Sr. made his family's commitment to philanthropy permanent, when he and sons Josiah K. Jr. and Eli Jr. donated stock to create the Lilly Endowment, a private foundation. Today the endowment, with holdings in excess of $7 billion despite Great Recession tumult, consistently ranks among the wealthiest private foundations in the world. And it supports, following the wishes of its founders, three causes: religion (by which Josiah and sons meant Christianity), education, and community development. It also places a high priority on helping the people of Indiana "better their lives." Indeed, the endowment has such a distinctive focus on Indiana that it has made *Lilly* a household word among the state's residents and a ubiquitous plaque within its educational, health, and religious organizations.

An endowment of Lilly's magnitude can readily convey its priorities and accomplish its goals. And this holds true for all of the endowment's divisions, including religion. Since its inception, the religion division has supported a range of Christian organizations, from Eli Lilly's childhood parish — Christ Church, now Christ Church Cathedral and the seat of the Episcopal bishop of Indianapolis — to organizations like the Association for Theological Schools, which is the accrediting organization of graduate theological schools and seminaries. Beginning in the 1990s, with the hiring of Presbyterian seminary professor Craig Dykstra as vice president, the division had two foci. The first involved enhancing theological education and scholarship on American Christianity, supporting seminaries across the United States, and underwriting hundreds of scholarly projects. I was a graduate student at Princeton University then, privileged to study with one of the nation's foremost scholars of American Christianity — Robert Wuthnow — and I both witnessed and benefited from the endowment's support for scholarship during the 1990s. The division's second and current focus, begun as the twentieth century wound down, involved strengthening American congregations, and their clergy in particular, on the view that excellent pastors are essential to vital congregations.

It is therefore a short journey from congregational and pastoral leadership to the endowment's interest in the theology of vocation — since it is this theology that describes how Christians hear the call of God to various endeavors, including pastoral ministry. Investing in seminary scholarships thus made sense, as did summer ministry programs for churchgoing teens. But program officers in the endowment's religion division were concerned that the median age of seminary students was rising sharply and that "too few" of the top graduates of liberal arts colleges were considering a career in pastoral ministry.[4] So these officers began conversations with college leaders and educators, to explore how colleges might regain their role in sending top students on to seminary education. Those conversations, along with the success of a pilot grant for a campus center for vocational exploration at a liberal arts college, sowed the seeds of the division's Programs for the Theological Exploration of Vocation (PTEV) initiative.

To start, the religion division identified thirty-seven religious colleges recommended by a pool of consultants. These campuses had widely varying denominational affiliations and even more widely varying enthusiasm about these affiliations, were located chiefly in the Midwest, and were to be invited by the endowment to submit proposals for campus-based exploration programming. At that moment, a roaring stock market intervened, nearly quadrupling the endowment's annual mandatory payout. These three dozen colleges, instead of receiving the usual private foundation request for proposals costing $500,000 each and lasting three years, received invitations to propose five-year programs at costs of up to $2 million each! "It was like opening the mail and finding a letter from Santa Claus," one development officer confided. "We were stunned! And then we ran across campus to recruit a [proposal] writing committee."

The endowment did not set the award at $2 million just to meet its mandatory payout, however. It consulted with college leaders about what size of grant would help applicants "be creative" in the design of their programming, and ultimately settled on a $2 million figure to have that "wow" effect (though endowment officers judiciously phrased it as "getting the attention" of colleges). The invitation letter also enumerated the endowment's goals clearly, asking these thirty-seven colleges and universities to "establish or strengthen programs . . . that (1) assist students in understanding their future work in light of their faith commitments and in terms of vocation, (2) identify talented young people and provide them with opportunities to explore ministry, either lay or ordained, as their life's work and (3) enhance a school's capacity to draw on the resources of its mission, heritage and religious tradition in preparing a new generation of leaders for church and society." While some of the initial thirty-seven campuses chose not to apply, most submitted proposals eagerly, and the endowment awarded $39.7 million to twenty colleges in the fall of 2000 to implement vocational exploration programs.

The foundation staff's weariness following this first round of awards made no difference to the stock market, which continued to expand and led the endowment to issue a second invitation. Seeing this as an opportunity to expand this campus experiment further, the Lilly Endowment identified 50 church-affiliated colleges and universities that were more geographically distributed and sent them an invitation similar to the initial pool's. Once again, a few campuses chose not to apply, but most did, resulting in a $57.3 million award to 29 additional colleges—and still the stock market rolled on. So in 2002, the endowment announced an open competition, and 326 four-year, accredited, church-related colleges and universities submitted proposals. The division's external grant readers and internal staff worked from early morning to late at night to give each proposal the fairest review possible. "It was amazing," said one external reviewer. "An office used to handling a few dozen proposals at a time now had to juggle hundreds of them." In this third and final round, the endowment made its largest award yet: $79.2 million to 39 church-related colleges. Taken as a whole, nearly half of the religiously affiliated colleges and universities in the United States (414 out of some 900) submitted proposals, with 114 receiving $50,000 planning grants and 88 institutions receiving $2 million implementation awards—an extraordinary rate of participation for a population that intently pursues its own agenda.[5]

Sustaining a Large Initiative

To oversee the work of these eighty-eight programs, the endowment funded a separate coordination office to handle paperwork, share information, organize assistance, plan conferences for program directors, form an advisory board, and launch a website and online community. This reduced the direct oversight burden on Lilly Endowment officers, yet they remained in contact with this coordination office and program directors alike, attended conferences and visited many of the programs personally. Addressing the first gathering of these program directors, attending with a team of four additional representatives from each campus (which included two senior administrators and two representatives from the faculty and staff), then vice president Dykstra waxed eloquent:

> I sense before we are even barely begun that we are already partners in a fascinating and promising conversation and enterprise. . . . You have taken what we thought to be important questions and made them your own. But you have done so in diverse ways — in ways consistent with the traditions and ethos of your own schools and in ways that are appropriate for your students, faculty and staff. The questions are not, by any means, all answered. The programmatic experiments are just getting started. But it is clear that you are all on to something significant.[6]

Dykstra was also honest. "What does Lilly mean by 'theological exploration of vocation'? The honest answer to the question is this: we don't exactly know. That is what we hope *you* will figure out. . . . [It] is for us, at this point, more an important question to ask than it is an answer we have some way of providing. Much less is it, in our minds, a specific program that we are hoping, through this funding, to seduce you all into conducting" (emphasis in the original). To the audience of program directors, senior administrators, faculty, and staff that heard this address, such openness to diversity was undoubtedly reassuring.

Moreover, Dykstra delivered these words with fully half of the colleges' presidents in attendance (a $2 million award nets personal attention from all but the wealthiest schools' presidents). Eighty-eight college delegations, then, including their presidents or provosts, were asked to participate in a conversation "that includes many voices, that draws on profound traditions of moral, religious, and spiritual wisdom, and that brings to bear the experience and insights of a wide variety of people, including not only your faculties and staff, but also — and perhaps especially — your students." In other words, they were asked to rediscover what it was that drew them into their present work, to engage scholarly texts on purpose and vocation, and to talk about these with one another and with their students. Who in academia could object to such a conversation? So converse these colleges and universities did, and they did so with creativity, thoughtfulness, and the finest of refreshments ($2 million buys a lot of tea and cookies!).

Observing this initiative unfold over the next few years, the Lilly Endowment was pleased by what it observed, and to embed this "good work" more deeply, announced the availability of sustainability grants. These were grants of $500,000 each, offering 50 percent funding for an additional three years of programming. To obtain these grants, campuses had to select their most successful program components, allocate internal funds for their continuance, and outline how these programs would, at the end of the sustainability grant, become subsumed into ongoing activities and operating budgets. Eighty-three campuses received these awards, evidence of administrative support as well as of the endowment's belief (to the tune of $41 million more) in the efficacy of these programs in general. The sustainability grants, combined with grants for the coordination office and related projects, brought the total investment by the endowment in PTEV to $225 million — making it the single largest grant initiative by the endowment's religion division.

Inviting Evaluation

Lilly Endowment officers were clearly pleased with the effects of this initiative, but they wanted their knowledge independently confirmed by an external evaluator, who could also "tell the story" of this effort to a wider audience. That is where I enter the picture. I was certainly external, because when then Lilly program officer (and now vice president) Christopher Coble walked up to me at the 2005 Annual Meeting of the Society for the Scientific Study of Religion in Rochester, New York, and asked if I was familiar with PTEV, I replied, "Familiar with *what*?" Then I recovered: "No, I'm not familiar with it — tell me about it." You see, like the presidents of church-affiliated colleges above, researchers in American religion are *always* interested in what a program officer at the Lilly Endowment has to say. One foundation president described this phenomenon humorously in Paul Brest and Hal Harvey's *Money Well Spent*:

From 1987 to 1999, Paul Brest, coauthor of this book, was the dean of Stanford Law School. During these twelve years, a day hardly went by when students, faculty, or alumni didn't tell him what he was doing wrong—and at least once in a while they were right. Then in 2000, he became president of Hewlett Foundation and, within a matter of months, underwent a personal transformation and, by all external signals, achieved perfection. The danger of his believing this was mitigated by a framed Yiddish proverb sent to him early on by a colleague at another foundation: "With money in your pocket, you are wise and you are handsome, and you sing well, too."[7]

Thankfully, I remembered how well Coble could sing, and I sat with him for conversation later that day. Both he and Craig Dykstra knew me from my Louisville Institute sabbatical award (the institute is funded by the Lilly Endowment), and they knew I was then writing a book about teens, American culture, and life trajectories. Our conversation began a six-month process that culminated in a 2006 planning grant award, followed by a 2007–10 implementation award for an external evaluation of PTEV under my direction.

That means I have personally benefitted from the same endowment whose initiative I evaluate here, and suggests I have a material interest in the evaluation's outcome. I will not pretend to be unaffected by this. At the same time, I have carved out a reputation for empirically driven sociological research that bluntly describes the sizable gap between what people assume and what the evidence demonstrates. So here is how I mitigate the effects of this bias. First, I describe the bias plainly. Second, I employ standard, social scientific methods of data collection and analysis. Third, I report the full range of results—blunders as well as successes, setbacks as well as progress (see especially chapter 6). Fourth, I position this book as but one voice in a much larger conversation about how to increase higher education's effectiveness and improve its engagement of the public good—a conversation to which I invite all readers, sympathetic and critical alike, to contribute as well.

To the endowment's credit, it funded a range of colleges and universities, from an assortment of denominational traditions, to implement highly varied exploration programming. That meant my evaluation had to encompass sufficient representation of this diversity and plumb varied forms of reflection, yet be sufficiently general to make comparisons across cases. So I selected chiefly qualitative methods of campus visits, document analyses, focus group interviews, in-depth individual interviews, and telephone-based alumni interviews, and supplemented these with follow-up campus observations, in-depth interviews, and a web-based survey of program participants. Our initial campus visits ranged from two to four days, and I selected campuses using a grid to ensure representation of colleges and universities from across denominations and regions of the United States, and across levels of perceived success (as indicated by internal experts). For example, my Roman Catholic subsample includes Jesuit, Franciscan, Augustinian, and diocesan schools; located in settings both urban and rural and north and south; spanning large research universities and small liberal arts colleges, some praised for their adherence to traditional Catholic practice and others for their "independence from Rome"; and variously classified by insiders as strong, weak, or moderate programs. Of course, I made my own judgment about program quality (which diverged significantly from that of the insiders); nonetheless, their initial ratings helped me visit a range of more and less effective programs.

I conducted half of the site observations personally, and hired two ethnographic researchers to conduct the other half. One was Keith Brown, then a PhD candidate in sociology at the University of Pennsylvania and now assistant professor of sociology at Saint Joseph's University in Philadelphia; the other was Anna Bradshaw, a MDiv graduate from the University of Chicago and now MSW candidate at New York University. All three of us met to evaluate the first site jointly and compare notes, to ensure that we understood the site-visit protocol and deployed a common approach to field notes and final reports. Several trained interviewers (including the ethnographic researchers) conducted telephone interviews, professional transcribers converted over four hundred hours of audio recordings into text documents, and research assistants double-checked transcriptions for accuracy and coded them using qualitative analysis software. (For more detailed information, see appendixes 2–4.) I personally supervised all data analysis, using both qualitative and quantitative software to assist in the gargantuan task. The writing and analysis proceeded iteratively, with each informing the other and the process ensuring my confidence in the findings described herein.

Scholarly and Educational Implications

During the six months between Coble's first conversation with me and my submission of an evaluation proposal, I wrestled with several questions. First, what if I discovered that the initiative was a colossal waste of money? Second, even if the initiative was successful, who would be the audience for a book about this initiative, and what publisher would be interested? Third, did I wish to invest the next few years of my career in an applied project, setting back the more traditional research project on young adults I had in mind? That the reader is now holding this book indicates positive resolution of these questions, but let me explain how I came to it. First, the Lilly officers insisted that I conduct a thorough evaluation and report its findings honestly, whether positive or negative. Second, they stated that if my findings did not comport with their view of the initiative's success, an internal report would be sufficient to meet my commitment to them. Third, they promised that I could retain use of the data I collected for my own research into life after college, thus supplying about half of that project's data.[8] And fourth, my growing understanding of issues relevant to this initiative convinced me that if it was successful, it would have important implications for central issues in both higher education and social science, and a wide potential readership. As I close this chapter, then, I describe this project's implications as an example of applied positive sociology that investigates the social, cultural, and organizational contexts that facilitate human flourishing and maximize human agency, for the efficacy of cultural trajectories in the study of emerging adults, for regaining the public trust by leveraging higher education's formative capacities, and for the study and engagement of purpose and spirituality in higher education.

Toward an Applied Positive Sociology

Few academic endeavors have captured attention and scholarly momentum like positive psychology. Since the 2002 publication of Martin Seligman's *Authentic Happiness*, there has been an outpouring of discussion, publication, and critique regarding this paradigm shift in psychology. The enthusiasm is fitting. Psychologists have documented dysfunction extensively; well-being surely merits equal attention. Unfortunately, my own discipline has not engaged in a parallel discussion of the social, cultural, and organizational contexts that facilitate human flourishing and maximize human agency—despite our long tradition of praxis sociology and the considerable contribution we could make to such an endeavor.[9] We are not exceptional in this, however. There appears to be little sign of a positive economics, positive anthropology, or positive political science either.

Perhaps the skeptical pose of social science hinders us; it beset me during the initial years of this evaluation, as I struggled to reconcile my empirical skepticism with the wide and enduring positive results I kept encountering. Even after a preponderance of evidence resolved that, I found writing comprised a second challenge, as I could fluently summarize pessimistic results, but had little experience articulating positive results in a robust manner. The applied positive sociology I recommend does not come naturally. But it is a necessary endeavor, if sociology and her sister social sciences wish to become more valued for their contributions to public life and social institutions. It is also a promising undertaking, since positive psychologists have demonstrated that motivation, persistence, and positive engagement are learnable skills, which formal organizations and larger social institutions can leverage readily.

We now understand that certain individuals possess intrinsic motivation to engage opportunities from an early age, and to do so in a positive and sustained way; but such individuals are statistically rare. Based on a national study of American adolescents, Stanford University psychologist William Damon reports, "What is too often missing—not altogether absent but evident only in a minority of today's youth—is the kind of wholehearted dedication to an activity or interest that stems from a serious purpose, a purpose that can give meaning and direction to life."[10] Positive and sustained motivation, Damon argues, requires a clear sense of life purpose. Harvard psychologist Daniel Goleman draws similar conclusions from studies of Olympic athletes, violin virtuosos, and chess grand masters, who maintain motivation across years of practice, setting these individuals apart from the majority of other athletes, musicians, and chess players. For Goleman, sustained motivation is born of high emotional intelligence, a cluster of abilities that "includes self-control, zeal and persistence."[11]

Damon and Goleman both cite studies demonstrating that the most fulfilled individuals are those who become absorbed with challenging activities that in turn make valuable contributions to the world.[12] They argue that sustained motivation is a learnable skill that results from a clear sense of life purpose and self-awareness. What neither delineates are the social and cultural contexts that facilitate the exploration and identification of life purpose, however. This is a project for applied positive sociology, of which this book is an example. I describe how well-designed and engagingly presented programs provided an inviting space to consider the idea of life purpose, which in turn led participants to pursue new courses of action or creatively reengage with activities that once wearied them, producing multiplier effects as participants shared their enthusiasm with friends and colleagues and even generating a local norm of purposeful reflection and engagement.

Sadly, disengagement if not disillusionment so pervades college and university populations that few can imagine campuses where the majority of students, faculty, and staff demonstrate intellectual curiosity and engaged citizenship. Results from the National Study of Student Engagement (begun because of low student engagement) indicate that four out of five college students do not devote even an hour of study for each hour they spend in class.[13] Nor are students compensating for minimal study time with more hours in cocurricular, extracurricular, or athletic involvements, as only a third of students put in more than five hours weekly on these activities. Professors likewise have little time for engagement. Today 69 percent of college instructors are contract employees, and overwhelmingly part-time. That leaves 31 percent of college instructors as tenure-track or tenured professors,[14] each facing pressures to publish or win grants so as to raise the institution's profile in national rankings, to advise students from their own as well as part-time instructors' classes,[15] and to serve on the scores of committees that govern even the smallest campuses. Many full-time faculty burn out, and many don blinders — focusing on select priorities, meeting core obligations, and ignoring everything else. Rarely do campus populations see themselves as part of a larger endeavor; the contemporary university is not an ocean liner that delivers essential goods and personnel to distant shores but rather a flotilla of rafts loosely tied together while their thousand pilots grab a share of the cargo.

It may seem odd that programs encouraging reflection on life purpose would have the effect of knitting together members of campuses and fostering their local and global engagement. Perhaps upon such reflection, many Americans realize that self-prioritizing lives do not provide the fulfillment that meaningful connections to others offer. Or perhaps the self is now so ascendant in American culture that efforts to move Americans beyond the self must now (ironically) begin with self-reflection. Whatever the explanation, we have an indisputable need for its effects. If college graduates do not become the purposeful, resilient, and globally engaged citizens that America needs, traditional collegiate education will find itself a luxury rather than a necessity. That cheaper credentialing alternatives are now expanding could put tomorrow's college administrators in a position not unlike that of print newspaper editors today—with falling revenues, fewer subscribers (read: students), an expensive physical plant, and a payroll that is impossible to meet.[16] I do not wish to be alarmist, but we must not ignore the writing on the wall. The disengaged campus-as-usual is no longer an option for American higher education.

Purposeful Life Trajectories

The laws of physics allow us to perfectly predict the trajectory of a physical projectile. Predictions about human trajectories from youth to adulthood are by contrast less than perfect. And yet, more often than not, youth follow the general arc established by their structural and cultural contexts—by the resources and life orientations of parents, educators, peers, and localities. Based on a 2003–6 study of collegiate young adults, sociologist Mary Grigsby described three cultural trajectories into which these young adults distinctly clustered. The majority trajectory was "individualist," wherein private life and leisure consumption were foci; the second trajectory was "traditionalist," wherein fulfillment of traditional gender, work, family, and religious roles was central; and the third and smallest trajectory was "interdependent," wherein a middle path of intentionally joining (or if necessary creating) other-oriented communities generated a sense of belonging.[17]

That the traditionalist trajectory was not the largest category, Grigsby argues (following Anthony Giddens[18] and Zygmunt Baumann[19]), was a consequence of our globe's constant economic change and its attendant cultural instability. While I do not discount the significance of macroeconomic churn, I grant culture more autonomy from economics than Grigsby does, and find Robert Bellah et al.'s claims about the ascendancy of American individualism and the diminishment of social institutions like religion and politics with their broader moral languages that call for contribution to the common good to be equally compelling.[20] Sidestepping this interpretive difference, however, what I find particularly intriguing for this book's purposes is Grigsby's *interdependent* trajectory. It seems to embody Robert Wuthnow's argument that American social capital is not collapsing (i.e., Robert Putnam's *Bowling Alone* thesis[21]) but changing, and that we are bound by "loose connections."[22] Might this interdependent trajectory be elective? That is, might it be a trajectory that purposeful individuals can opt into—seeing it as a middle way between a traditionalist trajectory that pursues a nostalgic fiction and a consumerist trajectory that is superficial and narrow? The interviews with this project's young adults answer that question, illuminating individual agency as not only structurally variable but also capable of acquiring both cultural and structural resources, which individuals can then leverage strategically.

Leveraging Institutional Impact

That social institutions influence, form, and even define identity is a sociological truism; as inherently social beings, we cannot help but be affected by how others view us. This is easily seen in the lasting individual impact of participation in total institutions like the armed forces, psychiatric hospitals, or prisons. But it is also apparent in corporations, families, and colleges and universities. Institutions cannot avoid influencing those who pass through them—they vary only in the attention and intention they give to their formative role.

For centuries, universities served the interests of elites, grooming their offspring to assume positions of power and to do so, ideally, with largess. The democratization of access and curricula that began in the late 1960s was thus necessary and commendable. But when the institutional pendulum swung away from elitist formation, it swung toward disavowal of formation—imprinting that era's "Do your own thing" into the fabric of higher education. In other words, when colleges and universities did not assert the primacy of preparing citizen-leaders over the disciplinary and professional agendas of its faculty and staff or the upward mobility desires of its students, they opened the formative floodgates to American privatism, careerism, and consumerism. It should not surprise us, then, to learn that the early 1960s represent the high-water mark of public respect for education as well as its scholarly sibling, science, or that approval for both has declined ever since (see fig. 2.1).

Today, the American public holds a startlingly low view of higher education.[23] A national survey reported that 60 percent of Americans agree that colleges are "like most businesses and mainly care about the bottom line," with only 32 percent agreeing that colleges make "sure students have a good educational experience."[24] The reasons for this are many, but minimal learning, bewildered graduates, and disengaged campus populations are arguably

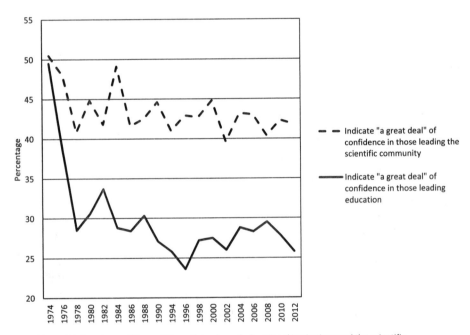

Figure 2.1. American public confidence in leaders of educational institutions and the scientific community. Item sample sizes range from 813 to 1,993 and are nationally representative samples of noninstitutionalized American adults age eighteen and over. Remaining item response options were "only some" and "hardly any." Neither item was included in the 1992 survey.

Source: Author's analyses of General Social Survey cumulative data file. Tom W. Smith, Peter Marsden, Michael Hout, and Jibum Kim, General Social Surveys, 1972-2012 [machine-readable data file]. Principal investigator, Tom W. Smith; co-principal investigator, Peter V. Marsden; co-principal investigator, Michael Hout. Sponsored by the National Science Foundation. NORC, ed. Chicago: National Opinion Research Center [producer]; Storrs, CT: Roper Center for Public Opinion Research, University of Connecticut [distributor], 2013. 1 data file [57,061 logical records] + 1 codebook [3,432 pp.]. National Data Program for the Social Sciences, no. 21.)

part of the equation. Students come to college hoping for engaging classes, but encounter massive lecture courses, busy faculty, and well-established methods to minimize effort and still achieve satisfactory grades. Professors encounter student resistance to intellectual challenge, sour campus politics, and few rewards for commitment to teaching or campus citizenship. Campus staff grow weary of bureaucratic inertia and the organizational restructurings that accompany each new administrator. To be sure, there remain dedicated students, professors, and staff on every campus who prioritize learning and campus engagement, just as there remain friendly critics who call universities to reclaim their public purpose, but few agree about where or how to begin.

For many, rebuilding the public's trust begins with reprioritizing undergraduate education. "The public has finally come to believe quite strongly that our institutions — particularly our leading universities — are not making the education of students a top priority," stated Derek Bok, at the end of his Harvard University presidency in 1991.[25] And one would be hard-pressed to find a college, university, or accrediting commission that disagreed. Neither do I. But after two decades of attention to pedagogy and learning assessment, gains in the public's trust have been slight (to wit: a gradual 5 percent uptick in education confidence from 1996 to 2008, followed by a 3 percent drop from 2008 to 2012; see fig. 2.1). A sustained rebound in the public trust will require more than teaching workshops and learning assessment.

A sustained rebound, I argue, requires three things: as formal organizations, colleges and universities must unequivocally prioritize students, faculty, and staff *as whole persons*; these persons must, in turn, prioritize the organization's mission; and all must prioritize local and global citizenship. On a macro scale, that may seem as likely as winning the Powerball jackpot. But the odds can shift markedly at the meso, or formal organizational, level. Consider that as hard as the American financial industry was whacked by the 2008 economic crisis, in regions across the nation, select small banks were unfazed because they understood their customers, their mission, and their local context — and now serve as models for the industry at large. Similarly, individual campuses, with effective leadership and grassroots support from campus constituencies, can thrive even as what Keeling and Hirsch call "throughput" comes to dominate higher education's priorities. Individual campuses *can* be marked by a faculty that understands students, teaching, and mentorship as well as it understands its disciplines; by students who desire to learn as much as they desire good grades; and by staff who recognize that meaningful interactions with students are as important as meeting deadlines and managing data. Individual campuses *can* be led by men and women who indisputably value faculty, students, and staff as whole persons and can be praised by communities near and far for their enduring contributions. I do not write this from the island of Pollyanna—I have seen it myself, and I am now seeing these campuses become models to others. What will become of this ultimately I do not know, but as the inexorable challenges felt by higher education send ever more campuses looking for long-term solutions, I am optimistic that some will encounter the creative, campus-based programs of purpose exploration evaluated in this volume, and find their promising outcomes worthy of emulation.

Purpose and Spirituality

After decades of obscurity, the topics of purpose and spirituality have reasserted their place in higher education scholarship and practice. Perhaps it was the reflections of so many university leaders, like Harry Lewis, former dean of Harvard College; Anthony Kronman, former dean of Yale Law School; Harold Shapiro, former president of Princeton University; or Derek Bok, former president of Harvard University.[26] Perhaps it was the anxiety that struck the nation after September 11, 2001, packing university religion courses to the gills and confronting us with religion's global durability. Or perhaps it was the looming retirements of prominent higher education scholars Arthur Chickering, Alexander Astin, Robert Nash, and George Kuh; grants by the Teagle Foundation or the Fetzer Institute; and the ubiquitous campus lectures of Parker Palmer and Sharon Dalos Parks that turned attention to existential questions.[27] Whatever the cause, likely all of the above and more, the effect has been indisputable—increasing attention to issues of purpose and spirituality in higher education.

Much of this literature is apologetic, underscoring the importance of purpose and spirituality to human well-being and arguing for engaging these in higher education. But much describes empirical and pedagogical results, including the prevalence of spiritual and religious activities among college students and faculty (see chapter 1), the association between purpose or spirituality and positive student engagement, and the positive outcomes when professors and educational programs engage these matters. This book joins this growing literature and expands it in several ways. It relays the results of an eighty-eight-campus effort to engage students, faculty, and staff in thoughtful conversations about purpose and vocation—a larger undertaking and program evaluation than any previously reported in this literature. It also links this scholarly literature with the scholarship on emerging adulthood—which has not been done and which holds vital implications for colleges and universities. And it reveals the distinctive capacity that systematic conversations about purpose and vocation have for broadening engagement both on and off campus and for assisting young adults in intentionally calibrating their life trajectories and anticipating setbacks during their pursuit of the same.

Some in the academy reject the idea that purpose or spirituality merit discussion in higher education settings or academic research. They may argue, with psychologist Steve Stewart-Williams, that "we are here because we evolved, but we are not here for any purpose,"[28] or insist on a "wall of separation" between church and state. Others may accept discussions of purpose in educational settings, but only if they steer clear of purpose's spiritual or religious dimensions. I do not concur, for philosophical and empirical reasons. In chapter 5, I discuss the dated, modernist views of secularism that insist on a public space that banishes religion, and relay stories of faculty members who were skeptical of their campus's efforts to engage undergraduates in exploration of purpose and vocation—until they witnessed the positive effects of these explorations. These professors eventually became their campus exploration program's biggest fans, even as some continued to struggle with the cause of the program's positive effects. In the end, it is the empirical evidence that justifies this conversation's place on campuses and within scholarly circles, and I submit this volume to consideration in both settings.

Looking Forward

Some readers have had their appetites whetted by the theoretical and practical implications described above; others have struggled to keep reading. Both types, and everyone in between, should find the next three chapters of keen interest. These chapters describe purpose exploration programming as campus stimuli, then examine their impact on students, faculty, and staff. These chapters supply the evidence for this book's claim that purpose exploration can deeply engage and positively influence campus members of every sort, and do so on particularist to nonsectarian campuses. Gathering these data was a rewarding, often exhausting, frequently exciting, and occasionally moving endeavor. Conveying it in this volume is my privilege.

3

Matters of Design

Garden State

The perfect antidote to winter malaise lies an hour's drive from my New Jersey home: Longwood Gardens. This horticulturalist haven, established more than a century ago by members of the Du Pont family and long open to the public, boasts acres of stunning *indoor* gardens. Stepping inside its enormous conservatory, one is enveloped in perpetual spring: blooming tree blossoms, flowers of every variety, rolling lawns, quiet brooks, and the sweet fragrances of its twenty distinct gardens. As I breathe in deeply, strolling around slowly, my spirits are lifted. I am viscerally reminded that spring will return, and I am grateful for the horticulturalists and managers who make Longwood Gardens such a remarkable place. Each time I visit, I am slow to depart, and each time I return, I wish I had done so sooner.

Gardens can have that effect, especially when they are thoughtfully designed and carefully tended. In this volume I have likened purpose exploration programs to gardens, since both require attention to design and commitment to ongoing maintenance, and both provide visitors with spaces to rest and reflect. This chapter examines the design and implementation of four successful programs, and then broadens to the general initiative. Readers will learn that programs varied in design from one another, and that the process of each program's implementation was important to its success. Readers will also learn the significance of a program's location within its organizational structure, understand the common repertoire from which campuses designed programs, and gain insight into personnel factors. In other words, this chapter examines purpose exploration programs as stimuli, while the next two focus on student, faculty, and staff effects.

Meaningful Work Initiative at Phi Beta College

Many campuses were stunned to hear that they were awarded a grant to discuss purpose and explore the theology of vocation, but few were more stunned than Phi Beta College. That is because students, staff, faculty, and even most administrators do not think of Phi Beta as a religiously affiliated college. A few old-timers could recall when work crews dismantled the chapel's steeple, removed its pews, and converted its sanctuary into a black box theater. The chapel's bronze dedicatory plaque was left, however, specifying the role of Reverend *This* and Bishop *That* in founding Phi Beta College and helping to spread Methodism. Though obscured by a hedge, this bronze plaque gave Phi Beta's public relations director a suitable image to accompany the grant award's press release, which she dutifully distributed.

On similar campuses, long accustomed to thinking of themselves as unaffiliated, announcement of a grant to discuss a theological idea triggered a backlash. Faculty leaders would demand to know who submitted the grant proposal, and staff would whisper in anxious tones: *Was the president trying to turn back the clock? Was this the work of trustees aligned with the religious right?* This did not occur at Phi Beta, however, for several reasons. First, the author of the grant proposal was its prolific professor of religion, Susan Huffington, who had the respect of faculty and students. She was Phi Beta's best-known scholar and was, frankly, as politically and socially liberal as they come. Second, Huffington had designed the program around the value of seeking and doing meaningful work. Drawing from Methodist pragmatism, the Socratic notion of an examined life, and students' career aspirations, Huffington proposed the "Meaningful Work Initiative." Third, this initiative was scaled so as not to overwhelm Phi Beta—a college of just over one thousand undergraduates. Huffington applied for $1 million rather than $2 million, kept program goals focused, and left the faculty's feathers unruffled. Fourth, Phi Beta was located in a religiously and culturally conservative region of the United States and had long enrolled students from that region's most prominent families. Other locations and other student bodies afford their faculty the freedom to view religion as a premodern relic, but not Phi Beta. Rather, Phi Beta faculty interacted daily with students, alumni, parents, or neighbors who publicly expressed their religious commitments, and thus a program that encouraged students to consider the connection between their religious values and their future occupations struck everyone as a good idea, or at least as not warranting complaint.

The story of the Meaningful Work Initiative at Phi Beta, then, involves a small endeavor that won over its entire campus. It did not seek attention using celebrity endorsements or promotional giveaways as Ignatius University's Rebound retreat did in chapter 2. Rather, it drew upon the genteel respectability of its mainline Methodist roots, and graciously invited participation in a few programs of good quality. Nor did it tap a cross section of faculty scholars and student life professionals to draft its proposal, as IU did. The proposal committee began and ended with Huffington herself. Phi Beta's academic dean did provide feedback on drafts that Huffington shared with him, and its president signed the proposal's cover letter, but Huffington was the proposal's unmistakable author and architect. Consequently, she became the agent of its implementation.

Becoming project director was not Huffington's plan, however. She had expected to hire a director and oversee from a distance. But it was clear to Phi Beta's academic dean, who convinced Huffington after two fruitless months of interviewing, that the program had to be rolled out by Huffington herself before she could hand it off to a manager. It was sage advice. Huffington became a flurry of activity during the project's first year, making excellent headway on a number of fronts. Chief among these was creation of a religion elective, Work and Meaning, which fulfilled a Phi Beta degree requirement and served as a gateway to internships, an undergraduate fellowship program, and international service projects. With the triple advantage of Huffington's popularity as an instructor, meeting a core requirement, and access to desirable resources post–course completion—every section of Work and Meaning filled with eager students, and by the time I visited Phi Beta, one out of three Phi Beta students had taken this course. That a single professor could teach so many was possible only at a small college. But it was also evidence of wise scaling: Ignatius University harnessed its size and sports prominence to good effect; Phi Beta deployed its star professor and tapped degree requirements to similarly good effect.

So what would students enrolling in Work and Meaning learn? They would learn about how different people define work; how work affects identity construction and community creation; who benefits most and least from work; how work varies by class, gender, and race; and how various theological traditions make sense of work. Woven through the course, too, were discussions about the reasons for working, about materialism, and about the "soul" of capitalism. The course, in other words, careened between Barbara Ehrenreich, Saint Francis of Assisi, Christopher Lasch, and the book of Ecclesiastes; watched eye-opening documentaries about worker movements and sweatshops; took a field trip to a job-training program for recovering addicts; and required students to subsist for two days on a minimum-wage budget. After observing one class, I wanted to take the whole course. Huffington was a master teacher; the eighty-minute session flew by, and I had to remind myself that my role was to observe, not participate. It was easy to see why Phi Beta students regarded the Meaningful Work Initiative so highly.

Following the Work and Meaning course, students could apply for credit-bearing internships, weeklong international service projects, spiritual reflection groups, or upper-level service-learning projects. Two merit special attention. The internship program bore no resemblance to typical listings of available internships. Rather, students would meet with two full-time staff members, who would administer personality tests and counsel students about career interests. Once students settled on a single area of interest, these two staff members would tap alumni to generate a placement. And since Phi Beta College had alumni in leadership positions across the region, there was virtually no internship request these two networking-savvy staffers could not fill. Rebecca, a dual science and economics major at Phi Beta, relayed this story about her internship experience:

I realized one day that I had too many goals that I wanted to achieve and too little time, and I was just, like . . . I know what I want to do but I don't know *exactly* what I want to do. I needed someone to help me to narrow down my choices, because I wanted to be, like, a marine biologist, wedding planner— all kinds of crazy stuff. [I even] did an internship through [Major US Bank] and realized that I didn't want your typical desk work. . . . So I decided to join [Huffington's] class, and when I got in there, I found it really difficult because I knew what I wanted to do; I just needed help narrowing it down. So [Huffington] pulled me aside and told me about [the initiative's internship] again, and I said, "Well, I guess I'll give it a try." . . . I listed one thing for entertainment marketing, and it was really hard to place me [until they] thought about [R&B Record Company]. . . . I fell in love with the gospel division, and I've been there since last February . . . ; I plan on getting my MBA after I finish here and pursuing it focused on the music industry.

A few hours after Rebecca shared her story, the internship director confirmed it (without my prompting) — relaying how his associate staff member, a prominent local socialite, tapped a lawyer acquaintance who once represented R&B Record Company. She called this lawyer, who called the company president, who arranged Rebecca's internship. The internship director's point was to illustrate how far his office would go to make student internship wishes come true. Individual attention like this is not inexpensive, but few experiences have more lasting impact on students' lives than transformative internships — making them a staple of many purpose exploration programs.

Phi Beta's service-learning component also merits attention. On most campuses nationwide, service-learning clusters in lower-level general education courses and takes the form of low-skill volunteer work, with few upper-level courses involved. At Phi Beta, however, service-learning courses were concentrated at the upper level, and made use of the higher-level skills of their students. For example, a professor of computer science enthusiastically described how his senior seminar students were rewriting the local school district's student database, removing it from archaic mainframe engines, linking student records from kindergarten through high school, and constructing user-friendly access that met school and parent needs. A biology professor divided students into two teams, one measuring toxin levels in local waterways, the other tracking the spread of nonnative botanic species, then had both teams present their findings to state and local officials. Similar assignments could be created at most colleges, of course, but rarely are because the initial setup and coordination work is too time-consuming for faculty who must also publish, win grants, advise, and serve on committees. A grant-funded staff member at Phi Beta assisted faculty members with service-learning assignments, however, and soon a critical mass of faculty had infused service-learning projects into their courses, generating a positive buzz that drew in more with each additional semester. The Meaningful Work Initiative did not give birth to faculty interest in service-learning; what it did was nudge pre-existing faculty interest and generate momentum.

Finally, Phi Beta created a Work and Meaning Fellowship program, for students who had completed the course, completed a credit-bearing internship, and participated in either an international or local service project. This program attracted prominent student leaders who served as mentors to students in the Work and Meaning course, as ambassadors to new students about the Meaningful Work Initiative, as leaders of service projects, and as administrators of minigrant funds. I met a cohort of these fellows, and they impressed me with their intelligence, graciousness, accomplishments, and future plans. They were every professor's dream students—those who make the most of opportunities at college, and who had made the most of the Meaningful Work Initiative specifically.

Accomplishing this much among students was impressive in its own right, but the initiative did not restrict itself to students. It saw college teaching as meaningful work, worthy of dedication and attention. To that end, Huffington created a biweekly Teaching Buffet, using a simple format: reserve a comfortable lounge, order lunch, invite faculty members, and recruit one of them to give a twenty-minute presentation about his or her teaching. The program was a rousing success. More than half of the Phi Beta faculty attends regularly, and there is a core group of two dozen that never miss a meeting. "I'm not a religious person at all," a political science professor told me, "but I do think teaching is a calling—and I'm grateful to [Huffington] for creating this [Teaching Buffet]." Huffington described its appeal differently: "If you feed them, they will come." But free food only explains so much, and only the cheapest professor would keep attending if food were the sole benefit. Rather, the program's success was indicative of deeper realities: first, it affirmed and implicitly thanked professors who took their teaching seriously;

second, it convened like-minded professors and created a teaching-as-calling community among them; third, it built upon preexisting goodwill among the faculty. Too often, colleges that profess to prioritize teaching live a different reality; the Teaching Buffet put shoes on Phi Beta's commitment to classroom excellence. As for good morale at Phi Beta, I should note that the necessary ingredients were in place: the academic dean was respected by the faculty, the campus and buildings of Phi Beta were well tended, local costs of living were comparatively low, and there were generally sufficient resources for most faculty to succeed. What Huffington's Teaching Buffet did was take these existing ingredients and create a dinner party.

There is one additional element that is important to understanding the Meaningful Work Initiative's success: it restricted its exploration of theology to the initiative's most advanced undergraduate programming, and operationalized calling as personally fulfilling and socially meaningful work. Huffington prefers to say she kept the theological underpinnings "implicit" and avoided "Christo-centric" language. Still, Huffington made it work at Phi Beta while similar campuses struggled. Her genteel implementation and focused goals, combined with the prevalence of religiosity in the wider region, helped her win over the campus. She even raised a half-million-dollar endowment for the program, and had good prospects for the balance. While her departure would be a setback, she gave the Meaningful Work Initiative a solid foundation and its programs could continue without her. Indeed, Huffington successfully transitioned several programs to new leadership, so she could pursue other activities. I am confident that the remainder, with sufficient oversight from Huffington, would transition smoothly.[1]

Discerning Vocation at Pullman College

A thousand miles from Phi Beta, and equally distant in religious orientation, one finds Pullman College. The college's name evokes diner cars and railroad conductors, and its buildings sport names of one or another regional industrialist. Naming buildings after benefactors is standard practice, of course, but Pullman seemed eager to do so. Perhaps because Pullman's denominational history tracks back to John Calvin, the Protestant reformer and theologian who exemplified industriousness and austerity, and whose early followers, according to Max Weber, gave rise to the spirit of capitalism itself. Subsequent scholarship has challenged Weber's causal argument, but not the applicability of his "Protestant work ethic" label to these early Calvinists. Consequently, Pullman College celebrates the industriousness of its donors, even as its faculty and students articulate diverse opinions about capitalism.

Because Pullman College embraces Christian faith and Calvinist theology in particular, it had no reservations about using theological terms or encouraging theological study of vocation and calling. Indeed, a core element of the Protestant Reformation was the sacredness of all vocations. Pullman therefore began its programming where Ignatius University's programming, for example, ended. Most campuses participating in this initiative were not as religiously homogeneous as Pullman, but about one-fourth were, and any reader connected to a college or university possessing an equally prominent religious identification should find Pullman's story valuable.[2]

Pullman's president could have passed the Lilly Endowment's invitation to a dozen members of his campus. That he passed it to his dean of the chapel, who was a member of his executive cabinet, who in turn had no difficulty recruiting faculty, staff, and denominational leaders, speaks volumes about the centrality of the chapel in Pullman's culture. (By contrast, on most religiously affiliated campuses, passing such an invitation to its marginalized chaplain would be its kiss of death.) Pullman's planning team agreed that the invitation was an *enhancement* opportunity — that is, an opportunity to strengthen what Pullman already did, not to launch costly programs it could not sustain. The planning team also agreed to meet to discuss common readings and to hear from national experts and observation teams it sent to purpose exploration programs already in place. (Pullman was in Lilly's second round of invitations, giving it twenty first-round campuses to visit.) Particularly astute was Pullman's early involvement of seminary and denominational leaders; this was not the college's first encounter with the Lilly Endowment — it understood the endowment's interest in increasing clergy recruitment and pulled all the right levers.

Pullman designed a distributed rather than centralized program. It assigned financial administration to the director of a preexisting center with parallel goals, and delegated program oversight to a dozen existing departments. Thus, faculty development programs were assigned to academic affairs, curricular efforts to deans' offices, residential life initiatives to hall directors, and so on. The proposal clearly appealed to the Lilly Endowment, which funded Pullman's Discerning Vocation program in the fall of 2001. I doubt it was a difficult decision for the endowment. But, I wondered, what did the endowment expect to gain by doing so? Given the campus's devout starting point, what did Lilly hope the grant would accomplish? Endowment officials explained that they awarded these grants to campuses like Pullman in order to be inclusive. But that inclusiveness accomplished something else, too. It helped define the outer boundaries of what purpose exploration might add to undergraduate education; it would establish how far proexploration undergraduates, faculty, staff, and even colleges as a whole might travel. And as Jeff Johnson's story illustrated in chapter 1, that was quite far indeed.

Pullman is forthright about its mission to "glorify God, follow Christ, and serve others"; backs that up with mandatory chapel services and restrictions against alcohol, drugs, and sex on campus; and consequently enrolls students who are predominantly evangelical in faith and practice. They enter Pullman with the view that their skills and talents are "gifts from God," to be used for God's purposes. Pullman's first-year experience program — orientation week, freshman retreat, residential life, and first-year seminar — therefore used grant funds to feature discussion of vocational theology and to nurture a wider awareness of the world's pressing needs. The former helped to deepen shallower understandings of vocation among first-year students, while the latter broadened student perspectives — a frequent goal of liberal arts colleges. World-broadening efforts generally fail among first-year college students, however, for developmental and cultural reasons I described previously.[3] Pullman College succeeded, however, because it embedded these goals within a framework of God imparting to faithful followers a measure of agency and efficacy. In other words, a Pullman student would hear that God equipped and called *her* to serve others, and by doing so, *she* became an agent of God's work in the world. She thereby acquired an intrinsically religious motivation to understand the world's diversity and its compelling needs, as did many of her classmates.

Consequently, we observed a palpable other-directedness among student participants in Pullman College's exploration programs. In contrast to students on other campuses, who spoke chiefly of self-understandings and future endeavors, Pullman students told a more continuous story of long-standing service activity and skill development, of present activities that demonstrated their sense of calling, and of how these present activities fit with their future plans.[4] Kara, a recent Pullman alum, connected environmental activism begun during high school to her degree in science education, which connected in turn to her current job directing "clean and green" water projects in three African nations that were underwritten by album profits from a consortium of gospel musicians.

Zach took a more circuitous route. Zach led chapel music during his senior year, and was known for carrying his guitar everywhere on campus. Then he graduated and landed his "dream job" doing animation programming in Hollywood. For a couple of years, he logged eighty-hour weeks. That got him promoted, but it left his guitar gathering dust and Zach feeling one-dimensional. Recalling discussions at Pullman about balance, Zach cut back his hours and accepted a position leading music for a multiracial congregation in the blighted neighborhood adjacent to his Hollywood office. Zach reported he was "happier than ever," and despite cutting back hours, he received a second promotion at the animation studio.

Helping to fuel Pullman's other-directedness were mentorship groups, an internship program, a vocation-themed career office, residential housing for preministry students, a pre-PhD mentoring program, urban service project trips, an annual service trip to Ghana, and a lecture series featuring humanitarians from around the globe. These programs spawned a veritable "culture of vocation" among students, according to its chaplain, which was confirmed by 73 percent of student survey respondents agreeing or strongly agreeing that "students on campus often use terms like *vocation, calling,* or *purpose*"; 77 percent indicating a commitment "to making a positive contribution to the church both now and in the future"; and 82 percent confirming "helpful conversations" about purpose and vocation with faculty or staff advisers.[5]

As striking as this provocational student culture was, the promentorship culture we observed among faculty and staff was even more so. Every one of Pullman's full-time faculty members participated in voluntary faculty development programs on mentoring students' exploration of vocation, and most of its staff participated as well, making for a high level of employee involvement. Nor were there shortages of employee volunteers for other grant programs. To be fair, Pullman is a campus one-fifth the size of Ignatius University, so its per capita funding was much higher. Still, other participating campuses had equivalent per capita funding ratios and much lower faculty, staff, and student buy-in, so impact cannot be attributed to per capita funding alone. Rather, Pullman strategically leveraged grant resources to accomplish its purpose exploration goals.

Pullman concentrated program efforts toward three goals: (1) fostering campus-wide involvement in undergraduate mentoring, (2) expanding off-campus contexts in which students "could experience and express their vocation," and (3) enlarging academic programs and curricula so students could consider the "important spiritual, moral, and political commitments that may necessarily accompany one's vocation." Accomplishment of the first two explains the broad student enthusiasm for vocation. Accomplishment of the third explains the enthusiastic buy-in among faculty and staff, and is most responsible for vocation's prominence at Pullman postfunding. It is easy to see how: at an institution where resources are always limited, populated by employees committed to mentoring students, arrive abundant resources to support exploration of one's purpose and vocation. The result was dozens of new courses, revised academic programs, innovative service-learning projects, multiple symposia, partnerships with external constituents, and exploration-linked scholarly projects.

Like the 1982 Weather Girls hit song "It's Raining Men," it rained program funding on Pullman faculty and staff. There was money for a new major in nonprofit management; for an urban semester complete with courses, internships, and a residence hall; for symposia on social justice with the Catholic university across town; for new minors; and for a few faculty hires. There were some ideas that had only nominal exploration content, most of which were rejected but some of which slipped through. But Pullman employees on the whole embraced the idea of vocation. In fact, when Pullman's academic dean proposed open conversations around the idea that "spiritual formation is a primary purpose of a liberal arts education," the faculty eagerly participated. On most campuses, such an idea would have been met with derision; even faculty on religiously affiliated campuses that received exploration grants would balk at such a notion. Not the Pullman faculty—they practice a liberal arts reminiscent of the founding clergy of Harvard, Yale, and Princeton, and prioritize making an impact on students. While similar rains occurred at other participating campuses, the Pullman rain was neither unwanted nor too much; it was just right to produce a record harvest of purpose exploration and mentorship.

What might we conclude about the outer limits of campus impact by a purpose exploration grant? A single case is insufficient for a final determination, but it suggests the following. First, virtually all students welcome self-knowledge and will connect that with their future plans. Second, a sizable minority of students—which I estimate to be one-third of Pullman students—will embrace the self-transcendence, seeking to express their sense of life purpose through service now and in the future.[6] Third, this sizable minority will generate a provocational community that spans campus sectors and occupies large pockets of student life. Fourth, faculty members will not only value mentorship, but generate new courses and academic programs to prepare students for the worlds they will enter and the complexities they will confront. Fifth, staff will eagerly restructure nonacademic programs, finding in exploration programming an affirmation of the commitment they have long sought to express. Sixth, senior administrators will enjoy greater consensus about organizational mission and operative strategies, and may even explore ways to reengage with elements of the educational experience that fueled their interest in educational leadership. These are powerful effects, and their emergence is predicated upon the long-standing cultural consensus of Pullman College. Yet powerful effects are possible on religiously heterogeneous campuses, even those with wide swaths of religious indifference—as demonstrated at the College of Douglass and DuBois.

Seek and Pursue at the College of Douglass and DuBois

The pew was vibrating—literally. A bass guitarist and two percussionists created a funk rhythm, two keyboardists added middle- and upper-range harmonies, a soloist who needed no microphone nevertheless sang into one set at full volume, and a gospel choir forty voices strong belted out a rousing song about the children of Abraham. I was sitting in "freshmen assembly" at the College of Douglass and DuBois, a mandatory weekly gathering in the college's storied chapel for first-year students, and this week the Seek and Pursue choir along with the chaplain had a message they planned to share *with power*. "We ARE the children of Abraham," Chaplain Jones shouted. "We've suffered under many pharaohs and wandered in many wildernesses, but God—OUR GOD—has opened up the Red Sea and delivered us into the Promised Land!" She continued, "So the question is, are you going to live like one bonded in Egypt, or like a citizen of the Promised Land?" In between sermon snippets, the choir launched into carefully selected songs that illustrated Jones's points. It was in many ways a characteristically black worship service, but it lacked one thing: an enthusiastic congregation.

This was not a church, but a chapel used for a mandatory school assembly of first-year students. The audience was not a cross section of ages all sporting their Sunday best, but eighteen- and nineteen-year-olds with the sagging shorts, large engraved earrings, and other accoutrements that comprise urban fashion. Academic advisers stood in the aisles taking attendance and enforcing decorum. And except for one song when a soprano soloist held a note so high I thought the stained-glass windows would shatter, two-thirds of these first-year students sat stoically throughout the entire assembly. None of that deterred the chaplain or the choir, however; they were certain about the message these freshmen needed to hear. It was, in many ways, the same message freshmen would have heard in the chapel of the College of Douglass and DuBois (CDD) more than a century ago.

CDD is a historically black college (HBC) affiliated with Methodists as well as the Disciples of Christ. Freshman assembly has always been a part of CDD's tradition. It is where CDD begins its unabashed efforts to mold students into "CDD men" and "CDD women." In loco parentis reigns supreme at black colleges like CDD, and so do titles and polite forms of address. Faculty members would address *each other* as "Dr." or "Professor," the college president was called "President Johnson" even by her vice presidents, and employees were required to call students "Mr." or "Miss" (not "Ms.") followed by their surnames. First names were never used except between students. Adding to this verbal formality was a strict dress code that left employees looking more like bankers than college faculty or staff. To be honest, CDD felt like an upward mobility boot camp.

I was struck by the unapologetically moral language that infused employee speech and campus discourse. Elsewhere, colleges and universities avoid moral claims and normative language, save for progressive educational ideals. Not here; CDD swam comfortably in deeply normative waters. Consequently, the chapel held a prominent place at the college, as the religiosity of the black church infused the campus culture. While this may make CDD sound similar to Pullman College, the two were quite distinct. At Pullman, faith was individualistic and had a public dimension chiefly through the assembly of like-minded employees and students. At CDD, faith was public and part of the historic identity of its people; familiarity was considered a component of what it meant to be black. In fact, many CDD students did not practice any religion, and many employees had a nominal connection to a congregation only (church membership was a job requirement). Yet CDD's culture was so fused with the discourse and practices of the black church that no student or employee in good standing would ever disrespect it — regardless of his or her personal views. One could say Christianity is to CDD what the armed forces are to the US Congress: officially respected — even as individual politicians support or oppose specific military actions.

With this in mind, one can understand why the chaplain was assigned to generate and oversee CDD's purpose exploration programming, and why theological terms like *vocation* or *calling* faced no opposition on campus. One does not become a Martin Luther King Jr. or a Thurgood Marshall without a clear sense of calling. The chaplain's challenge was penetrating campus members' religion-friendly veneer to "truly engage" them with the idea of vocation. If only she could draw them into the chapel, Chaplain Jones knew they would appreciate this message.

The enticement, Jones decided, would be a top-notch gospel music choir. Jones believed that music was the pulse of black youth identity, and that an excellent gospel music program would draw an audience. So Jones wrote a proposal that included a full-time director of a gospel choir along with a gospel artist series and a guest preacher series. Since Jones had a captive student audience regularly — freshmen orientation, freshmen assembly, all convocations, and black history events — Jones knew that consistently excellent music at these events would attract a larger audience to voluntary Sunday services, and those larger audiences would then hear good preaching and quite a bit of the theology of vocation.

Jones's plan worked. She hired an alumnus who was a gospel recording artist to become the chapel's music director; he in turn selected only the best singers and instrumentalists for his Seek and Pursue Choir, and he rehearsed them long into the night. In less than two years' time, Sunday chapel attendance went from fifty to four hundred, with 90 percent of the audience being CDD students. Easter and Christmas services had to be moved to the gymnasium, and a midweek chapel service begun as an experiment regularly drew more than two hundred student, faculty, and staff attendees. The Seek and Pursue Choir became the college's most competitive choir to join, attracting more voice majors than the music department's own concert choir. The music faculty was none too happy about this, but when the dean told them they could not require voice majors to sing in the concert choir, they voted to "loan" interested voice majors to the Seek and Pursue Choir for as long as its director "needed them."

Learning all this left me with two questions. I asked the choir director the first one: why, given the choir's popularity, did the students sit so stoically during the freshmen assembly? The music director did not hesitate. "Oh, that happens every year. They're new to the college and just trying to be cool. By next semester, they'll be up clapping and shouting like the rest of the students. We already had more of them clapping today than we did during our Welcome Week chapel service [two weeks earlier]." While his explanation sounded plausible, I checked the choir's reputation with upper-class students. One told me, with a dozen others nodding in agreement, "Everybody at [the College of Douglass and DuBois] loves Seek and Pursue [Choir]— they're so good, they travel everywhere and win all sorts of awards." Another added succinctly: "It's a *bomb* choir." (That is, the choir is so good, it'll blow you away—like a bomb.)

My second question was whether exploration of purpose and vocation had increased the way Chaplain Jones believed it would with a fuller chapel. This was harder to answer definitively. I did confirm the increase in students' chapel attendance, which is a powerful indicator of students' *voluntary* behavior, and can attest to students' use of terms like *calling*, *vocation*, and *purpose* when I visited. Clarice, who sang in the Seek and Pursue Choir, said she often talked about seeking and pursuing her own calling with other members of the choir. Other choir members concurred. But as the musical accompaniment to dozens of exploration-themed sermons each semester, it would be hard to imagine these ideas not impacting the choir. Web survey respondents overwhelmingly (87 percent) agreed that "through participation in [vocation] programs, I developed a better sense of my vocation, calling, or purpose"; the same proportion agreed that CDD's vocation programming "has helped me identify my skills and talents"; 93 percent agreed or strongly agreed that it "has encouraged me to both see and serve the needs of others"; 60 percent indicated they had a faculty or staff adviser "with whom I have helpful conversations about my vocation, calling, or purpose"; and 47 percent agreed that "because of my participation in [CDD vocation programs], I altered my life plans." Such figures are impressive—but with relatively few responses to that web survey, the results remain suggestive rather than determinative.[7]

In the end, evidence for deep impact of exploration programming at CDD is less systematic than it is from other campuses. I include the college here, though, because of something that Chaplain Jones said to me:

> Y'know, Tim, a lot of students here are hanging on by the slenderest of threads. They are academically underprepared and many times come from situations and backgrounds that make me shudder. They do not have the luxury to think about how they want to impact the world; they just want to pass their classes and somehow pay their tuition bill. For a lot of these students, *just staying in college is their calling.* They're doing everything they can to just stay here. And if somehow [our program] can give them the lift they need to keep going another day, another week, or another semester—then I know I'm accomplishing what this grant is all about.

Her words were powerful. Up to that point, I had spent a lot of time talking with students across the nation whose chief vocational challenge was deciding which opportunity of several they should pursue. But honing a sense of purpose should not be a luxury; it should not be the province of the elite. Purpose encompasses far more than career decisions; purpose is the grit that keeps weary men and women holding on despite enormous odds, because they understand what they need to do and why. At CDD, 99 percent of students receive financial aid; just 70 percent make it back for their sophomore year, and only 35 percent return for their junior year. These students may lack the nuanced awareness of global needs that Pullman students possess or know little of the philosophies of work with which Phi Beta students are familiar. CDD students were encouraged to understand purpose far more immediately—as the floating plank that kept their heads above the floodwaters until they reached dry land. CDD students had a visceral understanding of their callings.

Chaplain Jones explained that an esoteric program of self-reflection and self-transcendence would be of little use at this point in her students' lives. What they needed was a program that shouted "Hold on . . . there's dry land just around the bend" as it tossed plank after plank into the floodwaters of its students' lives. Chaplain Jones used her program grant to fund a rescue operation primarily. Other contexts and populations require different forms of purpose exploration. The Seek and Pursue Choir would draw an appreciative audience if it were to visit Richboro University, to which I turn my attention in the next section. But it would not transform Richboro's privileged, pressured, and anxious students. Those students needed time to reflect, personal mentorship, and a caring community to embark on their exploration of purpose and vocation.

Purpose Exploration Hall at Richboro University

Downtown Richboro could give Rodeo Drive a run for its money: Brooks Brothers, Tiffany, Versace, and Coach boutiques intermingle with day spas and sidewalk bistros offering valet parking. This is a wealthy area, and Richboro University, set on a hill overlooking the community, has a price in excess of $50,000 annually—making it one of the fifty most expensive universities in the United States at the time of our visit. And yet, the campus was less attractive than our ride through Richboro's town center led us to expect. Buildings were designed for function primarily, and landscaping was an afterthought at best. The expense of Richboro University lay in high living costs and their corresponding salary demands.

Since World War II, Richboro University's target market has been upwardly mobile Catholics seeking professional careers. Its schools of business, engineering, law, and education are its best-known programs, attracting graduate and undergraduate students; it also has a solid record of medical school admissions. During the 1970s and 1980s, Richboro focused on its graduate professional programs, neglecting its undergraduate programs and pushing aside its mission to develop students as whole persons. In short, Richboro moved so far from its Jesuit origins that the majority of employees viewed the university's Catholic identity as a fading relic. Its trustees, however, did not.

So in the early 2000s, the trustees installed a new president. This president, though a Jesuit priest like his predecessors, was clearly different. He was outspoken about the need to educate students as whole persons—because it was "the right thing to do," and because rebuilding Richboro's declining undergraduate enrollment demanded it. When $50,000 covers tuition for a bachelor's degree at the local state college, the university had to convincingly explain the value added of a Richboro degree that cost four times as much. The president's answer was to make a Richboro education different—to return it to its mission of nurturing students' minds, bodies, and hearts. To faculty and staff cynics, it meant spirituality had become a marketing gimmick; but to the president and the trustees, this was a serious priority. Cynics soon realized just how serious—as the new president personally interviewed all prospective faculty, hiring only those who supported Richboro's mission of holistic development, and directing staff to implement Richboro's mission or move on.

How do purpose exploration programs fit into this story? They precede the new president's arrival, in fact, and dovetail with its trustees' concern about undergraduates' experience. Here is what transpired. Richboro's outgoing president handed Lilly's invitation to Father Francis, the charismatic director of campus ministry. Father Francis then gathered a handful of like-minded theology professors and campus administrators, posing to them the idea of creating a themed sophomore residence hall. This hall would create an intentional community around issues of purpose exploration, featuring small discussion groups led by faculty and staff mentors, monthly dinner presentations, resident Jesuit advisers, full-time hall program coordinators, exploration-infused courses taught by faculty affiliates, enrichment trips, and two mandatory retreats. Interested first-year students would apply for residence in the hall, which would be renovated to support this programming, and, if accepted, would receive guaranteed housing for their sophomore year in the nicest and best-located dorm on campus, living among similarly motivated students. Finally, hall programming would avoid the term *vocation*, for the same reasons as at Ignatius University.

Father Francis readily convinced the planning team of his idea's merits, and did the same with the Lilly Endowment. He then recruited first-year students to apply for the hall's inaugural year, and these students in turn recruited friends, with the result being a Purpose Exploration Hall (PEH) populated by enthusiastic Richboro student leaders and student ministry volunteers, which coalesced into a warm community that relished its time together. Within weeks, the hall council held a logo design contest, and sold hundreds of T-shirts, hats, and lanyards. From that point on, it was impossible to walk across campus without seeing PEH-imprinted items worn by

Richboro's most involved and popular students. The hall's trajectory was up-ward ever since — surviving the departure of Father Francis (who left in obe-dience to a higher call by his order) — and generating so much positive pub-licity that Richboro University quickly raised $3 million to endow the hall's programming in perpetuity.

Among those observing the quick success of PEH were Richboro's trustees, many of whom were alumni and practicing Catholics, and some of whom were Jesuits. They were delighted to receive reports of increased applications, matriculation, and retention — attributed in part to PEH. The program director who followed Father Francis insisted it was the program's success that *specifically* led the trustees to hire a new president who empha-sized whole student "formation" and undergraduate education. I am not en-tirely convinced, but a reasonable case can be made that PEH underscored the trustees' interest in strengthening the university's Catholic identity and in their perception that Catholic identity could be an asset rather than a lia-bility in solving the university's recruitment and retention problems. It was true that Richboro's new president cited PEH's success in many venues, as it fit perfectly with his efforts to reestablish the university's Jesuit identity.

None of the forgoing implies that PEH was without flaw. It struggled to get faculty involved, save for a dozen faculty affiliates who taught the exploration-themed courses that residents must take. Its effects were also restricted to 20 percent of Richboro's sophomores, who self-select to par-ticipate. But what PEH lacked in breadth it made up for in depth. What it accomplished among residents was a two-year gain in maturity compared to nonresidents. This was demonstrated by PEH's top-shelf evaluation team, Richboro alumni who were employed at one of the nation's best educational research and testing firms. These evaluators administered a battery of psycho-logical indicators to a random sample of Richboro students and all residents of PEH. Residents had maturity scores that statistically exceeded those of Richboro's sophomores in general, and matched those of its seniors. Some of this was a selection effect: residents entered the hall with higher matu-rity scores than nonresidents. But much of it was not. Residents made sig-nificant gains during the course of their year, moving them from somewhat more mature than peers to much more mature. That is an impressive benefit: instead of leaving recipients with regrets about opportunities missed during college, it grants them a two-year head start in which to seize opportunities, augment courses of study, and devise postcollege plans within the resource-rich environment of the university.[8]

An example is in order. Carrie was a PEH resident who so enjoyed her experience there that she became a student adviser during her junior year (i.e., she helped with hall programs in exchange for room and board). As a result of purpose exploration exercises both years, Carrie decided to explore working with underprivileged children, and secured an internship with Head Start during her senior year at the university. Her good experience there prompted Carrie to seek full-time work in a similar setting following graduation, and she accepted such a job in a city a hundred miles away from her parents' home, finding an apartment, roommates, and making moving arrangements.

When we spoke with Carrie a year after her graduation, she relayed that her interest in a day-care career had begun to wane, yet she was staying on to establish her work history while she explored other avenues of interest. Particularly striking was how well Carrie adapted to independent living in her new location, including managing finances and maintaining good relationships with her roommates, and how calmly she spoke about this career change. This may not seem remarkable to some, but in comparison to emerging adults in general, Carrie's financial independence, sustained employment, and calm career exploration are rare.[9] Carrie's life was more comparable to those three years beyond their graduation from college than it was to those just one year out.

Fostering maturity among students is valuable in its own right, but administratively inclined readers will be interested to learn that this residential program jolted student satisfaction rates upward—which in turn improved recruitment, retention, and even alumni giving. Several hall residents told me how close they had come to transferring out of Richboro University after their first year, only to change their minds when they were admitted to the hall program, and then to become the university's biggest boosters just weeks into their sophomore year. Today, every campus tour passes through PEH. It has become a signature element of Richboro's student life, and many admitted students identify the program as a reason for their decision to matriculate.

Prospective students are not the only visitors to the hall. Richboro's development officers regularly walked donors through the hall to meet its residents, hear their stories, and see firsthand the evidence of the program's accomplishments. That these officers had little difficulty raising a $3 million endowment to sustain the hall's programming, or even enticing the hall's young alumni to become annual contributors of a modest sum, further affirms its contribution to Richboro University. I do not relay this to encourage Machiavellian adoption of purpose exploration on other campuses, however. Exploration programs should be undertaken for their intrinsic value and impact on students. My point is that one good outcome can lead to other desirable outcomes, and in this case, it did.

Location, Location, Location

Richboro located its exploration program in residential life, CDD chose the chapel, Phi Beta opted for academic affairs, Pullman scattered components across the campus, and IU created a freestanding center that reported to the vice president for mission. All five program locations had lasting effects along with inherent, structural limitations. Richboro's program deeply impacted two hundred students per year, but struggled to involve more than a dozen faculty. CDD got 50 percent of its students to attend vocation-themed, voluntary Sunday chapel services, yet had few roles for faculty or staff except to cheer from the sidelines. Phi Beta's program involved one-third of its students — many quite intensely, provided pedagogical support to half of its faculty, but its avoidance of the limelight made it harder for new students to find. Both Pullman's and Ignatius's programs impacted thousands, but Pullman's distributed structure made it difficult to distinguish program impact from Pullman's culture in general, while Ignatius's Rebound retreat divided the campus into participants and nonparticipants.

Across the initiative, a program's location within its organization's structure proved quite consequential. Housed in academic affairs, programs had a direct impact on curricular offerings and faculty development, with indirect impact on students. Housed in religious life, programs emphasized ministry opportunities for students and theological discussions. Housed in student affairs, programs prioritized service projects or residential life. Not that exploration programs sought to restrict their impact; most hoped to transform their campuses as a whole. But for reasons well known to organization scholars, it is easiest for an organizational unit to impact itself, then its own division, and finally the organization at large. It is fairly simple, for example, for me to initiate projects within my own department of sociology, takes more effort to do so within my school of humanities and social science, and requires broad participation and senior administrative support to do so across the institution. The same holds true for any organization with hundreds or thousands of employees. Pressure to prioritize one's own unit and division is strong; going beyond requires persistence, wide collaboration, and executive endorsement.

A program's organizational location generates inherent limitations. Broad impact thus requires program directors with collaborative skills *and* senior administrators who endorse the program's mission. The presidents of Ignatius, Richboro, and Pullman were unequivocal supporters, as were the chief academic officers at CDD and Phi Beta. Because these leaders made their support apparent, their programs had the latitude to impact their campuses more broadly. Executive support is thus a necessary condition for broad impact. Without it, impact might still be deep, but it was restricted to the organizational division that housed the program.

Programmatic Repertoire

At first, I did not discern patterns in the programmatic tools that each campus deployed. After all, a gospel choir is quite different from a themed residence hall, and both are different from a general education course on work and meaning. But after studying twenty-six campuses and reviewing all eighty-eight program proposals and reports, I identified eleven ways programs drew members of their campuses into purpose exploration. Six focused on students: curriculum, internships, service-learning, themed residence halls, mentorship programs, and seminary semesters. One focused on employees: faculty and staff development programs. And four were deployed equally with students or employees: retreats, personality assessments, minigrants, and campus events. Since examples of many appear above, I will describe those not yet discussed, then make a few structural observations about repertoire choice and impact.

I have come to appreciate, from other evaluation work, how difficult it is to create mentoring relationships programmatically.[10] That is because the deepest mentor/protégé relationships occur spontaneously, of their own volition, and extend years and even decades. Valuable advisory relationships *can* be fostered programmatically, however, and many campuses facilitated these by providing funds so advisers and students could share meals or attend campus events together, by teaching students how to maximize their advising meetings, by organizing students into groups that met weekly with an adviser, and by training faculty and staff advisers. Other campuses developed fellowship programs, like the one that chapter 1's Melody Thompson participated in, requiring common courses, off-campus activities, and regular meetings with the fellows' academic advisers. And a few campuses formed spiritual exploration programs, assigning interested students to faculty and staff volunteers for weekly conversation and prayer. Given the national erosion of faculty hours devoted to advising and the concomitant rise in student complaints about inadequate advising,[11] these advising enhancements were widely appreciated by students (see chapter 4).

Affecting fewer students, but quite deeply, were programs that allowed students to enroll for a semester in a seminary and count seminary coursework toward their undergraduate degrees. Potentially, but indirectly, affecting students were development programs for faculty and staff. These included seminars, teaching workshops, new-employee orientation programs, service appreciation luncheons, teaching release awards for vocation research or curriculum development, and administrative release awards for program development.

Many campuses used personality inventories as a part of their vocation programs. Particularly popular was the Gallup Organization's Strengths-Finder test, which has a specific version (StrengthsQuest) for use with college students; some campuses administered this test to all students and employees, providing follow-up meetings as well as individual counseling.[12] Completing the programmatic repertoire were minigrants for exploration-related projects. Students or employees could apply for a few hundred to a few thousand dollars to support service projects, curricular innovation, campus events, and more.

Just as choice of repertoire can enhance or undermine a musical performance, so, too, can it facilitate or weaken exploration of purpose and vocation. A few observations about programmatic repertoire are therefore in order.

First, programs that prioritized student impact had the clearest and deepest effects. Provide a student, for example, with an opportunity to work three months in Mother Teresa's clinics, and his life is changed forever. Nurture a reflective community among service trip volunteers, and one will observe students who recalibrate life trajectories to embrace global citizenship. Such programs can struggle to gain visibility beyond the borders of student affairs, however, since those most impacted tend to be juniors and seniors who may no longer reside on campus and who are close to graduation. Programs exclusively available to students, and focused on off-campus activities, were particularly vulnerable to budget cuts and closure.

Second, and by contrast, programs that prioritized faculty and curricular development had longer-term institutional effects. Get a faculty member to embrace the value of purpose exploration, for example, and she will infuse it into the way she teaches, the way she advises, and even the way she researches; she will become a sturdy oak in her campus's purpose exploration garden (see chapter 6). Faculty and curricular effects on students can be broad and self-sustaining, but they can be uneven and difficult to observe.

Third, and more specifically, exploration-themed campus events can generate broad attention, but require clear connections to ongoing programming to capitalize on that attention.

Fourth, and all other things being equal, minigrants and participation incentives can foster a critical mass of students or employees who embrace exploration of purpose and vocation.

Fifth, understanding one's audience is crucial: programs that targeted undergraduates during their sophomore and junior years, when they were less distracted by entering and exiting processes, accomplished disproportionately more of their goals. Programs that targeted new employees and recently tenured faculty, who are setting priorities that will guide their careers for years, were also quite effective. (See chapters 4 and 5 for a fuller discussion.)

Sixth, good public relations are essential. Programs implemented with careful attention to their public message had more participants and wider campus support than programs implemented without attention to these matters. I develop these observations in chapters 4–6 (see also appendix 5).

Personnel Matter

Salaries comprise the lion's share of higher education budgets, and rightly so. Learning is an interactive and individual process, and research tells us the most effective educators are marked by a passion for their subjects, basic organizational skills, and emotional intelligence (also known as emotional quotient, or EQ). Persuasion experts confirm the centrality of passion, while the necessity of organizational skills if teaching more than a handful of students speaks for itself.[13] Less obvious, but equally important to effective teachers, is the self-awareness, social awareness, character, and interpersonal skills that comprise emotional intelligence. Professor Huffington, Chaplain Jones, Father Francis, and IU's Steve Wright possessed emotional intelligence in abundance, as did directors of other successful programs. These program directors were at ease conversing in hallways, on sidewalks, and in quads; they knew everyone's name, and everyone seemed to know them. The only exceptions were on campuses that chose distributed programs, like Pullman College. On these campuses, the officially designated program director served in an administrative role, shifting the burden of EQ to team members who delivered specific programs.

Personnel with commitment to campus-based purpose exploration and high emotional intelligence are not uncommon, but these traits can take time to discern—thus, campuses that hired internally tended to reach effectiveness more quickly than those that did not. The one caution shared with me on several campuses was to avoid "wannabe professors" as program directors. Wannabe professors had doctorates and often adjunct faculty appointments—but their true career goal was full-time faculty appointments, and they used exploration programs to demonstrate scholarly prowess more than foster campus exploration. This happened infrequently, but it hindered a couple of programs. I expand on personnel factors in chapter 6, but introduce these here because effective personnel were essential to program impact.

Intelligent Design, More or Less

Good program design was organic; it tapped the history and strengths of a campus, developed programs that strategically leveraged existing and new resources, and divined the questions about purpose and vocation most likely to arise from its students, faculty, and staff. Good program design was also creative and reflexive; it kept overarching goals foremost, not pet projects.

Observing these programs helped me understand all that campus-based purpose exploration programs could encompass. But understanding this triggered bigger questions: How does purpose exploration affect students, staff, and faculty? Are its effects broad or narrow? What is its staying power? Does it make a difference in students' lives after they graduate? Does it make a difference in mentors' lives? Do exploration programs persist after grant monies are gone? Such questions are the focus of the next two chapters. Their answers reveal whether exploration programs are like cut-flower arrangements that bring a few days of pleasure before wilting, or like perpetually blooming gardens whose inspiration remains fresh and vital.

4

Students

Danny and Danielle

Danny sat at the end of the front row, while Danielle preferred a middle seat in the back—both well positioned to observe class-mates while pondering their own contributions to the class dis-cussion. They were the kind of students who make teaching re-warding, because they worked to understand course ideas and integrate them into their lives. Both were students in my Religion and American Culture course, and with a dozen equally engaged classmates, they made the course a special joy to teach. During our first-day introductions, I learned Danny had been raised a Lutheran and was now "exploring options," while Danielle had been raised a "hippie Quaker" and was now "generally agnos-tic." Prudent descriptions, as they offered specifics about the past but kept current statuses vague, but also honest, as they com-ported with Danny's no-nonsense, forthright discourse and with Danielle's earth-toned sundress, sandals, peace sign earrings, and progressive political buttons that covered her recycled book tote.

As the semester unfolded, however, both Danny and Danielle opted to share more of their religious identities and questions on the course blog.[1] It was there I read about Danny's long-standing service as a volunteer fire-fighter, of his decision to get engaged midway through the course, and of his concerns about joining his fiancée's church—which required a public pronouncement of his faith. It was also there that I learned of Danielle's employment in a New Age boutique that sold spiritual books, incense, crystals, and ritual oils, and of her warm friendships with an array of passionate outsiders: atheists, Campus Crusaders, and potheads.

Particularly impressive was the way Danny and Danielle used course concepts to see similar social processes at work in different religious communities, identify the epistemic assumptions upon which cultural worlds are constructed, and recognize the mechanisms by which social networks recruit members. This led Danny to research the theology of his fiancée's church, to attend a campus debate between atheist Christopher Hitchens and Christian apologist Frank Turek, and to ultimately become a member of his fiancée's church. And it led Danielle past a facile rejection of "organized religion" to a nuanced view—as she found herself genuinely moved during our visit to a black church and saw great value in the work that church did in its local community.

Wanting to deeply understand the course materials and integrate its ideas into their lives distinguished Danny and Danielle from the vast majority (80 percent) of American college students, who view college coursework as little more than a series of hurdles on the path to desired careers and lifestyles.[2] The minority (20 percent) who diverge appreciate classes as opportunities to learn, to investigate the world's complexities, and explore matters of identity. Their specific motivations vary, of course, as Danny's enthusiasm for learning was rooted in the identity implications of graduation and his decisions to get engaged and join a church, while Danielle's enthusiasm was rooted in fostering a more peaceful, tolerant, and inclusive world—through education and democratic activism. Yet, despite wide variability in student motivation and academic behavior, one can discern overarching patterns. Mapping these patterns provides insight into college student culture and offers a framework for understanding students' exploration of purpose.

Six Student Types

This is not the first, nor will it be the last, typology of American college students.[3] To create it, I formed a cultural field with a horizontal axis representing students' instrumental versus idealistic educational orientation and a vertical axis representing students' prioritization of educational performance (see fig. 4.1). Most students cluster toward the instrumental side of the instrumentalist/idealist continuum. And while there are students obsessed with their educational performance (i.e., grades) and others who minimally attend to the same, most cluster in the middle — desirous of good performance but moderating concern for grades in light of other concerns. This creates six broad types of students:

- Obsessive, Compulsive (OC) Achievers: These highly stressed students seek the best grades possible, because they view grades as essential to long-term career goals. Often in preprofessional tracks, these students are highly competitive and will do whatever is necessary to obtain the best grades. That may include arguing for higher grades with instructors, completing extra-credit assignments, or compromising their academic integrity.[4]

Figure 4.1. Six college student types.

- Utilitarians: These students care about grades, but balance them against other priorities—such as employment, family obligations, relationships, or extracurricular activities. Education is valued because it facilitates occupational advancement. This approach is dominant among nontraditional-age commuter students, but it is also quite common among traditional-age college students. Such students attend class regularly, complete their assignments, study for exams, and usually earn good grades.
- Minimalists (i.e., "Beer and Circus" types[5]): These students believe that college should be the "best four years of your life," and maximize pleasure through substance use and sexual gratification. They orient their week around sport games and Greek life. They meet minimum academic requirements to stay enrolled and satisfy their families.
- Future Intelligentsia and Reforming Activists: These students are regularly profiled in college advertising, because they embody higher education's ideals. The Future Intelligentsia are those deeply engaged and passionate students who become the next generation of professors, creative elites, and allied professionals (such as deans, counselors, or journalists). Reforming Activists are likewise engaged, but their passions lie beyond the academy. Their cause may be civic or political; it may involve matters of race, gender, or sexuality; it may be religious; or it may be a combination of these. Both types are intelligent and passionate, differing chiefly in the focus of their passions and therefore in their prioritization of grades.
- Rebels: These students reject mainstream culture for its superficiality, academia for its hypocrisy, and reform as unattainable. Student Rebels can be politically aligned, they can be immersed in illicit drug cultures, or they can be members of otherworldly or isolationist fringe groups. On occasion, they find a class engaging (because its topic or professor is rebellious), or join a broader cause (e.g., antiwar protests, efforts to decriminalize marijuana). But they generally occupy the margins of campus life.

Individual students can and do vary, moving from one type to another during their course of study, or even combining types. Utilitarians can discover a passion midway through their college years, for example, and become Reforming Activists. Or future members of the literary intelligentsia may demonstrate only utilitarian concern about their lab science requirements. Individual colleges and universities likewise vary in the proportions of each type they attract, with commuter campuses heavily populated by Utilitarians, for example, and elite schools dominated by OC Achievers. Individual and campus variation notwithstanding, these six types differed systematically in their interest and involvement in purpose exploration programming.

That I encountered no Rebels and only former Beer and Circus types during my visits to campus exploration programs came as no surprise. Rebels are rare on campuses today—though tuition increases, unemployment, underemployment, or resurrection of the Occupy Wall Street protests may reverse this—and Beer and Circus types have little use for reflection. Yet each semester, a few Beer and Circus types "hit rock bottom," and in their quest to alter behavior patterns, they sometimes found exploration programs. Somewhat similarly, OC Achievers whose intended paths collapse (e.g., premed students who fail organic chemistry) would also seek out purpose exploration programs, taking comfort in them. The core participants in exploration programs, however, were Reforming Activists and Future Intelligentsia. Such students would embrace these programs because they affirmed their passions and connected them with like-minded students. That is not to say OC Achievers or Utilitarians stayed away; they would participate, sometimes in droves, but managed their participation so as to not sidetrack the former's long-term goals or consume too much of the latter's time. Those who did not limit their participation did not long remain OC Achievers or Utilitarians. Like chapter 1's Melody, Jeff, and Rosa, they became purpose-driven Future Intelligentsia and Reforming Activists.

View from the Upper Deck

Of course, no amount of demand from any student type can generate $2 million in exploration programming. Evaluation of student impact therefore considers demand as well as *supply*, as quality programs attracted diverse participation on many campuses (see below and chapter 1). I found this quite challenging in the beginning. Because campuses designed purpose exploration programs keyed to their distinct contexts, traditions, and needs (see chapter 3), effects varied from campus to campus. As my tally of site visits increased, however, it became clear that student effects clustered into four categories: retention, trajectory calibration, social norms, and maturity. Because these are interwoven effects, I begin with the view from the upper deck before moving down to the field level.

I did not expect to observe a link between exploration programs and student retention, nor did the majority of those who designed these programs for their campuses. We expected student effects to cluster around academic decisions and postcollege plans—and they did, but more broadly than I anticipated. Students used exploration programs to select majors and identify careers, to better understand the world, to reinforce their fascination with a discipline or art, and to embed postcollege decisions within a larger framework that included career, family, service to others, and personal development. I call these trajectory recalibrations, since they frame individual decisions within broader engagement with the world. I also observed pro-exploration student communities among students in professional fields like nursing or teaching, and among those active in campus religious life or volunteer programs. On a few campuses, I encountered a protobacklash about exploration "jargon," student "God squads," and excessive exploration funding. I call both types social norms, as they illustrate recurring patterns of student behavior.

I was most surprised by the maturity effects, which I introduced in chapter 1. Many program leaders hoped that students' purpose exploration would pay dividends after graduation day. None, however, articulated the hope that purpose exploration would produce more intentionality, resilience, and life satisfaction. This was the home-run effect. I watched with amazement as the purpose-exploring team's rookies blasted the ace pitcher's welcome-to-the-real-world fastball over the outfield fence, then circled the bases with ease and humility. Home runs do not win baseball games single-handedly, of course. They must be joined by solid fielding, pitching, and batting skills. I therefore examine the foundation effects of student retention, planning, and norms that make the longer-term maturity effects possible.

Retention

It was an unseasonably hot April evening. I was in a stuffy lounge on the third floor of a residence hall, fiddling with the room's ineffective window air conditioner, when three male students burst into the room. "Hey, are you Dr. Clydesdale?" When I responded affirmatively, one smacked another upside the head and said, "I *told* you it was in this room!" I was then treated to an impromptu wrestling match, while the third explained, "They do this *all* the time," then hollered, "Yo, guys—this is a guest, OK?" Seeing that I was more amused than annoyed, they proceeded with the wrestling match for several minutes until a female student walked in and said, "Knock it off, Ryan. Let go of him, Jon," and the now sweaty Ryan and Jon collapsed onto the lounge's duct-taped couches. Rita introduced herself, and speaking authoritatively said "the rest" would arrive shortly. She was right: two more college men and six more college women entered moments later—without pausing from the funny story one had begun en route while the rest interjected one-liners. Not all focus groups begin this energetically, but I am happy when they do, as relaxed participants are essential to successful interviews.

Rita, whose words ended the wrestling match and who apparently corralled ten students to this meeting on time, introduced herself and then introduced me to the group—which had settled onto the couches and quieted themselves so I could speak. After a few words of introduction, I explained what this focus group was and distributed informed-consent forms. "Awesome!" one student said. "Cool!" another exclaimed, and they pumped their fists in the air. That is not a common response to informed-consent paperwork, but these two were happy they would receive fifteen dollars for participating, and this was the first they'd learned of it. They were also excited to hear I was writing a book, and that they might be "in it." With their questions answered and consent forms signed, I started the audio recorders and asked students to introduce themselves by stating their course of study, explaining why they came to this college, and why they stayed. This helps transcribers identify voices and gets the conversation rolling, and I added "and why you stayed" on the spur of the moment. I had not an inkling that this question would reveal doubts about persistence from these jubilant students.

Ryan, the wrestling instigator, was the first to speak—sharing his preferred (but unused) nickname as "the Beast," and then silencing the entire room when he said, "I had some rough times last year." He explained how the first year of college "you just want to have a good time, party, and y'know, live up freedom from your parents." He elaborated a little, then said, "But as the year goes on, you realize you can't live that kind of life and maintain [your grades]." Being placed on academic probation led Ryan to some soul-searching, and a decision to participate in the university's exploration programs—which became "the light at the end of the tunnel that people can just go into and come out better people." The young woman seated next to Ryan hugged him reassuringly, and I thanked Ryan for his answer. I then asked Jon to share his answer, and he proceeded to bury the emotional intensity needle. Jon was nearly expelled for actions unspecified to me but clearly known to others in the room, and with tearful eyes he said that if "this program never existed . . . I might be commuting to community college at home right now." Getting involved in the university's exploration program represented Jon's final opportunity to change direction. Emotionally overcome, Jon choked out, "So to me, it's priceless."

Rita spoke up next, saying, "If this university didn't have" these exploration programs, its "freshman class going into sophomore year would drop off by at least one hundred people." Many times, Rita explained, new students would say, "I was thinking of transferring at the end of my freshman year, and this [exploration program] was, like, the last straw—'We're gonna see if this works.'" And "six months later, [such] people are, like, 'Because of this I'm staying, because I got to see a whole different side of [this university], and [a] whole different side of people, and I got involved [on campus] through it.'" Susan added that "if your living situation sucks, it's over. . . . I wanted to transfer; I just couldn't stand where I was. My roommate was . . . , you know, . . . coming back with [sex partners], . . . going out on whatever day of the weekend, coming back and throwing up all over the room." Susan's salvation was the campus exploration center, which helped her remember why she came to the college in the first place, and connected her, as she gestured to those seated around her, with "amazing friends."

The entire focus group was not this emotionally intense, and a couple of students soon lightened the mood with humor as we turned to other topics of discussion. We talked about the Catholic affiliation of the university and their day-to-day experience as students; we discussed the purpose exploration programs they participated in and how they heard about them; we considered what was beneficial about the campus's exploration programs and what they would change; and we talked about what might happen if these programs were to cease. I found these eleven students to be forthright in answering all my questions—explaining how most decided to enroll "despite" the university's Catholicism, how some subsequently found that affiliation to be central while others were gaining respect for it, how they appreciated the mentoring and community-building components of the exploration program but were less satisfied with exploration-linked course offerings, how they loved the program's staff and were growing fond of the program's awkward but well-intentioned priest/faculty adviser, and how disappointed they would be if these programs ceased. These were not starry-eyed idealists, in other words, but young men and women with practical appreciation for the friendships that these exploration programs fostered, respect for *intentional community* (a phrase nine of the eleven used), and an appreciation for the exploration of purpose and the theology of vocation they had begun. Jon described it this way:

> I never really thought I was ever gonna answer the [purpose exploration] questions. [Yet] I *have* answered them. They're not questions you answer completely.... "*Whose am I?*" I knew I'm God's ... but what I learned was that I'm not *just* God's, I belong to a *community* of people, not just at [this university] — wherever I'm living. And [the questions] are helping me figure out who I am [and the importance of] living in community with other people. And I think that's what people want. When you're twenty years old, you have no idea what the world has for you. And I think everyone does want to know where they're going to be, and it's about ... trying to answer those questions.

Another female student said it was through "divine intervention" that she joined these programs. Having heard about the university's exploration programs during orientation, she vowed "There's no way *in hell*" she would participate in them. She kept that vow for a year, until her two best friends wore down her resistance, for which she is now grateful. "It's definitely changed who I am. I've learned a lot about myself this year, so I guess I'm a convert." Not all the students used theological vocabulary, to be sure, but none seemed rattled by it either. Both religious and nonreligious exploration terms had become part of the toolkit that all knew and variously used as they considered their identities, explored their futures, and forged a shared life together.

I did not uncover retention effects on all campuses. But that starter question about why participants stayed at their campuses elicited quite a few retention stories. Students on other campuses shared stories of dissatisfaction and wishing to leave, deciding instead to "invest" and "give it another chance," and finding that the campus's exploration programs provided a "niche" from which they could restart and "grow":

> I stayed because I really didn't like it at first and so decided to invest myself in the college and give it another chance, and then I got so invested that I didn't know who I would be if I left!
>
> (*Senior female, philosophy and English double major*)

> I've had friends that left, [but this exploration program] has opened so many doors and opportunities for me to explore what I really want to do that I feel like I can just grow more by staying here.
>
> (*Junior male, broadcasting major*)

> My first choice was U. Penn, but I got wait-listed. . . . [So] in the back of my mind, freshman year I still was like, "Oh, I can transfer out and go somewhere else." But I got really involved with [the campus exploration programs], and sort of found my niche. So I didn't want to leave, and now I'm absolutely obsessed with [this university].
>
> (*Sophomore female, biology/premed major*)

I also heard, on a couple of campuses, from students of color who used exploration programs to help them work through feelings of outsiderness. One Latino student said:

> I stayed because I definitely knew this was where God had [meant] me to be. I tried to leave a few times because I just felt like I didn't belong culturally. I loved the [campus's religious affiliation,] but I just felt out of place. . . . [Yet] I'm so happy that Christ helped me stay here because I've just grown in leaps and bounds — not only spiritually, every other way.
>
> (*Senior male, marketing major*)

When I asked him to elaborate, he relayed a story from his first year about an exploration lecture that challenged business students to use their careers not just for personal betterment, but to "advance God's kingdom" and positively impact the world. "Those words [struck] me because . . . I didn't want to just get caught up in the rat race of trying to advance, and then stuck in the nine-to-five, no-time [routine]." He accepted the exploration center's offer to find student internships in nonprofit organizations, spent that summer interning in a faith-based nonprofit that served at-risk teens, and now seeks to replicate that organization's work in his hometown. Another senior, an African American female studying youth ministry at a different college, said she "never felt comfortable" at her college, but stayed because each year the college "pushed me out of my comfort zone and caused me to grow each and every semester." Gaining a sense of personal purpose, then, helped some students find their niche and fortified others to press on despite difficulties.

Problems of adjustment and fit were not exclusive to students' first years. One young man told me he had had a great first year, only to see his sophomore year head south:

> By the end of sophomore year, I was fed up with [my roommates]. They'd gotten into a decent amount of drugs, and they were borrowing my car at times when they didn't tell me, and it just got out of control. My room turned into the party room, and they would just tear it apart. . . . By the end of sophomore year, I almost didn't want to come back. . . . [Then] I went on this [exploration] retreat, . . . had a blast, and met some new friends, and . . . it changed my college experience. My junior and senior years were unbelievably better than my freshman and sophomore year[s] . . . so I was pretty lucky. I was pretty close to leaving and . . . [the retreat] was just a huge, huge influence on me. . . . It's something that I've been trying to live by.
>
> *(Senior male, management major)*

Indeed, nearly one out of five college students nationally drops out during or after his or her sophomore year.[6] Sophomore-year experiences loom large, then, in many students' decisions to persist.

To test these qualitative retention findings systematically, I obtained six-year graduation rate data for all eighty-eight campuses that received an exploration grant, along with eighty-eight randomly selected campuses. Such data are available through the US Department of Education's Integrated Postsecondary Education Data System (IPEDS), which required submission of six-year graduation rate data beginning in 2002.[7] The 2002 data thus report the graduation rate of the entering undergraduate cohort of 1996, allowing 150 percent of the expected time-to-degree for that cohort to graduate, with the 2003 data doing the same for the entering cohort of 1997, and so on. I pooled data for cohorts entering college from 1996 to 1998, compared them to data for the 2001–3 cohorts, and then compared funded campuses to those selected randomly. An equal number of campuses (fourteen) from the funded population and random sample saw no statistically significant change in their graduation rates during this period. But fewer funded campuses saw their graduation rates decrease compared to randomly sampled campuses (thirteen campuses compared to twenty-one), and more funded campuses saw their graduation rates increase (sixty-one campuses compared to fifty-three; see fig. 4.2). In other words, about one out of five funded campuses posted better six-year graduation rates than comparable campuses selected at random. This is, to be sure, a crude experiment—since the funded campuses' higher retention rates could be a "Hawthorne effect" where addition of new programs (rather than their content) made students feel more appreciated and more educationally productive.[8] By the same token, three of the twenty-

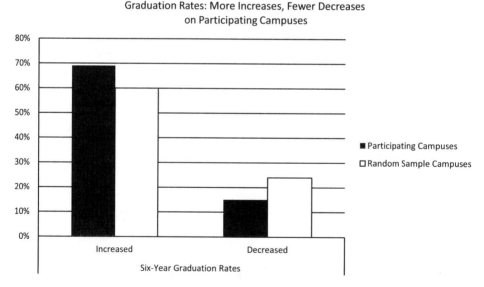

Figure 4.2. Comparison of six-year graduation rate increases and decreases.

six campuses I studied had weak exploration programs,[9] which, if proportionately true of the eighty-eight, would diffuse the retention effects of campuses with average to excellent exploration programming.

That exploration programs possessed notable retention effects is remarkable, since this initiative was not launched to improve retention. There were three funded campuses that sought to use their exploration programs to expressly improve undergraduate retention, in fact, and none succeeded. I suspect their feeble approach to purpose exploration (i.e., an Oprah-esque, ahistoric spirituality designed to appeal to everyone) failed to engage their campus's Future Intelligentsia or Reforming Activists, who elsewhere were the first and most enthusiastic participants in exploration programs. Questions of purpose and vocation, absent a connection to a community of students, are unlikely to appeal to students considering withdrawing from campus. Tangible matters like a new roommate, an emergency loan, permission to switch classes, or having friends to sit with during mealtimes are far more salient for struggling students. Direct approaches to retention must be in place before exploration programs are added, since exploration involves individual reflection primarily and can generate diverse results. One staff member, who ran a highly successful exploration program, put it this way:

> I have a love/hate relationship with the way our modern universities are going toward assessment almost exclusively. Meaning everything has to be quantified, and if it can't be quantified, it's not valuable.... I had a colleague from [another] university call me and say, "Hey, we'd like to start [an exploration] program down here.... Can you help us?" So I helped him start up a program down there. And he called me ... two years ago and said, "We're having a bit of a problem here. I've heard back from the Board of Regents, and they want me to justify my program and specifically prove how it helps retention." I told him at that point, "I can tell right now you're probably going to lose your program. It's not that I don't believe that this program absolutely helps retention, that it's making life-changing development in students' lives. This is a powerful program, but if they're going to only address you on those grounds, you'll probably lose." And he did. It was one of those things where ... the university, being run as a business and doing assessment as a business, [found] there just wasn't room for any sort of student development.

His conclusion may be extreme, but his larger point is valid. There is nothing inherently retention-related about purpose exploration; its retention effects lie in its community-building effects, which were not part of the exploration program's focus on some campuses. One program director told me about a college senior so moved by the human needs he witnessed during a January service project that he withdrew from his final semester to accept a full-time job doing relief work. That is an exceptional story, to be sure, but it is an important reminder that purpose exploration can have effects of all sorts[10] — which can include fostering community and thereby increase student retention, but not necessarily.

Life Trajectories

It is no picnic to grow up a "military brat" or a "preacher's kid." Tracy Turner had the dubious distinction of being both — the youngest child of a military chaplain. So *fourteen* times during her first eighteen years, Tracy and her family moved — out of one military chaplain fishbowl, across the country, and into another. Tracy's father had a unique career: a Lutheran minister with excellent conflict resolution skills, he specialized in rebuilding troubled chaplaincies. Tracy adored her father, but the nearly annual relocations left Tracy with few deep friendships, and her Pentecostal grandfather's rejection of her father's progressive Lutheranism strained kin relationships. Perhaps this was why Tracy grew enamored with novels, and why she chose to study literature at Mennonite College. That was where I met Tracy, a thoughtful young woman who appreciated her college's pacifist heritage, its tradition of hospitality to the needy, and its seriousness about matters of faith — even as she found the college more theologically conservative than she was.

Tracy entered college, therefore, already marked by idealism and self-reflection, and found her way to Mennonite College's exploration programs early. Tracy, to use my student typology above, was a Reforming Activist and core participant in her campus's exploration programs. Idealistic students like Tracy were the core of every campus's exploration program. But they were not its modal student type. Most students approach their college educations instrumentally, making Utilitarians or OC Achievers, like James Nwosu, the modal type. A second-generation Nigerian American, James attended college with a singular focus — to prepare for a career in international finance.

An only child, James enjoyed an affluent lifestyle and attended elite private schools. James's father, a successful engineering consultant, made it clear that James was to study law or finance—a demand at which other adolescents would bristle, but that James accepted, because he intended to surpass his father's success.

We met James in the spring of his senior year, during our visit to Richboro University. That he chose a university known for its school of business, with no concerns about its sticker price, confirms his affluence. So, too, did his impeccably chosen designer clothing, his presumptuous announcement that he needed to "cut short" our prearranged interview for "something important," and his self-flattering description of a job offer from a major Wall Street corporation. Both of my research assistants, with less affluent upbringings and interests in public service, described James as "arrogant" in their field notes, as did my otherwise silent transcriptionist. Though I did not conduct this interview personally, I met James along with these assistants, listened to his interview, and concur that James made several arrogant remarks. His complaint about "too much rain" during his spring break, which he spent at his aunt's Paris time-share apartment (and made after hearing that his student interviewers had spent their breaks working), was particularly so.

At the same time, James enjoyed his leadership role in Richboro's Purpose Exploration Hall (whose modest stipend would have provided little motivation; see chapter 3), described weekly service activities, and spoke genuinely about the program's impact on his life. Nor did he actually cut the interview short, but answered every question fully. Since James was an early interviewee, I struggled to make sense of him. My assistants alleged his exploration involvement was little more than *résumé* padding, and I do not doubt that James's *résumé* cited campus involvements. But it would be foolish for a student not to list his or her service activities. Moreover, James had ample choices of less demanding and more prestigious activities at Richboro University, nor could James's statements about the impact of his exploration program participation be dismissed as desire to please his interviewers (he seemed to possess little concern for their feelings). It was not until later, after meeting similarly driven students and devising my student typology, that I recognized James as an OC Achiever who discovered affirmation for undernourished values and interests during his involvement in exploration programs. Yes, James enjoyed an affluent lifestyle and sought a lucrative career—

but those things were not the sum total of James's identity. James also wanted to make a difference, to "provide people some of the opportunities that I've been provided." Most of these people, James explained, would not act on those opportunities, but at least he wanted to expose "at-risk" teens "to a trading floor . . . [where] you can make a million dollars by thirty." And that desire to broaden opportunity found affirmation in James's consideration of his purpose and vocation.

The issues that James and Tracy sought to discern were nearly opposite. Tracy was sorting out which career and what manner of living she should pursue given her long-standing values, while James was sorting out his values and how to incorporate them into the financial career and lifestyle he deeply desired. For Tracy, that meant applying to a two-year preministry fellowship program, which placed her into a seminar with twelve students who interned at churches during the academic year and devoted their summers to full-time ministry. For James, that meant applying for the Purpose Exploration Hall, initially to network with some of its wealthy alumni mentors, then discovering that these alumni asked hard questions about life purpose. James's mentor, in fact, challenged him to see the economic difficulties of a developing economy firsthand, which James did during his junior year. In short, both James and Tracy had sophomore- and junior-year experiences that were intense, placing them on trajectories they continued to calibrate as college seniors.

Part of what Tracy identified was a "severe" interest in ministry and community development, but that would not take the form of a pastoral career:

> I know that I have *severe* interest in pursuing a ministry and an outreach
> in some capacity. I'm not sure how that'll end up looking. My father is a
> [Lutheran chaplain], and so I've grown up in a very liturgical, church-based
> setting. But I don't see myself in that capacity *at all*. I'm very drawn to com-
> munity development and even the idea of living in community. . . . I'm a very
> externally focused person in that I don't feel comfortable if I'm not interacting
> with people or if I'm not trying to meet a certain need. So I think that a "severe
> interest" is kind of even linked to my own personal survival. I don't think that
> I would be at all self-actualizing if I weren't focused on the other. I wouldn't
> know what to do with myself if I didn't have another person's interest at heart.

Some of Tracy's interest in community development, she admitted, had its root in her "nomadic" upbringing, since "there's no place in America that feels like actual home." Some of it stemmed from "discussing the idea of belongingness and place" in her seminar as well as with friends. But the largest part of it came from her summer internship, which had her serving downtrodden residents of a rust-belt city while repairing the long-empty manse adjacent to a once-prominent city church:

> There were about five of us, and we lived in this old, gutted-out manse. It was in complete disrepair, so we spent a lot of the summer fixing it up, repairing it, and just focusing on each other, and then [doing] outreach to the external community. There's something very organic about that. . . . We didn't put our names on any of the food items and everyone's closets were open for anyone to take anything, which was a . . . jarring environment for some of us to be in. But for someone like me, it felt extremely right. I really like the idea of not putting an emphasis on the individual's possessions. I guess the model in the [biblical] book of Acts, the early church setting, where everything goes into the pot and everyone is taken care of out of that pot, is very, very appealing to me.

Tracy admits that her interests in ministry and community development "weren't really whetted until coming to college," but that the process of ongoing conversations, community service, and her fellowship helped her identify her career path. That still left Tracy with a couple of big questions—like "Where?" and "Doing what, exactly?"—but she took advantage of her senior year to investigate international as well as local opportunities for community development. Many seniors voice anxiety and "panic" about the future, especially when fielding a series of interview questions about it. Tracy was unflappable, however. She told us she had "absolutely" identified her "calling," defining calling as a "theme that will overshadow the different places that you come to and different jobs that you have," and identifying her calling as "ministry and community development." Tracy's confidence in her life's calling thus calmed her even as she stood at the threshold of many unknowns.

A similar calmness characterized James, though its expression was a tad arrogant. He confidently postponed giving an answer to his Wall Street job offer, defying his father, to await the outcome of his international fellowship application. That fellowship, which required James to create a project proposal, was infused with service. If it was awarded, James would not only embellish his educational credentials and international experience, but also implement his ideals of exposing needy youth to advancement opportunities. James described it this way: "Globalization is happening; there's nothing we can do to stop it," so we need "to prepare the people . . . the masses . . . with the knowledge and the resources to succeed." James did not use religious language, as Tracy did, for his religious beliefs were vaguely defined at best. But James's desire to serve differed from Tracy's in degree only. Tracy sought to live simply within a needy community, which she would also serve through a helping career. James sought a financially successful life marked by weekly visits to a needy community similar to the one in which Tracy planned to reside, where James could help to expand opportunities. James, just as much as Tracy, sought to lead a laudable life, and both deserve commendation.

Trajectories in General

Many of the 1,340 participants from nine funded campuses who relayed their experiences on my web-based survey sought equally laudable ends. Fully 84 percent of these participants confirmed that discussion, reflection, or reading about purpose or vocation had been personally "helpful" or "very helpful," and 74 percent reported that they had a faculty or staff adviser with whom they had valuable "conversations about my vocation, calling, or purpose" (see table 4.1). Both are potent indicators. The former demonstrates that even those reared in a postmodern and pluralistic culture find value in exploring framing narratives. Sorting out the world and one's place in it is an undertaking from which most college students hide, defaulting into traditionalist or individualist cultural trajectories (see chapter 2), but that some students will engage, finding the projects of self-knowledge and self-transcendence embedded in purpose exploration to be invaluable. The latter demonstrates that exploration programs substantially boost advising satisfaction above the 49 percent national rate of satisfaction with "academic and career advising."[11] Indeed, five surveys of academic advisers employed at 3,019 institutions of American higher education, conducted between 1983 and 2003 by the National Academic Advising Association, reveal little achievement of, and nominal gains in, "assisting students in considering life goals by relating interests, skills, abilities, and values to careers, the world of work, and the nature and purpose of higher education."[12] How is it that purpose exploration programs accomplished what the National Academic Advising Association could not? Exploration programs aimed wider and deeper, inviting faculty, staff, and students into conversations about life purpose, infusing institutionally organic exploration languages and methods of meaning-making storytelling to facilitate those conversations.

That more than half (52 percent) of the 1,340 survey respondents agreed or strongly agreed that "students on campus often use the terms *vocation, calling,* or *purpose*" underscores the importance of this exploration language. And conversations involving that language, in turn, foster student community and facilitate student development. Four out of five student participants reported that their campus's exploration programming "encouraged me to see and serve the needs of others," two out of three credited exploration programs with helping them "identify skills and talents," and one out of three indicated that exploration programs led them "to alter [their] life plans" (see table 4.1). That represents invaluable learning at the beginning of emerging adulthood, when it can inform identities, shape behaviors, and direct life plans for what

Table 4.1 Student and alumni participants in purpose exploration programs

	Percentage
Discussion, reflection, or reading about vocation was "helpful" or "very helpful" to me.	84
Campus vocation programming:	
helped me identify skills and talents.	64
encouraged me to see and serve the needs of others.	82
led me to alter my life plans.	33
Students on campus often use the terms *vocation, calling,* or *purpose.*	52
I have a faculty or staff adviser with whom I have helpful conversations about my vocation, calling, or purpose.	74

Notes: Percentages, except as indicated, pool "agree" and "strongly agree" responses. Survey respondents $N = 1,340$.

one clinical psychologist labels as arguably the "defining decade" of one's adulthood: ages twenty to twenty-nine.[13] Previous research indicates that college students show little interest in deeper questions of identity or one's place in the world;[14] these results suggest that introducing campus populations to a moral language with which to frame these questions, fostering storytelling as an ideal means of answering these questions, and seeding campuses with a supportive community of mentors and peers makes a world of difference.

Write-in comments from survey respondents underscore these percentages, not only in content but in sheer quantity, as 410 (31 percent) current and former student participants opted to write what was most personally helpful to them. One wrote how "the mentoring program helped me find out who I was, and not just what I wanted to be like, because others might think more highly of me." Another explained how:

> discussions of vocation at [my university] helped deepen my understanding of our work in the world. Prior to my time in [the program], I assumed work was only about self-interest, about making my way in a "dog-eat-dog" world. Now I see how work is not an isolated sphere separated from my values and my concern for the common good. This has proved enormously helpful in making my own way, and in discussions with fellow pilgrims making their ways in the world.

Still another wrote simply of "the power of this [purpose/vocation] concept to help give direction to an aimless life." Had only a few students volunteered such comments, they would be outliers, but when 403 (98 percent) of the write-in comments were positive, they merit attention.

Most frequently identified was the writer's own reflection on questions of purpose and calling. Students appreciated "the idea that what we do is not just about having a job, but having a calling," approaching "my career with more intentionality than I may have without education in the idea of calling," and acquiring a deeper understanding of the connection between work and identity:

> Since matriculating at [this university], I began to think of my life as a life of calling and purpose—and without that seed planted early on, I may not have

even thought about it. To most of the world, a job is just a job—but vocation is who you are.

Such reflection was nearly always linked to the influence of mentors and peer conversation partners. Students praised "one-on-one discussions with faculty members that took a personal interest in me"; peer discussion groups, "because I get to share my beliefs and learn those of others"; and courses whose texts were "more than helpful, [as they] cause you to reach down deep into who you are and ask yourself questions that you thought you already knew the answer to." Students praised professors and staff by name, complimented exploration-themed courses, and lauded specific exploration programs. Nor was subtlety the goal of many students' comments; they liberally inserted intensifiers like "amazing," "immensely helpful," "fantastic," and "incredibly inspiring," at times deploying all capital letters to make sure I would understand their point.

Students also described positive impacts of service activities and internships, retreats and fellowship programs, and spiritual insights. Some wrote about service trips that "opened my eyes to many new experiences and peoples, [and] helped me reflect on my life and how I want to spend it." Others highlighted internship seminars that ran during the semester:

> I think that the discussion groups that accompanied the [program] internships were extremely helpful to me because they gave me a chance to really reflect on the work that I was doing in terms of discerning my calling. Without the structure of the groups and insights from my classmates, instructor, and the required readings, I think I would have missed out on a lot of what I was learning about myself and my vocation through my internship.

Still others named retreats and fellowship programs as invaluable, because they combined learning experiences, discussion, and guidance, and imparted tools that simplified implementation of one's purpose. "The framework provided by the [retreat] . . . makes it much easier to think about direction and goals in life," one student writer explained, because it "makes my future planning more concrete and reasonable to deal with without being utterly overwhelmed."

Spirituality had a strong showing in student comments. Many wrote appreciatively of their college's efforts to foster purpose exploration, like the student who was grateful for "a university that is not just interested in getting you a job but about helping you figure out where the passions that God has given you meet the world's needs." Other students wrote of spiritual insights gleaned from courses, professors, staff, and texts:

> [Tracy Kidder's] *Mountains beyond Mountains* and [Bruce Olson's] *Bruchko* were really insightful books[15] into where God's purpose can take you and how you need to trust him with your future — something that really speaks to me right now.
>
> I realized that people struggle with their identity and purpose quite often, and have throughout history — hence, the seemingly endless writings and discussions about it. I also realized that I am truly blessed to know exactly where Yahweh is leading me and what I'm created to do.

Still other students wrote about newly acquired spiritual practices, like the one who explained that "the idea of prayer and its role in the choosing of a vocation has had a great impact on how I make decisions." While spiritual comments came most often from students attending evangelical campuses, they did not come from them exclusively. Students at religiously diverse campuses also expressed their appreciation for spiritual insights they had gained.

Perhaps the most striking comments came from alumni. I was concerned at the beginning of this project that ideas of purpose and calling might be maladaptive, hindering efforts to choose a path and secure a paycheck in the "real world." The opposite was true, as purpose exploration nurtured intentionality among alumni, like this one who saw vocation as the driving force in his career search:

> People talking about vocation so frequently [at the university] makes it feel like a common thing that everyone has and deserves. To pursue one's vocation becomes the norm, and, even after graduating and leaving that environment, I cannot fathom doing anything else. Friends from other universities, however, hardly understand the word, let alone the way it drives my search for a meaningful, fit-for-me career!

This man wrote as if he had found a secret path to meaningful work, and wished his friends could understand vocation's orienting role in his career search. Other alumni described how exploration programs helped them clarify "inchoate thoughts and aspirations" and of the "liberating" effect of exploration "language":

> Although I had given some thought to questions of vocation prior to [college], it was my [college] community that nurtured these inchoate thoughts and aspirations and gave me a place to think broadly and deeply about where my abilities match up best with the world's needs. Playing a central role in this reflection was my participation in [a college exploration program] and my informal conversations with [one staff member and two faculty members].
>
> Being given the language for the feelings that I already felt was incredibly liberating. I had only heard the word *calling* used in relation to ordained ministry. I knew that I felt I was being called to something, but I also knew that it was not ordained ministry . . . so I didn't really know what to make of it. Having the opportunity to be in conversation about my gifts and talents and how/where they might meet the needs of the world really set off a fire inside me. Even six years after graduation, I consistently find myself drawing upon my experiences in the [exploration program] to make big decisions in my life.

These three endorsements join those of 157 other alumni who had participated in campus exploration programs. It was feedback from alumni like this that most convinced me of purpose exploration's efficacy in a campus setting—as alumnus after alumnus described their sense of purpose or vocation as the driving force behind their deep thinking and passionate citizenship—outcomes that a liberal arts education is supposed to foster, but only rarely produces.

At the same time, I cannot ignore students who wrote complaints. There were seven. They wrote statements that the school needed to move beyond "touchy-feely" ideas about purpose and focus on "achieving through hard work and perseverance," complained about being "yelled at" for not participating in purpose exploration programming, or ranted against the school and religion in general.[16] To these seven I add another twenty-three survey respondents who indicated that reading and discussion of vocation was "unhelpful" or "very unhelpful" without writing comments, which gives a total of thirty, or 2 percent of student participants, who were dissatisfied with exploration programming. This is surely an underestimate, as others who felt similarly may not have received the survey or opted not to complete it. But it may not be a gross underestimate, for it comports with our experience during site visits: despite concerted efforts to find students who were critical of exploration programs, we found very few: students overwhelmingly settled into enthusiastic or ambivalent camps. This fits with the emerging adult norm of niceness — especially with regard to personal choices and during conversations with researchers — which dominates the discourse of college students, a phenomenon that other scholars have noted.[17]

Decisions, Decisions, Decisions

That the overwhelming majority of participants appreciated and often enthused over exploration programming is clear. The reasons for this, however, merit consideration. From student responses, we know that students gained self-knowledge about their talents, that they learned ways to apply those talents to a needy world, and that they experienced both reassurance and challenge in thinking more deeply about the paths their lives could take. We know, too, that students valued conversations with professors, staff, and supportive peers. But why do these things strike such a chord of appreciation? I propose two reasons, one normative and one practical. The normative reason, which I described above and elaborate in the first and final chapters, is that concepts of purpose and vocation impart a meta-narrative that infuses the arc of one's life with meaning and provides a base for constructive engagement with the world. Ideas like purpose and calling give students a respite from popular drones of American achievement and acquisition, affirm individual agency, and broaden the horizon of proactive pathways.

The practical reason, which surfaces in many written comments, is that exploration of purpose or vocation reduces the stress that surrounds student decisions. Some readers might think, "Stress? In college? I should be so stressed!" But consider the context in which today's college students make decisions. First, these are among the earliest decisions with longer-term career implications that college students, many of whom are still teens, must make. Second, because cultural scripts place career choice at the center of life satisfaction, and college as the locus of career preparation, students often infuse academic decisions with a sense of permanence and even irreversibility. Third, since each generation must earn its own place in a capitalist system, schooling becomes a major site of class-based angst[18] that elevates school decisions far beyond their limited role in life outcomes. Even though career counselors and campus advisers repeatedly intone that today's workers will change careers eight times over the course of their lives,[19] most students are convinced they must identify their lifelong career while in college. All too often, students approach college as a maze with multiple exits, with their life satisfaction determined by finding the right exit and doing so quickly. A premed student who makes every turn correctly and does not waste a minute, for example, will wind up at the exit where the bus for Harvard Medical School sits waiting. The premed student who dallies will be lucky to catch the bus for a third-tier medical college, while the one who makes a wrong turn will spend her career selling real estate. Such thinking is exacerbated by immaturity, but it is very much the product of larger economic and cultural forces.

Consequently, the stakes have become quite high for today's college students—which those who attended college during economic booms or eras marked by less global competition may not appreciate. Students have much at risk, for gains that are unknown and losses that are undeniably expensive. And while college students may not realize the staggering reach of global economic change, they are certain that there are no good jobs for those without college degrees, and that the most prestigious jobs require graduate degrees. It should not surprise us to learn that anxiety levels have reached an all-time high among college students. Nationally, three out of ten entering freshmen report that they "frequently felt overwhelmed by what they had to do," and just over half (52 percent) report "above-average" mental health—the lowest figure since this question was first asked in 1985.[20] Likewise, national surveys of college psychological counselors confirm a dramatic uptick in the seriousness of mental health issues among the students they treat.[21] Gone are the days when simpler relationship and adjustment issues filled counselor caseloads, as serious anxiety-related disorders now dominate caseloads and every campus has a suicide watch list. Perhaps this helps to explain why nearly one out of two students binge-drink—to drown their anxious feelings—and why rates of binge drinking among college women, who consistently report lower levels of mental health than college men, have risen so rapidly.[22] Alcohol relieves anxiety, but only temporarily and inconsistently, and generates anxiety-provoking complications of its own, further increasing consumption.

For many students, then, college is an anxious place, and they seek relief wherever they can—including in exploration programs. One student became alarmed "because people are freaking out as sophomores, as juniors and seniors in college . . . [trying to] figure out what they want to be right now." So he opted to participate in a purpose exploration workshop, which featured a panel of adults "who have been on this vocational journey throughout their whole lives and . . . [did not find] what they felt they were truly called to be until they were forty years old." Hearing their stories was "very reassuring" and "comforting . . . [because] maybe the path is winding to actually get there, and you need to go through a couple jobs." Another student described how, during her final semester of college, she "realiz[ed] that I wasn't really fond of my major." Thinking that "everything was gonna fall apart because I had wasted four years," she met with her campus's exploration staff. After several conversations, and more than a few tears, this young woman "found other options that felt right," was accepted into a one-year service program in a nearby city, and was beginning to "see the good that came out of stuff I didn't think was good." To these two stories I could add scores more; anxiety about decisions was the push that sent students seeking relief, and word of mouth about exploration programs made these a major draw.

My in-depth interviews suggest that OC Achievers had the highest rates of anxiety, with Utilitarians running a close second. The reasons are not hard to imagine. Such students seek practical, measurable outcomes from their college education: job offers, acceptance into corporate training programs, professional school admissions, and high scores on standardized tests. But these outcomes occur, if at all, at the conclusion of one's college career. In the interim, such students experience a daily gap between the practical outcomes they seek and the impractical education they receive. "Why do I have to learn this stuff?" becomes their mantra, illustrating disappointment with the impracticality of their courses and anxiety about insufficient preparation for the careers they seek. By contrast, Future Intelligentsia and Reforming Activist interviewees expressed less worry about the specifics of their future, as long as they could foresee ongoing engagement with their interests in the future. They may be more sanguine because their idealism is isomorphic with the deeper structure of higher education. That is, because higher education relies upon a supply-side model of student development, providing an enriched environment to benefit students with passionate interests and the desire to "make the most of college," there is a reassuring fit between idealistic students and collegiate institutions.

OC Achievers and Utilitarians thus welcomed—and sometimes flocked to—exploration programming that reduced anxiety and offered practical experience through internships or service. Personal reassurance and hands-on opportunities are scarce goods on campuses, and appreciated by students when found. At the same time, practically oriented students kept unsettling questions about meaning, purpose, and obligation at an arm's distance—as too much thinking about these matters could alter their culturally mainstream life trajectories. As a former OC Achiever observed:

> It requires a lot of reflection time to think about vocation and understand where you want your life to head and how you're going to be your best self. . . . I think a lot of people are lost in . . . this "achieve-a-tron." We are going and going and going, and some people don't stop to think "Is this really what I want to do? Is this the path, really, that I want to follow?" A lot of people are driven by money, families, [and] social pressures to do a lot of things that they do . . . just going through the motions and oriented [to] where they're expected to go, not necessarily where they should be going vocationally.

Another frequent participant in exploration programs was blunt about "the majority" of her classmates: "They have a plan, they want to stick to it, they want to reach the gold, and that's it! Like, don't tell them there's an alternate route; they're trying not to hear it." Idealistic students, by contrast, embrace alternate routes, like the Future Intelligentsia who told me:

> Someone asked me why I wanted to get my PhD [in child psychology] and waste all that time in school when you could be in the business school and make millions of dollars after two, three years out of college—but that's not what I want. I'm not here for me, I'm here *for others*. I'm also here to show my

parents that their hard work is paying off in terms of me wanting to help other people. There's just a lack of that in the world, and it's unfortunate, especially for children that need you.

Still another idealistic student described his switch from computer science to religious studies, despite earning outstanding grades in his computer courses, because he had "a lot of questions about religion and faith and so I just became a religion major and started questioning things more deeply." The problem, however, was that he had no idea "what I was gonna do with [a religion major,] and I didn't know why I was in it, other than the simple fact that I had questions." Involving himself with his campus's exploration program helped him see "college as something that lets you think and engage the world, [and see] that the money will always come wherever you go." I doubt instrumentalist types would reduce their anxiety with such thinking, yet this young man was positively serene that his intellectual interests in religion and his computer skills would converge in a rewarding and income-generating career.

Passionate Saints, Contingent Moralists

If there is a general pattern to the purpose exploration that college students did, it is this: idealistic types, like Tracy Turner, know their passions, but want to explore them more fully and use them to guide their futures — to find employment linked to their passions, locate communities that share these passions, and draw loved ones into these passions; instrumentalist types, like James Nwosu, embrace mainstream goals of satisfying careers, comfortable lifestyles, and familial intimacy, so they seek to identify their career path, align their present activities with that path, and (at least among those finding their way into exploration programs) incorporate into that path some contribution to others. Idealists, in other words, envision an uncompromising pursuit of their passions that resolves into meaningful work, livable incomes, happy families, and community-engaged lifestyles, while instrumentalists believe that pursuit of their career, lifestyle, and familial goals will bring them success and happiness. Future Intelligentsia thus lose themselves in learning, Reforming Activists pursue passion-linked endeavors, and Rebels seek a new world order, while OC Achievers focus on high-status careers, Utilitarians anticipate middle-status careers, and Minimalists dream of easy jobs that pay well.

What strikes me about this pattern is its parallel to the public-good experiments of economists. In these experiments, conducted internationally among university students, economists found that three types emerge: "knaves," or free riders, who behave selfishly unless sanctioned; "saints," or altruistic individuals, who sacrifice for the good of the whole; and "moralists," or contingent actors, who behave generously *if the system supports* generosity, and self-protectively if it does not.[23] Free riders comprise one-fourth of most students rather consistently, saints another one-fourth, and contingent moralists the remaining half. Saintly types like Tracy Turner will touch many lives because of the personal sacrifices they are willing to make, and colleges happily nurture young adults like her. But Tracy's path is possible through the support of contingent moralists like James Nwosu and a social system that supports contingent moralists' desires to augment personal success with giving to others. In other words, the charitable organizations, foundations, government social programs, and fair-trade businesses that fund the livelihoods of saintly Tracys would not exist without the economic life that contingent moralists like James generate and the resources that they share. As much as my heart leaps to hear Tracys speak of their plans, the more pressing need is for educators to leverage their many Jameses so that social institutions that undergird the public good maintain voters' support. Tracys appear to be plentiful; sufficient Jameses to support Tracys and the organizations that employ them, however, do not. This is a serious problem indeed.

The results of these public-good experiments suggest there are many Jameses who wish to do good. What these Jameses lack, however, is encouragement that their wishes can be meaningfully actualized in the career and lifestyle they pursue. What they need are examples of others in similar careers who have combined individual success with public contributions. And they need to understand that larger systems must be maintained to support the public good. This is a large-scale undertaking, and deserves a place in college curricula and cocurricular activities. A student like James should not have to search outside his school of business to find support for these ideals. He should have multiple options within it, as should students in other schools. There are courses, institutes, and cocurricular activities that support such ideals sprinkled throughout the academy, so models for this exist. At the same time, these programs are sprinkled rather than mandated.

Educators are also hamstrung by dated secularist/modernist assumptions that religious or spiritual discourse, which motivates many who seek the public good, must be banished from the classroom. Thankfully, philosophical work on coherent understandings of secularity has entered discussions of the liberal arts, and as these trickle down to classrooms, students will be freer to bring their authentic selves into the classroom and explore specific connections between their normative hopes, our world's many needs, and their future purposes.[24]

Social Norms

Hugs, boisterous conversations, comic bantering, and lots of flirting: these are the staples of college student sociability. They signify affection and belonging. And with few exceptions, recent college graduates tell me that easy sociability is what they miss most about college. At no other point in privileged Americans' life course is one surrounded by so many others of similar age, upbringing, academic abilities, and interests. Some of this interaction is wholly informal, begun haphazardly and maintained by choice. But much of it has its basis in structured contexts, such as athletic teams, student organizations, or required courses, which produces fairly predictable peer groups. College football players, sorority sisters, and premed students, for example, are three well-known peer groups whose common perspectives and broadly identifiable behaviors are products of their shared structural contexts. Such peer groups can significantly impact the identities of their members, and often lastingly—with former members reenacting social patterns decades later at reunions. It does not take a sociologist, of course, to appreciate the lasting identity effects of one's young adult group memberships.

With that backdrop, consider the impact that student groups with pro-exploration norms might have. Imagine a group of students united in friendship, each believing that his or her skills and talents are gifts to be enjoyed, developed, and used for the benefit of others, and who convey that belief through word and deed. Such a group would underscore the purpose explorations of its members, even generate a synergy around exploration and its possibilities. My evaluation team encountered several groups like these during our campus visits, and they assumed three forms. The first were profession based, comprised of students studying to become health professionals, teachers, business leaders, or clergy. The second clustered around chapels and religious life programming, where devout students (the *religious virtuosi*,[25] sometimes known as the campus's "God squad") immersed themselves in campus ministries and religious outreach. The third were service based, found among students dedicated to ongoing volunteer work or short-term service projects. Such groups, often in existence before their campus's exploration programs began, had a natural affinity for purpose exploration, were quick to engage exploration programs, and flourished with the infusion of grant resources.

We did not anticipate encountering proexploration student groups when we began our site visits. Rather, they found us. "Could you tell your students to turn down the vocation language? It's starting to freak out some of the principals." The statement was from a school superintendent, relayed to me by one university's career counselor, after a half dozen education students had used *vocation* and *calling* language during job interviews in his district. The superintendent was personally amenable to the language, being an alumnus and religious himself. But his nominally religious principals did not know how to respond to job candidates who claimed that teaching was their "vocation" or who declared, "Teaching is not a career, it is a *calling*!" These education students had so internalized the ideas of purpose and vocation that they employed them liberally during their job interviews. A focus group later that day confirmed students' comfort with these terms, and a zeal for them among students in the school of education. The spark was that school's exploration-infused first-year and senior seminars. This career counselor did relay the superintendent's message to the school's seminar instructors, but more as a point of information than as an alarm. "After all," she told me with a grin, "he hired four of them, and was calling to get me to send him some more."

Subsequent campus visits introduced me to proexploration student groups in nursing, education, business, campus ministry, and volunteer service. Students in these groups would use the language of purpose and vocation freely, in reference to themselves as well as friends. "[Jen] definitely has a calling to work with special-needs children," one student told me about another, and then elaborated with a touching example from a volunteer experience at a community health center. I could not determine if there was a gendered component to the appeal of proexploration norms, unfortunately.

We know from the social scientific study of American religion and spirituality that women have consistently higher levels of belief and practice,[26] and I know of one supplemental project funded by the Lilly Endowment to study male college students' interest in purpose and vocation exploration.[27] Students preparing for teaching and nursing careers were largely female on the campuses we visited, while proexploration groups of future teachers and nurses were almost exclusively so. But proexploration business majors, ministry groups, and service groups had more gender-balanced participation. Perhaps the male dominance of the executive suite as well as the senior pastorate, combined with the "muscular" nature of many service projects (New Orleans–rebuilding projects were especially popular due to the overlap between this initiative's launch and Hurricane Katrina), helped to foster male participation in these areas. A definitive answer about the gendered appeal of proexploration social norms must await another scholar's efforts.

I did observe elements of a protobacklash against exploration programs on three campuses. All three were campuses that required students to participate in purpose exploration during orientation, as a part of obligatory first-year courses, or via mandatory convocations. While mandatory participation did not always produce a backlash, it appears to be a necessary condition. Nor was the backlash severe: it mostly consisted of joking about exploration "jargon," about being "called to dinner," or "called" to ask another student "on a date." A couple of students voiced more serious complaints about "all this money for vocation" but no money for efforts to "go green," "fight poverty," or "reduce violence." I sympathize with these students, as their campus had a minimal budget to support student activities, which made even moderate expenditures like using tour buses or providing refreshments seem lavish. On the whole, however, backlash elements seemed shallow and sporadic, not as influential as proexploration student groups, and in their own way confirmed the reach of purpose exploration on these campuses. "At least they know the language," one program director offered in response to my inquiry about exploration jargon, "and maybe later, it'll become meaningful to them." At the time, I struggled to not laugh at his Pollyanna-ish perspective. But after fifty-nine follow-up interviews with alumni from exploration programs and sixty-four alumni from comparison campuses, my data suggest he might be right — at least for some of these jokers.

Maturity

"With a bachelor's degree, especially from a good school, I thought that you'd just walk out — you'd be this prime candidate for a job; . . . I just wasn't prepared for how difficult it would be." The words came from a recent graduate of one of the world's top universities, but similar sentiments were legion among recent graduates of colleges of all ranks. A wannabe journalist who graduated from a respectable college and spent her next year "working retail . . . in the mall" told me plainly, "I always say graduating from college was the worst thing that ever happened to me." Of course, global economic competition has kept college graduate wages flat and made paths to financial independence increasingly difficult for more than three decades — but the combination of American individualism and young adult disengagement from economic and political information had prevented this reality from trickling down to these college students' everyday consciousness. Hence, the frequent voicing of disappointment and frustration among recent college graduates did not surprise me.

What did surprise me was how little disappointment I heard from recent college graduates who as students had spent time exploring questions of purpose and vocation. Surely, if recent graduates who did not have opportunities to explore questions of purpose and vocation felt disappointed, then those who had spent time pondering these idealistic notions would be even more disappointed by the gap between their ideals and the realities of life after college. Yet, I observed nothing of the sort. Recent graduates who participated in purpose exploration programs as students voiced longer-term perspectives and demonstrated persistence in spite of setbacks. Participation in purpose exploration programs fostered not a maladaptive idealism but a grounded idealism that anticipated longer paths as well as setbacks, in turn generating broader satisfaction with these graduates' life-at-present.

Life after college is a story of setbacks and disappointments. To hear young adults describe these can be quite illuminating. Occasionally, setbacks were of lasting significance, like a serious health condition or death of a loved one, and young adults were powerfully and understandably altered by them. But for the overwhelming majority of these college graduates, setbacks took the form of closed-off opportunities — that is, applications declined by prospective employers or graduate schools. To these setbacks, I encountered three responses. A few recent graduates withdrew and spent months bemoaning their rotten luck, many lowered their expectations and began devising backup plans, while some granted themselves a couple of days to feel sad before reassessing their options and charting new courses to their original ends.

Tracy Turner and James Nwosu's stories offer two cases of reassessment and recharting. Catching up with both a year after they graduated from college, I learned that Tracy did not find work in international community development, and James did not win the international graduate school fellowship for which he had applied. Both were disappointed, but only briefly, and both were quick to reorient their efforts in positive directions. Tracy and James realized the many opportunities that still lay open to them, the privileged position they occupied as college-educated young adults, and the lifetime they had to pursue their goals. In other words, Tracy and James shared a perspective that helped them show resilience while identifying points of satisfaction in their present setting, both of which are important in successfully navigating a globalizing and postmodern world.

After receiving their disappointing news, James accepted his Wall Street job offer while Tracy arranged housing and recruited other seniors to live in and serve a needy community near Mennonite College. James had the golden backup plan, or so it seemed, except that the "[financial] world ended" in September 2008, two months into his employment. That is, Lehman Brothers collapsed, financial insurer AIG was put on federal life support, and his own company received so many resignations and issued so many layoffs that James was left without an identifiable supervisor for nearly a month. Tracy, meanwhile, discovered that launching an intentional service community with young adults is arduous without any support from an umbrella volunteer organization, and watched it nearly fall apart when participants realized the significance of not having health insurance. Her project survived, but at the cost of its members securing jobs based on benefits and scaling back community service to nights and weekends. As stark as the foregoing sounds, our conversations with James and Tracy were anything but. They were delighted to speak with us, to share all that had transpired since their first interview, and genuinely optimistic about the future. Though some ascribe optimism as a generational trait,[28] I argue that James's and Tracy's grounded idealism helped them accept these setbacks and move forward without surrendering their goals. James's and Tracy's perspective on themselves and their role in the world, in other words, nurtured their intentionality and persistence.

This perspective helped James and Tracy maximize the good in their current circumstances, adapt their future plans, and put the negative in context. For James, it meant enjoying his work as a financial analyst, where he was learning how international finance works and was party to financial transactions in the "millions of dollars." It also meant appreciating his lucrative income, which put him on a fast track to be debt-free in two years. Of course, James did not become uniformly mature, as he purchased a sports car on a whim one day, which he now must pay to garage and which he "never drives." Because he lived in New York City, he did not need a car—he used the subway to get to Wall Street, began his days there at 6:00 a.m., and often ended them as late as 10:00 p.m. He was also there most weekends. This work schedule put an end to his relationship with his girlfriend of three years; it also ended James's plan to work in international finance his entire career, as he watched the company's senior partners put in as many hours as he did.

> I have to sit right next to him, the guy's a millionaire ten times over, and when I'm there, like, ten o'clock, eleven o'clock at night, nine times out of ten these partners at [Big Bank], which is arguably one of the best investment banks in the world, are sitting right next to me. So, technically, I guess they can take off when they want, but because it's such a competitive environment, when you do take off, that puts you at a competitive disadvantage to your peers.

James had a different plan in mind: in two years he would move to the developing country he spent a semester in, either by company transfer or by quitting and joining an international organization to teach English. After that, James would start his own company, then sell it at age forty, so that he could "give back and actually have a true purpose in life." In short, James's time at Richboro University inculcated the language of purpose, his time abroad sensitized him to the underbelly of globalization, and his daily walk on Manhattan's sidewalks underscored his commitment to both. "Down on Wall Street," he told us, "you can be walking right next to a millionaire and in the same breath you can sit there and see a homeless person that has nothing, and is fighting to survive." For now, James understood that he was in training—for a purpose larger than himself and for people who have never had the opportunities that James refused to take for granted.

Tracy spent her first year after college doing the service that James planned for his short- and long-term future. So Tracy did not lose her appetite as James did when walking past homeless persons—because she was not walking by them to dine at her city's toniest establishments with other investment bankers; she was walking beside them to a church pantry to help them obtain food and other essentials. For this, Tracy was grateful. She was also grateful for the old Lutheran church that donated use of its manse to Tracy and four other young adults in exchange for their volunteer work. Her first year after college had not been without its challenges—chiefly financial— which she relayed in her characteristically thoughtful way:

> You want to be working toward some sort of overarching goal in the end. What is hard about that, and what I think a lot of people my age have been having a difficult time with, is making ends meet while trying to live intentionally. I never once thought I would be talking about health insurance as much as I've talked about it since graduation. Every day I'm, like, "Oh my gosh, I just need benefits!" and I hate it that the finances really do rule so much of the choices that I've made. I would've gone to Europe much, much earlier in my life if I had had the capital to do so. [Yet] what I like about where I am is [that] I'm with a group of people who are trying to make the best of their own personal situations and trying to make the best of the community situation so that life squeaks past a little easier for everyone. And I like being invested in that so young. It's a choice that I would make again if I had to.

Tracy eventually found a job that offered health insurance, but in the suburbs of her rust-belt city, leaving her only nights and weekends to do the community service she cherished. She also owed a "thousand bajillion dollars" in school loans, the ironic product of a college "where for four years . . . [we] talked about how to live into my faith and how to practice peace and social justice and community development and service." And yet, Tracy was not resentful. "It's difficult to make ends meet, but it's difficult for everyone . . . and I don't feel particularly victimized by that reality." Nor was she resentful about not finding international work, for her frequent moves as a military chaplain's daughter left her "hungry for a sense of belonging and place," which spending a fifth year in the RustBelt City region was beginning to impart. If there was any resentment in Tracy, it lay in the gap between her long-term desire to marry and have children, and the current absence of a boyfriend. In the interim, however, "I feel good about the quality of life I lead, and I think that I have a life that is centered in faith." She then added with a laugh, "But I am also just out of college, I live in a household of postcollege friends, and there's wine!" Though her purse was empty, her heart was full, and Tracy found daily validation for her way of living. I was confident that her vivacity, along with her dense social network, would soon connect her with potential suitors.

Satisfied to Flourishing

A skeptic might argue that Tracy and James would have proceeded along these lines without any purpose exploration—that these two young adults were more resilient, intentional, and mature to begin with and that purpose exploration added nothing to these preexisting traits. In the first chapter, I addressed this by (1) acknowledging that participants did enter exploration programs slightly higher in maturity than nonparticipant peers—but made substantial gains over the course of their participation, and by (2) pairing three participants in purpose exploration with three nonparticipants, and demonstrating the very different pathways of students with fairly similar entrance characteristics. Rather than repeat this with additional pairs of college graduates, for which I would hit page limitations and reader fatigue, I describe a more encompassing approach to this issue.

Our follow-up interviews with 123 recent college graduates included questions about graduates' satisfaction with six broad areas of life: their work or graduate school life, their finances, their living arrangements, their social life, their love life, and their religious or spiritual life. On the whole, all interviewees indicated they were more satisfied than dissatisfied with these six areas of life—an unsurprising result given the privileged position from which a college graduate engages the world and the general optimism of young adults. *Those who had participated in purpose exploration during college, however, expressed broader satisfaction with life after college than those who did not participate*, a statistically significant result that held firm even after controlling for respondents' gender, race, age, socioeconomic status, and attendance at

religious services.[29] Since participants and nonparticipants in purpose exploration were not selected at random, these results are suggestive rather than
determinative.[30] What they suggest is telling, however: purpose exploration
has enduring and beneficial effects on graduates' overall life satisfaction.

That recent graduates were on the whole more satisfied than dissatisfied with their lives is a positive outcome. But it is a modest outcome, too.
What parents and citizens seek, and educators promise, are college graduates who flourish — that is, young adults with positive goals for the short and
long term, who show independence, responsibility, and active engagement
with the community. For flourishing to be possible, one must observe broad
levels of life satisfaction — as flourishing is incompatible with limited levels
of satisfaction. It was here that participants in purpose exploration surpassed
their nonparticipant peers — as participants had a median satisfaction score
of 4.9, while nonparticipants had a median satisfaction score of 1.8. That is a
three-point difference, on a scale where each point signifies satisfaction with
a major dimension of one's life. Participants in purpose exploration were not
modestly satisfied with their lives; they were broadly satisfied with them —
they were, I argue, flourishing. Their nonparticipating peers, by contrast, were
not (see fig. 4.3).

This is a striking result, but it must be examined for confounding influ-

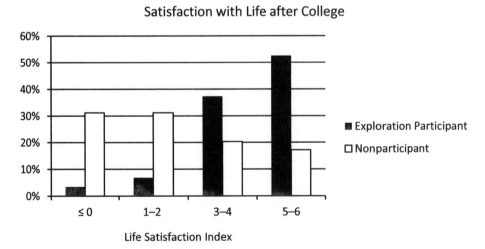

Figure 4.3. Comparison of life satisfaction levels one year after college graduation.

ence by age, gender, race, socioeconomic status, and pregraduation religiosity. That one's life experience varies by age, gender, and race is indisputable. The same holds for socioeconomic status.[31] I expected these confounding factors to be statistically significant and to diminish the difference in life satisfaction between exploration participants and nonparticipants, but neither age, gender, race, parent educational attainment, nor parent occupational status confounded life satisfaction scores (see fig. 4.4). That these demographic and social indicators showed no statistical significance is good news for US citizens, for it suggests a degree of social equality in initial life satisfaction among recent college graduates. This also turns a lot of deterministic thinking on its head, but only among those who completed four-year degrees in their early twenties, and perhaps only for the first few years after college, before graduate and professional school students complete the advanced degrees that widen gaps between themselves and the rest of the workforce.

Since participants in purpose exploration chose to attend religiously affiliated colleges or universities (sometimes for, and sometimes in spite of, that affiliation), I added controls for pregraduation religiosity — creating a three-point ordinal scale for interviewees with regular, occasional, or no religious

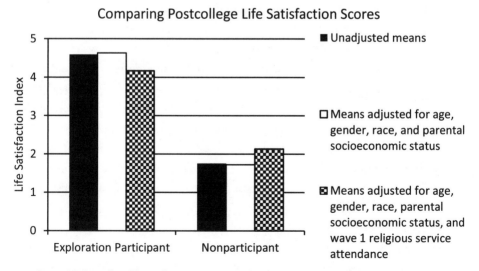

Figure 4.4. Postcollege life satisfaction comparison of exploration participants and nonparticipants.

service attendance at the time of our first interview.[32] Readers familiar with the research literature on religion and life outcomes[33] will not be surprised by the significant, positive, and sizable relationship between religious participation and postcollege life satisfaction. But congregational participation, while it reduces the predictive power of purpose exploration on life satisfaction, still leaves a sizable two-point gap in life satisfaction between exploration participants and nonparticipants (see fig. 4.4). In fact, 43 percent of the variation in interviewees' postcollege life satisfaction can be explained by two predictors: how frequently they attended religious services while in college, and whether they participated in purpose exploration.[34] For readers without statistical expertise, that may not seem like much—but consider that the SAT test, which is central to college admissions, explains 15 percent of the variation in first-year college grades. Quantitative social scientists agree that multivariate results above 15 percent, when working with individual-level data, are rare and respectable.[35]

So what does it mean that both purpose exploration and regular worship attendance during college possess such significant, positive, and sizable influence on postcollege life satisfaction? One interpretation is the old Marxist saw about religion being the "opium of the people." That is, religion legitimizes the economic status quo, leaving adherents blindly satisfied with their lives and the wider world. I reject this blanket interpretation, however, for the following reasons: exploration participants possessed a keen awareness of the world beyond their immediate circles, often dedicating their lives to the pursuit of a more just world; they recognized the many failings of institutional religious forms and practitioners; and they freely expressed dissatisfaction with areas of their lives when warranted. Ignorance about the wider world and preoccupation with their own lives was, if anything, more common among nonparticipants. *A more apt interpretation is that purpose exploration produces a pattern of examined living, that regular participation in congregational worship reinforces that pattern and encourages positive engagement with others, and that purpose exploration combined with congregational involvement increase the odds that emerging adults will flourish after they graduate from college.* While this is a bold claim, it is essentially a variation of an ancient truism. Since Socrates, educators have labored to facilitate thoughtful self-examination within their students, convinced that "the unexamined life is not worth living." Exploration of purpose and vocation provides a constructive mechanism for life examination, appeals to a wider swath of students than traditional liberal arts curricula do, and when combined with regular involvement in a congregational community (or surrogate[36]), fosters relationships that sustain lives worth living in spite of setbacks.

Longitudinal Effects

One of the most enjoyable parts of this evaluation project was conversations with campus program directors. These religiously and philosophically diverse men and women were resolute in their commitment to the flourishing of college students, and united in their view that purpose exploration contributed to student development. Each genuinely valued the ways students appropriated concepts of purpose and vocation to sort through decisions about majors, overseas study, internships, and graduate school applications. And yet, I often discerned a wistfulness in their words, as they sought to convey ideas that would not be fully appreciated "until ten, maybe twenty years down the road." It was not, as one director put it, as hard as "trying to sell life insurance to twenty-year-olds"—but there were "days when it felt that way." They hoped students "will remember" what they learned about purpose exploration, and "draw from it" as they made decisions with more serious and long-lasting effects. My educator's heart sympathized, but my social scientist's brain filed this under wishful thinking and gave it no further thought. That is, until I analyzed alumni results, discovering that one out of five exploration participant interviewees had married within a year of graduating from college, and that participants' use of purpose and vocational "discernment and reflection" increased the longer they were out of college. These phenomena indicate that purpose exploration holds value over time, at least among a sizable share of those exposed to it.

Exploration participants married at four times the rate of nonparticipants—a striking result in light of international increases in age at first marriage among young adults. Many of these marriages were between religiously conservative young adults, who often marry sooner than religiously progressive and nonreligious peers. But many were not. Exploration participants, having spent time as undergraduates reflecting on the long-term direction of their lives, were ready to make a variety of long-term commitments—including marriage. Equally striking, exploration participants were three

times as likely as nonparticipants to report being satisfied with "no" love life —
because they would consider romantic attachments to marriageable prospects only. Paul, for example, reported "no" love life because he was focused
on building community with other year-round staff at the camp where he
worked as maintenance manager. There was a summer counselor with whom
he had begun a romance, and for a month they tried a long-distance relationship. But they soon "realized more things about ourselves . . . and didn't want
to develop that into a deeper or more serious relationship," so they agreed
to part ways. That Paul evaluated this relationship in light of its long-term
potential speaks volumes; he talked as intentionally about this two-month
relationship as chapter 1's Melody, Jeff, and Rosa did about their marriages.
Paul realized he needed more face-to-face time with a potential girlfriend
to know whether she was marriageable, and although disappointed at first,
dating a marriageable woman was more important to him than simply dating.

I note that exploration participants and nonparticipants had the same
proportions (one out of four) engaged or talking about marriage seriously.
The twenties are, of course, prime years for pairing off. Yet, several nonparticipant interviewees told us their conversations about marriage had been
triggered by news of others' engagements: "Like, all the sudden, my friends
are *all* getting engaged or married — and that's really upped the pressure!"
Friends' engagements can have that effect, but it seemed the exploration participants did not need others' engagements to trigger thoughts or conversations about marriage; those were present from the beginning. I also observed clarity in the responses of exploration participants about their love
life, which was often missing from nonparticipants' responses. A number of
nonparticipant female interviewees would, for example, answer our query
about the seriousness of their reported relationship with "Well, it's serious
to me" or "*I* think it's serious." These are answers that illustrate the instability
of contemporary romantic ties. Their virtual absence among exploration
participants was thus striking. And since exploration programs focused on
undergraduates' career decisions and engagement with global needs, this intentionality in interviewees' love lives may represent an important spillover
effect of purpose exploration.

That any college learning spills over afterward merits close attention.
Comedian Don Novello, playing Father Guido Sarducci on *Saturday Night
Live*, introduced millions to his "Five Minute University . . . [where] in five

minutes you learn what the average college graduate remembers five years after they're out of school." His sketch hilariously illustrated the truism "Use it or lose it." So when three-quarters (72.4 percent) of alumni exploration participants agreed that "since graduating from college, I have drawn upon vocational discernment and reflection to guide my decisions," we have intriguing results about the usefulness of purpose exploration. Might that utility vary by respondents' gender, race, field of study, overall grade average, religious service attendance, or months since graduation? There are mountains of research indicating that social phenomena differ across gender and race. Project directors also speculated that openness to purpose exploration varied by field of study, grade point average, or time since graduating. And the multivariate analysis above uncovered a relationship between religious service attendance and postcollege life satisfaction that merits its evaluation as well.

Using ordinal logistic regression, a statistical procedure that evaluates the simultaneous influence (or lack thereof) of the above factors on use of reflection and discernment to guide decisions since graduation, I found no effects for gender, race, field of study, or overall grade average.[37] That means discernment and reflection are not practiced disproportionately by women over men, persons of color over white Americans, graduates in arts and science fields over graduates in professional fields, or those wearing honor cords over those squeaking by with the lowest grades permissible. To put it simply, purpose exploration is equally useful to a wide range of college students and alumni. Statistical analysis did reveal that use of discernment and reflection increased with religious service attendance and with months since graduating from college. That is, the more regularly alumni attended worship services and the *more* time elapsed since they graduated from college, the more likely they were to have drawn upon purpose exploration practices as they made decisions. This makes sense intuitively, as alumni would hear ideas of purpose and vocation reinforced during worship, and as they would face more life decisions the further they were from graduation day. These results also suggest purpose exploration is "sticky": it stays with alumni years after their graduation; gets reinforced through religious participation; and holds appeal without regard to gender, race, field of study, or academic performance.

Purposeful Citizens, Missional Campuses

Inviting undergraduates to explore purpose and vocation brings lasting benefits to students and to their campuses. The evidence for ongoing effect is straightforward: 88 percent of campuses I visited continued their exploration programs, with their attendant costs, two or more years after their Lilly Endowment award ended. Despite the draconian higher education budgets of the Great Recession, fully half of the campuses I visited continued their exploration programs with minimal changes, and another 38 percent continued most programs, leaving some intact and while restructuring others (see appendix 4).[38] Particularly striking were turnarounds by three average programs—two hired new directors and successfully relaunched, and the third saw its organizational antagonists dismissed and their department reorganized under the exploration program director. Purpose exploration does not just stick to alumni—it sticks to college organizational charts and campus cultures. It even helps to stick campuses together, with two-thirds of campuses that received grants, along with a hundred others, paying annual dues to participate in the Network on Vocation in Undergraduate Education, to enhance and expand purpose and vocation exploration among undergraduates.[39]

Purpose exploration does not appeal to all students. But the anxious waters that invisibly flood every campus lead the OC Achiever and Utilitarian student majority to seek relief wherever they can; this usually means binge drinking but can mean purpose exploration and reflection. The contingent moralist majority, if the public-good experiments of economists are correct, will support the common good—but not sacrificially and not if free riders run unchecked. These contingent moralists need affirmation for their inclination to good, including reflection on purpose, and guidance in operationalizing good works. We must not forget that these students become the popular majority that supports, or dismantles, the work of education, scholarship, and social justice.

This is not to say Future Intelligentsia and Reforming Activist students should be ignored. Such are the stars of campus and scholarly engagement! Too many of their names are missing from the campus marquees, however, because too few campuses know how to engage them successfully. This chapter demonstrates that inviting students to explore purpose and vocation draws in Future Intelligentsia and Reforming Activists. It demonstrates that quality exploration programs reinforce idealistic motivations while simultaneously helping pragmatic types convert vague desires to do good into tangible commitments. Exploration programs deserve careful consideration by any campus serious about holistic development and lifelong citizenship of its graduates.

Young adults have become the subject of intense attention, both scholarly and otherwise. Some fall into an aimlessness illustrated in popular media and books like *Quarterlife Crisis*, while many delay commitments and spend years "tinkering" with identities, careers, and relationships.[40] These wider realities underscore the intentionality, resilience, and maturity that graduates of exploration programs demonstrated above: their adulthood is not emerging; it is realized. They have consciously chosen interdependent life trajectories, while peers default into individualist or traditionalist life trajectories (see chapter 2). Although chronologically in their early twenties, exploration participants reasoned and spoke as if several years older. Such wisdom can be traced to the faculty and staff who, inspired by purpose exploration themselves, chose to fully inhabit their educational roles and embed themselves within the larger mission of their college or university. Their stories, conveyed in the next chapter, are as intriguing as the student stories that comprised this one.

5

Faculty and Staff

Herding Cats?

The first time I heard a university dean liken his job to herding cats, I laughed out loud. Cats seemed a perfect analogy for faculty, with their independence, territorialism, and readiness to bolt out the nearest door. And the image of some poor sap attempting to herd such creatures seemed an apt summary of a dean's impossible work. But nothing kills a good joke like repetition, and after two decades of hearing it, I am eager to toss "herding cats" onto the pile of tired academic clichés, along with "burned-out bureaucrats" and "administrative inertia." That is *not* to say the conditions that generate these clichés have disappeared; quite the contrary. I am weary, rather, of their hopelessness and of how they obscure the persistent efforts of many faculty, staff, and administrators to deliver a quality education. I have visited more than fifty colleges and universities across the United States, and at every institution, I have encountered dedicated educators, and a goodly number of them. I have observed faculty cooperating to enact major curricular changes, professional staff creatively collaborating on new initiatives, and administrators genuinely guided by institutional missions. Wise, innovative, and cooperative work is not impossible in higher education—but it requires ideas that inspire and draw together academic communities. And since citizens of academia like to analyze and dispute, these ideas must withstand exhaustive analysis while simultaneously tapping these citizens' desires to educate their students well. Questions of purpose and vocation, when introduced organically (see chapters 3 and 6), did this. This chapter describes the effects such purpose exploration had among hundreds of college faculty, staff, and administrators across the nation.

And yes, I wrote *hundreds*. I would estimate thousands of faculty, staff, and administrators were impacted across the eighty-eight campuses at large, but will restrict my claims to the hundreds of faculty and staff whom my evaluation reached directly: the 595 faculty or staff from eight campuses who voluntarily responded to my web survey, and the 274 faculty or staff from twenty-six campuses who participated in focus group or individual interviews (which gave us 790 unique faculty or staff respondents[1]). The campuses that participated in the web survey spanned denominational affiliations, regions, and campus sizes (see appendix 2, "Methodology"). And while I acknowledge that representativeness of web surveys is unknown, nearly 600 busy faculty and staff members chose to participate in this survey, so I begin with their responses.

What is an apt descriptor of lopsided percentages? Six times in American history, a presidential candidate received more than 55 percent of the popular vote—Lyndon Johnson (61.1 percent) in 1964, Franklin D. Roosevelt (60.8 percent) in 1936, Richard Nixon (60.7 percent) in 1972, Warren Harding (60.3 percent) in 1920, Ronald Reagan (58.8 percent) in 1984, and Theodore Roosevelt (56.4 percent) in 1904—and each win was described as a landslide. I selected *overwhelming*, since an overwhelming 86 percent of faculty respondents agreed or strongly agreed that their campus's vocational programs had "positively impacted my own work at [this school]"; 75 percent agreed that their participation "helped me hone my own sense of 'vocation,' 'calling,' or 'purpose'"; and 85 percent said that participation "deepened my appreciation for the mission of [this school.]" Cats, indeed! Percentages were even higher among staff respondents, coming in at 90 percent, 84 percent, and 93 percent, respectively (see table 5.1). I doubt few survey items, aside from a raise in pay, could generate higher approval rates.

Remember, this grant initiative was not designed to impact faculty and staff per se. Its goals were nurturing purpose exploration *among* students and enhancing the mentoring *of* students. Participation of faculty or even staff, beyond those necessary to deliver exploration programs, was not required. A few campuses, in fact, involved no more than a dozen faculty or staff volunteers, with a onetime advising workshop or mentoring lecture as a nod to the initiative's aim to improve mentoring. Most campus program design

Table 5.1 Faculty and staff participants in purpose exploration programs

	Faculty percentage	Staff percentage
Exploration programs "have positively impacted my own work at [this school]."	86	90
"Participation in [exploration programs] has helped me hone my own sense of 'vocation,' 'calling,' or 'purpose.'"	75	84
Exploration programs "have deepened my appreciation for the mission of [this school]."	85	93
Exploration programs "have had a positive impact on my department or program."	62	78
Faculty have been "generally" or "extremely" welcoming of the [purpose exploration] grant."	80	45
Staff have been "generally" or "extremely" welcoming of the [purpose exploration] grant."	44	79
"The impact of [these exploration programs] will be felt long after the grant money is gone."	80	87
[Active adviser of students only:] "Engaging concepts like vocation, calling, or purpose has helped me move advising/mentoring conversations into deeper and more important matters."	86	89

Notes: Percentages, except where specified, pool "agree" and "strongly agree" responses. Survey respondents N = 595.

committees, however, saw wide faculty and staff participation as essential if student exploration was to be as robust as it ought to be, and if purpose exploration was to persist after grant funds expired. And the evidence suggests their designs succeeded, with 80 percent of faculty and 87 percent of staff agreeing that the impact of their campus's exploration programs would "be felt long after the grant money is gone," and 62 percent and 78 percent, respectively, reporting "positive impact" by exploration programs on that employee's department. More specifically, 86 percent of faculty and 89 percent of staff respondents who regularly advised students agreed that engaging concepts of purpose or vocation "helped me move advising/mentoring conversations into deeper and more important matters." In the process of reaching students *through* faculty and staff, exploration programs reached a lot of faculty and staff.

Write-in comments by faculty and staff respondents supplied specifics. A female math professor wrote how exploring purpose has become "integral to my sense of self . . . [and] part of the everyday working here." A male law professor stated that exploration programs "have had a very significant impact on faculty and students . . . [and] enabled me to advise students in a far more meaningful way than I had prior to participating." A female career counselor said the programs "rekindled" her "love" for the school, "refreshing" and "bringing joy to all that I do." And a male student life professional wrote, "Thank you. . . . [Exploration] programs have made a strong impact on me, . . . [and] changed the way I work with students; [the] program is just wonderful." Some 198 faculty and staff took the option to write in comments about their campus's exploration program, nearly all of which were positive and most of which cited personal benefits in addition to job and campus-wide benefits.

And yet, for all the positivity toward exploration programming, survey results also indicate an unpleasant reality: faculty and staff inhabit separate and often unequal campus spheres. That became obvious when nearly 80 percent of faculty or staff respondents indicated their respective peers have been "generally" or "extremely welcoming" of the purpose exploration grant, but fewer than half could say the same about their staff or faculty counterparts (see table 5.1). Why? Because most faculty respondents did not interact with sufficient staff to venture an opinion about their general views of the exploration grant, nor did most staff respondents possess knowledge of enough faculty to estimate the faculty's response. This faculty/staff divide, also obvious during site visits (see chapter 2), illustrates the centrality of organizational structure to employees' experience. I am convinced that differences across institutions of higher education are *for students* largely differences of degree, but for faculty and staff involve *differences of kind* that define the nature of employees' work. Institutional type, in other words, is highly salient to a proper understanding of faculty and staff.

Consider how national accreditation requirements and consumer expectations bring commonality to the student experience. A psychology major will have a similar course of study at a rural liberal arts college or an urban research university. She will also enjoy similar options such as athletics, student organizations, and campus-wide events; rely on the same social media and mobile telephones for her social life; and purchase goods and services that are equivalent to her research university counterpart. But a psychology professor at the first institution, teaching nine courses per academic year, with two disciplinary colleagues and extensive campus service expectations, has a very different work life than her colleague at the second institution, who teaches four courses per year, manages relationships with two dozen departmental colleagues, and serves his department principally. Similarly, the lone career counselor at the first institution must serve all students, while his counterparts at the second institution may have a single counselor who specializes in psychology-related careers. Understanding the effects of purpose exploration programs on faculty and staff thus requires close attention to institutional context.

Institutional Context

There is a linear relationship between faculty or staff specialization and institutional size and mission, a fact so obvious its significance is often overlooked. Small institutions require faculty and staff to be generalists, while medium-sized institutions expect employees to balance specialization with generality. This would not be a problem if the graduate training of faculty and staff attended to both equally. But it does not, privileging a silo mentality that rewards specialization and producing graduates structurally mismatched to most colleges and possessing limited teaching skills. Most institutions resocialize new employees, therefore, using a combination of informal mentoring and orientation programs. Staff members resocialize more quickly, since their evaluation cycles are shorter and the absence of tenure forces resistance to take subtle forms. But faculty can miss or dismiss resocialization efforts entirely, because institutions need their faculty's scholarship to maintain or improve external rankings, and because tenure—primarily attained by faculty scholarship—provides autonomy from many institutional demands. This produces an "exiles from Eden" phenomenon brilliantly described in Mark Schwehn's book of the same title, and hilariously spoofed in novels such as Richard Russo's *Straight Man* (1998).[2]

The structural mismatch between specialized graduate training and most institutions' need for generalists produces a distinct employment context, which I map by intersecting occupational orientation with daily work pattern. Occupational orientation, which signifies employees' professional frame of reference, extends from "local" to "cosmopolitan," while daily work pattern, which captures employees' modal performance, runs from "hyperbusy" to "in a rut" (see fig. 5.1). This analytic field locates several higher education types: "campus stars," who enjoy prominent reputations outside the institution but display limited interest in the institution that houses them; "insti-

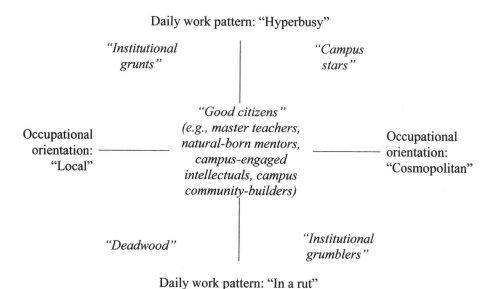

Figure 5.1. Work patterns and occupational orientations of college and university employees.

tutional grunts," whose robust work ethic is beloved by their supervisors but whose focus is restricted to the immediate context; "institutional grumblers," whose alienation from the institution but not from their profession leaves them preoccupied with greener pastures elsewhere; and faculty or staff "deadwood," whose alienation encompasses the institution as well as their profession, who retire in spirit long before their bodies depart the institution.

At the center of this analytic field one finds an institution's "good citizens": those employees who embody the professional orientation of their respective occupations yet fully participate in their local contexts, who chart a healthy course between extreme multitasking and mindless routinization. These good citizens are master teachers, natural-born mentors, campus-engaged intellectuals, and campus community builders, and they represent every university's sustaining, human core. Master teachers are those faculty and staff who intuitively understand how to spark student curiosity; they make understanding students a priority and continually hone their teaching skills. Natural-born mentors are sought out by students for their good counsel and genuine concern; they are the ones students turn to when crises strike, they are the first to hear students' triumphs, and they are sought out by alumni at homecoming. Campus-engaged intellectuals facilitate conversations about substantive matters; they share their knowledge with campus groups, and organize events that tap experts to address interesting and timely questions. Campus community builders provide the social glue that knits together employees, students, and community partners; they round up participants for talent shows, organize life-changing service projects, and link distinct social networks.

Good citizens can excel at multiple roles: master teachers are often natural-born mentors, for example, and campus intellectuals frequently nurture good community ties. Good citizens faithfully execute their own responsibilities while effectively working with others, keeping the university they serve well-connected and moving forward. Their efforts, unfortunately, are often missed because those in the corners of this analytic field draw a disproportionate share of attention on campus. That leaves a lot of good citizens feeling underappreciated—questioning why they work so hard while some do only the minimum, and frustrated by the praise heaped on institutional grunts or campus stars. Our site visits revealed weariness far more often than vitality among campus good citizens.

I emphasize those at the center of this analytic field because there are multiple organizational and cultural forces that pull faculty and staff out of the center—and few that draw them back. There is the bureaucratic weight of sustaining a complex formal organization, where policies, procedures, and paperwork exert a routinizing force. There is the American workplace praise for busyness, which celebrates productivity but ignores the unhealthy patterns that often accompany it. There is the economic and affective pull of the local, as paychecks get issued by brick-and-mortar employers, and obligations to coworkers and dependents exert a profound immediacy. And there are the universalizing norms of professions and academic disciplines, embedded during graduate training and sustained by external peers and the idealized pleasures of distant academic Edens. To remain in the center demands continual resistance, which does not produce organizational praise. What dean is happy when a faculty member refuses a committee appointment? What vice president is pleased when a staff member declines advanced training? Exploration programs, however, affirmed good citizenship and centered lives—conveying a message that is all too rarely communicated on college campuses today.

Exploration programs did more than affirm faculty and staff, however. They also challenged them with intellectual and practical projects keyed to religion's place on campus. That is, they presented intellectual questions and practical challenges that probed institutional and employee engagement with the campus's religious affiliation. For some campuses, the affiliation was active, specific, and permeated the campus culture. For other campuses, the affiliation was present but restricted to a defined sector of the organization. For still others, the affiliation existed in archives only, with religious life regarded as a purely private matter. (Hereafter, I refer to the third category as virtually unaffiliated campuses, the second as church-affiliated campuses, and the first as evangelical or ethnic campuses.) The place of religion on campus, organizationally and culturally, determined the deeper intellectual and practical project that exploration programs pursued among faculty and staff. In contrast to students, who were challenged to self-knowledge and self-transcendence across all eighty-eight campuses, faculty and staff were challenged to intellectual and practical projects determined by their campus's relationship with religion.

Exploration programs on virtually unaffiliated campuses pursued a project I call *legitimating faith and spirituality as valid topics of public conversation and activity* (see table 5.2). These campuses had no objection to faith or spiri-

Table 5.2 Intellectual and practical exploration projects among faculty and staff by type of institution

Type of campus	Intellectual and practical project	Programmatic tools	Most likely participants
Virtually unaffiliated (i.e., historically church-affiliated but resolutely nonsectarian campus)	Legitimating faith and spirituality as valid topics of public conversation and activity	Reading groups, discussion groups, lecture series, spirituality programs, religious diversity programs, progressive service activities	Good citizens—especially devout adherents of any religious tradition and resolute postmodernists
Church affiliated (i.e., actively church-affiliated but religiously diverse campus)	Drawing in faculty and staff to embrace and implement the institution's mission to develop whole persons	Employee retreats, seminars, and themed trips; grants to support pedagogical and scholarly engagement with purpose exploration; service-learning and community-engagement support centers; mentoring programs; minigrants	All of the above, plus good citizens from humanities, social science, education, health professions, student life, or career service departments
Ethnic or evangelical (i.e., theologically or ethnically distinctive campus)	Deepening faculty and staff knowledge of their tradition's theology of calling and vocation, and fueling efforts to more effectively engage a globalizing and pluralistic world	Integration seminars and programs, faculty or staff development awards, curricular and program enhancement grants, mentoring programs, minigrants	Any faculty or staff, but especially chapel staff, theology and religion faculty, and service-oriented faculty

Source: Author's analysis of 790 unique faculty or staff participants in web survey, individual, focus group, or telephone interviews at twenty-six campuses that received exploration programming grants.

tuality as private pursuits by their students, faculty, or staff—sometimes employing a chaplain or spiritual life staff to support the same. Nor did they object to scholarly study of religion—vibrant religion departments testified to that. But virtually unaffiliated campuses expected their members to remain publicly silent about their own spiritual beliefs and practices. Referencing one's faith or using spiritual language was considered inappropriate in the classroom, unwelcome during work conversations, and offensive if part of a public event. The goals were to protect public settings from exclusivist discourse, and to enforce a secularism that requires public spaces to be "scrubbed free of religion."[3] The former is reasonable, as some with devout views use languages that inhibit civil conversation,[4] but the latter reveals an anachronistic adherence to modernist theories of secularization that are "philosophically incoherent and phenomenologically inaccurate."[5] Such a modernist secularism would prevent luminaries such as Dr. Martin Luther King Jr., Mohandas Gandhi, or Mother Teresa from teaching courses on social justice on these campuses—that is, unless they checked their religious discourse at the classroom door. That students would need to be protected from the religious frameworks of instructors such as these, rather than be invited to join these instructors and classmates in a rich conversation about various bases of social justice, illustrates the absurd implications of modernist secularism.[6] Purpose exploration programs on virtually unaffiliated campuses rejected this absurdity, as had most faculty and staff on these campuses, and invited faculty and staff to engage notions of purpose and vocation, explore the rich literature in these areas, and encourage students to do likewise. As graciously as this was introduced, it was nonetheless a culturally subversive project with the potential (sometimes realized) to provoke faculty and staff whose epistemologies were rooted in mid-twentieth-century modernism.

A different exploration project characterized actively church-affiliated but religiously diverse campuses. On these campuses, exploration programs encouraged faculty and staff to embrace the institution's mission of developing whole persons and implement the same through curricular, cocurricular, advising, and residential life activities. Whole student development (or "formation," as some campuses called it) had once been a lived priority on these campuses, staffed as they were by clergy, members of vowed religious orders, and devout laity. But as these faculty and staff retired and were replaced by employees with areligious orientations to their jobs, whole student development faded from all but these campuses' mission statements. This created a gap into which exploration programs were more than happy to step. Exploration programs helped faculty and staff appreciate student development from a scholarly perspective, reclaimed whole student development as central to the institution's mission, and deployed grant resources to expand whole student development into all areas of the institution. At the same time, these programs expressed unequivocal respect for the religious diversity of the campus population. Whole student development was missional to these institutions because of their particularist histories, but was welcomed by pluralistic faculty and staff because of its applicability to students of any or no religious commitments.

A still different exploration project characterized campuses with active church affiliations and evangelical or ethnically distinctive populations. Because evangelical and ethnic campuses attracted special populations and inhabited distinct subcultures, exploration programs sought to deepen faculty and staff knowledge of their own tradition's theology of vocation, and fuel efforts to more effectively engage a globalizing and pluralistic world. These programs did not need to convince faculty or staff about the value of purpose exploration or developing students as whole persons. Rather, they reclaimed as their guiding framework helping students identify their callings, and pressed for deeper engagement with the wider world—crucial tasks given the ahistoric pragmatism of American culture and encapsulating tendencies of its subcultures.

It was important, given faculty and staff audiences, that all three projects were intellectually intriguing and practically engaging. One could host various symposia around these ideas or plan a series of practical workshops. And, in effect, that was what these exploration programs did, engaging faculty and staff substantively as well as methodologically while seeding a community of purpose exploration among them. Community is a buzzword in higher education, perhaps because it exists in such limited supply. Busy offices combined with large physical plants squeeze all but the rhetoric of community out of most colleges and universities. The faculty and staff we interviewed, however, praised the community that these exploration programs created and the rich conversations that languages of purpose and vocation made possible. Indeed, these were the most frequent remarks during our field research with faculty and staff, and in their survey comments. It took a grant about the exploration of purpose and the theology of vocation to create what many faculty and staff called the most vibrant liberal arts conversation they had ever participated in on a campus. This is a bold claim, and not true of all campuses, but true more often than not.

"It Feels like Real Liberal Arts"

The words were spoken by Katya O'Connor, a popular professor of biology and natural-born mentor, about the campus lectures, the biweekly coffeehouses, and the annual "Journey" weekend—all sponsored by the purpose exploration program on campus—which she regularly attended. "I like the way that they bring [an] expanding-your-mind feel to them," Katya told us. With young children, Katya could not attend all of the exploration programs, but she made it a priority to attend the lecture series, participate in the "religious understanding" coffeehouses, and help lead the Journey weekend. "A big theme" in this weekend conference for fifty students was "that life is a journey and a lot of the [program was] about that journey from different viewpoints." From attendee evaluations, Katya knew that "on average, the students get a lot out of it, but I know I get a lot out of it too. I'm, like, I hope they're having a great time—but I know I am." We asked Katya to describe what she gained through her involvement. She described her department as caring but "exclusive," and Katya valued the wider community that the Journey Center fostered. She also valued how the center helped her "reconcile a career in science with raising a family," and improve the "hallway advising" she did with female biology majors who often asked her about the same thing.

O'Connor taught at Marble College, a nationally respected institution with a distinguished list of alumni and an impressive endowment. Marble severed ties with its mainline Protestant sponsors nearly a century ago and removed the cross from its chapel without objection some twenty years ago. Katya was one of a dozen faculty members, and two dozen staff members, who supported and participated in programs by the Journey Center. We interviewed eight of these faculty and staff members, and they shared Katya's enthusiasm. Sally, a campus community builder who directed Marble's tutoring center, appreciated how the exploration program encouraged a "broader perspective" and helped "folks step away from busyness and their normal routines." Her point of entrance was through an exploration reading group.

"I joined the [center] reading group, and part of it, truthfully, was curiosity about who else was going to go, who else wants to explore these issues." The reading group included faculty and staff of every religious persuasion and none, and Sally "was pleasantly surprised that people were grappling with these kinds of issues that I'm not sure they would on an everyday basis; that we could all say, 'Well, from my perspective and with my upbringing, this is how I see this issue.'"[7]

Because of Marble's exploration grant, Sally reported that "a lot more of the campus has thought about their life's calling—about how they can reconcile making money and doing things that make positive change in the world, [and] how they can hopefully do both." Matt, a natural-born mentor who directed career services, agreed. He said students come to his office to talk about "conflicts that they're having between their love of something and 'Am I going to be successful?'" and found that the center's language of purpose and vocation assisted in these conversations. Rick, a professor of communications and a campus-engaged intellectual, expanded on the value of the center's vocabulary:

> It's going to be incumbent upon college communities to figure out how to relate to those students in the richest, most meaningful kinds of ways. What [the Journey Center] can do well and [must] continue to do well is to give faculty and staff a vocabulary and resources to foster those relationships as they relate to matters of life of the mind, life of the spirit, life of the quest—however that shakes out. Because the students are going to keep coming, and I think the worst thing that we could do is to throw up our hands and say that those questions don't have a place at a college campus . . . [to] say, "Well, we don't speak that language." Our students want to talk that language, and I think it's incumbent upon our community to try to understand it and keep the conversation going.

Sally added, "If [the center] ceased to exist . . . it would send a message that [this college] isn't about that sort of value seeking and the whole student." Unfortunately, Sally observed, faculty members such as Rick are all too rare: "When I talk to students, they seem to think that when they get in the classroom, faculty really care about their experience in regard to gender, socioeconomic background, race, sexual orientation—all these other things. But if they bring up religion, or a conversation they had with their minister or priest or priest or something, that that somehow isn't valued . . . ; [students] feel like that isn't as highly regarded as other parts of their identity."

Religious and spiritual language can make classroom discussion awkward. Allowing it in a pluralistic classroom is not unlike "breaking the fourth wall" in the theater; it can feel alien and uncomfortable. But I suspect it felt like this the first time educators addressed race or gender identity issues with students, and can still feel that way when inexperienced instructors do so. Instructors need guidelines and best practices, and I continue to explore these myself. Still, permitting full engagement of student identities merits classroom consideration, and I encountered campus educators of two types who were most open to this idea: devout employees of any faith, and resolute postmodernists (i.e., those who accept the full implications of discursive equality). Most educators on virtually unaffiliated campuses, however, fear engaging students' religious identities in class, being unsure about the right to express faith or spirituality in public settings, with some educators quite adamant about their exclusion. This produced a grant backlash on a couple of virtually unaffiliated campuses—of which Marble College's backlash was most extreme.

The local newspaper made it sound as if Marble College were about to become a seminary, which shifted the rumor mill into overdrive: "The board wants to get rid of the Jews and the atheists"; "It's an attack by the bishop and his consorts"; "The president is trying to turn back the clock." Never mind that Marble no longer had formal ties to any religious body or that it was a board of trustees decision to remove the cross from the chapel. The faculty did not trust the administration, and the poorly written press release about Marble's $2 million exploration grant did nothing to help matters. The faculty senate meeting that followed the article's publication was raucous. Senators waxed on about the Enlightenment, the separation of church and state, and academic freedom; demanded that the writing committee "explain itself"; then shouted down the committee chairperson's (admittedly flippant) responses. The result was a resolution demanding the college return the money, passed by two-thirds of the faculty senate.

No college president was about to return a $2 million check, however, especially when those demanding such an action had little understanding of the actual proposal. Instead, he convened a task force that combined outspoken opponents with select faculty from the proposal-writing committee (but not its irascible chair). Within weeks, the opposition backed down and cleared the grant-writing committee to hire an external project director. It did so, bringing in an easygoing fellow with an Ivy League divinity degree and publications about interfaith dialogue. The chair of the writing committee, a senior religion professor, offered his interpretation of the affair six years later: "You have to keep in mind [that] the context of [this area] is by and large Christian fundamentalism, and there's always a worry of *that* being identified with *this*. It seems to me that 'X' number of our colleagues hastily jumped into that identification. We all know it's false identification, but nonetheless, [these colleagues made it]. I mean, the biggest new church in [town] is a very fundamentalist Baptist church; they just pack them in." Though a Bible Belt location is not necessarily a hindrance to purpose exploration programs (cf. chapter 3's Phi Beta College), it is a core factor in the institution's larger context (see chapter 6). The best exploration programs had leaders who navigated around these issues and avoided provocation, but a couple, like Marble College, spent years rebuilding the goodwill that a careless press release and flippant remarks undermined.

How campuses introduced exploration programs was of upmost importance, because on every religiously diverse campus, one will encounter secular "hawks"—that is, staff and especially faculty members who are devoutly secular and who watch carefully for transgressions of institutional boundaries. Marble's explosive reaction was led by its secular hawks, who were offended by one grant element in particular: fellowships for faculty to explore connections between their scholarship, teaching, and the theology of vocation. Such fellowships were common in proposals by church-affiliated campuses, and well received by their faculties. But at a campus as far from church affiliated as Marble, such awards infiltrated the center of these secular hawks' territory. The task force agreed to review these awards while allowing them on a pilot basis during its review. After eighteen months, Rick, the professor of communications quoted above, said they were "taken off the table . . . to appease folks who were not happy." Rick had received one of these awards, and mourned their elimination. Ceasing this program, Rick lamented, "uncoupled questions of vocation and call and put them in a programmatic sphere, rather than saying they could be intellectual questions that are taken up in a serious kind of way." Exploration of purpose and vocation was permitted to occupy adjacent, cocurricular realms (such as public lectures or student programming), and faculty were free to engage these ideas there—but they could not engage faculty at the center of their academic work. While a felt loss to Rick and like-minded faculty, this decision defined the boundaries of the exploration project at Marble. And to everyone's surprise, exploration flourished as a cocurricular and student program.

Only Marble College, of the virtually unaffiliated campuses we visited, attempted to infuse exploration into the center of faculty's work. The rest let exploration become what Steve, a campus-engaged intellectual who was a librarian at another such campus, called an "in-the-cracks" program. That is, a program that took students' "development of competency in a particular discipline" along with their "social side" with its "friends and parties and so on," and became the "integrat[ive] element that pulls all that together and also connects them with their own deepest passions, their vocational visions, their relationships to one another, and their relationships to the larger community—and if they have a religious vision, then their relationship to God." Steve was delighted by his campus's "Deep Conversations" program, which met biweekly to hear short presentations and discuss these in small groups. This "created a kind of life that you don't find otherwise" and cannot find outside of a "true community." A philosophy professor concurred: "We always talk about getting students out of the [campus] bubble, and there's a lot of ways to do that, but the [exploration] programs do that really well; [they are] the only place that really networks together students and faculty and community people." To which an African studies professor added his personal appreciation for the "intellectual and physical space" the program created, for the "contemplative spirituality" those spaces fostered, and for the program's deft avoidance of the kind of rhetoric one would find at "Bible Thumper U."

Contemplative space and a community engaged with valuable questions had broad appeal. Jeff, a director of one campus's physical plant, relayed a story about his crew's involvement in purpose exploration. It began with the exploration program's need for renovations, but took an unusual turn when the program's staff invited the director and his crew to participate in reflection exercises. The staff wanted to introduce the program inductively, and, intrigued, Jeff's crew agreed to join them. When the exercises were over, the program staff asked the crew to design and build a physical space conducive to contemplative exercises as well as conversation. The crew and Jeff were honored and astonished. Few of the crew had ever thought about their work "as a calling," and rarely had they been so respected for the construction knowledge they possessed and contributions they made to campus. Consequently, they put special effort into renovating a large old house into a beautiful space, which years later some crew members still visit. In fact, Jeff regularly participated in the Deep Conversations program. "The asking of questions like 'Who am I?' and 'What am I doing here?' and 'What is my place in taking what it is that I'm learning and applying it in a way that matters to me?'—nobody's teaching that, and . . . [it's] a very important thing!" This campus was atypical for its outreach to the physical plant staff, however. The most frequent targets for purpose exploration were staff with direct student involvement. Marginalizing support staff was a strategic blunder, which I discuss again in chapter 6.

I was impressed by the sincere concern for students that employee participants in exploration programs expressed. Employees would speak of the deep personal joy they felt when they saw students benefit from purpose exploration programming, sounding not unlike parents describing a child learning to ride a bike. Cheryl, a natural-born mentor and an associate dean of students, wanted us to know that she appreciated the employee retreats and staff conferences she attended. But "the greatest thrill," Cheryl said, "is working with students, helping them discover this [exploration] program, and then . . . seeing how the program affects their lives. I mean, for some of them, this is the catalyst that gets them connected to the academics, that gives them a reason or purpose to be here, to discover themselves, [and to] start thinking about the future. That's been extremely rewarding." Employee participants such as Cheryl often revealed the settled identities and other-directedness (chosen or imposed) of middle adulthood, which stood in contrast to the personal explorations and interpersonal priorities that dominated the traditional-age students occupying the early years of emerging adulthood (see chapter 6).[8] I found it encouraging to meet so many mature, generous, and altruistic adults during our campus visits; it was a pleasant change from the conversations about organizational politics and personnel disputes that can dominate academic life.

There are two additional observations that, while not unique to virtually unaffiliated campuses, took distinct form on these campuses and merit attention. The first involves the breadth of thinking and range of implications that frequently accompanied faculty and staff exploration of purpose;

the second involves the separate spheres of faculty and staff. With respect to the first, purpose exploration by faculty and staff functioned like intellectual "Miracle-Gro"—taking fledgling ideas, adding exploration nutrients, and producing sizable research undertakings or substantial pedagogical innovations within a fortnight. This effect was so large on one campus that a poetry professor doubted this evaluation's capacity to "quantify experiences that are very holistic, . . . [that] deal with social justice issues . . . creat[e] global connections that will benefit our students for the rest of their lives, and . . . jumpstar[t] our research in very exciting ways—bringing a lot of creativity, a lot of open spaces that haven't been on this campus before." She explained how purpose exploration "is about being a full person . . . [yet] most of my conversations with others are about the fragmentation of our lives. . . . [Purpose is] very revolutionary—as gentle as it may look on the surface. But if you dig a little deeper, oh my God, it brings up all the issues." Stimulated in a more applied way was the school of business dean who declared, "Anybody that thinks religion is not going to be part of this international global marketplace in some significant way—their head is in the sand!" Elaborating, he explained, "If you force your marketplace to be neutral with respect to religion, you're really doing the organization harm, because you're asking people to bring less than their whole self into that marketplace, and . . . you don't get the full value out of the people that are part of the organization." Consequently, this college "needs to push the conversation in each program of study about the connections between that field and issues of faith, religion, and spirit." What has kept this conversation from occurring thus far has been a "lack of practices, even a language" for it. He had begun those conversations in his school, however, and was resolute about sustaining them.[9]

That faculty and staff inhabited distinct perspectives on their work was apparent early in this evaluation. On virtually unaffiliated campuses, these differences had a "rawer" expression. Staff would speak about faculty as "they" or "them," complain of being "shut out" of important campus decisions by faculty or academic deans, and attribute illogical organizational practices to faculty petulance. One associate chaplain generalized that "our faculty think that *religion* is a bad word," relaying how she "almost came to blows" with her sister and brother-in-law, who teach at another college, because "they don't have respect for a lot of staff." Faculty, by contrast, rarely mentioned staff—they seemed invisible, which confirmed staff members' complaints.

The caveat to this gripe was "present company excepted"; that is, the faculty and staff who participated in exploration programs valued the good citizenship they saw in each other. Those outside the program, however, were assumed to occupy the corners of the employee mapping discussed above (see fig. 5.1). These separate and unequal spheres, which intensify with size of organization, are common on campuses. On church-affiliated campuses, however, it seemed that the legacy of "Christian charity" kept alive a language of family, partnership, and community when speaking about fellow employees. That the exploration project on these campuses had less divisive potential likely helped as well.

"It's Helped Us Integrate the Curricular and the Cocurricular"

About ten years ago, the president of Cornfield Lutheran College recruited Joe Williams, a campus community builder par excellence, to lead Cornfield's international programs office. By all visible indicators, Joe has been highly successful—doubling both the number of students who study abroad and faculty-led international trips. He also remained active in the classroom and the concert hall, his discipline being choral music. With one foot in the cocurricular world and the other in the classroom, Joe enjoyed a wide perspective on the college and its constituents. He valued the classroom, but he also valued the rehearsal room, the concert tour, and the international experience. Joe knew valuable learning happened in Cornfield's classrooms, and equally valuable learning happened outside them.

When the president of Cornfield first approached Joe, there was no mistaking the school's religious affiliation. It was manifest in the college's name and underscored by the symbolism in its logo. Unlike virtually unaffiliated campuses, which require archival research to identify their religious origins, church-affiliated campuses have active and apparent church affiliations. College guidebook descriptions, admissions materials, centrally located chapels, and degree requirements in religion or theology make these affiliations obvious. Consequently, these campuses attract a disproportionate number of students and employees with corresponding identifications. At the same time, "disproportionate" does not equal "majority." These campuses insist that persons of all faiths and none are welcome to join their institutions, and they enroll and employ majorities who are unaffiliated with their institutions' official denomination. Or, to put it simply, most people at Lutheran colleges are not Lutheran, most people at Presbyterian colleges are not Presbyterian, most people at Methodist colleges are not Methodist, but one will find more Lutherans, Presbyterians, and Methodists at these respective institutions than on public campuses. Joe fit this pattern: born a Congregationalist, he described himself as more spiritual than religious, yet attended an Episcopal church for its excellent music.

When Cornfield's purpose exploration director approached Joe to create a "Reformation Legacy" tour for faculty and staff, Joe was intrigued. The tour would follow commencement, last two weeks, include visits to significant Lutheran sites in Germany, require readings, and feature presentations on Lutheran history, theology, art, and music. The trip's goal, the project director explained, was to help faculty and staff leaders better understand Martin Luther and the Protestant Reformation so that they could draw upon the Lutheran tradition in their various roles. Joe agreed, even as he had reservations about the purpose exploration that was to frame the trip. Those reservations evaporated when Joe made this connection early in the trip:

> This whole idea of communities, service, civic engagement—it's something that's always been a part of me, but I never integrated it with my sense of spirituality; I never understood it as part of the Lutheran heritage. . . . It was fundamental to Luther's way of thinking to engage in . . . critical inquiry—how you're most faithful when you challenge your own faith and yourself. And it was like a lightbulb in some ways for me. Not to mention that it was just great fun to be in the company of nineteen other people who were on this same journey. I mean, it brings a sense of solidarity that was a privilege to experience.

By the end of the trip, Joe reported, "An ethos . . . evolved" among fellow travelers that unified previously distinct components of their work and their lives in general, and "helped us integrate the curricular and the cocurricular."

Joe doubted, like the poetry professor above, whether this evaluation could capture exploration's impact on him or the college in general. "I can't measure it" or "understand [it] for myself," he said. Joe explained how exploration programs on campus had woven together student development, spirituality, community-engaged learning, intellectual engagement, and global awareness. His colleague Anne, a master teacher and a professor of nursing, agreed, describing how purpose exploration conversations led her department to shift its framework from "bio-psycho-social" to "bio-psycho-social-spiritual—looking at the whole person and helping our students to look at that spiritual component along with the psychology, the sociology, the environment . . . and seeing that as part of a whole." Jennifer, her colleague and a professor of humanities, likened purpose exploration to a set of tools for teaching and thinking:

> I think the one thing that made it very real to me was understanding that the Lutheran heritage is very academic. . . . It really resonated with me when I read people like [Philipp] Melancthon and Luther and [Timothy] Lull and [Martin] Marty, that the whole idea of social justice is completely embraced— regardless of whether people think this is affiliated with a church or not. The whole idea . . . gave me a lot of hope when I went back into the classroom to be able to say, "Well, I can be an advocate of what it means to be an academician in Lutheran higher education." Before that I didn't have the tools to talk my way out of a brown paper bag, so I just didn't talk about it. People would say, "Do you want to talk about spirituality?" I said, "No—I'd rather light myself on fire, and run the other way! No, I don't want to talk about that!" But now I have a much better understanding of it. . . . I can join the two together, or if I want them to remain separate, that's fine as well.

Jennifer, Anne, and Joe all attended Cornfield's Reformation Legacy tour, and they and their travel mates infused a palpable energy into the rollout of the campus's Citizenship Center that fall. A two-week trip abroad for twenty faculty and staff leaders was an undeniably expensive way to begin. But the program designers considered it an investment in faculty and staff that would seed the campus with enthusiasts for purpose exploration, who in turn would make the school's Lutheran heritage, as Jennifer worded it, "part of our lexicon."

That exploration programs used incentives such as trips, minigrants, or stipends to attract staff and especially faculty participants may not, at first blush, seem praiseworthy. Employee participation should be based on program merit, not personal gain. In the end, merit was what sustained employee participation, but project directors insisted an incentive was necessary to get busy employees' attention. Given the common use of honorariums as inducement and reward for work outside official employee duties, the repeated requests for participation that pass through faculty and staff in-boxes daily, and the untested and unusual nature of exploration programs—I can appreciate this view. The only place slow-moving and esoteric university life exists is on the silver screen; the reality of American higher education is heavy responsibilities and conflicting demands. Incentives can cut through the daily hubbub like a piccolo pierces through the sound of a full orchestra. Incentives draw employees in, but it takes program merit to sustain their involvement.

At Cornfield, the twenty employees who took the Reformation Legacy trip became early adopters of the Citizenship Center's programs, helping it become a "one-stop shop" that coordinated volunteerism, community-engaged learning, and alternative spring-break service projects. They also were the first to tap community project grants, which facilitated curricular and cocurricular projects. The athletic director, for example, created a joint staff position in leadership development and athletics, and filled it with an assistant football coach/volunteer coordinator who drew dozens of male athletes into previously female-dominated service programs. Two professors created an "Education and Service" conference that involved scores of employees, students, and off-campus educators, which has become an annual event. Cornfield's exploration program netted a high yield from its Reformation Legacy trip.

Five years later, those who attended were still enthusiastic about their experience. At the same time, they were honest about the gap between the reflective lives they desired and the hectic workdays that dominated their organization. "We say that we want this vocational, faith-based, healthy approach to life, which is holistic, but that's not how we organize ourselves as a college." The demands of a complex formal organization run counter to reflection and healthful living. Once the initial flurry of posttrip programmatic creativity died down and the novelty wore off, maintenance of new initiatives consumed employee attention. Gratitude for the exploration grant remained high, for "helping save our mission, . . . keeping some of our strengths, and . . . [preserving] our soul and the heart of the gifts we've always carried along as an institution," since market pressures had led Cornfield to add professional programs and merge liberal arts programs. Employees understood that the latter were necessary, but they nonetheless weakened morale, especially among faculty in consolidated departments.

The chief flaw in Cornfield's exploration program was its decision to offer the Reformation Legacy trip only once. This resulted in weaker enthusiasm for purpose exploration among those who were not part of the trip. Employees not on the trip would tap exploration programs, but they lacked the "ethos" and proexploration bonds that Joe and fellow travelers possessed. That single legacy trip rooted exploration programs on Cornfield's campus. But had it been repeated a couple of more times, an exploration ethos might have permeated the employee culture generally and encouraged more creative responses to Cornfield's increased professionalization. At other church-affiliated campuses, repeatedly offered seminars and retreats fostered pro-exploration communities among employees, generating enthusiasm for holistic student development and injecting new energy into cocurricular activities.

That church-affiliated campuses fostered an ethos of holistic student development among employees makes sense, given their organizational missions. Its spillover into expanded cocurricular activities puzzled me at first, however. Why observe increased activity here? Nick, a master teacher and professor of management at a Roman Catholic college, helped me locate an answer in organizational theory. He explained, "For any kind of organization, as soon as you ask anybody to pick up something that's secondary to their primary task, it's going to be hard. . . . It's going to take a lot of work." When an organization's resources contract, which has happened on all but elite campuses over the past two decades, employees prioritize primary assignments and reduce secondary efforts such as cocurricular activities.[10] Nick personally valued the purpose exploration program at his college, and created two cocurricular events with its support. But the exploration program at Nick's college did not nurture an exploration ethos among employees, as the Reformation Legacy trip or the faculty and staff seminars at Ignatius University did (see chapter 2). Not surprisingly, the exploration program at Nick's college was only minimally continued after grant funds were depleted. On campuses where employee seminars, retreats, or themed trips were offered repeatedly, however, a critical mass of faculty and staff emerged who defined their primary task as holistic student development and mutually reinforced that definition. Once holistic student development was located at the center of faculty and staff work, cocurricular engagement and its integration with the curriculum became a logical site of faculty and staff activity.

All Are Welcome

Worth special note was the inclusivity of retreats, seminars, or themed trips offered by exploration programs on church-affiliated campuses. Persons of any faith, no faith, or anywhere in between were warmly invited to explore ideas of purpose and vocation. Verena, an assistant professor of art history, was an active Roman Catholic at a Protestant college. Tom, professor and chair of political science, was a "radical atheist" at a Lutheran college. Mike, a newly promoted associate professor of religion, was a "queer Episcopalian" at a Methodist university. Yet all three were affirmed in their identities by their campuses' exploration programs, and reported that their participation made a significant contribution to their scholarly and educational activities. I profile each, as they illustrate the creativity with which faculty tapped into exploration programs, before switching to the different effects of participation among staff members.

Verena's love of art had its source in the icons and architecture of the Roman Catholic cathedral in which she was reared; of that she was certain. Verena also spoke of the mysticism that attending Mass still fostered, and of the spiritual dimension she always sees in the art she studies—which she had to "bracket" during her PhD program. When Verena went to interview at her Protestant college, she was happy to learn she would not have to "check her faith at the [classroom] door." But Verena had "no idea" how much her campus embraced holistic development until she and her husband enjoyed an entire week at the college's mountainside conference center during her new-faculty orientation. At this program, new faculty read and discussed historical, pedagogical, and theological texts; considered their own roles as faculty; heard from prominent scholars; and forged bonds while hiking, whitewater rafting, and visiting wineries. Underwritten by the exploration program and supported by administrators for its capacity to reengage the institution's religious affiliation, this orientation trip had observable effects on Verena: it convinced her to add a service-learning project to her art history classes; it connected her to an undergraduate fellowship program whereby outstanding students assisted faculty with research; and it affirmed her desire to produce excellent scholarship, mentor students, and start a family according to her own time frame, not the tenure clock. Verena was a master teacher, a natural-born mentor, and an active scholar; she could be a poster child for Ernst Boyer's definition of a "teacher-scholar."[11]

By beginning her employment with purpose exploration, Verena gained distance from "that battle . . . to get this grant, to get my funding" into which her graduate and postdoctoral training had socialized her. For years, Verena lived by the mantra "I'm going to teach at Harvard, I'm only going to do research, I'm going to focus only on this [project]," but this orientation experience reminded her that "I've always had this vocation to be a teacher and a researcher, and to have an impact on young people's lives." Not that "research isn't important," as Verena's scholarly record was and continues to be impressive, but "you could actually bring your students into your research." Doing so takes "time and energy," yet she loves seeing her students learn during their service-learning experience teaching art at a Roman Catholic city school that cannot afford an art teacher. Verena also loves the mentoring relationships she has, relaying a story about a young woman from an affluent family whose parents and older brother attended Yale. This young woman "was desperate" to attend Yale herself, but was not admitted and enrolled at Verena's college as her second choice. Assigned to Verena's first-year seminar, this young woman said the college's emphasis on serving others made no sense: "How is anybody going to make a living? Are they kidding?" But after several classes with Verena, a year assisting with Verena's research, and long conversations, this young woman said she had come to understand the college's motto: "Now I live it, I really feel it—it's transformed my outlook on life." At commencement, she gave the valedictory address, making selfless service the theme of her speech. And she concluded by thanking Yale for not admitting her—as she had "gained so much more" from her education at Verena's college.

I asked Verena if she might have shaped her career along these lines without participating in an exploration-infused employee orientation week. "I'm not so sure—I think after a few years you might start to sense it," Verena answered. But she was convinced that "it really did take that kind of gathering" for her to remember and develop her calling. Verena was thankful that her college encouraged faculty to "aspire to be the best that they can be," and closed our interview by saying she "feel[s] comfortable being the person who I really am here," before dashing out to pick up her daughter from preschool—a reason for departure as revealing as the interview itself. Themes of comfort and fit were not unique to Verena, however. They also emerged during interviews with other faculty, including Tom. Tom taught at a liberal arts college in a town so small that the college tripled the community's population when classes were in session. Some of Tom's comfort was rooted in his own rural upbringing, but much of it he found by happenstance, when he accepted a one-year teaching position at the college while completing his dissertation. When the professor Tom replaced took a job elsewhere, Tom was offered a full-time position and accepted. Unlike the enormous lecture halls that characterized his public alma mater, Tom discovered that small classes and a close community facilitated the sort of transformative education he'd only dreamed might exist.

Tom's dreams were limited partly by his blue-collar upbringing. Neither his grandfather nor grandmother, who reared him, had finished high school—so they were happy that Tom finished high school and never said a word to him about college. Nor did Tom broach the subject, as he saw little value in college and enlisted in the armed forces instead. Two years in a combat zone reversed Tom's view, however, and he enrolled at the local state university upon his discharge. To his surprise, Tom completed bachelor's, master's, and doctoral degrees. His view of higher education was not the only thing that changed, either. Raised in a fundamentalist church by his grandparents, Tom converted to Catholicism during high school, rejected that for nihilism during his military and college years, and today embraces "social constructivism," which, he explained, requires him to do all that he can to reduce injustice. Peppering his interview with coarse language, Tom told us he considered ideas of purpose and vocation to be "epiphenomenal post hoc justifications," and kept his distance from the college's exploration program when it first appeared. But Tom grew impressed by the progressive community engagement sponsored by the exploration program's Journey Center, and the center's two full-time staff encountered numerous individuals who pointed them to Tom, who was a provocative, campus-engaged intellectual. When the three finally had lunch, they discovered kindred social concerns and much to like about one another. Before lunch ended, Tom agreed to create a course around the idea of "journey" and introduced the Journey Center staff members to the staff at a community organization he had founded.

All of this preceded our visit to Tom's campus by several years. By the time we arrived, Tom had become a core faculty participant at the Journey Center. He even made broad use of exploration language (he called it "values talk") in his classroom. We asked why, given his views on religion and spirituality. Tom said his goal was to get students to "engage socially" with the world, and that the students who attend Tom's college needed a "moral orientation, whatever that is," to do so. Purpose and vocation provided that, so Tom used that language, even though he privately regards these ideas as "goofy." The bottom line was expanding justice and equality, so Tom was happy to talk this way if it moved students into working for justice. Tom told us the exploration grant was the "best thing" that ever happened to his campus — expanding the college's involvement in the immediate area, providing Tom with resources to create an academic certificate program in social justice, and promoting this certificate and community involvement among students in general. "It's been quite a *journey*," Tom concluded with a wink and a smile, knowing his comment embodied multiple meanings.

Life journeys can be that way, taking interesting turns and passing through unexpected places. That was how Mike felt. A newly tenured professor in the religion department of a Methodist university, Mike was buying a loft with his partner in a Bible Belt city. He'd never intended to stay at the university, only wait out a lull in the academic job market and "challenge the cultural scripts" of the provincial students and employees he assumed predominated the campus. Mike encountered few provincials on campus, however, as this red state university had a left-leaning reputation that was appreciated by its students and employees. He was also pleased to discover a small but progressive urban scene about forty-five minutes away, which he quickly made his home. Still, Mike kept an eye out for infringements of his scholarly and normative "space," and joined the grant-proposal-writing committee, not because he valued purpose exploration, but to ensure that any proposal it generated would not constrain his academic freedom. One can file Mike's action under the adage "Keep your friends close and your enemies closer."

To support the committee's work, Mike contacted a divinity school classmate who taught in a summer program for teens exploring seminary education. This classmate relayed how the program challenged the achievement myth and taught the underside of capitalism. Mike loved it, and proposed using this framework to challenge the OC Achiever students who dominated his university (see chapter 4). The writing committee concurred, and crafted a proposal to unsettle and reorient the university's preprofessional students. When Lilly funded the proposal, Mike worked on several aspects of the program, creating its Engaging the World religion seminar. Mike was unprepared, however, for just how unsettling this seminar would become.

Mike had come to this Methodist university expecting his biblical criticism courses and his sexuality to unsettle students, but students accepted both with a yawn. When Mike shifted his iconoclasm to achievement, however, he provoked anxiety in and out of the classroom, found himself moved by the "fragility" of his students, and revised his classroom demeanor from provocation to gentle exploration. Sorting through the "questions evoked" by this, Mike received a brochure about a sister campus's conference on vocation and the academic life. Mike rearranged his schedule to attend, and found the conference "really helpful." It encouraged Mike to "reflect on [his] vocational commitments," redefine his teaching as "mentoring in the classroom," and see iconoclasm as one of many tools professors can deploy to facilitate student learning. The experience moved Mike from institutional grumbler to master teacher, a transformation not uncommon among the faculty we encountered on participating campuses. Purpose exploration engaged educators too, even educators quite sure about their purpose.

Some might be surprised by a religion professor being wary of a grant to explore purpose and theologies of vocation. Mike's watchfulness was, however, common among religion professors, who were as religiously diverse as these campus populations in general. We heard a lot of faculty stories such as Mike's and Tom's: wariness, followed by guarded participation, followed by enthusiastic support. Staff, by contrast, were often first to participate in exploration programs. Carol and Ron, the respective directors of admissions and fine arts facilities, each had more than twenty years of service at a Presbyterian college. Carol, a lifetime member of the Presbyterian Church, told us how the purpose exploration program increased respect and appreciation for the campus's church affiliation across the university. "It's not that we were ashamed that we were Presbyterian, but now we're very proud." Elaborating, Carol adds, "I think we're intentional about our heritage and our history, [while] we might not have been as intentional before." Her favorite program occurs Tuesday nights in the newly renovated, multifaith chapel, where an employee relays her or his "vocation story." A campus community builder, Carol loves how these talks have opened up the faith dimension of employees' lives and stimulated conversations about spirituality among students and employees.

Ron agreed. His lifelong involvement with fine arts had nurtured a profound sense of spirituality, though he struggled to translate that spirituality into words, much less a system of thinking. Ron reported that the exploration program on campus had "created a climate in which it's OK to talk to people about faith things; I hear conversations, and people have engaged me in conversations, and vice versa, just sitting and eating lunch." For years, students talked to Ron about their "callings as actors," as musicians, and as visual artists, linking these to their faith or spiritual traditions, but Ron—a natural-born mentor—felt ill at ease during these conversations. Now Ron feels equipped to join these conversations—to the benefit of students and himself. Might that have happened anyhow? Ron said no. Without the campus's exploration program, "It would not be as free an environment, . . . [and] the people that would be impacted the most are the people who are alone in their faith, the ones who are walking in that direction but not quite sure and almost afraid to say things or let people know that they actually have beliefs." After three decades of service, Ron was delighted by a new openness that "allow[s] people to discuss freely their heart and their soul—faculty *and* students." Not all participated in these discussions, but for the "[one-]third" of faculty, staff, and students who did, Ron said it was really valued.

Purpose exploration programs conferred permission to speak publicly about faith and spirituality on many campuses, which some faculty and staff seized more quickly than others. Ron's openness to spirituality was characteristic of many faculty and staff in the arts; perhaps it is the creativity of the arts, or millennia of intertwinement between art and religion that stimulates the receptivity of those in fine arts fields to spirituality. Others seemed prompted by denominational pride, such as Carol. We met many staff amenable to, if not directly affiliated with, their employer's sponsoring denomination during our campus visits. On some Roman Catholic campuses, for example, we received internal survey reports that showed staff as most allied with Catholicism, followed by students, followed (distantly) by faculty. Perhaps this affinity was intentional, a product of senior administrators privileging denominational adherence in staff hiring, to show fealty to the sponsoring denomination or to counterbalance low rates of adherence among faculty. Perhaps it was the result of differences in graduate training, with lower animosity toward faith and spirituality in the professional programs that train most staff.[12] Or perhaps it was the broader settings in which staff encounter students, and the wider freedom students feel to discuss faith and meaning outside the classroom. Regardless of the reason, the effect was the same: staff were notably more accepting of purpose exploration programming.

Two Divergent Patterns

The exploration project on the majority of church-affiliated campuses involved fostering an ethos of holistic student development, and creating thereby a space for individual purpose exploration. But we did observe two divergent patterns, which illustrate the dynamism of a campus's church affiliation. On three campuses, we saw exploration programs championed by senior administrators, because these programs strengthened administrative efforts to "re-Christianize" (one dean's term) the institution. These administrators described how "hiring for mission" had faded in the 1970s, as their institutions mimicked research universities. The current administrators sought to reprioritize undergraduate education and student development, however, hiring faculty and staff with matching priorities, and deploying orientation programs and exploration seminars to underscore the connections between these priorities and the organization's religious heritage.

At another campus, a different project was under way. Here, the senior administration had no objection to religious life "per se," but wanted to loosen up the college's degree requirements in religion. This could have been done directly, but two senior religion professors refused all suggestions to revise the required course and pressured junior colleagues to toe the line. So the dean and president did an end run. The president instructed the public relations office to feature exploration programs in the alumni magazine and arrange for student participants to speak to the board of trustees. And the dean presented revisions to the college's degree requirements, which broadened the religion requirement to a course in religion, philosophy, or ethics. It was a savvy strategy: religious trustees were thrilled by the student presentations and prominent magazine coverage, and accepted the degree revisions without objection. The exploration program thus provided cover for a necessary curricular revision that could have been avoided had the two senior religion professors not been stubborn. This is less a case of institutional desacralization, then, than it is professors' organizational incompetence, and raises the question of how many other church-affiliated campuses removed religion requirements for similar reasons (there being no national shortage of stubborn senior professors).

In contrast to assumptions about religious declension on American campuses,[13] this evaluation reveals that campus religious affiliations can be quite dynamic. The above discussion also illuminates two additional lessons. First, exploration programs did not drop onto generic campuses, but emerged from distinct contexts molded by local personalities, administrative priorities, organizational histories, and interorganizational politics. Exploration programs were subject to forces beyond their control and uses beyond their original intentions. Second, faculty and staff are more than just employees; they embody institutions as a whole. A campus can see every building and every policy manual destroyed by a natural calamity, but can rebuild and emerge stronger because of the commitment of its faculty and staff. By contrast, were a ghastly epidemic to wipe out an entire college's faculty and staff, new employees inhabiting old buildings could never recapture the identity and mission of the original college. This is why exploration programs sought faculty and staff involvement; one cannot change an organization without changing the people who comprise it.

That a few campuses were "re-Christianizing" was precisely what Mike and secular hawks feared. Their fears were rooted in stereotypic understandings of campus church affiliations, however. There are many options for campus church affiliation between "Bible Thumper U" and religious declension; this evaluation demonstrates that active church affiliations were not incompatible with commitments to religious diversity or academic freedom. The last thing academics have to fear is a challenge to academic freedom by the Evangelical Lutheran Church in America, the United Methodist Church, the Presbyterian Church in the USA, the Society of Friends (Quakers), or the American Episcopal Church. These denominations pride themselves on their openness to intellectual and scientific inquiry, and have decades of evidence to support the same on their affiliated campuses. Faculty at Roman Catholic colleges and universities likewise enjoy wide academic freedom, as few Roman Catholic institutions have implemented the bishops' recommendations for faculty hiring, and most have curried favor with their bishops in other, nonacademic ways.[14] The re-Christianizing effort on two campuses was, as best as we could discern, driven by market loss; that is, the region's religious high school graduates were choosing other religious colleges, so these two campuses emphasized religious life programs and course offerings to woo them back. This had zero effect on faculty beyond a few more religious high school graduates in their courses.

Nor do faculty members need to fear "hiring for mission." Hiring for mission is common to most organizations,[15] even if not explicitly called such, as it ensures that new hires understand the organization's primary focus. This is quite different from requiring allegiance to a denomination or doctrinal statement, a practice at evangelical colleges only. Verena, for example, was a Catholic applicant for a job on a Protestant campus, and sailed through her interview with the dean. Her dean explained how hiring for mission did not prevent him from hiring faculty from other Christian traditions, non-Christian traditions ("I just hired a Jewish professor last week!"), or no religious tradition. Rather, he sought employees who would respect the distinctive mission of the college, support its concern for global needs, and embrace holistic development of the diverse students the college "has [admitted] and always will admit." The college wanted "campus citizens . . . [not] disciplinary tribalists." Verena said meeting with the dean was "one of the best parts" of her interview—as she found the dean's passion for liberal arts and for challenging students to become global citizens quite inspiring. That the dean affirmed Verena's Catholicism, encouraged her to bring her "authentic self" into the classroom, and explained how he wanted thoughtful engagement with religious, spiritual, and normative traditions to be what set the campus apart pushed the job to the top of Verena's list. Hiring for mission, at least as this dean practiced it, helped him recruit good campus citizens—of which no campus can have too many.

The exploration project on church-affiliated campuses was, in short, a more assertive and practically elaborated version of the exploration project on virtually unaffiliated campuses. Its discourse was "Our students need and deserve" to explore their sense of purpose or vocation, not "Please consider." At the same time, this discourse did not become policy. It was undergirded by "exploration apologetics"—arguments that it is right and good to engage college students with questions of purpose and vocation, and that all sorts of resources, including theology, can help students answer those questions. Employees' own participation in exploration programming, on virtually unaffiliated and church-affiliated campuses alike, very much depended upon these apologetics. That makes their absence on ethnic and evangelical campuses all the more striking. Apologetics were unnecessary because helping students find their purpose was embedded in the distinct cultures of these campuses. Employees on these campuses knew the value of engaging students with ideas of purpose and vocation. A different exploration project thus characterized culturally distinctive campuses.

"We Can Dream a Little Bit; We Can Explore Things with Our Students"

Employees at ethnic and evangelical colleges have always understood their role to go beyond guiding students through degree requirements. Many, in fact, do not use the phrase *holistic student development*, preferring terms such as *student formation, moral development,* or even *student discipleship.* They consider their primary purpose to be forming student character and nurturing student futures. I can still see the perplexed faces of the dozen employees attending a focus group interview at the College of Douglass and DuBois (CDD; see chapter 3) when I asked if there was staff resistance or faculty backlash when the purpose exploration grant was announced. After an awkward silence, a philosophy professor bluntly asked, "You realize that you are on a *black college*, don't you?" The chorus of "That's right," "Um-hmm," and "Yes," combined with incredulous head shakes, made it clear that CDD practiced a form of higher education different from most campuses. At CDD, the language of calling and vocation long predated its exploration grant, as it did at every other ethnic or evangelical college we visited.

That does not imply there was nothing for exploration programs to do on culturally distinctive campuses. Only that exploration programs needed no apologetics and encountered no resistance. Thus, they pursued a project of deepening faculty and staff knowledge of their campus's theological tradition, affirming all employees' work as a calling, and supplying resources to foster more creative and effective engagement with the world. Deepening knowledge of the campus's theology of vocation was essential. It might seem odd, given the preexistence of vocation language among employees on these campuses, but this language had lost most of its connections to theology. These employees were not that different from American citizens who "know" that the Civil War is important to understanding America, but would struggle to provide more than a couple of facts about this definitive national event. Reconnecting employees with their campus's theological tradition supplied the foundation for affirming faculty as scholars and staff as educators, which in turn undergirded their intelligent and innovative engagement with the world.

Ebony Jackson, the athletic director and women's basketball coach at CDD, was not a woman to be missed. At six feet two inches tall, Ebony towers over her female colleagues and most of her male colleagues. But beyond her physical presence, Ebony speaks with a passion that commands attention. Ebony made it a priority to participate in my focus group interview, because she wanted to tell me about her "calling" as athletic director. She was committed to "building character," "training students for life," and "win[ning] games too." Having coached at an NCAA Division 1 school previously, Ebony hated how "it's just all about winning and screw everything else." Ebony was thrilled to accept the athletic director position at CDD, where she found "Christian support" to bring "the spiritual, the academic, and the physical" together. She was particularly happy with the purpose-infused leadership conference that she requires her athletes to attend. "We do not have as much staffing as we'd like [in athletics] to do programs that would help grow our student athletes." Yet, "Student athletes are often ambassadors for [CDD] whether they want to be or not. They're very visible, probably one of the most visible groups on any campus. . . . So, for me, training these young people to understand what it is they do and help them to find their way in life is very important." Ebony is grateful for the deep understanding that the leadership conference brings to ideas of "find[ing] a purpose" and building "character," jump-starting conversations that she and her coaches continue with athletes in season and off. "Coaching is really teaching," Ebony declared, and by all accounts, Ebony was a master teacher whose partnership with her campus's exploration program strengthened her nonclassroom pedagogy.

On ethnic and evangelical campuses, exploration programs often invited employees to generate better ways of mentoring students, then underwrote their innovations. This happened with Ebony, and it happened with Jacob, a professor of youth ministry whose quote about dreaming opened this section. Jacob had toiled for two decades to strengthen the youth ministry major at his evangelical college, and he was proud of what he accomplished. Yet he was haunted by recurring stories of alumni burnout or moral lapses. "It wasn't the majority of alumni, not at all, but over the years you hear stories of this graduate or that graduate doing this or doing that — and you'd ask yourself, 'Is there anything more I could be doing to prevent this?'" Relaying his concern with faculty colleagues over lunch one day, Jacob was intrigued when a psychology colleague suggested he run a battery of personality tests on his students — to increase their self-awareness and to identify students with personality disorders that would make youth ministry a poor career choice. Four minigrants later, Jacob and his psychology colleague were handing me data tables from four waves of a youth ministry capstone course — which implemented this battery of tests — and relaying stories of successful ministry placements as well as successful interventions and career redirections.

These minigrants were not costly, a couple of thousand dollars each, but they covered fees for five psychological tests for forty students annually, costs to track students, and expenses for travel to present results at professional conferences, and in the end, they helped produce a coauthored book. That represents excellent value relative to cost. These minigrants, to be sure, sat atop a larger exploration program that emphasized integration of scholarship, theology, and mentoring via summer writing seminars for faculty, in addition to multiple student programs. Together, they embedded exploration language as well as its practice at this college. Yet, it was the minigrants that most imparted "permission to dream," seeding the campus with resources to support innovation. For that, faculty and staff on Jacob's campus and other distinctive campuses were grateful, and not just a little grateful — overwhelmingly so.

That expressions of gratitude occurred with greater frequency on evangelical and ethnic campuses underscores two observations: more constrained budgets and wide employee support for campus mission. Financial resources are limited everywhere — but especially so on evangelical and ethnic campuses, with narrower donor pools and more disadvantaged student populations. Salaries are lower, and expectations for employee involvement are higher too. Employees tolerate this work-harder-for-less environment, however, with little complaint. It was their overwhelming gratitude for professional development resources that highlighted their heavier work obligations. Brian, an English professor at one evangelical college, expressed profound appreciation for a teaching release grant that enabled him to write a book. That, in itself, was not remarkable — until I learned that Brian wrote his book with a single course release, which dropped him from four courses to three courses for one semester only. To be fair, Brian wrote a one hundred–page textbook and not a four hundred–page monograph—still, this illustrates the rarity of teaching releases, and how far resources were stretched on these campuses.

Writing a textbook was not Brian's only accomplishment during his teaching release; he also collaborated with another professor and four student assistants to film a documentary to accompany the textbook. Those students traveled with their professors to interview prominent scholars and visit historic sites, all the while being talked to about graduate school and aided in building their portfolios. Students at an ethnic college expressed similar enthusiasm for a local writers seminar developed by their professor, Athena, which included visits to the places about which these authors wrote and conversations with local historians. Athena, whose graduate training was in classics, created the seminar because she was interested in the literary connections between Latin classics and their influence on writers two millennia later:

> I think we are in a unique environment, and sometimes we take for granted what we have around us. But the students haven't had the experiences that we've had, so it is a nice opportunity to go out into the world and . . . into our communities [to see the writers' contexts . . .]. I really believe, from a vocational point of view, you get to experience the journey that these writers have had—both inward and outward—and for our students to consider those journeys and look at their own journeys is important.

Athena's own research stagnated when she began at the college two years ago, due to the demands of teaching as well as running a writing center. This seminar was therefore the most intellectually stimulating project Athena had participated in since being hired. She planned to "write up" her experience, so others could benefit as well. While pedagogical scholarship is often belittled by scholarly traditionalists, this project was Athena's intellectual lifeline, providing a rich learning experience for her students and likely impacting more lives than another treatise on Aeschylus ever would.

Limited resources and heavy workloads can make employment on ethnic or evangelical campuses overwhelming. Selena, a student life administrator, relayed how her friends "constantly ask, 'Why are you still working there? Good God, why don't you go find another job?'" Selena replied, "I have a lot of faith that this campus is a great campus. I have faith that even though there are some decisions made by administration that I don't necessarily agree with, I have a love and a devotion for the job that I do and for the students that I work for." Selena's devotion was not always this strong, however. She was updating her résumé when she chose to participate in an employee workshop that her university's exploration program sponsored. "It was those times of reflection and some of the sessions with [the exploration program] that helped me restore my faith that every business, every institution is going to have situations or times when there's going to be a little bit of dissension." Similarly, Ursula, a professor of theology born and educated in Germany, said her students often ask how she could "leave Wittenberg" for [Peoria]. "Well, I answered, 'How could Jesus leave heaven for Bethlehem? If he made it, I will make it too.'" In fact, Ursula was "happy to be here—I've never had a work environment that was so in favor of this integration of faith and learning," and loves the freedom she has to present not only Lutheran points of view "but also the point of view of other religions; I think that is just fabulous." Ursula appreciated how her campus, and especially its exploration program, affirmed her scholarly contributions, just as Selena appreciated her exploration program's message that *all* employees are *equally* educators. While professors on these campuses mainly teach and advise, and staff members mainly administer, to be recognized for one's scholarly and educational contributions goes far in making inherent organizational frustrations tolerable.

Scholarly and educational affirmations of employees also helped to fuel innovative engagement beyond the campus and subculture's boundaries. At Mennonite College (see chapter 4), for example, efforts to deepen understandings of the Mennonite tradition uncovered an undeveloped theology of social justice. "There's a huge amount of student energy for spiritual and religious kinds of things," one professor explained, "but it hasn't always been directed to the good of the world." In response, a couple of faculty scholars tapped Mennonite concern for "reconciliation" and deployed it to engage economic and racial disparities. Others opted to engage Catholic social teaching, hosting a joint conference for Catholic and evangelical college students on "vocation in the world." One professor who attended this conference remarked how the Catholic college students "were head and shoulders higher" than the evangelical students in thinking about the world. The students from Roman Catholic schools were "better thinkers, better informed than any other students there," including their own Mennonite College students. In short, evangelical college faculty at this conference identified two challenges confronting their traditions. They had to devise better models of engagement with the world and structure that engagement to begin with service and thoughtfulness, not condemnation and callousness.

Engaging the world took a different tack at ethnic colleges. Exploration programs emphasized connections to and service within one's community, as a way of tapping the strength of one's heritage, and knowing *in detail*, as one exploration program put it, the stories of "those who have gone before" and blazed trails that "we may follow in their footsteps." Faculty and staff participants in exploration programs were thus encouraged to share their own life stories, and to draw on their community networks to variously demonstrate vocation in action. In other words, increased solidarity was the fuel for expanded community service and leadership development.

This solidarity certainly fueled the service and leadership of Kimberly, a social work professor, who led students on an alternative spring-break trip to New Orleans. While there, Kimberly not only helped students anguished by the devastation from Hurricane Katrina understand that "bad things happen to good people all the time, so the question is 'Why does God have you here to help?'" but guided students through a polite confrontation with a white electrician whose truck sported a racist bumper sticker. Kimberly tapped into the public theism of her campus's tradition to redirect students from anguish to agency, its prophetic tradition to channel rage into "speaking truth," and her own professional expertise to facilitate positive group process. It was "one of the most rewarding experiences" Kimberly ever had as a professor, and it underscored the value that the chapel and a vibrant religious life — enhanced by the exploration grant — brought to "the entire" college.

Patterns of engagement with the world thus differentiated culturally distinctive campuses, with ethnic campuses practicing engaged solidarity, and evangelical campuses fostering microinnovations. Or, to put it differently, ethnic campuses engaged by busloads in a few shared endeavors, evangelicals by vanloads in scores of distinct projects. It was a curious pattern, given the religious diversity on ethnic campuses and the religious homogeneity on evangelical campuses. But it revealed the root identities of these campuses, which are the common history, shared language, and collective experience of the larger ethnic tradition, and the shared doctrines and biblical texts of evangelical religiosity. Thus, ethnic campuses privilege, for example, black Protestantism or Latino Catholicism in their public discourse, yet affirm the religious diversity of their campus populations. And thus, evangelical campuses proclaim doctrines embraced by all members of campus while granting freedom in the enactment of those doctrines inside and outside the evangelical subculture.

To my surprise, I discovered more commonalities to employee experiences at ethnic and evangelical campuses than differences, and consequently a common intellectual and practical project pursued among employees on both types of campus. Limited financial resources, high commitment to campus mission, and preexisting concern for holistic student development granted exploration programs a supportive faculty and staff, who infused exploration into the curriculum and student life programming at evangelical campuses, and into campus ministry and the wider public culture at ethnic campuses. Expecting to find "ceiling effects" for exploration on evangelical campuses, I observed instead faculty and staff who raised their campus's ceilings. Not satisfied with purpose exploration gardens tended by a few gardeners, employees on evangelical and ethnic campuses reassigned entire swaths as campus exploration nurseries and organized themselves into expert teams to support this preexisting but extraordinarily enhanced campus undertaking.

Altruistic Educators, Dedicated Professionals

For too long, the higher education community has allowed its faculty to be typecast as cats and its staff to be pigeonholed as bureaucrats. This needs to stop. I observed and heard from hundreds of faculty and staff committed to an excellent educational experience for students and the highest standards of professionalism. There are good citizens on every campus, and a goodly number of them: one study at Cornell University, for example, reported between 4 and 22 percent of its faculty participated at least monthly in an out-of-class, nonresearch activity with undergraduates, with one-third indicating that these activities greatly enriched their own lives and another third indicating moderate life enrichment.[16] These are self-reports, to be sure, yet they reveal that, even at an Ivy League university, there are between one out of twenty and one out of five faculty members who value broad engagement with undergraduates. On teaching-prevalent campuses, one can expect the proportion of similarly engaged faculty and staff to be significantly higher.

Many good citizens feel unappreciated,[17] however, and weary from continually resisting organizational and professional pressures that would draw them away from their good work as master teachers, mentors, campus-engaged intellectuals, or community builders. Purpose exploration programs are not the only way to affirm and provide resources to the good citizens on a campus—but I have encountered no other campus initiative that intrigued, inspired, and united campus good citizens as well as these programs did. If this interests you as much as it fascinated me, read on. The next chapter will help educators of every sort understand the strategic blunders these programs made, the larger ecologies these programs inhabit, and the evidence-based recommendations I offer to improve or implement campus-based exploration programming.

6

Strategies and Ecologies

Cacti, Not Roses

It does not take a degree in horticulture to know that cacti, not roses, are the native species of the American Southwest. Nor does it require master gardening skills to appreciate the beauty of cacti, bougainvillea, or succulents. This does not mean that roses cannot grow in Phoenix, only that a rose garden will require close attention and consume precious water resources to thrive. In chapter 3, I likened campus exploration programs to gardens, and relayed the stories of four organically designed, carefully implemented programs. Not all exploration programs experienced the same success as those four, however. Some had to replace roses with lower-maintenance native species, others had to redesign their gardens, and a couple had to relocate their gardens due to poor drainage and insufficient sunlight. This was to be expected, given the novelty of these projects and newness of their gardeners. Nor do adjustments undermine the value of gardens in general. Even visitors to modestly successful gardens reported value in the time spent there. Gardening difficulties represent learning opportunities, as their identification will help future gardeners avoid similar problems, and provide insight into the larger organizational ecologies that constrain new campus endeavors.

Consider this chapter, then, an exercise in *applied, positive sociology*. Positive psychology is the social science of individual flourishing, and it has grown exponentially over the past decade, creating a void in corresponding attention to the *contexts* that facilitate individual flourishing by the broader social sciences of anthropology, economics, political science, or sociology.[1] There are few institutional sites more amenable to positive sociological analysis, moreover, than higher education. Student flourishing is a universal ideal among colleges and universities, but student flourishing is rarely understood to include purpose exploration. Rather, a flourishing student is understood as actively engaged with learning, self-confident, and without psychological dysfunction, presumably indicated by degree completion and a clean disciplinary record.[2] Many colleges and universities seem content, therefore, to have a couple of dozen exemplary student citizens to profile in marketing materials and respectable graduation rates. A few poster boys or girls and a steady flow of graduates, however, fall far short of the ideals that most educators and many students have for higher education. By strategically engaging issues of purpose exploration, campuses can foster contexts in which students, faculty, and staff flourish, which in turn will generate, without exception, more and better citizens.[3]

This is not to say engaged learning and knowledge mastery are unimportant; over the centuries universities have created knowledge and fostered innovations that have improved the lives of humans around the globe. Self-confidence and degree completion are likewise important, as university graduates lead organizations and governments that shape the future. But universities and their graduates have also flooded the globe with knowledge that, absent purpose, has left many adrift in informational seas and lacking purposeful direction. Knowledgeable but purposeless persons generate factoids that enlarge informational seas. Knowledgeable and purposeful persons, however, develop navigational skills to chart courses through informational seas, benefiting themselves and aiding others. Campus-based purpose exploration programs are not the only way to nurture individual purpose. But they have this in their favor: positive, wide-ranging, and demonstrable effects among students, faculty, and staff. Analysis of its strategies to generate purpose-nurturing contexts, and understanding of wider campus ecologies, are therefore essential to replicating this programming's effects.

Not every campus that implemented exploration programming observed gains in the purposefulness of its population. There are many ways such programs can undermine their own effectiveness or be subverted by forces beyond their control. But we can be confident that continuing campus business-as-usual will do nothing to reduce instrumentalist, consumerist orientations among students and will deplete even further the ranks of good citizens on every campus (see chapters 4 and 5). It is a truism that those who study the past are less likely to repeat its mistakes. This chapter, therefore, offers an analytic review of exploration effects among individuals and within organizations, including strategic blunders. It then opens the lens wide, examining the cultural, political, economic, and organizational ecology of American campuses. And it closes with strategic recommendations, for those eager to engage campus populations, or portions thereof, with questions of purpose and vocation.

Strategic Change

It is a cornerstone of American popular culture: "Anyone can change." And in theory, any person, this side of death, can choose to change for the better. But the likelihood of individual change varies widely, even among the privileged citizens of collegiate campuses. In this section, I describe change among individuals as well as within formal organizations, identifying life course location, introduction and depth of exploratory conversation, and the emergence of proexploration communities as the most salient factors in individual and organizational change. For individuals to become more intentionally purposeful, they must be structurally open to change — which is largely determined by location in the life course — and appropriately introduced to purpose exploration. For formal organizations to become more intentionally purpose-nurturing, they must launch proexploration communities that forge coalitions to implement purpose-fostering change.

Location in the life course is particularly salient to exploration receptivity. I previously explained how most first-year college students, consumed by daily life management, resist questions of identity and meaning (see chapter 2). Likewise, college seniors, invested as they are in academic majors and postcollege aspirations, resist the deeper questions that are essential to purpose exploration. Seniors do not want to ask, for example, if a future in chemistry is the right choice after slogging through four years in chemistry coursework and publicly announcing plans to become a chemist. The prerequisites for meaningful purpose exploration are (1) being settled into one's college student status, but (2) less so into one's program of study or postcollege plans, which is most prevalent among college sophomores and juniors. The primary exceptions are Future Intelligentsia and Reforming Activists, who seem ready at any point to consider questions of purpose or vocation (see chapter 4). These types represent fewer than one out of five college students, however.

Settled faculty and staff, by contrast, demonstrate less interest in purpose exploration than those unsettled (even positively) by new jobs, establishment of professional careers, or promotions. The variance in receptivity between settled and unsettled employees is not as wide as it is among settled and unsettled students, however. Employees typically occupy middle adulthood, while students (on this project's studied campuses) typically occupy emerging adulthood. In middle adulthood, external transitions foster internal reassessment.[4] Middle adulthood is marked by more moderate adjustments to identity, with self-reflection focused on the means by which one expresses the statuses (e.g., scholar, teacher, neighbor, parent) one has achieved. Faculty and staff undergoing external transitions were interested and often eager to tap exploration resources as they considered questions of identity and role fulfillment. Emerging adults, by contrast, perceive overwhelming options for their lives and are anxious about the consequences of their career choices (see chapter 4).[5] External transitions appear to amplify emerging adult anxiety and hinder this age group's willingness to reflect. Research beyond what I report here is necessary to confirm this interpretation; nevertheless, openness to purpose exploration among middle adult employees ran opposite to that of emerging adult students.

One of the key accomplishments of exploration programs was fostering deeper conversations. At evangelical and ethnic campuses, this was a straightforward process involving theological texts, language, and oral narratives. But at church-affiliated and virtually unaffiliated campuses, with religiously diverse populations, particularistic conversations had to simultaneously affirm religious diversity. This appeared to require separate methods for employees and students. For faculty and staff, the road to deeper conversations began with institutional history, since campuses participating in this initiative had origins that could not be understood apart from devout founders and the religious movements they embraced. For students, the road to deeper conversations began with inductive religious practice (e.g., structured meditation) that was clearly explained to outsiders, and opened for participation by all. Engaging history with employees and religious or spiritual experiences with students led to deeper conversations, including introduction of theological ideas. The academy prides itself, of course, on examination of all ideas, which includes theology if it is properly introduced (i.e., with respect for audience diversity) and possesses content worth exploring (i.e., intellectual depth). Some campus exploration programs did not appreciate these separate stages, confusing the need for careful introductions with theology itself, and depleting theology of its substance—leaving a flaccid spirituality in its place. That drained respect for such conversation among faculty and staff, and among Future Intelligentsia and Reforming Activists who were core student participants in exploration programs elsewhere. An Oprah-esque spirituality is a nonstarter in academic settings; by contrast, theology, rightly introduced, can be intellectually and ethically generative, even though it takes particularistic forms.

Nearly every campus that submitted proposals expressed hope that their entire communities would be touched by exploration questions. Few campuses articulated a model, however, for how individual exploration would result in proexploration campuses. The missing link was proexploration groups and communities, forged from repeated programs that successfully introduced exploration questions, and populated by exploration-engaged participants. Campus change does not occur because disaggregated individuals alter their thinking; it occurs because close-knit groups devote themselves to implementing change and leveraging coalitions to accomplish their goals. As Margaret Mead famously said, "*Never doubt* that a small group of thoughtful, committed citizens can change the world."[6] If thoughtful, committed citizens can change the world, they can certainly change formal organizations. Proexploration communities can embed purpose exploration into organizational structures.

Proexploration communities represent the organizational corollary of teaching a man to fish so that he can feed himself. Among students, a disproportionate share of Reforming Activists, Future Intelligentsia, and student leaders (often, OC Achievers who were contingent moralists) participated in proexploration communities (see chapter 4). Among employees, master teachers, natural-born mentors, campus-engaged intellectuals, campus community builders, and those intrigued by good citizenship predominated (see chapter 5). Proexploration communities drew together individuals, facilitating good conversations, unexpected friendships, and generative thinking. Their members found common identity in purpose exploration and in efforts to pursue purpose. They not only agreed about the value of purpose exploration in higher education but sought to extend exploration into additional places and processes. They often succeeded. But occasionally such communities failed, and more often they never formed, because of the strategic blunders described next.

Strategic Blunders

We sat in the same row for the forty-minute van ride from the airport to the conference hotel. It was 3:00 p.m., but I had been awake since 3:00 a.m. to catch a flight for this convening of eighty-eight campus teams. I was tired, and she was too. But since the rest of the van was laughing like old friends, and we were heading to the same conference, the silence grew awkward. So I asked Stacy where she flew in from, and we recounted our early risings and turbulent landings. We chatted for a few minutes, until the topic shifted to my role as evaluator of this initiative. Stacy said, "Well, good luck with that," our conversation petered out, and we rode the rest of the way in silence. Famished, but out of sync with the restaurant hours, I registered quickly and sought food at the bar. Stacy was already there, her suitcase beside her, nursing a beer. This time our conversation flowed more easily. She had a divinity school degree from a prominent university, was an ordained United Church of Christ minister, but found that church ministry "didn't suit me." So she entered a ThD program, completed it, but could not find work as a professor because she was "too liberal" for religious colleges and "too religious" for secular colleges. She worked awhile as an adjunct professor, hoping for a full-time faculty position, when she saw an advertisement for a full-time director of a campus exploration program. Stacy applied, got hired, and had worked as project director the past four years.

I asked Stacy how the project was going. "Do you want to know the truth?" she answered cautiously. To my affirmative response, Stacy launched into a sad tale of faculty resistance, departure of the vice president who had championed the project, his replacement's refusal to hire her support staff, and her inability to launch several program components. Worse still, Stacy was assigned to an office in the rear of the chapel—a building in desperate need of repair, far from the academic buildings on campus, and long unoccupied by any employee. The office even lacked an Internet connection, forcing Stacy to trek back and forth to the library to use e-mail during her first two months. Frustrating circumstances, to be sure, and Stacy's bitterness was understandable. Her only comfort was the dozen students who found their way to the chapel to participate in two progressivist programs she oversaw. When I asked if she found support from other project directors or the initiative's coordination office, Stacy said no. There was just one person she felt a connection to, another project director who was sunning herself by the pool outside the bar's windows, and the unoccupied chaise beside this woman was Stacy's next destination. We finished our burgers, and bade farewell a second time. And as best as I could tell, Stacy and her sole colleague spent the entire conference, aside from meals, commiserating in their poolside chaises.

Stacy's story haunted me for quite a while. That I heard it near the start of my evaluation work, combined with my entering skepticism about enthusiastic claims, left me dubious about the initiative in general. Only later did I hear that Stacy and her poolside partner "directed the two weakest programs" in the entire eighty-eight-campus initiative, and that Stacy was "poorly matched" to her position's needs. I verified both claims independently. A report by program consultants[7] confirmed that outspoken faculty at Stacy's university opposed the exploration grant, and that a key vice president left right before Stacy's hiring. But the situation was nowhere near as bleak as Stacy had indicated. The report identified several promising avenues for development, a number of interested staff and faculty collaborators, and "much encouragement" for the initiative's goals from two current administrators. Stacy was somehow unable or unwilling to leverage these. In short, Stacy entered a chilly environment for purpose exploration, but had she deployed the emotional intelligence, organizational savvy, and creativity that other project directors applied to similarly challenging settings, she might have had a more rewarding experience (see chapter 3). I cannot say whether

Stacy lacked these traits, only that she did not use them. I can confirm that Stacy appended "adjunct professor of religious studies" to her job title, which was unique among project directors, and indicates her primary identification with the professoriate. "Wannabe professors," as one insider to this initiative called them, especially when hired from outside to administer exploration programs, did not make good project directors (see table 6.1). Stacy's chaise-mate, whose campus we did visit, was a wannabe professor who used every program opportunity to showcase her scholarly prowess. I am fairly confident Stacy was as well. At a minimum, Stacy was an ineffective director, and keeping her was that campus's biggest blunder.

Ineffective Project Directors, Inorganic Program Designs

Dynamic directors and organically designed programs were, without doubt, the most important factors in a program's depth and breadth of impact, and in its postaward continuation. A dynamic director, passionate about purpose exploration, possessed of emotional intelligence, and leading a program that was well matched to its campus's mission and culture seemed destined for success. That is not to say inorganic designs, such as a particularistic program on a religiously heterogeneous campus (see chapter 5), would necessarily fail, only that the effects of such programs would be restricted to a narrow band of students and employees. Similarly, ineffective directors did not eliminate program impact, only suppress a program's potential. Inorganic designs and ineffective directors, had they combined, would have been deadly—but among the twenty-six campuses we studied, we did not encounter this worst-case scenario. I did meet a socially awkward project director who, bereft of charm though not of good intention, presided over a program that performed rather well in spite of him. And Stacy's chaise-mate, her minimal commitment to purpose exploration notwithstanding, facilitated sufficient positive outcomes that a replacement was hired after she left and the program expanded under her successor's leadership. Organic designs can see success even when their leadership is ineffective.

On the whole, project directors most poised for success were those who helped develop the original proposal and design the exploration program. These internal hires possessed a deep understanding of the program, were known for their good citizenship, and were nominated to lead because their

Table 6.1 Inventory of strategic blunders

Blunder	Description
All eggs in one basket	Massive events/conferences that drew participants but did not produce deep or sustained impact.
Clumsy public relations	Failure to appreciate the campus and surrounding culture when introducing or describing purpose exploration programs.
Field of Dreams fallacy	Believing that "if you build it [a program], they will come." Incentives were necessary for initial participation on all but ethnic and evangelical campuses.
Ineffective project directors	Low emotional intelligence, turf-protective rather than enterprise-minded, defensive rather than open to feedback, "wannabe professors" more interested in showcasing their intellectual prowess than in developing exploration programming.
Inorganic program design	Implementing an exploration project that was mis-matched to college/university type (see table 5.2).
Marginalizing faculty	Because obtaining faculty buy-in was difficult during program design, some campuses excluded faculty and academic aspects of exploration programming.
Marginalizing support staff	Many staff work with students besides those in student life, supervising student workers and willing to contribute to cocurricular programs when informed of them.
No partners (outside the campus)	Not developing support for purpose exploration programming by establishing connections with sister denominational campuses, other campuses in general, sponsoring denominations, or the Council of Independent Colleges' Network for Vocation in Undergraduate Education.
No senior allies	Not leveraging (or occasionally not having) supportive presidents, chief academic officers, or other senior administrators to accomplish program goals.
Untended communities	Not fostering a community among participants by failing to repeat retreats, trips, or programs that built interpersonal connections, which, over time, created proexploration communities among student leaders and employee "good citizens."
Theology "lite"	In a misdirected effort to affirm religious diversity, theological concepts morphed into "spirituality lite," lacking substance or history.
Tough crowds	Targeting those least open to purpose exploration, such as new students consumed by the transition to college and semiadult daily life, seniors anxious about postgraduation planning, "beer and circus" students, and disgruntled faculty.
Too many baskets (with one egg each)	Widely distributed programming too diffuse to observe direct effects. Most effective programs had fewer than five strategic goals.

emotional intelligence made them well suited for such work. Several of these project directors were so winsome, in fact, that I questioned whether their program's success was a product more of personal charisma than of purpose exploration itself. After two such project directors were recruited to higher positions, with negligible effect on their programs' strong performance, I realized that personal charisma grew their gardens faster and drew more people to them, but it was the garden itself that kept visitors satisfied.[8] Externally hired project directors, by contrast, faced uphill battles. External hires needed to learn the culture and processes of their new organizations, form relationships, and find allies — taking months to arrive at the place from which emotionally intelligent internal hires began. If they lacked emotional intelligence, these external hires could labor for years before their respective programs produced observable results.

I was curious why emotional intelligence was so important among directors of exploration programs. Considerable research attests to the contribution of emotional intelligence to career success in general,[9] but it seemed particularly important to this work because (1) purpose exploration touches personal matters that require sensitivity; (2) disparate departmental agendas need skilled navigation; (3) programmatic creativity can generate public success or failure; and (4) the freedom most faculty feel to speak bluntly can rattle those unaccustomed to it. Those reflecting on their life's purpose can experience powerful emotions and relay sensitive personal information. This requires individual empathy and compassion, as well as organizational skills to devise methods of processing such experiences when dozens are involved. Emotional intelligence is also essential when, for example, directors of marketing sit beside professors of ethnic studies at a seminar table, and they voice opposite opinions. Affirming both opinions and both speakers demands not only intelligence but expertise in interpersonal communication. Programmatic creativity and experimentation require taking risks too, enduring creative failures and pressing on rather than retreating to safety. And it takes considerable emotional intelligence to tolerate the blunt discourse of faculty, to separate critiques of one's ideas from critiques of oneself, and to maintain good communication with persistent critics. These are all marks of emotional intelligence, and those possessing it nearly always directed successful exploration programs.

Tough Crowds, Untended Communities, and No Senior Allies

Three blunders ran second to the effects of inadequate project directors and inorganic program design: focusing efforts on those least open to purpose exploration, not fostering community among participants, and not leveraging the support of senior administrators. By the first, I mean focusing programs on those campus members least available structurally. That includes first-year and senior students preoccupied by their transition into and out of college, and employees in general rather than campus good citizens. Quite a few programs targeted first-year students, to little effect, because of the "myth of first-year transformation"[10] and educators' atypical undergraduate experience, which assigns the first year as the time for intense identity exploration. Programs that targeted seniors were likewise limited, as anxieties surrounding the end of one's college years kept seniors alternating between denial and pragmatic preoccupations. And programs that targeted employees *in general* were ignored by campus stars, deadwood, institutional grunts, and institutional grumblers, and often missed by campus good citizens because they manage commitments by disregarding most generic invitations (see chapter 5).

Several campuses, including chapter 5's Cornfield Lutheran College, failed to foster proexploration communities among their participants. By not repeating programs, or by not creating mechanisms to nurture the fledgling connections that formed through participation, these campuses missed opportunities to nurture proexploration communities that could sustain programmatic momentum. Programs could nurture such communities inexpensively: follow-up presentations, reading groups, and service trips reconvened exploration-attuned campus members, strengthening ties and embedding exploration language into the emerging group.[11] A couple of campuses opted to invest substantially in proexploration communities, such as Verena's university (see chapter 5), which had a deep and sustained effect. Without a proexploration community, program staff became the primary stimulus for purpose exploration on campus. While the skills of these staff often compensated for the lack of a proexploration community, this did not bode well for long-term purpose exploration on campus.

Failure to leverage support by senior administrators completes the second tier of strategic blunders. Campuses should encourage purpose exploration because of its positive contribution to students and employees, not because senior administrators support it. But some programs lacked appreciation for colleges and universities as *complex formal organizations*—that is, as social structures governed by formal procedures and characterized by a division of labor and tiered authority. Complex formal organizations require interdepartmental collaboration and executive support to effect new programs. Even straightforward changes, such as revising the orientation program for new employees, require cooperation from offices of human resources, conference and event planning, dining services, physical plant, business services, academic affairs, public relations, the president, and likely more. While a dynamic project director can visit departments and seek to persuade staff about the value of this undertaking, senior administrators are needed to convene these staff, work out processes, resolve differences, manage unforeseen problems, and authorize the change.

Foundations require grant proposals to include a letter of support from the organization's head, and this initiative was no different. In a couple of cases, the promise of support was insincere, but more often support was not tapped effectively. The most common cause was lack of organizational savvy: failing to vet ideas before formally proposing them or maintain regular communication with senior administration generated hard lessons for some project directors. But nearly as problematic were prickly "friends" of the exploration program, such as outspoken staff members or intransigent professors, whose associations with the program irked senior administration. Wise exploration gardeners (i.e., project directors) understood that senior administrators sit atop organizational bulldozers that can double the size of their gardens or plow through them to build a parking lot, and thus they invited bulldozer operators to garden picnics regularly and made sure any prickly friends of the program behaved. Unwise gardeners watched the bulldozers from a distance, hoping their operators would be too distracted to see the prickly friend who was mooning them from atop the garden's fountain. Senior administrators, even when busy with other matters, still scan the organizational horizon. Wise program leadership took responsibility for the whole exploration endeavor, addressing problems even loosely related to the project and maintaining regular communication upward. Unwise program leaders did not.

Clumsy Public Relations and Marginalizing Faculty

Serious, though less so than the strategic blunders above, were clumsy public communications and marginalizing faculty. There is a well-known pearl of American folk wisdom: "You get one chance to make a first impression." And first impressions, research shows, can be quite enduring.[12] If it is a positive impression, that is good; but if it is a poor impression, that is bad indeed. Chapter 5's Marble College struggled with exactly this. It takes skill to question the banishment of faith and spirituality from public conversation without offending listeners, especially on a nonsectarian campus. It also takes skill to convey substantive ideas about purpose and vocation to religiously diverse campus populations without being trite or exclusivist.[13] On some campuses, this meant never using the word *vocation* in public communication—like chapter 2's Ignatius University. Ignatius had extensive grant experience and the confidence to jettison the Lilly Endowment's language; many participating campuses did not have experience with grants of this magnitude, however. Consequently, some who spoke about vocation would stumble, and public misunderstandings resulted. Those misunderstandings set back the work of the exploration program by a few weeks to a couple of years, and those most easily offended were the faculty. This was ironic, given the offense that faculty bluntness regularly caused staff, but this irony was not appreciated by the project directors who had to mend communications. It is better to learn good public relations in advance rather than in regret.

And nowhere were good public relations more important than when attempting to cultivate faculty involvement. George, the vice president at one campus we visited, was genuinely self-effacing. At one point during our conversation, however, he vigorously quoted billionaire Ted Turner: "Lead, follow, or get out of the way!" The prompt was George's retelling of his campus's proposal-drafting process. He went out of his way to invite six faculty and six staff to develop the exploration proposal. But after the third draft got panned by these faculty, George had "had enough" of their "negativity and obstructionism." So he cut them out of the writing process, instructing the campus's grant writer to work only with student life and campus ministry staff to develop an exploration program for the campus. That decision was effective in the short term, as it helped his campus generate a coherent proposal that netted it major grant funding, but it was unwise in the long term. Unless a college secures endowment funds for exploration programming (which some did), the persistence of purpose exploration requires its infusion into the teaching, advising, and scholarly practices of its faculty. Senior administrators can dismantle nonacademic programs overnight, silence or dismiss troublesome staff, and ignore student complaints, knowing that most fade quickly. Not so with faculty or curriculum. Because of the golden handcuffs of tenure, and the curricular authority possessed by faculty, support for purpose exploration by professors is essential to long-term campus impact. The nursing department in chapter 5, for example, can use its purpose-infused curriculum for years no matter who occupies the college's presidential suite. Faculty are like the trees of a purpose exploration garden. While it requires more effort to plant them, and while they grow slowly, trees define a garden's landscape and are the only species that can stop bulldozers in their tracks. Exploration programs marginalized faculty at their long-term peril.

Field of Dreams Fallacy, All Eggs in One Basket, and Too Many Baskets

The fourth tier of strategic blunders involved the details of program design. As described above and in chapters 3 and 5, the most important design factor is a program's organic fit with the type and mission of the college or university. But even with organic design, some programs flourished while others struggled. I assign these blunders to the fourth tier because unlike an inorganic program design, which must be wholly revised, these could be fixed by a strategic reorganization. The first of these blunders I call the *Field of Dreams* fallacy, because, like the farmer played by Kevin Costner in the 1989 movie, those who make this mistake believe that "if you build it [a purpose exploration program, in this case], they will come." The truth is, participants will *not* come without incentives or peer recommendations, unless one builds it on an evangelical or ethnic campus.

On one campus, we met an exploration program committee member who had experienced a personal transformation with the help of a spiritual director (i.e., a member of a vowed religious order who guides inquirers' prayer and spiritual exercises). He insisted students would have equally valuable experiences with an exploration counselor, which he defined as a specially trained campus minister who would individually guide students through discernment of their purpose and vocation. Because of this committee member's persistence, and an untimely sabbatical by that campus's chaplain (who disavowed the idea that there would be student interest in such services), the committee approved renovations to create a meditation room and an adjoining office, and funding for a full-time exploration counselor. The hired counselor was a pleasant woman, well trained, and a consummate listener. But for two semesters cobwebs accumulated in her office and adjacent meditation room. They built it, but the students did not come. While the majority of college students devote no more than thirty-five hours weekly to classes and class preparation,[14] it does not follow that they lack for ways to fill their free time. Most students are employed, involved on or off campus, and preoccupied with the social life of emerging adulthood. Campuses can build exploration centers, but they must draw participants to them, and that often meant incentives.

Incentives did consume resources, but they gave exploration programs a strong start. Not all components of exploration programs required incentives; some campuses created incentivized courses, seminars, or retreats that served as gateways to opportunities without incentives. But wise leadership appreciated the five-year window of their program's availability and the many demands on student and employee time, and deployed strategic incentives to draw wide participation. These program leaders understood incentives as investments, and far less costly than unused renovated spaces, unvisited full-time employees, poorly attended retreats whose timing and substance had not been vetted with students, or empty lecture halls and costly speaking honorariums because the leaders did not secure cosponsors or recruit faculty to bring their students—stories we heard with some regularity during conversations with campus program leaders.

Closely related to the *Field of Dreams* fallacy is the "too many eggs in one basket" blunder. Two campus programs put extensive resources into organizing exploration-themed conferences featuring famous keynote speakers, breakout workshops, banquets, and published proceedings. Such conferences generated good publicity for their respective campus, but the lasting effects were minimal. A few dozen employees and students would join a larger audience to hear speakers convey information that they had already published or would soon publish. On one campus, the college moved the conference to a downtown hotel to accommodate demand, forgetting until the last minute to arrange bus transportation so interested students could attend. At best, twenty students showed up, yet that did not stop the public relations staff from putting a photo of the keynote speaker on the cover of the college's alumni magazine. I suspect this blunder was the product of too much faculty involvement in exploration program development; it is the sort of heady conference I would have proposed prior to conducting this evaluation. Scholarly types find intellectual stimulation in conferences like these—but few others do, and neither campus gained much from its investment.

The stock diversification approach (i.e., "too many baskets") was not, however, the antidote to the "too many eggs in one basket" blunder. Extensive diversification diluted the purpose exploration effect and made it difficult to see what the exploration programming added to the campus. This was the particular challenge of distributed program designs, where no central exploration office was created and existing programs received extra resources to add exploration to their programming. When these existing programs had a clear appreciation for purpose exploration, the distributed design worked effectively and campus-based exploration was well positioned for long-term sustainability. When these subcontracting programs did not possess this appreciation, it seemed as if some "Aunt Lilly" had bestowed money in tribute to the activities already under way. I did not observe a pure example of this, but at one evangelical campus with a distributed exploration program, I could not discern an added purpose exploration effect in about half of its component programs. And with no project director to goad these preexisting programs to infuse purpose or vocation better, there was no corrective mechanism. This campus did correct itself when it hired a project director from another school to oversee the sustainability phase of its exploration programming: he held subprograms accountable and accomplished more with the campus's sustainability grant than the hodgepodge of overseers did with an implementation grant four times larger.

Marginalized Support Staff, No Partners, Theology "Lite"

These final blunders have significant impacts, but are in the fifth position because they can be readily corrected. Support staff can be invited into the program, external partners for exploration programming can be found, and substantive theological concepts can be readily plumbed. Correcting these has importance for several reasons, the first being the proportion of college students who work on campus and how long they work. Even if students are employed only ten hours per week, those hours accumulate into a significant, sustained contact with campus support staff—from clerical workers to physical plant personnel to food services employees. Many of these support staff, moreover, seek employment at religiously affiliated colleges and universities because they value the mission of these organizations (see chapter 5). True, the accounts payable staff may not encounter many students directly, but the department likely employs a few student aides whom its staff come to know very well. Support staff should not be overlooked as potential mentors; the work they do is highly representative of what graduates will encounter when they enter the workplace.

Just two campuses officially recognized their support staff's contributions to purpose exploration mentorship: chapter 3's Pullman College, which trained staff as small-group facilitators, and chapter 4's Mennonite College, which invited its entire staff to a summer picnic to hear words of gratitude from the president, reflections on mentoring by three staff members, a keynote address about student learning beyond the classroom, and breakout sessions afterward. Both were evangelical colleges, so norms of nurturing students were widely shared. Still, working with students is a favorite part of staff members' jobs at most colleges, so supplying staff with exploration training could pay dividends for years to come. Summer picnics are common on many campuses, so programs similar to Mennonite College's are highly replicable.

Replicating good ideas is, of course, a benefit of interorganizational partnerships. The coordination office for this initiative sought to facilitate partnerships via annual conferences; an extensive website of recommended readings, films, course syllabi, and programmatic discussion; and funds for consultants. Most exploration programs took advantage of these resources. But a few did not, staying poolside rather than participate, and missing creative ideas and collaborative possibilities. Participation needs to be coupled with awareness of contextual differences, to avoid transplanting foreign species into one's garden. Still, there is much to learn from other gardeners, and especially from those working in similar soils and climates. Thus, Jesuits benefited from their own gatherings, as did Lutherans, Presbyterians, Methodists, virtually unaffiliated campuses, and evangelicals. That participating schools have, by their own initiative, coalesced into fee-paying members of the Council of Independent Colleges' Network for Vocation in Undergraduate Education (NetVUE), and the fact that they have attracted even more campuses that did not receive exploration grants confirms the value of conversation partnerships. Not all exploration-minded campuses participate in these conversations, of course, but many do.

Strategic Ecology

By using the phrase *strategic ecology*, I wish to signal the breadth of perspective necessary for effective campus exploration programs, and the interconnectedness of internal and external elements that influence colleges and universities. This is one section that practically minded readers ought not skip; it identifies five interconnected layers of campus ecology, and describes within each key factors relevant to exploration programming (see table 6.2). Those who oversee exploration efforts on campus, or who wish to implement such efforts, will find here a typological overview of ecological factors and phenomena that must be considered to launch, deepen, or expand a purpose exploration program.

Personnel

Most strategic blunders involved missteps by program personnel. I do not wish to belabor these, only reiterate the importance of program staff with enterprising orientations to programming, comfort with faculty discourse, effective interpersonal and public communication skills, programmatic and interpersonal problem-solving skill, and high emotional intelligence. Program directors who possessed these maximized the potential of the programs they oversaw. They used their garden soils, tools, budget, and assigned species, making well-designed gardens look extraordinary and blandly designed gardens look good. They could not, however, turn clay into topsoil, relocate buildings whose shadows blocked the garden's sunlight, or prevent damage from severe cold or drought. Those elements had to be addressed at structural and organizational levels.

Table 6.2 Strategic layers and associated factors affecting purpose exploration programs

Strategic layer	Associated factors
Personnel	Emotional intelligence of director and staff
	Entrepreneurial or enterprise orientation to programming
	Comfort with academic environment and faculty discourse
	Ability to receive criticism and make adjustments
	Oral and written communication skills
	Interpersonal problem-solving skills
	Proactive management of "problem employees"
Program structure and process	Organic fit with organizational history and current organizational culture
	Centralized versus distributed administration
	Receptivity to feedback and evaluation
	Willingness to adapt and experiment, to maximize successes and cut losses
	Focus on those most structurally and culturally amenable: sophomores and juniors, student leaders, new employees, newly promoted individuals, campus "good citizens"
	Incentives that match organizational culture
	Strategic goals not too diffuse or too narrow; 3–4 goals ideal
	Proexploration communities fostered
	Thoughtful theological exploration
Intraorganizational	Fit between program goals and organizational location
	Clear program boundaries and interdepartmental relations
	Senior administrative attention and support
	Employee morale and support for mission; faculty/staff relations
	Organization's recent past and near future trajectory
	Organizational profile/mission: liberal arts, research, or professional/vocational training
Interorganizational	Market ratings and rankings
	Competitive position vis-à-vis other colleges and universities
	Health of ties to sponsoring denomination, sister institutions
	Financial support
	Revenue diversification
Cultural, macroeconomic	Local and regional culture: public religiosity norms, rural versus urban, disengaged versus sociable, affluent versus poor
	Public support and accountability
	Dominance of research university organizational model (where disciplinary and professional memberships trump institutional/local citizenship)
	American pragmatism: student credentialism, consumerism
	Global economic expansion and contraction, Great Recession

Program Structure and Process

Well-designed programs aligned with the university's history and organizational culture, focused on those most structurally open to purpose exploration, and invested in strategically selected goals. They intentionally nurtured communities that would sustain exploration activities and ensured participants were invited to a robust examination of purpose and vocation exploration texts. For many campuses, a centralized office made the most sense, but a few evangelical campuses prospered with distributed administration. It was especially important to solicit feedback regularly and use it to make programmatic adjustments. As much as the evaluator in me wished rigorous social scientific evaluation methods were essential, they were not. What *was* essential was a habit of soliciting feedback and using it to improve program performance. Just as small businesses do not need formal market research if they know their customers well, exploration programs that knew their campus populations well did not need formal evaluation methods.

The final structure and process factor was predesigned flexibility and experimentation; programs needed to be modular and scalable to best serve participants and improve over time. Excellent design, when combined with outstanding program personnel, produced exploration programs with waiting lists of future participants. Even if combined with average personnel, well-designed programs still attracted many participants. New York City's Central Park is packed on a warm spring weekend, but a winter visit possesses its own charms and draws a decent crowd too. Frederick Law Olmstead's design is appreciated regardless of the undulating budget of the city's Parks and Recreation Department.

Intraorganizational Factors

Program design and staff did not exist in a vacuum. Factors inherent to complex formal organizations variously strengthened or undermined individual program effectiveness. Among these was the program's place in the organization chart. It was hard to draw faculty to a garden located on the far side of campus and surrounded by residence halls. But even when the garden was located near employee offices, low morale or interemployee tension limited employee participation. Low morale left employees suspicious of new ventures, and resentment between faculty and staff minimized their voluntary interactions. Low employee morale could even nullify the impact of senior administrative support for exploration programming, which was otherwise a positive factor in program effectiveness.

More unpredictable but quite influential was a college or university's recent trajectory. One campus we visited had launched new professional programs and consolidated liberal arts departments, so its exploration program was valued for preserving the campus's liberal arts tradition (see chapter 5). Another two campuses had severed official ties to their sponsoring denomination soon after receiving exploration grants, one of which valued its exploration program for illuminating paths forward, while the other saw its exploration program as a vestige of that affiliation. Rounding out the list of intraorganizational factors is the clarity of relationships between exploration programs and allied departments. Most exploration programs were distinct from religious life offices, because their strategic foci were different, but a few chaplains did not appreciate that arrangement. Similar frustrations were voiced by directors of career services and student life deans. Intraorganizational boundaries are watched closely and need ongoing clarification. From my own two decades in higher education, I have observed campus organizational change to be the norm and not the exception: departments reorganize, senior administrators come and go, staff members switch jobs, and budgets change with amazing regularity. To keep all parties on the same page and purpose exploration on the agenda requires ongoing attention.

Interorganizational Factors

If the democratization of access has been American higher education's indisputable bright spot over the last half century, then the commodification of higher education has been its unequivocal low point. Market position frequently trumps learning, teaching, or scholarly community. It generates college executives who publicly denounce ranking systems while privately manipulating institutional statistics to game these systems. It produces employees who privilege paychecks and professional recognition over teaching moments. And it recruits students who care more about a college's status and social life than its opportunities to learn. A few campuses that received exploration grants were internationally respected universities, whose market concerns focused on research, grants, and student amenities. Most campuses, however, were regional colleges, waging uphill battles against public universities that charge half as much while rebuffing flank attacks from for-profit colleges with slick advertising. On regional campuses, every program and every employee gets enlisted in the college's battle to maintain market position—including exploration programs and their staffs. On several campuses, senior administrators tapped exploration programs to help themselves and the organization rethink its mission and strategy; this represented the best-case scenario. On a few campuses, exploration programs found themselves shoehorned into student retention programs, then criticized for their weak performance; this was the worst-case scenario (see chapter 4). On most regional campuses, however, exploration programs were enlisted as available resources, and valued for their contributions to employee morale and student satisfaction. The bottom line for exploration programs is to enlist proactively in the battle for market position, because aside from elite institutions, every program finds itself drafted and can be assigned duties for which it is poorly suited.

Given the ferocity of the battle for market position, allies are invaluable. Those allies might include sister institutions, sponsoring denominations, or philanthropic organizations. Partnering with sister institutions can bring economies of scale, such as jointly run overseas or summer exploration programs. Sponsoring denominations can underwrite scholarship programs so youth interested in purpose exploration enroll, host exploration-linked conferences or other events on campus, and facilitate exploration-themed community involvement through local and regional congregations. And the value of philanthropic partners is self-evident. Exploration programs, with the sisterly connections they facilitated, the denominational ties they nurtured, and the philanthropic interest they attracted, found allies readily. Many campuses recognized this during their planning stages; others stumbled upon it serendipitously, receiving large gifts from devout alums pleased by the renewed enthusiasm for the institution's religious heritage, or discovering partners in purpose exploration among sister colleges and denominational service agencies. But some campuses missed these possibilities, and many did not maximize them.[15]

Cultural, Macroeconomic Factors

The outermost layer of an exploration program's strategic ecology is cultural and macroeconomic. Exploration programs can do little to alter these factors, but awareness of them can be invaluable. Local and regional culture was particularly important; failure to appreciate the prevalence of fundamentalism set Marble College's exploration program back nearly two years, while sensitivity to the same helped Phi Beta College's program gain a warm welcome (see chapters 5 and 3, respectively). A couple of programs miscalculated their rural community's needs, and one struggled to effectively engage its affluent and urbane local population. To these add increased public scrutiny of higher education, the dominance of a discipline-preoccupied academy, an American pragmatism that disdains intellectual life and tolerates permeation of marketplace logic into noneconomic relationships, and the tectonic shifts of the global economy. The dominant academic response to these is lamentation. But proactive engagement of these issues can seed critical and creative thinking.[16] And proactive engagement can facilitate emergency planning that mitigates disaster and speeds recovery. Higher education is one of the few places left in postmodern cultures that can foster proactive engagement, critical thinking, and creativity; when we lament rather than accept wider realities, we make finding forward paths even more difficult.

Strategic Recommendations

If I Ran the Zoo is a favorite Dr. Seuss book. In it, young Gerald McGrew recounts how he would enliven the zoo by replacing its lions, tigers, and bears with a fantastical assortment of creatures. It is a delightful contribution to children's literature, and its protagonist often springs to mind as I field inquiries from campuses about exploration programming. I wish, like Gerald McGrew, I could make recommendations without concern for empirical realities—but I can only describe strategies that offer the best odds of success and the most significant impact. In short, I recommend a three-stage process that (1) selects the exploration project appropriate to a campus's type (see table 5.2) and adapts it to the campus's particular history and organizational culture; (2) designs exploration programming to reach the most likely student and employee participants and foster self-sustaining, proexploration communities among them; and (3) solicits program feedback and regularly reviews the program's effects.

Since I review issues of organic design in chapters 3 and 5, I do not repeat them here. I simply underscore the inclusion of faculty in this organic process. Professors are the trees of a purpose exploration garden, rooting that garden most enduringly on campus. It is worth the time it takes to ensure their participation. At the same time, campuses are designing gardens and not arboretums, so faculty must not be the only or even the majority members of the design group lest they fall into the scholarly trap of designing a research center and planning international conferences. Research centers may spring from the purpose explorations of faculty participants (and have done so), but these should be the fruit and not the seeds of an exploration garden. I also advise that organic conversations be guided by keen understandings of the campus culture and its larger ecology, and not dominated by unique personalities. The former ensures strategic "fit" and valuable contribution, while the latter prevents quirky imprints upon the program design (see the "exploration counselor" discussion above).

As for the exploration programming itself, its overarching goal should be the nurture of self-sustaining, proexploration communities among students, faculty, and staff. There were various ways that exploration programs fostered such communities among students: undergraduate fellowship programs; exploration-infused undergraduate majors; postgateway program offerings (see chapter 2's Ignatius University and chapter 3's Phi Beta College), and themed residence halls. All had high impact, but the sophomore residence hall described in chapter 2 had the most lasting impact: that institution chose the ideal year to engage questions of purpose and vocation; the hall's central location and appealing activities made participation competitive; mentor groups created comfortable spaces for personal reflection; and dynamic faculty teaching in the hall's classrooms added academic gravitas. Particularly savvy was the program's choice of a themed residence hall, which is an established residential genre that needs little explanation and for which basic budgets preexist. It is therefore the easiest place, ceteris paribus, to launch the student component of a purpose exploration program. If I ran the zoo, an exploration-themed residence hall is what I would do.

To reinforce the impact of this exploration-themed residence hall, I would add: (1) curricular development grants so faculty could create exploration-infused courses and teach them within the residence hall; (2) community-engaged learning grants for upper-division courses, so faculty could tap advanced student learning and skills in purposeful service to communities local, national, and global; (3) minigrants so that students could continue the purpose exploration begun in the sophomore residence hall and expand it; and (4) first-year-student visit days, to introduce new students to purpose exploration and the themed residence hall. These programs, together with the exploration-themed residence hall, will generate waves of purpose-seeking sophomores, who then possess two years to further explore their purpose in the rich environment of a college or university. This program will not reach all students, I admit, but it has the potential to be contagious, reaching a "tipping point" on some campuses.[17]

Running parallel to this exploration-themed residence hall would be the faculty and staff program component. There are five essential elements here: (1) intellectual substance; (2) conversation leaders with interpersonal skill and intellectual respectability; (3) sufficient time to foster interpersonal connections; (4) incentives to draw a wide cross section of employees; and (5) involvement of new, newish, and newly promoted employees. It is critical that engagement of faculty and staff be intellectually robust and that conversation leaders keep all involved while preventing any from dominating the discussion. Though this may seem challenging, it is not that different from an interdisciplinary graduate seminar. And while this seminar can occur during a trip abroad, as at chapter 5's Cornfield Lutheran College, a weekly on-campus seminar can be as effective and foster interpersonal ties in the real context of daily university life (see chapter 2). Some campuses offered faculty and staff seminars as intensive summer experiences, which also seemed to work well. What was less effective were one-day "working retreats" or even weekend retreats; while favorably received, these lost momentum quickly because the interpersonal connections were too new to be sustained. As a general rule, there is no such thing as quality time when it comes to fostering faculty and staff community; it takes a *quantity* of time for relationships between faculty and staff to form and solidify.

To this faculty and staff exploration seminar, I would add support for curriculum development, community-engaged learning, working retreats for individual programs, pedagogical and advising workshops, interinstitutional purpose exploration conferences, and minigrants. Support for curricular development and community-engaged learning would make it easier for interested faculty to insert exploration into the academic side of the campus and draw students into the intellectual and ethical dimensions of purpose exploration. Working retreats would help individual academic programs take their curricular work a step further, reframing course sequences to foster students' purpose exploration. Pedagogical and advising workshops would convey best practices, and affirm these as valued campus work. Attendance at exploration conferences would foster dialogues that further stimulate faculty and staff thinking. And minigrants would encourage employee creativity, seeding innovations and fostering synergies that turn busy campuses into enriching communities. Not every employee will participate in a faculty and staff exploration seminar, nor will every participant take advantage of postseminar resources. But one can be sure that many campus good citizens will be energized by them and likely attract colleagues to them. One should expect student and employee proexploration communities to be mostly separate, due to life course and maturity differences, but encouraging these communities to overlap at strategic times (e.g., a joint retreat) will greatly benefit students and bring joy to faculty and staff participants.

I admit that I have never been a project director nor played a part in any campus's exploration program. These are general recommendations for actively church-affiliated campuses, based on high-level conclusions drawn from my site visits and additional observations of this initiative at large. Virtually unaffiliated, ethnically distinctive, and evangelical campuses will need to recalibrate these recommendations based on their unique contexts, with the former scaling back its expected curricular inroads to a few exploration course electives, and the latter two ratcheting up from a themed residence hall to a comprehensive sophomore experience program and a community-engaged, discipline-specific practicum or service tour for juniors and seniors. The precise design will be the organic product of each campus, guided by the goals of targeting likely participants and fostering proexploration communities among them. Soliciting feedback and regularly reviewing efforts must also be standard practice in every exploration program; programs cannot be guided by a "father knows best" mentality. Rather, they must become partners to dynamic communities centered around questions of purpose and vocation, which celebrate all who live out their answers to these questions, whatever form that living takes. Of course, change is inherent in communities, formal organizations, and campus ecologies. So these recommendations fit this particular moment, the present challenges to higher education, and this global era. Their applicability to specific organizations, future challenges, and global changes will vary.

Garden Essentials

There are on every campus, thankfully, good citizens dedicated to quality education, and a small but engaged proportion of students who seek a transformative learning experience as well. But with each passing year, these good citizens and engaged students find more reasons to abandon their good work; capitalism's commodification of higher education is unrelenting. Purpose exploration programs are no match for capitalism's effects or permeation. But they can provide a garden oasis where deeper questions can be pondered, thoughtful conversations enjoined, and journeys meaningfully charted. They can, that is, when organically designed and strategically deployed.

In trying times, practically minded persons question the value of gardens. What tangible product, after all, do gardens generate? What value do they add to a community, to an organization, or to a people? Gardeners can point to sonnets written, songs composed, couples engaged, and children inspired within their borders — but these cannot be recorded in an accounting ledger. Their value cannot be found in a spreadsheet. But their persistence, over time and around the globe, and their popularity, among millions of gardeners and garden visitors, can be (and has been[18]) relayed in the works of numerous historians and geographers. While necessity forces us to inhabit a utilitarian world most of the time, and to be its agents in much of our lives, our humanity refuses to abide that narrow world continuously. We escape to gardens of various sorts, find our humanity renewed therein, and sacrifice our utilitarian rewards of time and money to preserve these beautiful and restorative spaces.

Campus exploration programs helped thousands of students, faculty, and staff across the United States renew their humanity and enhance the lives of others. Could they have done so more effectively? Absolutely. This chapter has described more than a dozen ways purpose exploration programs could have better assisted their participants, and made specific recommendations about program structure. Could other programs or exploratory foci be equally effective? It is certainly possible. But that possibility does not negate the demonstrated impact of purpose exploration programs, and the accumulated wisdom from more than a decade of deployment makes them ready for serious consideration on campuses of every variety. In chapter 7, I explore the larger lessons embodied in the success of these exploration programs, and draw out implications for policy, practice, and mentoring of emerging adults in general. I conclude this chapter, however, by inviting all campuses to engage students in conversations about purpose and calling, and to do so by tapping the strategic analysis contained here and the exploration resources enumerated in appendix 5.

7

Larger Lessons

More or Less Anxious

At first, I thought it was strong winds off the ocean. But when I sat up, I could tell it was not the wind that shook my beach recliner back and forth. Voices all around asked, "What was that?" "Did you feel that?" Speculation raced in the absence of information: "It was an earthquake! It might be a tsunami! There must have been an explosion underwater!" In minutes, smartphones supplied the answer: a 5.8-magnitude earthquake struck the Piedmont region of Virginia shortly before 2:00 p.m. on August 23, 2011, shaking beach chairs at the Jersey Shore and rattling nerves and up and down the East Coast. Now that it was no longer a slow news day, the media kicked into high gear, reporting on the evacuation of the White House and Capitol, quelling rumors of bombs and terrorism, supplying images of damaged buildings, and finding incredulous East Coast residents to interview. "I was just standing there when everything started to shake."

By that evening, California residents and comedians were having a good laugh at all the hyperventilating on the East Coast.

And we deserved it, frankly. But it would be a mistake to conclude Californians or anyone else is fearless in the midst of an earthquake. Fear is a justified reaction to an earthquake, as are multilevel official responses, from construction code changes to rescue equipment purchases to emergency planning. Living near an active fault line has a sweeping effect on how people live, shaping zoning laws, public budgets, government agencies, business contingency plans, nonprofit foci, school policy and curriculum, and even household décor.

I relay this because tectonic shifts of a global economic and macrocultural nature have been rattling the First World with growing frequency, producing powerful effects on adolescents' transition to adulthood and generating wide anxieties about the cause of these tremors. In chapter 4, I cited the high rates of anxiety indicated in surveys of college students, which have been corroborated by surveys of besieged mental health counselors on campuses. But college students are not the only ones feeling anxious — many observers are worried too. The editors at the *New York Times*, otherwise quick to affirm lifestyle diversity, made this troubled observation on cover of its August 18, 2010, Sunday magazine: "They move back in with their parents, they delay beginning career paths, they put off commitments; what is it about 20-somethings?"[1] The article itself was carefully researched, quoting scholars of adolescence and emerging adulthood, and interviewing a variety of twenty-somethings. There was a young woman toiling to earn an advanced degree and accumulate the requisite experience for career success in a competitive global economy, as well as lethargic young men enrolled in an adulthood boot camp that banned media and required early rising, daily chores, and active job searching. But foremost was the article's concern about the societal impact: "Parents are helping pay bills they never counted on paying, and social institutions are missing out on young people contributing to productivity and growth. . . . We're caught in a weird moment, unsure whether to allow young people to keep exploring and questioning or to cut them off and tell them just to find something, anything, to put food on the table and get on with their lives."

While concern about youth can be found in a number of ancient texts,[2] perceived resistance to assuming adult responsibilities among twenty-somethings combined with cultural ambiguities about what it means to be an adult have intensified anxiety in many quarters. Data from the US census bears out the rapid social shift: in 1960, two-thirds (66 percent) of American men and three-quarters (77 percent) of American women had completed all five of the traditional demographic markers of adulthood by age thirty: leaving home, finishing school, getting married, having a child, and becoming financially independent. By 2010, fewer than three out of ten men (28 percent) and four out of ten women (39 percent) had done the same.[3] This is an extraordinary social change in just fifty years' time: America went from an overwhelming majority of young adults completing these five markers in 1960 to an overwhelming majority *not* completing them fifty years later. Moreover, of these five indicators, only financial independence is considered a certain indicator of adulthood today, underscoring this profound cultural change.[4]

I disagree with an implicit assumption in most discussion of young adults, however: that the lengthening path to adulthood is primarily the product of young adult choices. Nor do I find convincing claims that longer paths to adulthood are products of either the Great Recession or sliding academic standards (though these have certainly exacerbated matters). The lengthening path to adulthood is rather the result of (1) macroeconomic changes that have made financial independence elusive; (2) macrocultural shifts that have replaced traditional family formation with a menu of lifestyle options; and (3) insufficient socialization of youth by families, schools, and congregations for the altered economic and cultural landscapes that now exist. This phenomenon only appears to be recent because the college degrees and specialized credentials earned by the offspring of middle- and upper-middle-class Americans sheltered them for several decades from the increased difficulty of attaining financial independence.

Receiving more of the public's and economic pundits' blame for the travails of recent college graduates, but for the wrong reasons, are America's colleges and universities. It is true that colleges and universities have allowed academic standards to slide, when one in three college graduates scores "proficient" in national tests of adult literacy, 60 percent of full-time undergraduates in four-year postsecondary programs skate by with fewer than fifteen hours of weekly study time, and college students show "barely noticeable" improvement in critical thinking and reasoning after three consecutive semesters of full-time collegiate education.[5] It is also true that elements of college and university organizational structures have operated at less than peak efficiency. I do not think it unreasonable, then, that pundits express frustration with minimal learning or organizational inefficiencies in higher education given our exposure in these areas. But hear me clearly: neither is the culprit behind steadily lengthening and increasingly complex paths to adulthood, nor would full repair of them regenerate ample white-collar jobs or alter the "marked decrease in resiliency," "quarterlife crises," and wanderings of twenty-somethings "adrift" if not "lost in transition."[6] Where I argue higher education *is* culpable is in not creatively and systematically engaging students in a wide-ranging conversation about living lives of purpose in a complex, globally competitive, and deeply unjust world—a conversation with demonstrable capacity to improve campus engagement along with graduates' navigation of the long slog to stable employment and productive citizenship. These culprits, false and true, merit our careful attention.

There is more than sufficient evidence of minimal learning in college for accrediting commissions to take serious corrective action immediately. Students deserve college credentials that reflect academic proficiency, and that means requiring colleges and universities to demonstrate that graduates possess collegiate-level proficiencies. But reestablished academic standards, as important as they are for our credibility, will manipulate the supply of capable college-educated workers only. There is no guarantee that the global economy will generate increased demand for college-educated workers, or that it will do so in the locations, employment sectors, or career fields desired by graduates. The relationship between a nation's educational attainment and its economic development is complex and nonlinear;[7] despite politicians' reductionist claims, it takes more than well-educated citizens to spawn economic growth. Lengthening pathways to adulthood are, moreover, multinational phenomena, as evident in nations that restrict university education to those with the highest standardized test scores as they are in nations that emphasize broad access to higher education. We should not expect raised academic standards to reverse or even slow the lengthening paths to adulthood apparent across the First World; if anything, they may lengthen the time to degree due to remediation.

I must also observe, not as an excuse but for the sake of completeness, that market pressures, political demands, and cultural expectations to graduate ever-increasing numbers of students fostered ideal conditions for academic standards to be undermined. America prides itself on its decentralized system of higher education, and points to its elite universities' global prominence as proof that a system of self-regulating, organizational competition works. That decentralization offered little basis for preventing the erosion of academic standards by powerful waves of market incentives, political pressures, and rising aspirations, however. Accrediting commissions and scholarly associations could have and should have done more to take colleges and universities to task for declining academic standards, but the bottom line is this: an American college education became easier to obtain because America *wanted* it to become easier, and rewarded colleges and universities with money and customers (students) for making it easier.

During the heady decades of higher education's expansion, there was admittedly little incentive for colleges and universities to attend to the efficiencies of their organizational structures and processes. When flush with cash and students, it is easy for administrators to justify hiring staff to perform tasks that faculty no longer did, and ignore programs that cost more than they generated or made no contribution to undergraduate education. Just as homes need spring cleaning, so too do college and university organizations—which two decades of constricting budgets, followed by the Great Recession, appear to have accomplished handily. The assumption that higher education needs wholesale restructuring[8] to more effectively educate its students, then, gains no support from this evaluation's findings. Well-trained thinkers and dedicated citizens are not widgets that one rolls off a university or college conveyor belt on graduation day. Genuine learning is often inefficient, and authentic citizenship can derail the best-laid plans of students and educators. The genuine learning we observed on campuses led students to change courses of study, add internship or international experiences, and even suspend enrollment to serve special populations—all of which can lengthen degree completion. Likewise, the authentic citizenship we observed led students to modify career plans, join social movements, and divert their attention from grade point averages.

What limits students' genuine learning and authentic citizenship is not inefficiencies in colleges' or universities' organizational structures (about which most students are oblivious), but students' dominant orientation to their education. When students view college education as a means to an economic end and not as an opportunity to learn, explore, and investigate the world, even the most efficient college or university will not foster genuine learning or engaged citizenship (see chapter 4). Increased programmatic efficiency will do nothing to improve the learning and citizenship outcomes we expect of a college education, and likely undermines their attainment. Efforts to streamline delivery of educational content will only fuel student instrumentalism. While market efficiencies help to produce tangible goods and services more cost-effectively, they do serious harm when applied to intangibles such as learning, relationships, or citizenship. Genuine learning and engaged citizenship are economically irrational and gloriously inefficient; they are immune to organizational streamlining.

There is one place, though, where colleges and universities do possess responsibility for aimless and lengthy wandering by college graduates. That place is higher education's retreat from questions of purpose and vocation. I am not the first to claim this retreat, but I may be the first to link this retreat to the unnecessary and often harmful wanderings of newly college-educated emerging adults. By not engaging questions of purpose and vocation, colleges and universities leave the individualist and traditionalist cultural trajectories of American youth untouched, dropping graduates into active earthquake zones without drinking water or a map. It is no wonder why today's families have had to stretch like "accordions" to accommodate twenty-somethings — paying a "private toll" for global competiveness; why nearly half of emerging adults meet the criteria for at least one psychiatric disorder; and why so many are "adrift" if not "lost in transition" — living lives marked by consumerism, civic disengagement, and anomic morality (see trajectory discussion below).[9]

Colleges and universities must equip graduates for the long slog from commencement to stable employment and productive citizenship, because if they do not, in an era of reductionism and simpleminded accountability, they will find themselves culpable for the whole of the long slog itself. Where job fairs and résumé workshops once provided all that was necessary to put graduates on the path to financial independence (the baseline adult achievement), there must now exist systematic processes to help students identify their interests, understand global change, and launch interdependent postcollege journeys. A program of purpose exploration is not the only way for campuses to accomplish this;[10] but it is a demonstrably effective way to increase campus engagement and satisfaction, to focus attention beyond campus bubbles, and to supply a language, conversation partners, and generative resources that improve successful navigation of our highly competitive and complex world.

Since equipping college graduates for the long slog, as a formal and systematic undertaking, is a new iteration of a task abandoned by colleges and universities, some educators may be tempted to resist, thinking it better to wait out the economic doldrums, to identify gaps in other social institutions, or to attend to more immediate organizational challenges. This is not wise, for several reasons. First, lengthening paths to adulthood are not recent phenomena, as they predate the Great Recession and are evident across the First World.[11] Europe, Japan, Australia, and South Africa have all experienced lengthening paths to adulthood; the United States is behind the curve on this one. While an expanding economy may take the edge off the criticism of higher education, it will do so temporarily, until rising college costs and rising numbers of graduates drive any brief uptick in median incomes down again.

Second, complaining about other social institutions — such as families insufficiently preparing their offspring, businesses disinvesting in human resources, or governments reducing support for higher education or social programs — will provoke a fiery response that will singe much of what higher education holds dear and limit its ability to define and solve its own problems. Tenure is often viewed as a shield for professors' plush lifestyles, and academic freedom as a ruse to teach nonsense. We must defend these crucial tools of the academy, but the most effective way may be to shore up higher education's structural foundations (by raising standards and equipping students for the long slog) before complaining about other institutions that have been damaged by recurring macroeconomic and macrocultural tremors.

Third, while physical plants, enrollment, and revenue streams may press more immediately upon university administrations, the core of higher education's contemporary challenge is anxieties about the financial and domestic independence of young adults. College students invest significant resources in credentials that, based on the most current College Board projections, do not reach the break-even point until graduates are thirty-two, and yield a lifetime earnings benefit of $300,000 over those with high school diplomas only.[12] Meanwhile, students inhabit campus environments that do little to encourage healthy, long-term behaviors and relationships.[13] The economic necessity of a college credential remains, but its traditional residential form becomes increasingly akin to costly city hotels whose grandeur is yesteryear. While the city may be guests' more desired location, when hotel rates climb ever higher, value-conscious customers opt for the high-tech, utilitarian motels that entrepreneurs have built along the interstate. Their distance is not *that much* of an obstacle, and they meet current building codes for earthquake resistance.

A prudent response to America's anxiety about directionless young adults is to deploy every lever that demonstrably increases student engagement and improves postcollege transitions. In chapter 4 we learned that one in five students approaches education more idealistically, and one in two will contribute to the public good as long as the system rewards altruism. This book demonstrates the positive effects that levers widely neglected in higher education can have during critical moments in students' educational and life journeys. Different levers engage different students, and timing their use is important as well. But college educators are not in a position to ignore any effective lever. Thankfully, purpose exploration levers possess reflexive benefits, renewing campus good citizens and building community through the common language created and the permission to convey stories about individual and collective purpose.

There is much in the day-to-day bureaucracy of American higher education, and even more in the global context, that can grind down the idealism of educator and student alike. But engagement with questions of purpose can spawn a grounded idealism that sustains aspirations in spite of setbacks, and that calibrates interdependent trajectories that, over time, produce lives of service to others and personal satisfaction. Levers of purpose exploration will not engage everyone on every campus; there is work to be done identifying and deploying other levers that motivate and engage. At the same time, purpose exploration has engaged *many* different students and many educators on a *wide* variety of campuses, including campuses with particularist affiliations. Particularist history can be a powerful asset, if deployed descriptively and not prescriptively, and if presented as one of many ways to gain traction in exploring the deep questions of life.

For the remainder of this chapter, I summarize lessons learned from this national initiative to explore purpose and vocation on college campuses, and discuss implications for engaging purpose in higher education, for launching college graduates into adulthood, and for strengthening higher education. Along the way I draw out implications for the practice of higher education, for curricular design as well as cocurricular activities, and for mentoring of emerging adults. It is good that so many dedicated educators populate college and university campuses. But dedication alone is insufficient to reverse the deeply rooted instrumentalism of most American college students; it is limited even in its capacity to engage idealistic students on American campuses. Rather, educators need to foster new conversations around ageless questions of purpose and well-lived lives, drawing from the various levers deployed across this multicampus initiative, to nurture communities that refresh student, faculty, and staff leaders, who in turn inspire a critical mass of campus citizens.

College educators need to transform higher education from within, or watch as it is transformed from without. I throw my hat in with the first project, since the consequences of more market-driven colleges and universities make me shudder. Dislodging college students' disengagement may seem as likely as adjusting the earth's orbit, but I once watched eight-year-olds lift an automobile off the ground at a science museum, using a large lever-and-pulley system. Archimedes famously said, "Give me a lever long enough and a fulcrum on which to place it, and I shall move the world." For a goodly number of students, faculty, and staff, purpose exploration becomes a lever that produces remarkable movement.

Levers of Engagement

Campuses, students, professors, and staff are not monoliths, and neither are campus-based exploration programs. To understand the impact of the latter on the former, I disaggregated and labeled salient differences across campuses and within their populations. In this section, I review these analyses and summarize these programs' effects.

Campus Types and Project Types

With eighty-eight campuses participating, there were representatives of every sort: research universities and liberal arts colleges, commuter schools and residential campuses, densely urban campuses and those with acres to spare, student populations from a few hundred to nearly twenty thousand. There was also wide denominational representation: conservative to liberal Protestants, Roman Catholics of a wide variety, an Orthodox college, and nonsectarian colleges and universities that had Christian founders. We did not find that these variations, however, produced important exploration effect differences among participants.

The most important campus-level difference was rather the character of its religious affiliation: was the campus historically affiliated, actively affiliated, or culturally distinctive? The first identified colleges and universities that were currently nonsectarian but possessed historic connections to religion, the second included actively church-affiliated campuses with religiously heterogeneous populations, and the third consisted of campuses that served ethnically or evangelically distinctive populations. This difference determined the intellectual and practical exploration project pursued among faculty and staff (see table 5.2). At nonsectarian, historically affiliated colleges and universities, the exploration project nudged faculty or staff to accept, if not engage in, public conversations about purpose and vocation, including the religious and spiritual roots of these ideas. At actively church-affiliated yet religiously diverse campuses, the project emphasized holistic student development, which included exploration of purpose and vocation, as a core campus priority. And at ethnic or evangelically distinctive campuses, employees were invited to deepen their knowledge of their campus's cultural tradition and help students better engage a pluralistic and globalizing world.

Rather interestingly, the challenge posed to students did not vary by campus religious affiliation. All campuses sought to encourage self-knowledge and self-transcendence among students. This is likely an age effect: students eighteen to twenty-two years old dominated all eighty-eight campus populations, and these young adults confront similar tasks of development (see chapter 4).

Student Types

American college students overwhelming seek bachelor's degrees for their presumed career and marketplace advantage, with only one in five attending for more idealistic reasons. A decade of national surveys also confirms that 20 percent of college students at four-year institutions devote twenty-one or more hours weekly preparing (studying) for class, 15 percent spend five or fewer hours per week, with the remainder falling in between.[14] Juxtaposing these two critical student characteristics creates three subtypes of idealist students and three subtypes of instrumentalist students (see fig. 4.1). Idealist types include the next generation of intellectual and creative elites, whom I label Future Intelligentsia; those whose passions run toward social change, whom I label Reforming Activists; and those who reject core elements of the present social order, whom I label Rebels. Instrumentalist types include those who prized grades and occupational achievement, whom I label Obsessive, Compulsive Achievers; those who balance concern for grades with time for friends, family, jobs, and fun, whom I label Utilitarians; and those who regard passing their classes as the cover charge to a multiyear college party, whom I label Minimalists.

International public-good experiments provided additional analytic traction, revealing that one-quarter of young adults seek to "free-ride" consistently, another one-quarter sacrifice for the public good consistently, and the remaining one-half demonstrate contingent moral action—behaving sacrificially when sacrifice is rewarded, and selfishly when selfishness is rewarded. I label the latter group contingent moralists, and argue that it is essential for higher education to help contingent moralists find practical ways that they can support the public good via their individual careers and via change within their career organizations. While it is tempting for educators to focus on sacrificial types because of the idealistic lives they intend to lead, it is critical to swing contingent moralists toward support of the public good for our planet's long-term well-being.[15]

Faculty and Staff Types

College campuses possess distinctive work environments, and their employees enjoy considerable autonomy. This produces a range of orientations to work, from myopically local to globally cosmopolitan. At the same time, campus employees demonstrate an array of daily work patterns, from stuck in a rut to hyperbusy. Juxtaposing employee orientations with daily work patterns helped me identify eight employee types (see fig. 5.1), four of which occupy the corners of the array and four of which reside at the center. At the extremes are deadwood, who are faculty or staff with local orientations and highly routinized daily work patterns; institutional grunts, who are similarly local but exhibit hyperbusy daily patterns; campus stars, who are employees with cosmopolitan orientations and hyperbusy daily work patterns; and institutional grumblers, who are equally cosmopolitan but possessed highly routinized daily work patterns. These four employee types receive a disproportionate share of supervisor and coworker attention.

Often less obvious are campuses' good citizens. The forces of localism, cosmopolitanism, routinization, and overcommitment are strong, but these faculty and staff resist the campus centrifuge. Good citizens embodied one *or more* of the following roles: master teacher, natural-born mentor, campus-engaged intellectual, and campus community builder. The first and second characterize those who keep pockets of transformative education alive, the third characterizes those who use their expertise to benefit the campus at large (e.g., organizing biweekly symposia, film series), and the fourth refers to those whose sociability builds connections and coalitions (e.g., recruiting employees for charitable events).

Program Design

Important design factors include the program's organic fit with campus culture and history, its organizational location and structure, its strategic priorities, its selection of organizationally savvy and emotionally intelligent personnel, its solicitation of feedback, its willingness to experiment and adapt, and its attention to fostering proexploration communities. Exploration programs are like campus gardens; their design and plantings have to fit with the climate and soil, be tended regularly, attend to visitors' feedback, and consider changing weather conditions. And, like gardens, exploration programs do not exist in a vacuum, but reside in a larger ecology of intraorganizational, interorganizational, cultural, and macroeconomic forces — some of which they influence, most of which they manage, and all of which they must understand.

Effects on Students

Organically designed, well-managed, and ecologically attuned exploration programs attract students who find that thought-provoking conversations and affirmation of their potential encourage them to stay enrolled, work through short- and long-term decisions, connect with like-minded students, and calibrate meaningful postcollege trajectories. Exploration programs are particularly helpful to college sophomores and juniors, as they have completed their transitions to college, found stability within the collegiate context, and thereby acquire the confidence to ask deeper questions of purpose and vocation, before the exit transition of senior year undermines that stability.

Future Intelligentsia and Reforming Activists relish involvement in purpose exploration programs, because these programs affirm their intellectual and reforming ideals. Yet, many OC Achievers and Utilitarians find that exploration programs help them reduce decision anxiety and incorporate "making a difference" into their career plans. Since this grant initiative preceded the Occupy Wall Street movement and trailed the Free Speech movement, we did not encounter Rebels on our campus visits. We also observed that Minimalists had no use for purpose exploration, with one exception: the handful of Minimalists who, each semester, wake up in hospitals or jails, and subsequently find their way to exploration programs in efforts to redirect their lives. For recovering Minimalists such as these, exploration programs can be invaluable.

While purpose exploration helps students reduce decision anxiety, gain understanding of their own selves, and appreciate their connections to the wider world, the greatest test of exploration's efficacy comes after graduation — when plans must be implemented, adapted, and revised. This is where the effects of purposeful thinking become most striking: those who participated in exploration programs demonstrated — one year after graduating from college — greater intentionality, more resilience, and broader life satisfaction than those who did not participate in such programs. This was especially true of those who paired participation in exploration programs with participation in a congregation or congregational surrogate, as these underscored their intentionality and resilience. Analysis of alumni surveys reveals that the benefits of purpose exploration grow stronger with time as life decisions accumulate. As one campus program director told me, "The rubber really hits the road with this after students graduate"; as slippery as that road can be for young adults, purposeful college graduates found that self-knowledge and self-transcendence offered much-appreciated traction.

Effects on Faculty and Staff

The primary effect of exploration programs on faculty and staff was affirming and resourcing good citizens. This took various forms: staff reported respect from the faculty for their role as educators, professors spoke about support for pedagogical and scholarly innovation, and both mentioned deeper conversations they had had with each other and with students. Exploration programs granted faculty and staff permission to speak about purpose and vocation publicly, tapping a language that facilitated conversation while fitting with the campus culture. Faculty and staff especially appreciated how exploration programs helped students see faculty or staff members as whole persons (and not, e.g., as "grading machines" or "disciplinarians"), broadening their conversations with students.

There were a few patterns to faculty and staff engagement with exploration programs. "Early adopters" were those newly hired or newly promoted, the devout (regardless of faith tradition), and those resolutely postmodern. The reflexivity of these employees readily comported with the reflective invitation of exploration programs. The widest effects on faculty and staff occurred on culturally distinctive campuses and the narrowest on historically affiliated campuses, with staff more amenable in general to exploration programs than faculty. Once faculty did involve themselves, however, the depth and duration of impact was large — permeating instruction, program structure, advising conversations, and even scholarship. For this reason, I liken pro–purpose exploration faculty to trees in campus gardens — oaks that grow slowly, but whose sturdy branches offer shade for many years. Finally, faculty and staff participants in exploration programs deeply valued the mission of their college or university, and saw their individual work contributing to that larger mission.

Effects on Campuses

The above effects spill over to campuses in general. Students impassioned about their studies and employees who feel valued become seeds of improved morale and retention. Curricular offerings expand and new curricular programs begin. Cocurricular opportunities blossom, with expanding service opportunities, closer community ties, more international programs, new lecture or performance series, revitalized chapel programs, diversified religious life, and improved residential programs. Actively affiliated campuses tap their religious heritage to initiate exploration conversations while simultaneously affirming individuals whose affiliations differ. Purpose exploration can even infuse mission statements and reorient the delivery of student services. These are valuable effects in general, and particularly so for private, religiously affiliated campuses that face increasing market competition and constricting revenue streams.

Recommendations for Deepest and Most Lasting Effects

For lasting effects on individual participants, programs should focus on the most receptive moments in a student's or employee's life course, and make contextually amenable introductions. Among students, this means focusing on sophomores and juniors, and generating experiences that combine challenging conversations, personal affirmation, and authentic community. For faculty and staff, this means focusing on new and newly promoted employees, and on good citizens, encouraging these educators to share their own stories and inviting exploration of their campus's religious tradition and its view of a purposeful life. It also means supplying follow-up resources so that purpose explorations undertaken can be continued over time. For campuses to be lastingly affected, exploration participants need to coalesce into a self-sustaining community and possess an amenable senior administration that will support that community's well-being and consider its proposals carefully.

I recommend exploration programs, particularly in the form of themed residence halls for interested sophomores and seminars for faculty and staff, with follow-up programming and modest incentives to start the programs well. But I make these recommendations with three caveats: the program must fit with the organization's culture, it must be implemented by high-EQ and organizationally astute staff, and it must be tangibly supported by senior administration. Impact will be attenuated if any of these three is missing. Impact will be substantial, however, when all three are in place — as they were in the best programs this evaluation studied. These programs demonstrated the value of engaging purpose broadly, of helping students launch intentional trajectories, and of harnessing the formative and community-creating potential of college and university campuses.

Purpose Matters

Since 2006, some of the best-known scholars of American higher education—Arthur Chickering, George D. Kuh, Alexander W. Astin, Robert J. Nash, and Parker J. Palmer—have documented the value of engaging spirituality on campus, forming a veritable chorus about the positive effect this has on student achievement and engagement (see chapter 2). This volume joins that chorus, and extends its repertoire in two ways—identifying theologically embedded exploration of purpose and vocation that is especially generative among campus populations, and describing the broad impact that occurs when a critical mass of students and educators coalesces into a pro-exploration, self-sustaining community. This section takes a closer look at this scholarly chorus's repertoire to date, then describes theologically embedded exploration and its community-creating implications.

The foremost documentation of spirituality's educational impact is Alexander W. Astin, Helen S. Astin, and Jennifer A. Lindholm's *Cultivating the Spirit: How College Can Enhance Students' Inner Lives.* This book is the culmination of a decadelong national research project by the Higher Education Research Institute that Alexander Astin founded and for decades led at the University of California–Los Angeles. Many of Astin's early reports garnered wide attention, and I cite these results at several points in this volume. Using longitudinal panel data from a nationally representative study of college students, Astin and his colleagues reported wide and robust effects of students' spiritual development during college, including students' academic outcomes, leadership skills, satisfaction with college, and ability to understand and form positive relationships with people of different races and cultures. "The most striking finding concerns the spiritual quality of equanimity: when college students show significant growth in equanimity, their GPAs tend to improve." Spiritual equanimity, or feeling at peace and centered, increased intellectual self-confidence and psychological well-being, which in turn improved academic performance. Growth in spiritual "quest," or the search "for meaning and purpose in life," also generated growth in intellectual self-esteem and leadership scores.[16] Since purpose exploration reduces decision anxiety and engages questions of life's meaning, it spans equanimity and quest, which helps to explain why exploration programs facilitated such positive outcomes among students.

Astin, Astin, and Lindholm reported, however, that "engaging in such a search [for meaning and purpose] can at times prove to be frustrating and emotionally unsettling," lowering student satisfaction with college and psychological well-being. This is not surprising, given that very few campuses participating in Astin, Astin, and Lindholm's survey had purpose exploration programs.[17] By contrast, student participants on purpose exploration campuses reported extraordinarily high rates of satisfaction and campus engagement (and likely had higher rates of psychological well-being too, since well-being is a powerful correlate of campus engagement; see chapter 4). That does not imply that their explorations of purpose and vocation were free of unsettling moments, only that they found support during those unsettling times and resolved these positively.

Astin and his colleagues confirmed considerable student interest in questions of purpose across all types of campuses, and in the outward implications of spirituality. They reported an increase in spiritual quest from one-fourth of entering students to one-third of college juniors—underscoring my recommendation of exploration programming on every campus, and among sophomores and juniors in particular.[18] Astin, Astin, and Lindholm also reported that the more students increased in their "Ethic of Caring" and "Ecumenical Worldview," the more students were likely "to endorse the promotion of racial understanding, and to report significant growth in [their] ability to get along with different races and cultures." These were self-reports, to be sure, and behavior will vary. But these results comport with the service component built into every exploration program we visited, and our observations of caring, gracious,[19] and ecumenical worldviews prevalent among undergraduate participants.[20]

Prior to Astin, Astin, and Lindholm, the broadest study of spirituality's impact on college students came from George D. Kuh and Robert M. Gonyea.[21] They analyzed cross-sectional data from more than 150,000 student respondents to the National Study of Student Engagement (NSSE), and concluded that spirituality did not harm and likely promoted students' educational engagement: "Spirituality-enhancing activities do not seem to hinder, and may even have mild salutary effects on, engagement in educationally purposeful activities." They also found that religiously active students did not withdraw or self-segregate, but interacted with students with "very different religious and political beliefs and personal values" at a significantly higher rate than religiously inactive students. These findings are important in two ways: they underscore spirituality's outward-engaging effect, and refute popular assumptions about religiously and spiritually active students' withdrawal from campus life. The opposite, in fact, was true: students who were *inactive* religiously or spiritually were the most disengaged from "educationally purposeful activities." Since these data were cross-sectional, they cannot gauge individual-level effects as Astin, Astin, and Lindholm's did. Still, these national results demonstrate spirituality's positive effects on students' interaction with diverse populations, and neutral to beneficial effects on students' educational engagements.

In addition to these nationally representative campus results, one can add campus and classroom reports from Arthur W. Chickering, Jon C. Dalton, and Liesa Stamm's *Encouraging Authenticity and Spirituality in Higher Education*;[22] reports of successful classroom, student life, and campus-wide spiritual engagement in Parker J. Palmer and Arthur Zajonc's *Heart of Higher Education*;[23] and scores of anecdotes in Robert J. Nash and Michele C. Murray's *Helping College Students Find Purpose*.[24] Religious and spiritual skeptics may find Nash and Murray's book of particular interest, as the authors provide a secular case for the centrality of meaning-making to human life, describing therapeutic and secular approaches to meaning-making—logotherapy, narrative therapy, philosophical counseling, and positive psychology—and outlining pathways that any educator can follow in engaging these issues.

While I appreciate the increased scholarly attention to spiritual matters in higher education, I find its assemblage under the banner of *spirituality* to be regrettable. Nash and Murray use the term briefly, but most of this literature sprinkles the term like salt on French fries. Writers favor the term because it encompasses religious as well as nonreligious experiences of awe and transcendence. But the term's inclusivity becomes its undoing for three reasons. First, popular use of *spirituality* varies wildly and incoherently: from stirring experiences born of majestic vistas to penitent fasting to teen séances. Second, the term means little to the overwhelming majority (more than 80 percent) of adolescents and young adults, who struggle to even define it.[25] Third, the term's inclusivity leaves conversations without a place to begin or a method to deepen. In short, amorphous and untethered spirituality engages few people, and in two exploration programs that deployed it in well-intended efforts to be inclusive, it sent students and educators scurrying for the door.

The spirituality that animated this initiative sprang rather from exploration of theological ideas grounded in denominational narratives and traditions. It emerged, in other words, from narratives and practices that were descriptively but not didactically presented. Many assume theological particularism to be the enemy of inclusivity, but it need not be so. Particularism and exclusivism can be separated. What particularism specifies is a speaker or author's point of departure and her or his ultimate destination, but it does not preclude listeners or readers from appreciating the journey with its triumphs, travails, and discoveries. Perhaps an analogy might be helpful. I would never subject myself, for example, to the extreme conditions and inherent dangers that wildlife photographers endure, but that does not make me uninterested in their stories or their photographs—they fascinate me, in fact. Similarly, participants in exploration programs, students and educators alike, might share nothing in common with their campus denomination, yet could find the journeys narrated by denominational figures, with their theologically embedded insights about a life of meaning and purpose, to be quite generative.

That theologically themed narratives engaged diverse campus participants should not surprise us; stories have engaged people across cultures and over time, and theology is quite at home in campus settings. Theology is the scholarly discipline whose study historically launched the university centuries ago,[26] and it offers a robust starting place for conversations about meaning and purpose, which is what it did on the majority of actively or historically church-affiliated campuses that we studied. And since Christian theology comports with the religious preferences of two out of three American undergraduates nationally,[27] Christian theology offers a familiar port from which to launch conversations about purpose and meaning.

The chief obstacle to conversations about purpose and meaning is not their potential inclusion of particularist ideas, but professors, of whom only one in three nationally agrees that "colleges should be concerned with facilitating students' spiritual development."[28] While that represents a high proportion of the faculty, I would suggest it is the *term spiritual development* and not the process of spiritual development that is the true obstacle, since 60 percent to 80 percent of faculty nationally agree that "help[ing] students develop personal values," "develop[ing] moral character," "instill[ing] in students a commitment to community service," and "instill[ing] basic appreciation of the liberal arts" are "very important" or "essential" goals for undergraduate education, and these were the very goals of the exploration programs we studied.[29] Moreover, several scholars of higher education have offered empirical and anecdotal claims about the importance of "passionate thought," about educators' high reflexivity, and about professors' "crises of meaning" following tenure, which further indicates that the terms used to describe purpose exploration, rather than purpose exploration itself, are the primary obstacle.[30]

The significance of contextually appropriate terminology cannot be underestimated. Just as some campuses we studied kept the term *vocation* implicit, so also might some campuses keep the terms *spirituality, theology,* or *religion* implicit.[31] Exploration programs must establish themselves and their leaders must gain the trust of fellow educators, and while that process unfolds, there is no need to alienate potential allies by using terms that some regard as "loaded" and others as "baffling." But do not misunderstand me; I am not suggesting campuses detheologize or despiritualize purpose exploration programming. That would alter the stimuli that produced the positive outcomes documented by this evaluation, and nullify the asset that active, particularistic religious affiliations gave to campuses that possessed them (i.e., supplying places to begin exploration conversations and traditions to help these conversations deepen). Purpose exploration programs will accomplish little if they ban the theological metanarratives that most participants found so generative. What I am suggesting is that some campuses may need to begin with engaging questions, with stories of meaningful journeys by individuals and institutions, and keep theological and spiritual content in descriptive and historical forms. Once conversations about purpose are established and appreciated, more explicit theological and spiritual resources may be introduced.[32]

Engaging undergraduates with ideas of purpose and vocation is efficacious, but readers do not have to take my word for it. Leaders of more than 175 campuses nationwide have authorized payment of annual dues to access resources and training for vocational exploration since the 88-campus initiative ceased.[33] The reasons campuses joined are many, but prominent among them are (1) intuitive understandings of the ever more challenging tasks of attaining adulthood and consequent need to better equip college students, (2) awareness of the beleaguered and dwindling supply of campus good citizens, and (3) the necessity of withstanding market challenges and persuading prospective students of the distinctive benefits that enrollment brings. The next two sections underscore the significance of campus-based exploration of purpose and vocation—in light of lengthening pathways to adulthood and pro-exploration communities that colleges and universities are well suited to host.

Launching Matters

As sociologist Mary Grigsby reports, and this evaluation's interviews confirm, culturally mainstream American youth follow one of two default life trajectories: an individualist trajectory that defines life purpose privately and prioritizes personal intimacy and material consumption, or a traditionalist trajectory that prioritizes assuming responsible roles within families, work, communities, and congregations.[34] There are serious problems, however, with both trajectories. The first is their implicitness; they guide the overall direction of young adults' lives yet receive little explicit or critical attention by young adults or their educators. These are trajectories that youth acquire gradually rather than select intentionally. The second is their declining effectiveness; the secure careers, the long-term intimacy, and robust communities necessary for their attainment grow more elusive. The third is their datedness; lengthening pathways to adulthood and increasingly varied lifestyles are phenomena across the First World, and have been for several decades. Attempting to follow these cultural trajectories leaves too many college graduates "adrift" and "lost in transition," too many on paths that do not satisfy, too many struggling with poor mental health, and too many blaming higher education for insufficient preparation.[35]

Thankfully, hundreds of educators across America have helped college students recalibrate their trajectories, selecting destinations intentionally and recognizing the cultural and economic challenges that impact life around the globe. Their efforts, described in earlier chapters, are encouraging, but more important, they are replicable. College represents an ideal time and place for young adults to understand all that has shaped them thus far, to appreciate the complex world they inhabit, and to forge a life marked by personal resilience, social significance, and lasting satisfaction. Many participants of exploration programs selected an elective trajectory that drew upon their considered strengths and skills, engaged existing communities in a personally sustainable way, and united them with like-minded citizens to renew communities where needed. This section describes default and elective life trajectories, examines their consequences, and recommends purpose exploration as an effective way to help students launch lives that will make a difference and offer the best possible response to higher education's critics.

A life trajectory is a culturally inculcated image of the good life, combined with prescribed actions to attain it. Prophets and philosophers have expounded upon the good life for three millennia, generating a diverse library that has informed and enriched human life. But proportionately few humans spend time in that library, because survival does not afford most that luxury, and because the rest find the default answers of their culture to be satisfactory. Since American young adults attending college have generally met their survival needs,[36] most perceive evidence of the good life among fashionable, affluent, self-made professionals and celebrities, with a substantial minority finding it in the dedicated fathers, loving mothers, heroic firefighters, caring teachers, kindhearted Little League coaches, and faithful congregants of classic Americana (making Norman Rockwell the official illustrator of the traditionalist life trajectory). There are young adults who reject these default trajectories, calibrating interdependent trajectories based on alternative understandings of the good life, but they are relatively few and far between.

That the traditionalist and individualist default trajectories are based on social, economic, and cultural assumptions that no longer hold is a serious problem. Still worse, young adults do not evaluate the assumptions of these trajectories during adolescence or early emerging adulthood, when trajectories are most easily altered. Individualist young adults do not see, for example, how few career paths can supply their trajectory's high consumption expectations, how overconsumption does not produce well-being, or how difficult it is for resolute individualists to maintain lasting, intimate relationships. Traditionalist young adults, similarly, do not recognize that their idealized communities have been undermined by the economic and cultural individualism of global capitalism. So they seek jobs and assume responsibility within communities, oblivious to employers shuttering businesses, to kids opting for Xbox over Little League, to daily commuters with no time to volunteer in the firehouse, and to struggling congregations everywhere except for the megachurch located in the next county over. There are exceptions, to be sure. Some who follow default trajectories will find economic success, intimacy, vibrant communities, and overall well-being. But those exceptions will increasingly prove the rule: neither trajectory reliably delivers the good life it idealizes.

Unexamined life trajectories are not, to adapt Socrates's wisdom, worth following. The two variants of the good life these trajectories idealize are like a choice of blue or green hospital gowns: either one supplies a modicum of social respectability, but neither fits well or offers lasting satisfaction. Moreover, the years and effort that emerging adults devote to the pursuit of these trajectories could be far better deployed. Psychologist Jennifer Tanner reports that emerging adults have the highest risks and rates of poor mental health of any age group, and that college graduates are as susceptible to mental illness as non-college-attending peers.[37] Sociologist Katherine Newman describes "the private toll of global competition" paid by families of emerging adults as households expand and contract like accordions.[38] Sociologist Christian Smith writes of too many emerging adults damaged and wandering far and wide in a search for meaning.[39] Not all agree; developmental psychologist Richard Settersten argues that the years of exploration that characterize emerging adulthood eventually can produce successful and fulfilled adults, who in turn benefit society as a whole.[40] But even if true of some portion of emerging adults, the costs of this portion's success are high and too widely borne.

Engaging college students with questions such as "What makes a life meaningful and significant?" and then introducing them to purpose exploration resources with which to consider those questions, and giving them a firsthand opportunity to use their skills to assist others in need has been a promising and broadly effective intervention. Those who have engaged in serious purpose exploration report positive social engagement and greater life satisfaction. But potential enthusiasts must not underestimate the forces arrayed against such exploration. The macroeconomic and macrocultural changes that have made financial independence elusive and diversified family formation have intensified the status anxieties of late adolescents and young adults, which in turn have undermined willingness to consider larger questions at the ideal moment for their exploration. Most retreat to the manageable distractions of a college student's relatively comfortable life, making broad use of what I have called the "identity lockbox."[41] Proportionately few young adults (20 percent of adolescents, according to Stanford psychologist William Damon[42]) possess a clear sense of purpose that they can draw upon to guide decisions and structure their efforts. Exploration programs worked hard to engage students creatively with big questions, and to generate safe places in which students could consider them.

Since few young adults appreciate the purpose of purpose, or understand the tectonic economic and cultural shifts that have lengthened and complicated the path to adulthood, emerging adult wanderers and their troubled observers frequently blame higher education for insufficiently educating graduates.[43] Colleges and universities should ensure their graduates possess the core skills and knowledge promised during matriculation, and provide broad and nuanced measures of the "value added" of their campus's education. And many are working assiduously to do so. Neither will reverse the lengthening postgraduation transition to adulthood, however, and both will take years to complete. Equally important, and far more achievable, is to systematically address the exit transition of college students. This requires (1) planting seeds, even while recruiting prospective students, about effectively navigating the long slog from graduation to stable employment and productive citizenship; (2) defining one's campus as a place that takes seriously its obligation to effectively prepare students for life; and (3) sowing these seeds throughout the first year of college. It particularly requires (4) a structure and supportive resources for trajectory recalibration and test launching (e.g., internships, service learning) among sophomores and juniors. And it requires (5) attending to the practical aspects of recalibrated trajectories among seniors, within their academic or professional programs as well as in general, so that they can gird themselves for the challenges and inevitable setbacks ahead of them.

Positive psychologists have identified a characteristic that, better than any other predictor, distinguishes successful from unsuccessful individuals across fields and endeavors; they call it "grit." Psychologist Angela Duckworth defines "grit as perseverance and passion for long-term goals"; psychologist Martin Seligman, as "extreme persistence" that is most apparent in "time spent on task."[44] This is important, Seligman reports, because time on task is "malleable." Grit is not genetic nor a feature of certain personality types, in other words, but a product of individual agency. It can therefore be fostered by positive social norms and modeled by supportive communities. Grounded idealism—the combination of intentionality, maturity, and dedication to a

set of short- and long-term ideals observed among alumni of exploration programs—includes a generous helping of grit. But it was grit focused less on
private ends and more on shared ends. Grit that kept chapter 4's Tracy pursuing a life of service despite challenges of obtaining health insurance and living
on a low income, and that modified James's Wall Street ambitions to include
an unrelenting desire to increase opportunities among those who have few—
both here and abroad. Such grit was rooted in a resolute sense of life purpose;
one could call it other-directed grit, purposeful grit, or, given the theism of
most of its articulators, Godly grit.

If there is one thing young adults need in order to endure the long slog, it
is grit. And if there is one thing that young adults should possess if they wish
to make a difference in this world, both now and over the course of their lives,
it is grounded idealism. Perhaps young adults will stumble upon grounded
idealism of their own accord; perhaps they will recognize the high failure rate
of default trajectories sooner rather than later. But the press of everyday life
in our competitive global economy offers scant time for reflection. The ideal
time for young adults to calibrate life trajectories is during their college years,
despite the difficulty of this task due to young adults' powerful status anxieties. College is where intellectual and diagnostic resources are most widely
available, where potential trajectories can be tested, and where mentors and
supportive friends can assist. Intentionally calibrated life trajectories produce
lives that combine challenge, fulfillment, and impact; they produce appreciation for the launching received as a college student; and they represent exhibit A in the defense of colleges' and universities' contributions to society.

Institutions Matter

Social institutions form people; there is no place to hide from that reality.
Ideally, institutional effects should be positive: families should produce well-
adjusted children and youths, schools should produce motivated learners
with broad intellectual skills, congregations should produce members who
demonstrate kindness and integrity, businesses should produce employees
proud of their company and its services, governments should produce citizens committed to democracy and justice. But institutions are not always
healthy, and frequently have effects opposite from those intended. This is not
to deny the role of human agency or the nature of social interaction within

institutions. It is rather to underscore the role social institutions play in meeting societal needs and shaping the behavior and perspectives of their participants.

At a formal level, colleges and universities understand this, as each possesses a mission statement describing the nurture of productive citizens and future leaders as its contribution to the wider social good. And within a framework of social contract theory, the universality of this mission is a good thing. The problem, however, is that most colleges and universities give scant attention to the process by which they accomplish this outcome. The dominant model for fostering students' citizenship and leadership is a supply-side osmosis—admit students, require that they complete a structured set of courses, offer optional activities for their enrichment, hope that they encounter inspirational educators, and expect that these ingredients will combine to form gold (i.e., productive citizens and future leaders). The model is akin to building a deluxe grocery store in order to teach cooking—that somehow its well-stocked shelves, impressive cookbook selection, food demonstrations, and local chef presentations will transform everyone who shops there into an accomplished cook in four years' time. This may produce sufficient cooks to meet advertising and promotional needs, but most students barely nod at the demonstrators as they grab cereal and frozen pizza, visit the bottled-drinks aisle, and make a beeline to the express checkout lane. Supply-side osmosis is an ineffective way to nurture citizens or leaders; campuses must challenge individualistic and traditionalist default trajectories, invite students to calibrate interdependent trajectories of their own, and supply resources to permanently embed their recalibrations.

This book demonstrates that citizenship and leadership are spawned through participation in dynamic communities comprised of positively engaged peers, caring mentors, and thoughtful leadership, and marked by rich conversations. Citizenship and leadership, in other words, are more likely to be discovered in communities than stumbled upon by inquisitive individuals. And while proexploration communities cannot be created ex nihilo, it does not follow that college or university leaders cannot supply the resources and recruit the leadership that facilitates the emergence of such communities. Colleges and universities, as formal organizations that assign members to specific tasks requiring sustained effort and interaction over time, represent fertile soil for community formation. Add the seeds of good questions, supply the shovels of reflective practice, set aside a place and time, and recruit someone with gardening know-how to spearhead the effort—and a lively gardening community will grow. There are costs, to be sure, but nowhere near the $2.5 million invested per campus by the Lilly Endowment to launch this process. Promising paths have been identified in this evaluation, scores of campuses have posted best practices, and exploration-minded educators and scholars have created a variety of valuable resources (see appendix 5).

Rather than hoping for purposeful citizens by osmosis, an effective model initiates programs that draw together campus members and forms pro-exploration communities. There are many components to this process, but particularly important is a supportive senior administrator with a missional mind-set, willingness to (re)direct resources, and a light managerial touch. Senior administrators can recruit gardening leadership teams, present them with an intriguing charge, and make necessary supports available so teams can execute their charges. But senior administrators must themselves remain in the wings or they will alienate that segment of the campus that dislikes them or spawn a cohort of insiders who want access to senior leaders. Some readers may be dismayed by the leading role I assign to senior administrators, wishing for a grassroots movement. Formal organizations are not democracies, however, and new initiatives require resources sooner or later. Campus visit after campus visit made it clear that support by a senior administrator was essential to successful exploration programming and the coalescing of program participants into proexploration campus communities.

Institutions of higher education matter because they are ideal sites for formation of transformative communities, which are in turn effective in helping college students recognize the ill-fitting default trajectories that have guided their lives and recalibrate self-knowing, self-transcending, and interdependent life trajectories. This is not to imply that campus exploration programs or the colleges and universities that housed them were perfect. Not all formed self-sustaining, proexploration communities successfully, and those that did were populated more by idealist students than contingent moralist students (see chapter 4). Still, despite their imperfections, these campus exploration programs began invaluable work among students and educators that continues to this day, and that is being replicated at dozens of colleges and universities beyond the original eighty-eight participating campuses.

Readers Matter

I am patently aware that some readers are not employees of a college or university, and many may be affiliated with colleges and universities that will not implement exploration programs. I am grateful such readers have abided my focus on campus programming, and want to offer implications that educators, those who work with college students directly or in organizations that serve them, parents and extended families of young adults, and funders of higher education should find useful to their settings and tasks. Leading off is the individual efficacy of purpose exploration no matter the readers' location in the life cycle. Questions of purpose or vocation are questions worth continual consideration. Like a healthy diet and regular exercise, they are beneficial regardless of age or context. Appendix 5 includes a bibliography of texts and films prominently used in campus exploration programs; every reader should be able to identify one that merits personal exploration (or re-exploration).

Let me also suggest that readers seek conversation partners as they revisit questions of purpose or vocation. Supportive partners make eating healthy and exercising more enjoyable, and reinforce one's commitment to healthy habits. Likewise, those who read an engaging text together, discuss an engrossing film, or share a service activity can help one renew commitments or encourage a new undertaking. The currents of privatism and materialism run deep in American culture; individual kayakers can fight these currents, but most find their efforts are less tiring when joined by other kayakers. Purposeful living is a countercultural pursuit; finding support for such a way of life is essential if it is to have staying power.

To readers who teach, or plan to do so, I invite you to engage the questions of what makes a meaningful life both in and out of the classroom, and to allow students to engage their religious and spiritual identities when they answer. This may be a rough transition at first, which you can aid by modeling "I" language and particularist but not exclusivist storytelling. Some disciplines, the humanities in particular, will find conversations such as these easier to introduce. But even professional and scientific fields can infuse these themes of purpose or vocation into their courses. Imagine, for example, introductory courses in biology and business that began each class with a three-minute profile of a biologist or business executive who devoted his or her career to the public good, or who augmented a traditional career with regular pro bono work. Or imagine a semester-long seminar on "biology [or business] for the public good." Models for this do exist—just not in wide or frequent supply.

Still other possibilities include community-engaged learning, especially when it draws on higher-level student skills, collaborative programs with student life professionals, and advising that includes ways students can tap campus and community resources to actualize their desire to make a difference. Campuses are ideal sites for exploration of purpose, even if they lack formal gardens for such exploration; wildflowers can be as beautiful as planned gardens, many can thrive under the shade of a single faculty tree, and the sight of them can inspire other instructors to sow seeds of their own. In short, I recommend that instructors be strategic in the design of their courses and class materials, and intentional about mentoring; this will require effort, but it will pay dividends in the form of more students exploring their passions and pursuing lives of significance.

Readers who work with college students outside of classrooms—in student life, residential life, or religious life, or in nonprofit organizations that attract college students—have the advantage of knowing student lives more fully than most faculty, and of encountering students in more natural settings than the classroom. With one-fourth to one-third of students nationally interested in questions of purpose or vocation, part of these readers' privilege is encouraging thoughtful consideration of these questions as they arise in the course of everyday life. Affirm these questions, and do not be afraid to introduce them into conversations either; they are not far from many students' minds. Give particular attention to the programmatic models that appear in appendix 5; many of these can be readily infused into existing programs. Consider also forming a reading or film discussion group with amenable colleagues, drawing from some of the other resources in that appendix or cited in this chapter. And consider inviting classroom educators to join you; there are many who treasure their work with students on every campus, and they would be delighted to participate.

To parents and kin of young adults, understand that young adults' exploration and identification of a sense of purpose is of far greater importance than speedy completion of degree requirements. In my first book, I strongly endorsed a "gap year" following high school, to give teens an opportunity to identify a direction or purpose that would then guide subsequent years. I am even more convinced of the value of a gap year, of participation in campus-based purpose exploration programming, and of off-campus experiential learning. Internships, study abroad, short- and long-term service programs, and even dropping out of college for a semester or year to work, travel, or serve can be invaluable in young adults' crucial tasks of calibrating life trajectories. When young adults seek these as part of an intentional process of discovery, I encourage parents and extended families to offer the fullest support possible. A few months or even a year's "delay" during college can save years of wandering and costly pursuits afterward.

Trajectories are profoundly shaped by parents and families—often unconsciously but sometimes intentionally—and their calibration begins well before the start of young adulthood. For parents of school-age children and teens interested in these matters, I recommend William Damon's *Path to Purpose* and Richard Lerner's *The Good Teen* as outstanding resources for helping children and teens forge a sense of purpose.[45] I also advise parents and families seek out the support of community partners in this important work—be those partners civic associations, arts organizations, sporting associations, service agencies, or congregations—and to nudge as necessary these community partners toward issues of mentoring children and youth's sense of purpose. Finally, I advise parents and extended families to not assume that good grades and admission to college signify a sense of purpose that will guide the rest of a young adult's life. Those may signify little more than inculcation of an individualist or traditionalist life trajectory that will leave young adults spending much of their twenties attempting to follow a trajectory that will ultimately fail. Good grades and admission to college are relatively easy to come by; a well-honed sense of purpose, intentionality, and resilience are not—and these are the traits that separate lives of significance and deep satisfaction from lives of self-absorption and resignation.

To readers who fund higher education, and particularly those employed in philanthropic organizations, I suggest that one will enjoy broader and more sustained impact when recipients buy into strategic questions than when they are required to implement foreign methods or models. Strategic grant making dominates much of the philanthropic world, and in theory, I have no objection to it. Its practice is what causes much consternation. Educational historian Diane Ravitch excoriates several of America's largest foundations in her book *The Death and Life of the Great American School System*,[46] for dictating the design and methods of educational initiatives that they funded. Ignoring the skills and insights of educators "on the ground" in school systems around the country, these foundations forced innovations in public school systems that not only failed, but for which the foundations themselves had no public accountability. By contrast, this initiative of the Lilly Endowment strategically identified three questions, and encouraged applicants to be creative and experimental in their programmatic efforts to answer these questions. The results could not differ more: wide ownership of the questions, postgrant continuation of programs, and an ever-widening pool of interest on campuses across the nation. This is but one philanthropic case, but it is a significant one, and deserves close consideration by program officers across the philanthropic world.

Grounded Idealism

I have argued previously that a new epistemology hangs two questions over the lectern of every college professor: "So what?" and "Who care?"[47] Invisible to instructors, these questions appear like blinking neon signs to students who know they can locate dozens of experts to disagree with any statement of fact, and who view truth claims as nothing more than opinions held by many or few. This folk theory of knowing, with roots in American pragmatism and anti-intellectualism, pervades popular American culture. But its blunt questions reveal something else, something embedded in the existence and repetition of these questions: Americans yearn for truths that matter, truths that are worth caring about. And this yearning, I suggest, is what makes the idea of purpose so appealing to so many.

Since few instructors appreciate this popular epistemology, they assume students' regurgitation of facts and claims signifies acquisition of knowledge and intellectual skills, and as long as these instructors' grading distributions please students, they will hear nary a complaint. To alter this educational détente requires honest engagement with this epistemology's signature questions—"So what?" and "Who cares?" Master teachers engage these questions regularly, and Future Intelligentsia find that the answering of them can become addictive. This is good as far as it goes, but it amounts to nibbling around the edges of the problem. Students need a compelling reason to deeply engage their studies, educators need a powerful justification to pull the rug out from under teaching-as-usual, but neither have found the present array of intellectual or normative appeals sufficient.

To alter the business-as-usual of American higher education requires a different approach. It requires looking to old as well as new ideas, and to practices past and present. Among the past practices is purposeful education, and among the old ideas is the notion that life has purpose—education in other words, that engages the heart. Others have made this argument before; my contribution is that it works, that it inspires students and educators deeply and equally, and that it is effective on a wide variety of campuses. Higher education can and should call on purpose. That puts me, along with hundreds of college educators who have observed the powerful effects of educating with and about purpose, among higher education's grounded idealists. We are a guardedly optimistic group, but we welcome newcomers. I hope you will join us.

List of Participating Institutions
in the Lilly Endowment Inc.'s Programs
for the Theological Exploration of
Vocation Initiative, 2000-2009

Alma College

Asbury College

Augsburg College

Augustana College

Austin College

Azusa Pacific University

Baylor University

Bluffton University

Boston College

Butler University

Calvin College

Cardinal Stritch University

Catawba College

Claflin University

College of Saint Benedict

College of the Holy Cross

College of Wooster

Concordia College

Covenant College

Creighton University

Davidson College

Denison University

Dillard University

Dordt College

Duke University

Earlham College

Eastern Mennonite University

Elmhurst College

Evangel University

Fairfield University

Furman University

Geneva College

Georgetown College

Gordon College

Goshen College

Grinnell College

Guilford College

Gustavus Adolphus College

Hamline University

Hanover College

Hastings College

Hellenic College

Hendrix College

Hope College

Howard University

Indiana Wesleyan University

Lee University

Loyola University Chicago

Luther College

Macalester College

Manchester College

Marian College

Marquette University

Maryville College

Mercer University

Messiah College

Milligan College

Millsaps College

Mount St. Mary's University

Northwestern College

Occidental College

Ohio Wesleyan University

Our Lady of the Lake University

Pacific Lutheran University

Pepperdine University

Saint Bonaventure University

Saint John's University

Saint Louis University

Saint Norbert College

Saint Olaf College

Samford University

Santa Clara University

Seattle Pacific University

Seton Hall University

Simpson College

Spelman College

Transylvania University

University of Dayton

University of Indianapolis

University of Notre Dame

University of St. Thomas

University of the South

Valparaiso University

Wake Forest University

Wartburg College

Whitworth College

Willamette University

Xavier University of Louisiana

Methodology

This evaluation studied purpose exploration programs on twenty-six campuses located across the United States, via multiday site visits to twenty-four campuses conducted by individual ethnographers or ethnographic research teams. In addition to field notes, site visits included 284 audio-recorded interviews with current and former students and 274 audio-recorded interviews with faculty and staff members. Most interviews occurred in focus groups, but many took place singly in face-to-face interviews, and some had to be arranged telephonically. Sixty students who were interviewed individually were invited to participate in follow-up telephone interviews about one year after they graduated from college, of which 59 were successfully reinterviewed. For the sake of comparison, 65 students from campuses that did not receive grants were interviewed singly, of which 64 were successfully reinterviewed via telephone about one year after graduating from college. The field and interview data combined provided the requisite background to generate a web-based survey about campus-based exploration programming. This survey was implemented on nine campuses, and garnered responses from 2,111 students, alumni, faculty, and staff participants in exploration programs. In this appendix I present details about these data sources, within the context of the process by which the evaluation unfolded, and alongside reflections on the methodological and project management lessons learned.

An Iterative Process

Exploratory, qualitative research is inherently iterative, and this evaluation was no exception. I was invited to undertake this evaluation project because I was an outsider to these campuses and this Lilly Endowment initiative, and because I had an active scholarly interest in young adults, higher education, and American religion. External evaluation is best, but it should be built into a program from the outset (which the endowment encouraged at the campus program level, but did not pursue at the broader initiative level until it approached me in 2005; see chapter 2), and must allow extra time for the evaluator to gain a working knowledge of the program to be studied. The endowment's Programs for the Theological Exploration of Vocation (PTEV) was a large and varied initiative, far more so than I realized even after attending a convening of all eighty-eight project directors and doing pilot site visits. I thus misdesigned my initial methods, though it took time to realize that.

From a strategic philanthropy standpoint, the initiative's strength was its encouragement of creativity and experimentation in campus efforts to engage students and their mentors in exploration of purpose and vocation, and in its express avoidance of prescribing methods (see chapter 3). But that creativity made for wide program variance, on campuses that themselves varied widely. For example, North Carolina's five participating campuses included Catawba College, a liberals arts institution of 1,300 undergraduates affiliated with the United Church of Christ; Davidson College, an elite liberal arts institution of 1,700 undergraduates affiliated with the Presbyterian Church of the USA; Duke University, a world-class research institution serving 6,500 undergraduates and 8,200 graduate or professional students, affiliated with the United Methodist Church; Guilford College, a respected institution serving 2,600 undergraduates, split between traditional-age and adult learners, and affiliated with the Quaker tradition; and Wake Forest University, a rising national institution serving 4,400 undergraduates and 2,400 professional students, historically affiliated with the Baptist Church. These colleges and universities are a disparate set, and still they lack representation of Roman Catholic, evangelical, or ethnic-serving campuses. Had I restricted myself to twelve campuses, as initially planned, I would not have captured sufficient campus, program, and religious variation. I increased my sample size instead.

At the same time, repeated site visits, which I initially intended, did not fit the recalibration and destination-altering effects of purpose exploration. Inviting exploration of purpose is like pointing out a scenic byway not printed on a traveler's map, which leads to both original and alternate destinations, and not like acquisition of a skill, such as learning a foreign language. Repeated visits to campus would capture incremental skill acquisition, but were ineffective when the phenomenon was more or less bivariate: one either knows and uses the scenic byway, or does not know or care about it. Since a primary focus of this evaluation was student impact, and since most student participants indicated that the chief arena of purpose exploration was their postcollege plans, I ceased follow-up visits to campuses and began follow-up interviews with students one year after they graduated. Before making this switch final, I did conduct follow-up visits to four campuses, gaining insight into the ongoing adaptation and routinization of exploration programming, but little else. Follow-up conversations with project directors were just as helpful, and these were just as effectively carried out on the phone or in a separate location.

Site and Respondent Selection

I began my evaluation by devising a typology of campus religious affiliations, and intersecting that with a typology of perceived programmatic quality. This was not hard, but assigning campuses onto this grid was a more fluid process than anticipated. The line between actively affiliated mainline Protestant campuses and virtually unaffiliated campuses can be blurry, as representatives from the same campus will disagree about the prominence of its religious affiliation. There was also a gap between the view insiders gave me of programs' quality and what we found when we hit the ground: some programs had project directors with strong communication skills and so-so programs; others had great programs with soft-spoken project directors. Still, this starting classification schema offered a place to begin, and helped me select campuses that would represent the full range of these programs. I did not choose campuses at random, though at times I would roll a die to choose within a particular category. But selection of one campus sometimes put us within a two-hour drive of another campus, so I would schedule two site visits per trip when possible. What I lost in random probability I gained in sample size, which is generally not an ideal trade but it enabled us to observe sufficient campus and program variation, which was essential (see appendix 4).

Given the busyness of campuses when classes are in session, and the just restrictions of research ethics, I notified sites of our desire to visit them and requested their assistance in arranging appointments and meeting rooms. How project directors responded to this initial request was, in retrospect, fairly well correlated with the quality of their programs; those who responded immediately and enthusiastically had effective programs that they were eager to show off, those who responded more slowly had programs of moderate impact, and those who required follow-up efforts before responding had programs of narrower impact. Concurrent with these requests, my evaluation team pulled together a comprehensive file for each selected campus — including public statistics and related information about the campus, copies of its program proposals and annual reports, letters from external consultants that were copied to the endowment and coordination offices, postings by the program to the coordination office website, notes from presentations by the program at coordination office conferences, and program website materials. By the time my evaluation team reached what qualitative researchers call the saturation point, we had identified twenty-six campuses for visits, assembled twenty-six program dossiers, and visited twenty-four campuses (with three campuses visited twice and one campus visited three times).

That means there was one campus that did not cooperate with our visit request, and one that we studied telephonically (see below). The uncooperative campus took a passive approach at first, not replying to e-mails and phone messages. I received a response only after contacting a campus executive, who required proof that the Lilly Endowment had authorized this evaluation (though a general letter to this effect was sent to all programs, and I was introduced at the initiative's final conference — which this executive attended). I was then given information about submitting the evaluation to the school's Institutional Review Board, where the project director's "friend" —

who chaired the review board — demanded ridiculous changes to the evaluation protocol that would have hopelessly compromised data collection (for
example, he wanted me to submit my interview questions to interviewees *in
advance,* so they could "prepare" their answers). Rather than conduct a compromised evaluation visit, I withdrew my visit request. From the program
dossier, I determined that this campus used its grant monies to renovate its
chapel (hoping that a more attractive space would improve student usage
and thus students' explorations of purpose and vocation), host a conference
featuring internationally prominent figures (organized around an exploration
theme, but with few student registrants), and develop a residential program
for ten exploration-interested students (which took several years to effect).
In short, this program's accomplishments benefitted few students and no faculty or staff (except for its project director). It was not surprising that college
officials labored to keep me out. While I found this frustrating, one out of
twenty-six is a low refusal rate (4 percent).

There was a second campus that we visited telephonically. This visit came
about because one of my coethnographers had been regaled at one site visit
with stories of a "battle" between the chaplain's office and the exploration
program staff on another campus. We had not planned to visit this other
campus, and had sufficient representation from its cell in our selection grid,
but I thought it wise to create a program dossier and have phone conversations with several parties to get firsthand information. There was a conflict between a member of the chapel staff and the exploration project director, and a communication issue between the project director and the grants
office, which resulted in no sustainability award. Given what we learned over
the phone, I decided a campus visit would not be an effective use of evaluation resources or campus members' time. Several years later (after my travel
monies were depleted), I acquired evidence that a full-fledged exploration
program had been put into place at this campus, overseen by the same project director, to which the (new) chapel staff now reported. Several issues
hindered this exploration program, but its project director's persistence was
clearly not among them.

At the twenty-four campuses we visited, I did my best to assist project
directors in arranging our visit schedule by providing an outline of the persons, events, and activities we hoped to observe during our visit, and reviewing this outline over the phone. I asked for opening and closing conversations

with the project director, individual conversations with all other exploration program staff, a conversation with a senior administrator most familiar with the exploration program, a conversation with the on-site program evaluator, and a conversation with a tenured social science faculty member to discuss the general campus and student culture. I asked project directors to arrange separate focus group interviews with students, faculty, and staff and individual interviews with students. I asked project directors to arrange for us to observe grant programs, events, or affiliated courses; to supply contact information for several recent alumni who had participated in the vocation program; and to provide contact information for anyone who might not have been able to meet with us during our visit because of prior commitments or illness. I asked project directors to preserve open times during our visit as well, so that we could schedule conversations and interviews of our own. And finally, I asked project directors to send copies of all on-site evaluation reports and other printed or digital materials used in their programs. This was a demanding request, and the gift certificate I sent after our visit was far from sufficient for the scheduling and information-assembling work we asked of these project directors.

The structure of this request helped ensure that we would see as much of the program as possible and talk to as wide a range of participants and local informants as possible. It also gave project directors the opportunity to put their "best foot forward," and they made concerted efforts to do so. I was concerned that this would undermine the representativeness of the data we were collecting. But to be honest, it was not hard to uncover the real story. The key to acquiring it was (1) paying as much attention to what was omitted as to what was said or shown, (2) probing for specifics, (3) promising confidentiality at the start of focus group interviews, and (4) clarifying to all that this evaluation would not result in a campus-specific report that "took money away" but rather was national in its focus.

So when one site visit included four enthusiastic focus groups with students and one bland faculty focus group marked by late arrivals and early departures, for example, it was clear that the program had successful student programs and tepid faculty engagement. Or when a provost answered our opening question with a twenty-minute continuous reply that was breathless, energetic, supplied story after story and statistic after statistic—it was clear that grant's impact was having a campus-wide effect. And when students went "Huh?" when I mentioned one exploration center program, but were interrupting one another to tell me about their experience in another, staying afterward to talk further with me and e-mailing still more comments to me — it was clear the first program had failed to reach many students while the second was wildly successful.

I was struck, in short, by the helpfulness of focus group interviews in uncovering what was and was not happening with respect to purpose exploration on a given campus. There were some, usually comprised of staff, that featured big claims and little supporting evidence. But staff are the most organizationally vulnerable members of a college or university — so they are wise to be circumspect, especially when management is in the room. The presence of a boss usually undermined the usefulness of staff focus groups. This was less true when focus groups included staff of similar statuses; those focus groups were as helpful as ones with faculty or students — and may have been most enjoyed by participants because of the camaraderie they elicited.

Our focus group interviews with faculty were almost always insightful, blunt, and thoughtful, and our focus group interviews with students were almost always infused with passion and joy. The exceptions were faculty members with a pet project to protect, and campuses whose programs touched students indirectly (i.e., that focused on faculty development and thus effects on students were diffused). Most faculty focus groups seemed to tap their participants' love of talking, complaining, and thinking out loud — making these interviews quite revealing. And most student focus group interviews, thanks to students' general obliviousness to all things administrative and organizational, made us feel as if we were entering a parallel universe — as august professors were hilariously spoofed, soft-spoken staff members praised for their compassion, and project directors both critiqued and appreciated. Focus group interviews, when conducted in confidence among equals, revealed the "real story" better than a full day of official conversations and observations. Speaking in front of one's peers not only filters out a lot of "spin," but it also supplies the context that puts official information and events into perspective. I recommend focus group interviews to researchers planning to evaluate campus programming; they are efficient and effective ways to explore claims and acquire context.

I should note that we paid focus group interviewees and in-depth interviewees a modest sum in appreciation for their time, and explicitly asked the project directors to relay that information to potential interviewees as they arranged our interviews. Most project directors did so, though a couple did not (see chapter 4). I did this partly because everyone's time is valuable, it honors the gift that participants' time represents, and doing so increases the response rate, especially of those who may be less self-motivated to participate in evaluation research. Student participants would often express how much they appreciated these payments, confirming payments' usefulness in attracting participants. We did not hear this from faculty and staff participants; but we never had one refuse payment, so these incentives may have been just as useful in encouraging participation among faculty and staff as among students. Focus group participants received fifteen dollars, and first-wave in-depth interviewees each received forty dollars (see discussion of second-wave in-depth interviews below).

Aside from offering payments to improve representativeness of participants, we augmented the prearranged schedule with conversations and interviews of our own. The former was more common, as it was easier to stop by during a faculty member's office hours, visit a staff member's office, or approach students in the quad, dining hall, or student center to answer a "couple of quick questions" than it was to align the openings in our schedule with openings in a potential interviewee's schedule. The latter did happen, just not as often as we hoped. Still, even brief conversations were illuminating—conveying the perspectives of nonparticipants in exploration programs as well as the perspectives of participants who were not tapped (or could not attend) the scheduled interviews. These conversations helped us check both "hunches" and official claims, confirming claims about campus awareness as well as our doubts about unsupported claims. The same was true of follow-up phone interviews with alumni, who, despite being selected for follow-up by the project directors, were geographically distant and felt quite free to evaluate the strengths and weaknesses of their campus's exploration program.

On Sample Bias and Sample Selection

None of the foregoing eliminates the methodological charge of sample bias. I acknowledge that not all student, faculty, or staff participants in exploration programs may be as enthusiastic or as deeply impacted as those we studied, despite concerted efforts to augment this project's respondent pool. But this bias was inconsequential—as we had no trouble learning about short-comings, gaps, misses, and frustrations from the 558 student, faculty, or staff participants whom we formally interviewed on twenty-four campuses (an average of 23 per campus), or divining the same from the 2,111 respondents to a web survey implemented on nine campuses (an average of 235 per campus). I have worked eighteen years at my current institution, but I would be hard-pressed to recruit 23 students, faculty, or staff to talk enthusiastically about any topic during two consecutive business days, much less enthusiastically about a single topic, nor could I cajole 235 campus participants to complete a web survey from 235 unique Internet protocol (IP) addresses (see web survey discussion below). As charming as these project directors might have been, the rates of participation alone speak to genuine enthusiasm and appreciation among participants.

Related to sample bias is the issue of self-selection. One could argue that the positive impact of exploration programs demonstrated herein is attributable to exploration-minded individuals self-selecting into these programs, which is a claim I cannot disprove. But this volume's claims do not reside in the capacity of these programs to "convert" generic members of a campus population into purposeful grounded idealists (though that did occur sometimes). My claims lie rather in the positive effect that supplying quality exploration programs can have on students, educators, and campuses in general. I take as a starting point that there is a baseline interest in questions of purpose and vocation among a minority of students and educators, which research by Alexander W. Astin, Helen S. Astin, and Jennifer A. Lindholm demonstrates to be between one-fourth and one-third of college students nationally.[1] But no amount of baseline interest in these questions can create $2.5 million of exploration programming on campuses that lack such programs, nor does self-selection undermine the value of a program. A program's value is gauged by participants' self-reports and by comparisons of participants with nonparticipants, both of which this evaluation employed. What self-selection restricts is overgeneralizing a program's value or impact, which I respect by noting—repeatedly—the less than comprehensive appeal of exploration programming.

An analogy may be helpful. The Juilliard School has an international reputation for training outstanding creative performers. Yet Juilliard is marked by powerful selection effects: only the most talented high school performers apply and gain admission. Those selection effects do not negate the education Juilliard provides; what they do is prevent Juilliard from claiming that it can take any high school graduate and transform that person into an internationally acclaimed performer. Juilliard does not claim such educative impact, of course; it states that its mission is to "provide the highest caliber artistic education" to the "gifted" students it enrolls from around the world. In a similar way, the impact of campus-based exploration programs will be limited to those interested in exploring questions of purpose and vocation, using the resources supplied by a given campus's exploration program. That appears to be a sizable minority of most campus populations, and a majority of some campus populations; interest is these matters is distributed more widely than artistic giftedness, but nonetheless does not include all or even most members of most campus populations.

Panel and Comparison Interviews

To gauge the "real-world" impact of student participation in purpose exploration programs, I added two elements to my original evaluation design. First, I converted in-depth interviews to panel interviews, reaching out to all sixty of my in-depth interviewees one year after they graduated from college. (Thankfully, I had indicated the possibility of follow-up interviews on the informed-consent form that each interviewee received and signed, so this was not a surprise to the interviewees.) And thanks to an extraordinary follow-up interview team, we successfully completed forty-minute telephone interviews with fifty-nine of our sixty original interviewees (see discussion below). Second, I added comparison interviews, conducting ninety-minute, face-to-face, in-depth interviews with sixty-five students enrolled on campuses that did not have exploration programs. Interviews with nonparticipating students on campuses that had exploration programs would have been ideal, since they would have attended the same campus as participants, eliminating campus variation differences. My initial evaluation proposal drafts included a substantial budget request to that end. Unfortunately, that request could not be supported by the Lilly Endowment, so I conducted comparison interviews using alternative resources on ten reasonably similar campuses: a Roman Catholic university, a mainline Protestant liberal arts college, a mainline Protestant university, three evangelical colleges, an elite nonsectarian private university, a public college, and two public research universities. In most cases, knowledgeable insiders recruited participants for these interviews, distributing informational flyers that indicated forty-dollar honorariums. Some of these insiders were instructors, some were graduate students, and some were staff employees. Though imperfect comparisons, the range of campuses, the mix of insider selection and respondent self-selection, and the parallel timing of these interviews supplied interviewees whose responses were quite analytically helpful. And thanks again to my extraordinary follow-up interview team, we completed forty-minute follow-up interviews with sixty-four of the original sixty-five interviewees when they were about one year beyond their college graduations.

The extraordinary second-wave retention rate of 98 percent was a product of three factors: continued participation by my two site ethnographer colleagues, so that many interviewees were reinterviewed by the same person; an outstanding project manager and research associate who deployed the full range of social media to reach interviewees and convince them to participate (see below); and follow-up honorariums that began at sixty dollars and increased by twenty-dollar increments (with a maximum of one hundred dollars) to encourage participation. The vast majority of our interviewees agreed to our follow-up requests readily (some even contacted us first!); the few who agreed only after we increased the honorarium fell into two clusters — those who were extremely busy with their careers or graduate education (e.g., medical school students), and those who seemed to be embarrassed by their lack of professional accomplishment (despite the easy explanation of the Great Recession).

I chose to make the project's follow-up interviews forty minutes long and conduct them over the telephone for three reasons. First, the initial interviews captured background information about the interviewee's family, social origins, and education that we did not need to repeat. Asking interviewees to "bring us up to date" on their lives since we last spoke with them, with follow-up prompts to ensure they covered all the areas we were interested in (e.g., changes to health, family), gave us a broad update on our interviewees that was organized and expressed in their own words. Second, conducting interviews via phone was far less costly than traveling to conduct interviews, and far more convenient, though we did have to be flexible regarding our time availability. Third, having conducted forty-minute telephone interviews for another project, I knew them to be long enough to convey the importance of the interview without being unduly burdensome, and sufficient to get a broad sense along with considerable detail about the matters we wished to understand. A few interviews went longer, but only by the interviewees' own agreement, and most lasted about thirty-five minutes. It might be interesting for future interviewers to split follow-up interviews between face-to-face and telephone, and evaluate what difference it has on the quality of data collected with more precision. I am convinced of the efficacy of these telephone interviews, however, and their efficiency speaks for itself.

All interviewees received informed-consent forms before each interview, and all interviews were audio-recorded using two recorders. The two-recorder approach turned out to be one of our wisest strategies, as recording problems or postrecording mishaps affected 5 percent to 10 percent of all interviews, but only one interview simultaneously (which we recaptured the next day thanks to the interviewee's gracious accommodation). With the audio-recording applications now available on most smartphones, some of which can immediately copy recordings to remote servers, future researchers can readily deploy a digital recorder and a smartphone to create two high-quality audio recordings, and make technological redundancy a standard ethnographic practice. It is a simple way to eliminate virtually all data loss.

Ethnographers, Interviewers, and Analysis

It was a pleasant change from previous research projects to have ample financial resources. Those resources enabled me to hire outstanding ethnographers, professional research transcriptionists, research assistants, and (eventually) a project manager, as well as supply the requisite technology and analytical tools. I could not have been more pleased with the professionalism of the team I was able to hire, and the only thing I would do differently in a future project of this size is budget for a project manager from the outset — as the travel, correspondence, paperwork, and data collected required far more oversight than I had anticipated. Thankfully, a budget surplus enabled me to hire an outstanding project manager and research associate for fifteen months during the third and fourth years of this evaluation project. But the effect of my underestimating the management demands was a two-year delay in the completion of this project.

To make sure the coethnographers—Keith Brown, Anna Bradshaw, and I—approached site visits with similar eyes and ears, I had them read preparatory documents and studies, then spend four days with me conducting a joint site visit. We did focus group interviews, conducted in-depth interviews, observed classes, and had conversations with numerous site personnel—with me conducting these during the first day and coethnographers assisting, then switching those roles on the second and third days. We ate dinner together each night to debrief, then returned to the hotel to write field notes. On the fourth day, we discussed field notes and finalized the research protocol that would guide future site visits. This was a highly useful process, because spending so many hours side by side allowed us to discuss a myriad of matters both small and large, and because both coethnographers were brilliant individuals who alerted me to things that I might not have seen otherwise.

The joint site visit jump-started this project's data collection, and during the next few months we conducted site visits on our own, keeping in regular conversation about not only the "nitty-gritty" details but also sharing analytic reflections on processes at work and hunches that merited exploring. Some of our conversations were face-to-face at meeting points in the mid-Atlantic, some were over the phone, and some were via e-mail. My regard for my co-investigators doubled during this project, and I am grateful for the many inconveniences they patiently endured—from winter storms that wreaked havoc on flight schedules to sixteen-hour site visit days to reimbursement checks that got lost in the mail. The paychecks these coinvestigators received were insufficient for the dedication they gave to the project.

Equally dedicated were two professional research transcriptionists, who efficiently turned around audio recordings and took particular care to attribute the proper statement to the right person in focus group interviews. These transcripts were then double-checked by a small corps of undergraduate research assistants along with the project manager. This process confirmed the high quality of these transcripts to begin with, but was nonetheless essential because these transcripts became the backbone of this project's data. The most common errors involved organizational names and acronyms, with scholarly jargon running second. A student interviewee, for example, might mention receiving information through the campus mail, referring to the mail room by its nickname, *C-PO*, which was transcribed as "See Po (?)." Or a professor might mention a German philosopher whose name was rendered as "High Digger (?)." The transcriptionists alerted us by the addition of question marks, which my research assistants could usually correct independently, checking with me or the coethnographer as necessary. The project manager and I then read every cleaned transcript, spot-checking occasionally, which provided an additional layer of quality control.

Since I teach at a primarily undergraduate college, with no graduate program in sociology, I hired and oversaw small cohorts of undergraduates to do transcript cleaning, coding, and on several occasions join me during site visits to assist in field observations. Undergraduates do not possess the same analytical skills as graduate students — but they make up for that with enthusiasm about research, which, combined with their willingness to learn, made them essential contributors to this project. The majority of these research assistants have now gone on to graduate school, two are enrolled in PhD programs, and several have attained graduate research assistantships partly as a result of their experience with this project. Analytically, I found their contributions to be limited at the meso- and macrosociological level — but was impressed by their capacity to generate thoughtful interpretations of individual respondents' stories, and I intend to ask future undergraduate assistants to do even more at the individual level of analysis. I encourage future researchers to explore this individual-level analytic potential among their undergraduate assistants.

Interview transcriptions, field notes, program dossiers, and research assistants' interpretive essays were incorporated into Atlas.ti, which is qualitative analysis software. It is not the most user-friendly application, however, so I contracted with experts at ResearchTalk Inc. to offer a training seminar and provide software support during this project. They helped us appreciate the value of a limited code pool, of coding meaningful units of text, and of best practices in categorizing documents and generating analytic reports. With this training, I put undergraduate research assistants to work coding these documents — not the most thrilling research assignment, but an essential one (and counterbalanced by reflective journals I asked them to keep during the process, which drew my attention to a number of remarkable results). Both my project manager and I did coding as well, and also spot-checked assistants' codes to ensure their accuracy. Once the text was coded for content, Atlas.ti gave me a range of tools that allowed me to generate categories, contrast information across various categories, look within a category to identify patterns, and attach analytic memos to documents or categories as appropriate. I did the lion's share of analytical work with Atlas.ti, but my project manager was quite helpful in sorting individuals and programs into the typologies I generated.

I would be remiss if I did not relay the success of my postbaccalaureate appointment—which is a postundergraduate parallel to a postdoctorate. This was the fifteen-month project manager and research associate position that I created from a budget surplus, which I offered to my most outstanding undergraduate research assistant, Patricia Tevington. This young woman, now a PhD student in sociology at the University of Pennsylvania, had been my undergraduate research assistant for two years, so I was confident she would make an excellent assistant. The fifteen-month position I offered provided her with full-time employment from her May graduation through the following summer, and helped her decide that graduate study in sociology was the right choice for her. Given what we know about emerging adulthood today, and the competitiveness of graduate school admissions, a postbaccalaureate would be an appealing position for a new college graduate. It offers an apprenticeship in research that is intellectually stimulating, pays no worse than most entry-level jobs, offers pleasant working conditions, strategically positions the candidate for a graduate school assistantship, yet offers an easy exit should the candidate decide a scholarly career is not of interest. Should I ever conduct a project of this magnitude again, I will not only hire a project manager from the beginning, I will also embed into the project several postbaccalaureate appointments. I recommend that researchers with access to similarly talented undergraduate students do likewise; the quality of work that one will receive combined with the joy of mentoring make this a win-win proposition.

Web Survey

Some project directors told me the widely varied foci and activities of campus programs would make a single quantitative evaluation instrument impossible to create. In the beginning, I was tempted to agree with them. Campus programs did seem like "apples and oranges," and it was hard to see how a single instrument could span the programmatic variety we kept encountering. At the same time, we met site evaluators at each campus, some of whom were doing impressive quantitative work tracking participants' change over time. They graciously shared their instruments with us, and while these instruments were specific to their campus programs, in them I discovered the seeds of this evaluation's web survey.

The key breakthrough came when I focused on the self-reported value of participation and general outcomes. For students, that meant asking about their familiarity with ideas such as purpose and vocation prior to their enrollment, about the helpfulness of those ideas, and about their personal appropriation of these ideas generally and specifically (i.e., identifying skills and talents, seeing and serving the needs of others, altering one's life plans, serving the church, considering a ministry career). It also meant asking respondents about the prevalence of exploration language among students in general, and about the helpfulness of exploration conversations with one's faculty or staff adviser. There were open-ended response options in several places, including ones about recommended program changes and general comments, and finally a series of demographic and education questions. I repeated these same items for alumni, adjusting the tense to reflect that their participation had occurred during college, adding only two items—one asking whether the alum has had time to use purpose exploration skills since graduating, the other asking if the alum has drawn upon these skills in making decisions (see appendix 3, "Interview and Survey Questions," for the precise questions and survey sequence).

For faculty and staff, the survey questions went in a different direction. I asked if the campus's purpose exploration program "positively impacted" the employee's own work at the college or university; if it helped hone his or her individual sense of purpose or vocation; if it deepened the employee's appreciation for the mission of his or her college or university; if it positively impacted his or her department; if it was positively or negatively perceived by faculty in general; if it was positively or negatively perceived by staff in general; if it had made an impact on the campus as a whole; if the impact of the exploration program would persist after grant funding expired; and if the employee believed the exploration program encouraged preclergy students. I also asked faculty and staff respondents if the programs had improved advising and mentoring generally, if they were themselves student advisers or mentors, if they ever talked about issues of purpose or vocation with students whom they advised or mentored, and if engaging those concepts helped the faculty or staff respondent "move advising/mentoring conversations into deeper and more important matters." I closed by asking all respondents a series of demographic and education/employment questions.

I had several initiative insiders as well as a couple of survey experts review the instrument, and after making revisions, implemented the survey at one campus to start. I did this as follows: I contacted the project director and requested permission to conduct a web survey of the campus's students, alumni, faculty, and staff participants. The project director's role was to serve as liaison to his or her campus's Institutional Review Board (IRB); then, after obtaining its approval, to e-mail a letter of invitation with an embedded web survey link to as wide a pool of students, alumni, faculty, and staff participants as possible; and to e-mail a reminder message at one and two weeks after sending the initial invitation. To assist the project director, I supplied a sample invitation message and reminder message. And to improve participation rates, I promised a two-dollar donation per respondent to one of four charitable organizations (the American Cancer Society, American Red Cross, United Nation's Children's Fund, or World Vision), which the respondent could indicate at the end of the survey.

Based on feedback from the initial site survey, I added questions to allow future respondents to be more precise in the identification of their own religious and spiritual affiliations and practices, then (slowly) gained permission to implement the survey on eight more campuses. The web survey host provider, Survey Monkey, offered several features worth noting. First, it allowed only one survey response per IP address—which prevented a single individual from using the same computer to complete the survey multiple times. That meant a few married employees could not use their home computer for both survey submissions—but an easy workaround was for one spouse to use his or her work computer. Second, Survey Monkey offered an upgrade to a secure connection (similar to those used when making online credit card transactions), which I purchased because it ensured respondents' data would remain confidential. Third, it allowed me to track completion patterns, which would rise sharply for the first twelve hours after an e-mail invitation or reminder was sent, plateau for a day or so, then drop off substantially. From prior survey experience, I know that one invitation with two follow-ups is most efficacious; the first invitation produces the greatest number of responses, followed by the second, and trailed by the third. That the responses followed this pattern supports, though it does not prove, that 2,111 unique individuals completed the survey.

Web surveys are, by basic design, nonrandom. One cannot be certain who is completing a web survey—the intended target, his friend, her mother, or an insecure program director hopping from seat to seat in a campus computer lab (to get around the unique-IP-address restriction). Nor did I send the invitations myself, so I cannot calculate a response rate. These 2,111 responses are representative of no one other than the 2,111 individuals who completed them. At the same time, the opinions of 2,111 individuals are not inconsequential. (Had all of them voted for the Democratic presidential nominee in the state of Florida on November 7, 2000, for example, Albert Gore Jr. would have been elected president of the United States over George W. Bush, winning Florida by 327 votes rather than losing it by 1,784 votes.) College students, recent alumni, faculty, and professional staff are busy people who receive dozens of requests for their time each month; that they chose to respond—often writing in extensive optional comments—speaks volumes about the importance they ascribe to their participation in exploration programs. As for fraudulent responses, I have no doubt that there are some among the 2,111—but I doubt they comprise more than a fraction of the total, and would do little to alter participants' overwhelming endorsement of purpose exploration programming (see chapters 4 and 5).

The nine campuses that participated included conservative Protestant, mainline Protestant, Roman Catholic, ethnic Christian, and virtually unaffiliated campuses. The campuses were located in all regions of the United States, and in rural, suburban, and urban settings. I did not ask campuses that had distributed programs to participate, since they lacked records of participants, nor did I ask project directors whose skills did not lie in record keeping. I could have requested that such colleges or universities distribute my survey invitation to all students, faculty, and staff—but based on experience with other campus's IRBs, I knew that the likelihood of that request being approved was exceedingly low. Nor did I ask campuses with narrow programs to participate, since we had overwhelmingly met their participants during our campus visits; to do so would have compromised respondents' anonymity and, more important, disrespected the time and attention we had received during our site visit. That leaves more than nine campuses from which I could have requested participation, but I stopped because I did not see sufficient variation to justify continued surveying. The uniformly high evaluations of exploration programs across campuses, combined with the length of the IRB approval processes and program staff changes as grant monies were depleted, signaled to me that there would be little benefit, and limited participation, in further campus surveys.

The web survey's primary weakness is arguably the late start to this national evaluation. Had I begun my evaluation work in 2003 and not 2006, and hired a project manager from the outset, we could have generated a participant database internally that would have given us a clear sampling frame and a known response rate. Future evaluators would be wise to generate participant lists early in their program's life cycle. If they can conduct a web survey, it is hard to beat the efficiency of the design and implementation of such instruments. Web surveys have their drawbacks, but those are increasingly matched by declining response rates to other forms of surveying. I cannot say what the effect of the two-dollar charitable donation incentive was, but I suspect it underscored my population's willingness to complete a web survey. It merits at least a pretest.

Interview and Survey Questions

Included here are the questions we used to guide our focus group interviews and first- and second-wave panel interviews (i.e., in-depth interviews conducted with college students prior to their graduation from college, and repeated approximately one year after graduation). We did not limit interviews to these questions or this particular order, as we wanted these conversations to unfold as naturally as possible. But these provided a starting place for our semistructured interviews, and we would make sure that we touched on all of these issues during each interview. Web survey questions appear at the end of this appendix.

Student Focus Group Interview Questions

After informal chatting to set the tone as students arrived, we would offer formal welcome remarks, clarify our role and the guiding principles of the interview, run through the informed-consent process, and then begin the audio recording. *Opening:*

We've all introduced ourselves, but for the sake of the audio recording and transcriber, I'd like each person to state their name, tell us their class year and major, and then briefly explain why they applied to this college/university, and why they've stayed. (Prompts: Would anyone be willing to go first? [To that individual:] Should we go to your left or right?)

Q1: Tell me about the parts or programs of the Lilly grant [use local name] at this college that you've been involved in. (Prompt: How did you hear about these programs/activities?)

Q2: There are so many different things that you can get involved in at this college, why did you choose these programs/activities? (Prompts: Has your involvement been beneficial to you? Why?)

Q3: Is there anything you'd change about these programs? (Prompts: What, why? What would you keep the same?)

Q4: If I walked across campus today and randomly stopped students to ask them about [Lilly program name]—what would they say? (Prompts: How many would know about the programs? How many would have a positive view, a negative view? What if I could travel back two years in time and do the same thing—would I hear anything different?)

Q5: How important is the religious affiliation/heritage of this college (or university) to you? (Prompts: Has it become more/less important over time? Would other students generally say the same thing, or might there be some other voices/opinions than those I'm hearing around the table?)

Q6: Do you ever hear students, faculty, or staff using terms like *vocation, calling,* or *purpose* [or add other terms used by the local program]? (Prompts: Among whom? How often? Is talking about such ideas helpful? Who uses these terms the most—students, faculty, or staff?)

Q7: If, at the end of this semester, [program name(s)] ceased to exist— what would happen? (Prompts: Who would be impacted most? Who wouldn't even know? Would this college be different if [program name] had never existed? How?)

Q8: We've covered a lot of things today, but I may have missed something important. So I wanted to give you an opportunity to tell me what that "something" is, or what you think is the most important "take-away" lesson about [program name]. (Prompt: Anything else?)

Faculty and Staff Focus Group Interview Questions

Again, we would set the tone with informal conversation as participants arrived, then give formal welcome remarks, clarify our role and the guiding principles of the interview, carry out the informed-consent process, and then begin the audio recording.

Opening: We've all introduced ourselves, but for the sake of the audio recording and transcriber, I'd like each person to state their name, tell how they came to be employed at this college, and then explain why they've chosen to stay. After this, we won't go around the room but will just ask folks to jump in as and if they wish.

Q1: Tell me about the parts or programs of the Lilly grant [use local name] at this college that you've been involved in. (Prompts: How did you hear about these programs/activities? Has your involvement been beneficial to you? How?)

Q2: The Lilly Endowment, when it launched this initiative, encouraged recipients to be creative and experimental in its efforts to engage members of campus in the theological exploration of vocation. From the various places that you sit and the various students, staff or faculty whom you know, what have been the grant's hits and what have been the grant's misses? (Prompts: If you could change anything about the programs, their use of money, or their goals, what would you change? Why?)

Q3: How do your colleagues view your involvement in these Lilly programs, and what has been the extent of faculty/staff "buy-in" of the aims of the [program name(s)]? (Prompts: How many know about these programs? How many participate in these programs? How many are proponents? How many are opponents? What if I could travel back three years in time, and ask this same question—would I hear the same answers?)

Q4: The Lilly Endowment sought to enhance the vocational mentorship of students, and particularly enhance the capacity of faculty and staff to provide vocational mentorship of students. Some of you have been affiliated with the university for a long time, some of you are newer, but I'm curious, have you seen a change, has there been an enhancement, have conversations with students grown deeper?

Q5: Do you ever hear students, faculty, or staff using terms like *vocation, calling,* or *purpose* [or other terms used by the local program]? (Prompts:

How often? Among whom? Has talking about such ideas been beneficial? To whom? Who uses these terms the most—students, faculty, or staff? Has usage been meaningful, jargonesque, or both?)

Q6: How important is the religious affiliation/heritage of this college (or university) to you? (Prompts: Has it become more/less important over time? Would other faculty/staff say the same thing, or might there be some other voices/opinions than those I'm hearing around the table?)

Q7: If, at the end of this semester, [program name(s)] ceased to exist— what would happen? (Prompts: Who would be impacted most? Who wouldn't even know? Would this college be different if [program name] had never existed? How?)

Q8: We've covered a lot of things today, but I may have missed something important. So I wanted to give you an opportunity to tell me what that "something" is, or what you think is the most important "take-away" lesson about [program name]. (Prompt: Anything else?)

Panel Interview Questions (Wave 1: Pregraduation)

After introducing ourselves and thanking respondents for participating, we would go through the informed-consent process, then ask interviewees to complete a background information sheet, which collected contact, demographic, degree, and academic program information. Once the sheet was complete, we would start the audio recorders, using the following questions to guide the conversation.

Q1: Some young adults know what they want to do with their lives, others have no idea, and the rest fall somewhere in between. How about you? (*Probe extensively*, and use the follow-ups below if these issues do not get addressed.)

Follow-up prompts for those who "know":

- When and how did you realize this is what you wanted to do? (Probes: What is appealing about it? Did you always have this interest? Any other career/vocational interests? Any setbacks? [Get full description.])
- What factors helped you realize this? (Probes: role of family, friends, hobbies, school activities, voluntary activities, employment, specific

values (e.g., children, location, family, parents' wishes), religious faith. [Get full description.])

- Describe the specific work environment, the location, and the type of people you would like to work with in the future. (Probes: indoors/outdoors, occupational specialization, work sector [business/nonprofit/government], urban/suburban/rural, state or US region, type of boss, coworkers, clients.)
- If money was not a concern for you, would you still choose the same field? (Probes: Why? What would you choose to do? Why?)
- What about your future outside of your work life? Have you given thought to your goals or plans about this part of your life? What goals, plans, or hopes do you have?
- What kinds of decisions have you already made in preparation for your future? (Probes: Were any of the decisions difficult? Did you seek/receive advice?)
- What, if anything, are you passionate about? Explain.

Follow-up prompts for those who "have no idea":

- Do you have any general ideas or hopes about what you will do with your life? (Probes: Explain. Probe all vague ideas or hopes for more information and their possible sources.)
- Are there any fields or career areas you know you have little to no interest in? (Probe: How do you know you're not interested in these fields?)
- Does it ever concern you that you "have no idea" what you want to do with you life? (Probes: Explain. How does it make you feel? Have you ever taken steps to identify what you want to do? Explain. Did they help?)
- Does it ever concern others that you "have no idea"? (Probes: Who does it concern, what do they say, and how does it affect you?)
- Do you have a major? How and why did you choose this major? Was this a hard decision for you? Is your major the right decision for you? Why?
- Do you have any plan for the first year or so after college? Describe it.
- Do you have any plan for the time from now until you complete college? Describe it.

- What about your future outside of your work life? Have you given thought to goals or plans about this part of your life? What goals, plans, or hopes do you have?
- Do you have any current hobbies, activities, or involvements? Describe them. Have you ever considered a career that is related to these hobbies, activities, or involvements? Why?
- What, if anything, are you passionate about? Explain.

Follow-up prompts for those "in between":

- Would you say you are "in between" because you have multiple conflicting interests, no precise career in mind, or something else?
- Are there fields or careers you've ruled out? Why?
- What factors will be most important to you in choosing/deciding what you want to "do with your life"? What factors will be unimportant?
- Does it concern you that you are "in between"? Explain.
- Does it ever concern others that you are "in between"? Explain. (Probes: Is anyone pressuring you? Who and how? What impact does this pressure have on you?)
- When do you think you'll be more certain about what you want to do? What will make you more certain then?
- What about your future outside of your work life? Have you given thought to goals or plans about this part of your life? What goals, plans, or hopes do you have?
- Do you have any current hobbies, activities, or involvements? (Probes: Describe them. Have you ever considered a career that is related to these hobbies, activities, or involvements? Why?)
- What, if anything, are you passionate about? Explain.

Q2: Tell me about your background—your family, where and how you were reared, your schooling, and any particularly important experiences in your life. (*Probe extensively*, and use the follow-ups below if these issues do not get addressed.)

Prompts about family relationships:

- Where did you grow up? Who reared you? Do you have any brothers or sisters? (Probes: gender, age of each.)

- Describe your relationship with your parents [or the individuals who raised you] (e.g., close, distant, argumentative, respectful, etc.). (Probe: Can you give a recent example from your relationship that illustrates this?)
- Describe your relationship with your siblings (e.g., close, distant, argumentative, respectful, etc.). (Probes: Can you give a recent example from your relationship that illustrates this?)
- Besides your parents or siblings, are there other members of your family who have played an important role in your life? If so, please describe who and how. (Probe: Can you give a recent example from your relationship that illustrates this?)

Prompts about family status:

- Describe your parents' (or legal guardian's) occupations. (Probes: What do they do for a living? How long have they made their living in this line of work? Do they oversee the work of others in their jobs? If so, how many people do they oversee?)
- Did your parents [or whoever raised the student] graduate from college? (Probes: *If yes*, where and in what field of study? Did your parents get a graduate degree? Where and in what field of study? *If no*, tell me about their educational background.)
- What about other members of your family, both older siblings and extended family members—have they graduated from college? Where did they attend college?
- Have you lived in mostly urban, suburban, small-town, or rural communities? (Probes: Do your parents own their home, or do they rent? If you had to describe your family's social class, how would you do it? Did you attend public or private schools growing up? If private, what type?)

Probes about religion and spirituality:

1. Were you raised in any religious or spiritual tradition?
   A. If no: Would you describe yourself as either religious or spiritual today? (If yes, proceed through all questions in the next section. If not presently religious or spiritual, ask: Do you hold any religious or spiritual beliefs at all? Do you believe in God or any supernatural powers? What is your view of religion and spirituality in general?)

B. If yes:

- Tell me about your religious or spiritual upbringing.
- How would you describe your basic religious beliefs today?
- Do you have a religious preference at present? If yes: What is it? If not: Do you have any person or group with which you identify religiously? Who?
- What is your view of the Bible? (Probes: God's word? Error-free? Book of morals? Good literature? Etc.)
- Do you read the Bible? How often? Have you read it previously? When?
- Do you attend religious services? How often? Where?
- Do you pray or meditate? How often? How long? What did you pray about the last time you prayed?
- Do you have any devotional practices? Describe them.
- Are you involved in any religious organizations? Please describe, and explain why you are involved.
- What has been most important in your religion to you? Explain.
- Is "spirituality" very important to you? How? How do you define spirituality? (Probe: Anything else?)
- How does your commitment to your religious faith today compare with your commitment a few years ago? (Probes: Has it been consistent, or has it increased or decreased? Why?)
- What about the future? Do you think your commitment level will stay the same, increase, or decrease? Why?
- Have your parents or other family members played a role in your religious beliefs/practices? Describe how.

Q3: When you think about your future — say, ten years from now — how do you picture it? (*Probe extensively,* and use the follow-ups below if these issues do not get addressed.)

- Where would you like to live? Why? (Probes: urban/suburban/rural; type of housing/approximate size of house; region of country [Northeast, South, West Coast, etc.].)
- What would be your occupation? (Probes: If unsure, ask for a "type" of occupation: professional, business executive, small-business owner, skilled worker, etc. Why?)

- What factors would be most important to you in finding work? (Probes: role of income, prestige, adventure, flexibility, challenge, creativity, security, work schedule, vacation.)
- What educational goals do you hope to achieve?
- Will you be married? If yes, describe what you hope your spouse will be like.
- Will you have children? If yes, how many children? If no, do you ever plan to have children?

Q4: Tell me about your love life. (*Probe extensively* for long-term relationships, any current relationship, past relationships; possible impacts on the future. Use the follow-ups below if these issues do not get addressed.)

Prompts for those in a long-term relationship:

- How long?
- How did you meet?
- Are you sexually active with this person? Are you exclusive with this person?
- Would you describe this as a serious relationship? Why?
- Is there anything you'd say you've learned through being in this relationship? What?
- Has this relationship in any way influenced your future plans or what you think about your future?
- Have you ever thought about marriage with this person? What have you thought about it?

Prompts for those not in a long-term relationship:

1. Are you in any type of romantic or sexual relationship right now?
   A. If *in* some type of relationship:
   - How would you describe it?
   - How and when did it start?
   - Is there anything you'd say you've learned from this relationship?
   - Do you ever talk to this person about the nature of your relationship? If yes, what do you talk about? If no, why not?
   - Has this relationship in any way influenced how you think about the future? Explain.

B. If *not* in some type of a romantic or sexual relationship:

- Are you actively looking? Where and how are you looking for one? How much attention or time would you say you give to looking for a relationship?

- Do you ever hook up (i.e., engage in a sexual encounter that may or may not include intercourse, with another person whom you barely know or with whom you have no plans to pursue a relationship)? How often? Do you have any "friends with benefits"? How often do you take advantage of those benefits?

- If you are not actively looking, can you tell me why?

2. Have you previously been involved in a romantic or sexual relationship?

- How many and how long?

- How did you meet?

- Would you say any of these were serious relationships? Why?

- Is there anything you'd say you've learned from these previous relationships? What?

- Did these relationships in any way influence your future plans or the way you thought about the future?

Q5: Would you say your present life or future planning has been guided by some sense of purpose or direction? (*Probe extensively,* and use the follow-ups below if these issues do not get addressed.)

Prompts for those responding "yes" or near to it:

- Would you say your *purpose* or *direction* [use the respondent's term] is unique to you, or applicable more widely? (Probe: Explain.)

- How did you come to identify this purpose? Was there any process or information that was useful to you in identifying this purpose?

- Do you think this purpose or direction will change? Why?

- Would you say your purpose or direction is a "calling" or a "life mission"? If yes, how so?

- How would you describe this purpose or direction? Is it religious, spiritual, ethical, familial, highly individual? Which is it mostly?

- How strong is this purpose or direction? How clear is it? Has it become clearer or stronger recently? Why? (Listen for the vocabulary that the

respondent uses to describe it, and use that vocabulary—clarifying it
with the respondent if unclear.)

- Would you say this sense of purpose or direction is guiding you toward
certain paths, away from certain paths, both, or none? (Probes: Explain.
Get specifics.)
- Who or what has been most influential in forming or finding your sense
of purpose or direction? (Probes: Explain. Get specifics.)
- Have you participated in any programs or activities while at college that
have facilitated your sense of purpose or direction? (Probes: Explain.
Get specifics.)
- Did you ever have a different sense of your purpose or direction? (If
yes, how did it change? Explain. Get specifics.)
- Did you ever feel like you were resisting your purpose or direction?
(Probes: Explain. Get specifics.)
- Would you say that you hope your life "makes a difference"? What dif-
ference do you hope to make? How important is making a difference to
you?

Prompts for those responding "no" or "I don't know":

- Do you think having a sense of purpose or direction is possible or desirable? (Probes: Why? Explain.)
- Do you hope to eventually have a purpose or direction yourself?
(Probes: Why? If yes, when/how do you think you'll find that purpose
or direction?)
- Have you participated in any programs or activities at college that
encouraged you to think about the idea of "purpose" or "direction" in
life? What did you think of these programs or activities?
- Many things motivate individuals in life. What sorts of things motivate
you? (Probe: Is there anything else? Which things motivate you the
most?)
- Are there specific sorts of future activities you would not do? (Probes:
What are they, and why?)
- Would you say that you hope your life "makes a difference"? What difference do you hope to make? How important is making a difference to
you?

Q6: We've talked about a number of important things during this interview. But before we end our conversation, I want to give you the opportunity to add anything else that you think would be important for us to know, so that we understand you and your answers as fully as we can. (Probe any remarks here, too.)

Panel Interview Questions (Wave 2: Postgraduation)

After confirming the interviewee's receipt of the informed-consent documents and obtaining permission to audio-record the interview, we would ask the following questions.

Q1: It's been [about/more than] a year since you last spoke with us. Could you bring me up to date on what's happened in your life since then? (Probe extensively — not just getting the "facts," but exploring the "whys" behind experiences/decisions, exploring any setbacks/mistakes, and gaining a sense of how the respondent feels about his or her experiences during the past year. The goal here is to try to get the interviewee talking about the topics below on his or her own, using the interviewee's own narrative structure and expositional logic.)

Q2: [Ask if not covered in respondent's answer to Q1:] Would you say your first year after college is working out the way you hoped it would? Why?

Q3: [Optional; ask if answers to Q1 and Q2 have been brief:] What's been best and worst about life after college for you? (Probe to clarify if necessary.)

Q4: [Optional; ask only if answers to Q1–Q3 have been brief:] Do you ever talk with others about "life after college"? (Probes: What do you talk about? What prompts these conversations?)

Q5: I'd like to explore several different areas of life with you, and hear you talk about your level of satisfaction in each. Are you satisfied with your work life [or graduate study, if a full-time graduate student]? Tell me about that [*or* please explain]. Have you experienced any major changes in this area of your life during the past year? (Repeat "satisfied" question sequence for: financial life, living arrangements, social life, and religious or spiritual life.)

Q6: Would you say your experiences and decisions since graduating from college been guided by a sense of purpose or direction? (If yes or maybe: What is that purpose or direction? How has it guided you? Is this sense of purpose or direction religious or spiritual in nature? Explain. If no: Do you wish you had a sense of purpose or direction for your life? Explain.)

Q7: Do you believe you were well prepared for life after college? Why? (Optional follow-up, if respondent believes she or he was not well prepared: Is there anything you wish had been different?)

Q8: Any closing thoughts?

Alumni Telephone Interview Questions

After confirming the interviewee's receipt of the informed-consent documents and obtaining permission to audio-record the interview, we would ask the following questions.

Q1: Could you begin by telling me when you graduated; what your major(s) or minor(s) were; and any key programs, teams, or other involvements you had on campus. (Probe involvements if the respondent mentions purpose exploration programs.)

Q2: Tell me about the parts or programs of the [local Programs for the Theological Exploration of Vocation, or PTEV, program office] at [name of college or university] that you were involved in. (Prompts: How did you hear about these programs/activities? Was your involvement beneficial to you? How? Is there anything you'd change about these programs? What?)

Q3: Did your involvement in [name of exploration programs] help you make choices about your life after graduating? How? (Prompts: Do you think you would have made these same choices had you not been involved? Why?)

Q4: Would you say your life is guided by a sense of purpose or direction? Describe it.

Q5: Did you ever hear your classmates, faculty, or staff using terms like *vocation, calling,* or *purpose* [or add other terms used by the local program]? (Prompts: Among whom? How often? Was talking about such ideas helpful? How? Who used these terms the most: students, faculty, staff?)

Q6: If I were to call a random student who graduated in your class, to ask them about [the local PTEV program office]—what would they say? (Prompts: Would they know about the programs? Would they have a positive view, a negative view?)

Q7: Would your college experience have been different if [local exploration programs] had never existed? How?

Q8: We've covered a lot of things today, but I may have missed something important. So I wanted to give you an opportunity to tell me what that "something" is, or what you think has been the most important "take-away" lesson about [local exploration program name] for you. (Prompt: Anything else?)

Faculty or Staff Mentor Interview Questions

After introducing ourselves and thanking respondents for participating, we would go through the informed-consent process, then ask interviewees to complete a background information sheet, which collected contact, demographic, education, employment, and tenure information. Once the information sheet was complete, we would start the audio recorders, using the following questions to guide the conversation.

Q1: Tell me how you came to be involved with [local PTEV program name]. (Probe for length, breadth, and depth of involvement. Probe also for how important this involvement has been to the mentor.)

Q2: Does the language of *calling, vocation,* or *purpose* resonate with you? Why? (Probes: Does it resonate with students whom you advise or mentor? Does this language resonate on this campus? How do you know? Among the faculty/staff? Within your division/department?)

Q3: Tell me about your own religious/spiritual journey. (Probes: Were you reared in a religious tradition? Which? Have you experienced any religious changes or shifts since childhood? How would you describe your religious affiliation now? Your spirituality now? To what extent does your own religious/spiritual life comport or conflict with that of this institution?)

Q4: How do others view your involvement with [local PTEV program name]? (Probe extensively—positive/negative views; perceptions among peers, supervisor/deans, students.)

Q5: Has your involvement in [local PTEV program name] enhanced your vocational mentorship of students? In what ways? (Probes: Has it enhanced your work as a faculty member/staff professional? How? What do you do differently? How do you know it has been an enhancement?)

Q6: If [the local PTEV program office] were to close at the end of this semester, what would happen—on campus, in your department, to you? (Probes: How important is it to you that the activities and processes this office began continue? Why? Do you think these activities and processes will be sustained? Why? Will your own practice of vocational mentorship be sustained?

Q7: We've talked about a number of important things during this interview. But before we end our conversation, I want to give you the opportunity to add anything else that you think would be important for us to know, so that we understand you and your answers as fully as we can. (Probe remarks here, too.)

Web Survey Questions

These questions used the names of each campus, its exploration program, and its specific program activities or events. The questions were otherwise worded identically. After introductory information, respondents answered the questions listed below, which followed separate branches for students, alumni, and faculty or staff before reconverging on demographic questions.

Q1: Please indicate which [exploration] programs you participated in. (A list of five to fifteen programs and events followed, along with a write-in "other" option, to which respondents could check a box indicating participation.)

Q2: Indicate your overall evaluation for each program that you participated in. (The same list of programs and events followed, with six response options for each: did not participate, excellent, very good, good, fair, and poor.)

Q3: What is your primary position at [name of college or university]? (Response options: student, alumni, faculty, or staff.)

Student and alumni Q4: Before entering [name of college or university], I was familiar with concepts like vocation, calling, and purpose. (Response options: strongly agree, agree, not sure, disagree, strongly disagree.)

Student and alumni Q5: Has discussion, reflection, or reading about vocation [or calling, purpose] been helpful to you? (Response options: very helpful, helpful, neither helpful nor unhelpful, unhelpful, very unhelpful.)

Student and alumni Q6: Through participation in [name of exploration project], I developed a better sense of my vocation, calling, or purpose. (Response options: strongly agree, agree, not sure, disagree, strongly disagree.)

Student and alumni Q7: [Name of exploration project] programs helped me identify my skills and talents. (Response options: strongly agree, agree, not sure, disagree, strongly disagree.)

Student and alumni Q8: [Name of exploration project] programs encouraged me to both see and serve the needs of others. (Response options: strongly agree, agree, not sure, disagree, strongly disagree.)

Student and alumni Q9: Because of my participation in [name of exploration project] programs, I altered my life plans. (Response options: strongly agree, agree, not sure, disagree, strongly disagree.)

Student and alumni Q10: I am committed to making a positive contribution to the church both now and in the future. (Response options: strongly agree, agree, not sure, disagree, strongly disagree.)

Student and alumni Q11: My commitment to serving the church has increased because of my involvement in [name of exploration project] programs. (Response options: strongly agree, agree, not sure, disagree, strongly disagree.)

Student and alumni Q12: [Name of exploration project] programs encouraged me to consider full-time ministry as a potential option for my future. (Response options: strongly agree, agree, not sure, disagree, strongly disagree.)

Student (and alumni) Q13: Have you (ever) applied to a seminary, theological school, or rabbinical school? (Response options: yes or no.)

Alumni Q14: Are you presently enrolled in a seminary, theological school, or rabbinical school? (Response options: yes or no.)

Student Q14 (alumni Q15): Students on campus often use [*or* used] terms like *vocation, calling,* or *purpose.* (Response options: strongly agree, agree, not sure, disagree, strongly disagree.)

Student Q15 (alumni Q16): I have [*or* had] a faculty or staff adviser at [name of college or university] with whom I have [*or* had] helpful conversations about my vocation, calling, or purpose. (Response options: strongly agree, agree, not sure, disagree, strongly disagree.)

Alumni Q17: I really don't have much time for vocational reflection or exploration since graduating from college. (Response options: strongly agree, agree, not sure, disagree, strongly disagree.)

Alumni Q18: Since graduating from college, I have drawn upon vocational discernment and reflection to guide my decisions. (Response options: strongly agree, agree, not sure, disagree, strongly disagree.)

Student Q16 and alumni Q19: Please indicate which definition of *vocation* comes closest to your own. (Response options: [1] Vocation is an ongoing process of reflecting on one's joys, one's skills, and others' needs, and of taking steps to bring these three into harmony. [2] Vocation is a voice inside us, which we must listen to, to make sure we have found "the call" most appropriate to our own lives. If we listen to the "voice," we will know what to do with our lives. [3] Vocation is determining what is the one "will of God" for my life and answering that call. There is no guarantee that this call will fit with my skills or interests. [4] Vocation is the work we choose to do for a career, be it business, farming, teaching, or whatever we choose to call our profession. It implies regular employment, although the job may change from time to time. [5] Vocation is to embrace a life of radical discipleship as our Christian calling. It is to live lives that have been transformed and reach out in loving service to others.)

Student Q17 and alumni Q20: What, if any, changes would you recommend for [name of exploration project] programs at [name of college or university]? (open-ended, write-in response)

Student Q18 and alumni Q21: Do you have any final comments about the [name of exploration project] programs or the larger "Programs for the Theological Exploration of Vocation" Lilly Endowment initiative that you would like to share? (open-ended, write-in response)

Student Q19: Are you a _____? (Response options: freshman, sophomore, junior, senior, other [please specify].)

Student Q20: When do you expect to graduate? (Response options: 2008, 2009, 2010, 2011, 2012. or later.)

Alumni Q22: When did you graduate? (Response options: 2004 or earlier, 2005, 2006, 2007, 2008.)

Student Q21 (alumni Q23): What is [*or* was] your primary (or major) field of study? (Please don't abbreviate.) (open-ended, write-in response)

Student Q22 (alumni Q24): What is [*or* was] your secondary (second major, minor, concentration, etc.) field of study? (Please don't abbreviate.) (open-ended, write-in response)

Student Q23 (alumni Q25): What is [*or* was] your overall grade average? (Response options: A+, A, A−, B+, B, B−, C+, C, below C level, I don't know, or I'm not telling.)

Alumni Q26: What is your current occupation or job title? (open-ended, write-in response)

Alumni Q27: Are you currently serving as a religious professional (e.g., ordained minister, priest, vowed member of a religious order, rabbi, imam)? (Response options: yes or no.)

Faculty and staff Q4: [Name of exploration project] programs have positively impacted my own work at [name of college or university]. (Response options: strongly agree, agree, not sure, disagree, strongly disagree.)

Faculty and staff Q5: Participation in [name of exploration project] programs has helped me hone my own sense of vocation, calling, or purpose. (Response options: strongly agree, agree, not sure, disagree, strongly disagree.)

Faculty and staff Q6: [Name of exploration project] programs have deepened my appreciation for the mission of [name of college or university]. (Response options: strongly agree, agree, not sure, disagree, strongly disagree.)

Faculty and staff Q7: [Name of exploration project] programs have had a positive impact on my department or program. (Response options: strongly agree, agree, not sure, disagree, strongly disagree.)

Faculty and staff Q8: Overall, how has the [name of exploration project] been received by the faculty at [name of college or university]? (Response options: [1] Faculty have been extremely welcoming of the grant. [2] Faculty have generally been welcoming of the grant. [3] Faculty have expressed some resistance to the grant. [4] Faculty have expressed extreme resistance to the grant. [5] Faculty do not know enough about the grant to welcome or resist it. [6] Not sure.)

Faculty and staff Q9: Overall, how has the [name of exploration project] been received by staff at [name of college or university]? (Response options: [1] Staff have been extremely welcoming of the grant. [2] Staff have generally been welcoming of the grant. [3] Staff have expressed some resistance to the grant. [4] Staff have expressed extreme resistance to the grant. [5] Staff do not know enough about the grant to welcome or resist it. [6] Not sure.)

Faculty and staff Q10: How would you characterize the impact of [name of exploration project] programs on your campus as a whole? (Response options: [1] Lilly vocation grant programs have negatively impacted our campus. [2] Lilly vocation grant programs have positively impacted our campus.

[3] Lilly vocation grant programs have not impacted our campus. [4] Not sure.)

Faculty and staff Q11: The impact of [name of exploration project] programs will be felt long after the grant money is gone. (Response options: strongly agree, agree, not sure, disagree, strongly disagree.)

Faculty and staff Q12: [Name of exploration project] programs have encouraged students to consider full-time ministry. (Response options: strongly agree, agree, not sure, disagree, strongly disagree.)

Faculty and staff Q13: Advising and mentoring at [name of college or university] has been improved as a result of [name of exploration project] programs. (Response options: strongly agree, agree, not sure, disagree, strongly disagree.)

Faculty and staff Q14: Do you advise or mentor any students? (Response options: yes or no.)

Faculty and staff advisors only Q14a: Have you ever talked about issues of vocation, calling, or purpose with students whom you advise or mentor? (Response options: [1] Yes, I often talk about these issues with students. [2] Yes, I occasionally talk about these issues with students. [3] No, I do not talk about these issues with students.)

Faculty and staff advisors only Q14b: Engaging concepts like vocation, calling, or purpose has helped me move advising/mentoring conversations into deeper and more important matters. (Response options: strongly agree, agree, not sure, disagree, strongly disagree.)

Faculty and staff Q15–Q17: same as student Q16–Q18 and alumni Q19–Q21.

Faculty and staff Q18: Please indicate how many years you've been employed at this institution. (Response options: less than 3 years, 3–5 years, 6–9 years, 10–14 years, 15–19 years, 20 years or more.)

Faculty and staff Q19: Please indicate your level of education. (Response options: high school graduate, high school diploma, or the equivalent [e.g., GED]; some college but no degree; associate's degree in college, occupational/vocational program; associate's degree in college, academic program; bachelor's degree [e.g., BA, AB, BS, BDiv]; master's degree [e.g., MA, MS, MEng, MEd, MSW, MBA, MDiv]; professional school degree [e.g., MD, DDS, DVM, LLD, JD, DDiv]; doctorate degree [e.g., PhD, EdD, ThD].)

Faculty and staff Q20: In what field of study did you earn your highest degree (e.g., US history)? (open-ended, write-in response)

Faculty and staff Q21: Are you tenured? (Response options: yes or no.)

[No student Q24–Q27; no faculty and staff Q22–Q27.]

Q28: In the last *twelve months,* how often have you been attending religious services, not including weddings, baptisms, and funerals? (Response options: more than once a week, once a week, two to three times a month, once a month, many times a year, a few times a year, never, not sure.)

Q28a (asked of "never" and "not sure" respondents): Regardless of whether you now attend any religious services, do you identify with any particular religious tradition, denomination, or church? (Response options: yes or no.)

Q28b (asked of Q28a "no" respondents only, *then skipped to Q31*): Do you consider yourself to be an atheist, an agnostic, just not religious, or something else? (Response options: atheist, agnostic, not religious, something else.)

Q28c (asked of Q28a "yes" respondents only): Do you consider yourself to be Protestant, Roman Catholic, Jewish, Muslim, or something else? (Response options: Protestant, Roman Catholic, Jewish, Muslim, something else. *Those responding Roman Catholic, Jewish, or Muslim were skipped to Q30.*)

Q28d (asked of Q28c "Protestant" and "something else" respondents only, *then skipped to Q30*): With what religious tradition, denomination, or church do you most closely identify? (Response options: Assemblies of God, Baptist; Buddhist, Catholic, Christian or just Christian, Church of Christ, Church of God, Church of the Nazarene, Disciples of Christ, Episcopalian, Jehovah's Witness, just Protestant, Latter-Day Saint(s), Lutheran, Methodist, Mormon, Native American, Nazarene, nondenominational; Orthodox (Eastern, Greek, Russian, etc.), Pentecostal, Presbyterian, Unitarian-Universalist, Unity Church, Wiccan, other.)

Q29: With what religious tradition, denomination, or church do you most closely identify? (Response options: Assemblies of God, Baptist, Buddhist, Catholic, Christian or just Christian, Church of Christ, Church of God, Church of the Nazarene, Disciples of Christ, Episcopalian, Jehovah's Witness, just Protestant, Latter Day Saint(s), Lutheran, Methodist, Mormon, Native American, Nazarene, nondenominational, Orthodox (Eastern, Greek, Russian, etc.), Pentecostal, Presbyterian, Unitarian-Universalist, Unity Church, Wiccan, other.)

Q30: When it comes to your religious beliefs, compared to other religious Americans, do you usually think of yourself as _____? (Response options: very liberal, liberal, moderate, conservative, very conservative, not sure.)

Q31: Gender. (Response options: male or female.)

Q32: Race (you can select multiple options). (Response options: African or Afro or black American; American Indian/Native American/Alaskan Native; Asian American/Pacific Islander; Hispanic or Latino/a American; white or Caucasian American; other [write-in response option].)

Q33: Does your family identify with a particular ethnicity (such as Italian, Jamaican, Japanese, etc.)? If so, please indicate that ethnicity here. (open-ended, write-in response)

Q34: In what year were you born? Year of birth. (numeric four-digit-year write-in response)

Q35: To which charity shall we donate two dollars in appreciation for your time completing this web survey? (Response options: American Cancer Society, American Red Cross, UNICEF [United Nations Children's Fund], World Vision.)

APPENDIX 4

Visited Campuses, Program Participation, and Postaward Continuation

Campus	Course and curricular programs	Internships and service projects	Residential life programs	Mentoring programs	Seminary programs
Conservative Protestant:					
"Mennonite College"	A, PI, M: New	M: Fr	A	PI: premin fellows	A
"Pullman College"	A, M: Fr	A, PI	A	A, PI: premin/ research	A
CP3 College	A	A	A	A, PI	A
CP4 Univ.	A, M: Fr	A, PI, M		M: premin	A
CP5 Univ.	A	A, PI	A	A, PI: honors	
CP6 Univ.	A, M: Fr	A	A		A
Ethnic Christian:					
"C. of Douglass and DuBois"	M: Fr	A		A	A
"Mexicana College"	A, M: Fr	A, PI		A	A
E3 College	A, M			A	A
E4 Univ.		A		A	A, PI
E5 College	A	A	A, PI	A	
Mainline Protestant:					
"Presbyter College"	A	A, PI		A, PI: fellows	A
MP2 College	A, M: interns	A, PI		A, PI: student/ faculty research	
MP3 Univ.	A	A	A	A	
MP4 Univ.	A	A, PI		A	A
MP5 College	A	A, PI		A, PI	A, PI

Retreats	Strength and interest assessments	Minigrants	Campus lectures, events	Undergrad exposure estimate (%)*	Undergrad participation estimate (%)*	Program continuation postaward
		A	A, M	100	≥10	extensive
A	A		A	100	≥33	extensive
A, PI	M: New	A	A, M	100	≥25	extensive
	M: New	A	A	100	10	moderate
	A: New		A	87	≥10	extensive
A			A	100	≥10	moderate
			A, M: Fr	100	≥25	extensive, via grant extension
A		A	A	100	≥20	moderate
A, M: Fr	A	A	A	100	≥50	extensive
			A	75	≥7	extensive
			A	≥15	5	moderate
A	A	A	A	35	5	extensive
	A: interns	A	A	25–50	10–25	minimal
A		A	A	45	≥10	moderate
A		A	A	≥10	2	moderate
A		A		25	7	moderate

Continued

Campus	Course and curricular programs	Internships and service projects	Residential life programs	Mentoring programs	Seminary programs
Roman Catholic:					
"Ignatius U"	A	A, PI		A	
"Richboro U"	A, M: Soph partic.	M: Soph partic.	A, PI: Soph	M: Soph partic.	A
RC3 College	A, M: fellows	A		A, PI: premin fellows	
RC4 Univ.	A, M: some Fr	A, PI		A, PI: premin	A
RC5 College	A, M: Fr	A			A
RC6 Univ.	A, M: Fr	A		A	A
Virtually unaffiliated:					
"Phi Beta College"	A	A, PI	A	A, PI	A, PI
VU2 College	A	A, PI: premed, law	A	A, PI: premin	A
VU3 Univ.		A, PI: premin			
VU4 Univ.	A	A		A, PI: faculty/ student research	A, PI

Key: A = available, M = mandatory, PI = participation incentives; Fr = 1st-year students, Jr = junior-year students, Soph = sophomore-year students, Sr = senior-year students, New = all new students; extensive = most or all programs continued; minimal = a few programs continued; moderate = many programs continued—some intact,

Retreats	Strength and interest assessments	Minigrants	Campus lectures, events	Undergrad exposure estimate (%)*	Undergrad participation estimate (%)*	Program continuation postaward
A, PI			A	50	≥13	extensive
M: Soph partic.	M: Soph partic.	A: Soph partic.		≥30	≥20	extensive
A			A	60	≥7	extensive
A	A	A: premin	A	67	1	moderate, via grant extension
A			A	100	10	minimal
A		A	A	100	≥3	minimal
			A	≥35	≥15	extensive
A		A	A	5–10	≥3	moderate
A, PI			A	20–40	≥10	moderate
A, PI	A	A	A	14	≥2	extensive

others restructured, and some ceased; none = no programs continued.

*Undergraduate exposure and participation estimates drawn from program self-reports, or interpolated using extant and observational data. Interpolated figures appear in italics.

Resources for Purpose Exploration Programming

By Patricia Tevington and Tim Clydesdale

This book is an evaluation, analysis, and recommendation of campus-based purpose exploration programming; it is not a "how-to" book, however. It offers specific design recommendations based on observation of deepest and most self-sustaining impacts (see chapter 6), but these designs are secondary to a broad and organic process that fits purpose exploration into the organizational culture and structural ecology of a campus. In service to those organic processes, and to readers who wish to individually explore and engage these matters, we offer this annotated bibliography of resources most often deployed across the eighty-eight-campus initiative, descriptions of the most common programmatic tools (arranged in declining order of their prominence), and a selected bibliography of theological works on vocation. Educators are also directed to the Council of Independent Colleges' Network for Vocation in Undergraduate Education, which maintains a far richer repository of vocation resources as well as

conferences and training opportunities (see http://www.cic.edu/Programs
-and-Services/Programs/NetVUE/Pages/default.aspx).

Annotated Bibliography of Prominently Used Exploration Texts

Augustine of Hippo. *Confessions*. Translated by R. S. Pine-Coffin. New York: Penguin
     Classics, 1961. The autobiography and spiritual memoirs of a major figure in the
     world of Christendom, Augustine of Hippo's *Confessions* stands out as a resource
     for vocational reflection in Catholic, Protestant, and secular institutions of higher
     learning. Describing his conversion to Christianity from a life of worldly pleasure
     and adherence to Manichaeism, Augustine writes vividly of the work of God in his
     heart.

Badcock, G. D. *The Way of Life: A Theology of Vocation*. Eugene, OR: Wipf and Stock
     Publishers, 2002. Correcting misunderstandings, Badcock offers a theological
     explanation of vocation, drawing from Scripture as well as Protestant and Catho-
     lic sources. *The Way of Life* dismisses reduction of vocation to occupation and dis-
     tills vocation as Christ's call to love God and neighbor. Rather than asking what one
     ought to do, Badcock proposes that Christians ask who they ought to be, the answer
     being "a follower of Christ."

Bass, D. C., and M. R. Schwehn. *Leading Lives That Matter: What We Should Do and
     Who We Should Be*. Grand Rapids, MI: Eerdmans, 2006. An anthology commis-
     sioned by the Lilly grant initiative, *Leading Lives That Matter* is designed to draw
     college and university students into conversation about purpose. Sampling from
     classic and contemporary authors, Bass and Schwehn's volume is equally useful in
     religious and nonsectarian college and universities. Its selections guide students to
     consider significance, identity, and the meaning of work. A study guide is available
     through NetVUE.

Buckingham, M., and D. O. Clifton. *Now, Discover Your Strengths*. New York: Free Press,
     2001. Buckingham and Clifton, through an online personality test, help readers
     identify their top five strengths. *Now, Discover Your Strengths* invites readers to focus
     on strengths rather than weaknesses, using strengths to improve their performance
     at work and relationships in general. The book lends itself to discussions of pas-
     sions, talents, and gifts, and can be used in classrooms or career counseling.

Buechner, F. *The Sacred Journey: A Memoir of Early Days*. New York: HarperOne, 1991.
     Relays the "early days" of author Frederick Buechner's life, beginning with child-
     hood loss and culminating in his discovery of faith and entrance into Union Theo-
     logical Seminary. Buechner describes how God communicates through life events,
     leaving readers with an example of, and strategies for, vocational discernment.

Chittister, J. *Wisdom Distilled from the Daily: Living the Rule of St. Benedict Today*. New
     York: HarperOne, 1990. In the fifth century, Benedict composed a set of guide-
     lines for spiritual life. Joan Chittister, a nun in the Benedictine tradition, argues true
     spirituality is found in the daily experiences of ordinary life and offers the Rule of

Benedict as a helpful strategy in its pursuit. Prayer, work, and leisure are explored. *Wisdom Distilled from the Daily* can be easily appropriated by readers in other traditions who seek to infuse spirituality into daily life.

Day, D. *Loaves and Fishes*. Maryknoll, NY: Orbis Books, 1997. First published 1963. Dorothy Day's thirst for justice grew after her conversion to the Catholic Church. A former Socialist and unbeliever, Day helped to launch the Catholic Worker Movement, a religious community based on prayer, pacifism, and hospitality. *Loaves and Fishes* chronicles nearly thirty years of Day's own experience as leader of this group and editor of its newspaper.

Ehrenreich, B. *Nickel and Dimed: On (Not) Getting By in America*. New York: Metropolitan Books, 2001. *Nickel and Dimed* reveals the sobering realities that mark America's working class. In three of America's cities, journalist Ehrenreich passed herself off as a waitress, housekeeper, and retail worker, attempting to live off of the wages available to unskilled workers. Ehrenreich's narrative engages poverty, injustice, and social responsibility, while raising questions about the nature and meaning of work as experienced by much of the world.

Farnham, S. G., J. P. Gill, R. T. McLean, and S. M. Ward. *Listening Hearts: Discerning Call in Community*. Harrisburg, PA: Morehouse Publishing, 1991. *Listening Hearts* suggests the context within which the devout discern their God-given call. Drawing from a variety of spiritual traditions — including Orthodox, Benedictine, Ignatian, and Quaker heritages — it emphasizes remaining open to the will of God. The text is designed for use in group settings, such as classes or discernment groups.

Guinness, O. *The Call: Finding and Fulfilling the Central Purpose of Your Life*. Nashville: Thomas Nelson, 2003. Guinness addresses humanity's quest for identity and meaning, arguing this thirst cannot be quenched through any other avenue but God, who has a unique purpose for each person. Guinness addresses vocational misunderstandings of all varieties. A study guide accompanies the newest edition, facilitating its class or group use.

Hardy, L. *The Fabric of This World: Inquiries into Calling, Career Choice, and the Design of Human Work*. Grand Rapids, MI: Eerdmans, 1990. *The Fabric of This World* offers an evangelical perspective on the relationship between faith and work. Hardy contends understanding the meaning of work, given its ubiquity, is essential. He explores work with historical and cultural lenses, describing the classical and medieval preference for the "contemplative life" over that of labor, the Freudian assertion of work as self-denial, the Marxist view of exploited workers, and the Reformation declaration of all callings as sacred. *The Fabric of This World* considers practical implications of the latter, including career decisions that might be particularly relevant to college and university students.

Ignatius of Loyola. *The Autobiography of St. Ignatius Loyola*. Edited by J. C. Olin. Translated by J. F. O'Callaghan. New York: Fordham University Press, 1992. Recounted by Ignatius to Louis Gonzales da Camara, the *Autobiography* tells readers of Ignatius's wounding during military service and his long convalescence spent reading sacred texts. Moved by the lives of saints and Christ, Ignatius turns away from aspirations to worldly success and devotes himself to service, spending his next seventeen years in study, travel, and spiritual exercises. An appealing narrative for students, faculty, and staff in general, it was a popular text on Jesuit campuses.

John Paul II. *Laborem exercens.* Encyclical letter, September 14, 1981. Accessed March 2, 2010. http://www.vatican.va/holy_father/john_paul_ii/encyclicals/documents /hf_jp-ii_enc_14091981_laborem-exercens_en.html. Pope John Paul II's papal encyclical *Laborem exercens* (On human work) is important to any discussion of work and meaning. Following the Creation mandate, humans take part in the act of creation, which gives inherent value to their work. John Paul II asserts work cannot be judged solely by the social status or economic value that it renders; it must be judged by its Originator. This encyclical offers a theological reflection on the meaning of work, social responsibility, and human dignity.

Kidder, T. *Mountains beyond Mountains: The Quest of Paul Farmer, a Man Who Would Cure the World.* New York: Random House, 2003. *Mountains beyond Mountains* tells the story of Dr. Paul Farmer, a physician and anthropologist, and of his friends and collaborators, as they establish Partners in Health to serve rural Haitians and, over time, needy communities on every continent. An inspirational narrative, this book articulates issues of social justice while exploring the place of gifts, skills, and individual privilege.

May, W. F. *Beleaguered Rulers: The Public Obligation of the Professional.* Louisville, KY: Westminster John Knox Press, 2001. Ethicist William F. May asserts professionals wield enormous power in society due to their expertise, as marginalized as they sometimes feel. May calls professionals to forsake marketplace pressure, self-interest, and careerism, and return to public service, becoming not just dispensers of knowledge but stewards of truth and partners with their clients. May's work examines eight professions: physicians, lawyers, engineers, corporate executives, politicians, members of the media, ministers, and professors. May's call to service is relevant to courses in ethics or work, especially among students considering these professions. Faculty members should appreciate May's framing of professors as public servants.

Meilander, G. C., ed. *Working: Its Meaning and Its Limits.* Notre Dame, IN: University of Notre Dame Press, 2000. This is an anthology of seventy-five selections that engage the moral implications of work and its relation to life. Meilander assembles poetry, short stories, and philosophical essays. Of particular interest is discussion of the meaning of work, which explores work as cocreation, necessary for leisure, dignified but irksome, and leisure.

Neafsey, J. *A Sacred Voice Is Calling: Personal Vocation and Social Conscience.* Maryknoll, NY: Orbis Books, 2006. Neafsey argues that one's calling rests not in personal fulfillment alone, but in balance between internal and external indications of vocation. A true call incorporates satisfaction from responding to the needs of the world. *A Sacred Voice Is Calling* promotes vocation as a corrective to injustice. Neafsey's work is ecumenically accessible, as it draws from non-Christian as well as Christian traditions.

Palmer, P. J. *Let Your Life Speak: Listening for the Voice of Vocation*. San Francisco: Jossey-Bass, 1999. In one of the most widely read books on vocation, Parker Palmer defines vocation inwardly: as claiming one's true selfhood and inherent gifts, which have been present since birth. Vocation can be discovered by discerning sacred revelation within one's own life. Palmer uses his own biography to illustrate his claims.

Parks, L. A., S. D. Daloz, C. H. Keen, and J. P. Keen. *Common Fire: Leading Lives of Commitment in a Complex World*. Boston: Beacon Press, 1996. *Common Fire* examines 145 humanitarians, analyzing which factors led respondents to diverge from self-interest and insulated lives. Often, humanitarians had important relationships with someone markedly different from themselves, benefited from mentorship, and enjoyed a diverse group of like-minded peers and colleagues. This text offers much to educators who wish to instill a lasting passion for civic responsibility.

Placher, W. C. *Callings: Twenty Centuries of Christian Wisdom on Vocation*. Grand Rapids, MI: Eerdmans, 2005. Placher's anthology offers wisdom from Catholic, Orthodox, and Protestant traditions, from Tertullian to Karl Barth. Opening with biblical texts, this volume includes discussions of calling by the early church, the medieval church, during the Reformation, and today. With these resources, and Placher's cogent introductions, readers see the diversity and commonality of calling across time, space, and tradition. A study guide is available from NetVUE.

Sittser, J. *The Will of God as a Way of Life: How to Make Every Decision with Peace and Confidence*. Grand Rapids, MI: Zondervan, 2004. Breaking from conventional understandings of vocation as unraveling the mystery of God's master plan, Sittser calls readers to focus on living the will of God in the present via the capacities already revealed to them. Tackling human responsibility, the sovereignty of God, and suffering, Sittser advises readers how to discern the will of God now. The newest edition contains study questions for classroom or group use.

Smith, G. T. *Courage and Calling: Embracing your God-Given Potential*. Downers Grove, IL: InterVarsity Press, 1999. Gordon T. Smith identifies three "calls": a general call to love God and one's neighbor, a specific call to use one's unique capacities, and an immediate call of duties and tasks. Vocation is the second, and should be understood in light of both our general and immediate calls.

Steinbeck, J. *The Grapes of Wrath*. New York: Penguin Classics, 2006. Winner of the 1940 Pulitzer Prize, *The Grapes of Wrath* lends itself to conversations about privilege, justice, and the nature and meaning of work. Steinbeck vividly illustrates the plight of migrant workers and raises unsettling questions about the oppression of the poor, social responsibility, the dynamic of power, and the myth of the American dream.

Stevens, R. P. *The Other Six Days: Vocation, Work, and Ministry in Biblical Perspective*. Grand Rapids, MI: Eerdmans, 1999. Stevens argues that the frequent distinction between the clergy and laity is harmful. He deconstructs the foundations of clericalism, proposes a theology of vocation, work, and ministry, and calls for restructuring the church to better equip laity for daily ministry. Case studies and study questions are presented at the close of every chapter.

Terkel, S. *Working: People Talk about What They Do All Day and How They Feel about What They Do.* New York: New Press, 1997. *Working: People Talk about What They Do All Day and How They Feel about What They Do* contains transcripts of Terkel's one hundred interviews with American workers from all walks of life. The reader is invited to share their joys and sufferings, and see how workers find meaning in what they do regardless of their position. First published in 1974, it remains a thoughtful resource two score years later.

Tolstoy, L. *Death of Ivan Ilych.* White Fish, MT: Kessinger Publishing, 2008. First published 1881. The *Death of Ivan Ilych* is a poignant meditation on suffering, mortality, and significance. Written shortly after Tolstoy's own religious conversion, this novella recounts the life and death of an ordinary man. Preoccupied with societal mobility and worldly ambition, Ivan realizes only on his deathbed that self-interest impeded him from living a good life.

X, Malcolm, and A. Haley. *The Autobiography of Malcolm X.* New York: Penguin Modern Classics, 2001. *The Autobiography of Malcolm X*, as recounted to Alex Haley, is a narrative of the black leader's conversion from anger and despair to faith and hope. After experiencing vicious racism as a child, Malcolm falls into substance abuse and petty crime. Arrested and sentenced to prison, Malcolm encounters the teachings of the Nation of Islam, and becomes a radical advocate for black unity and separatism. Later, during his pilgrimage to Mecca, he worships alongside Muslims of all races and changes his views. The life of Malcolm X serves as a stimulus for consideration of social justice, political engagement, racial reconciliation, and personal faith.

Annotated Bibliography of Prominently Used Purpose Exploration Films

Bender, L. (producer), and G. Van Sant (director). *Good Will Hunting.* United States: Be a Gentleman Limited Partnership, 1998. Gifted with a genius IQ, Will Hunting (played by Matt Damon) makes his living through construction and custodial jobs in a working-class Boston neighborhood. When MIT professor Gerald Lambeau (played by Stellan Skarsgard) realizes that Will has been anonymously solving the complex mathematical equations left for his graduate students, Will begins a new chapter in his life. To avoid jail, Will agrees to work for Lambeau and see therapist Sean McGuire (played by Robin Williams). While Will is pushed by Lambeau to explore his academic potential, he is challenged by McGuire to confront his troubled past and map out a meaningful future. Will's loyalty to his friends, the potential that his latent genius offers, and the expectations of influential persons tie in to exploration of purpose. The exchanges between Will Hunting and therapist Sean McGuire are of special consideration, as the connections between desires, talents, responsibilities, and relationships are explored.

Betzer, J., and B. Christensen (producers) and G. Axel (screenplay). *Babette's Feast.*

Denmark: Panorama Film A/S, 1988. Fillipa (played by Bodil Kjer) and Martine (played by Birgitte Federspiel) are the beautiful twin daughters of the strict puritan pastor of a Denmark parish, who chose simple lives of piety in their father's village rather than romantic love and worldly success. Many years later, as the two lead their deceased father's aging congregation, they receive a Parisian war refugee as their housekeeper. This Catholic foreigner, Babette, spends the next fourteen years in loyal service to the sisters and the town. When Babette wins the lottery, she decides to create a luxurious French feast for the sisters and the parish's elders. Initially resistant to the perceived decadence of Babette's feast, the sisters and church leaders come to enjoy the physical and spiritual nurturing from the rich food and sacramental nature of the meal. Although the feast itself is of pivotal importance to the film, much of the story line concentrates on the lives and decisions of Fillipa and Martine. The audience is drawn into their decisions to place faith first, even at the cost of true love. The film also prompts reflection about the use of one's gifts, such as Babette's culinary prowess.

Braschi, G., and E. Ferri (producers) and R. Benigni (director). *Life Is Beautiful*. Italy: Cecchi Gori Group Tiger Cinematografica, 1998. Starring director Roberto Benigni himself, *Life Is Beautiful* is a powerful film set in 1930s Italy. Guido Orefice is a Jewish man who uses humor to win and marry his love. Years later, Guido uses wit and playfulness to shield his young son from the horrors that are unfolding as he and his family are taken to a concentration camp.

Burnam, D., and D. Dubcovsky (producers) and W. Salles (director). *The Motorcycle Diaries*. United States: FilmFour, 2004. Based on the memoirs of twenty-three-year-old Ernesto "Che" Guevara and accounts supplied by Che's best friend and traveling companion, *The Motorcycle Diaries* recounts a pivotal experience in the life of Che Guevara. In 1952, Ernesto (played by Gael Garcia Bernal) and Alberto (played by Rodrigo de la Serna) board an old motorcycle, seeking to cross the South American continent in pursuit of adventure. When their motorcycle breaks down, the two continue their journey and come face-to-face with the suffering of Latin American peoples. As upper-middle-class Che is exposed to repeated examples of dire poverty and oppression, he is transformed. The culmination of the boys' trip comes during their three-week internship at a leper colony. *The Motorcycle Diaries* provides rich fodder for discussion of privilege, injustice, the proper response to suffering, and ultimately, one's sense of purpose.

Carliner, R. (producer), and R. Duvall (director). *The Apostle*. United States: Butcher's Run Films, 1998. Sonny (played by Robert Duvall), a devout but deeply flawed Pentecostal pastor from Texas, learns his wife (played by Farrah Fawcett) is having an affair and conspiring to remove him from his position. Under the influence of alcohol, he attacks his wife's lover with a baseball bat and puts him into a coma. Sonny flees to Louisiana, where he adopts a new identity as "the Apostle E.F." Determined to do as much good as possible before he is uncovered, Sonny establishes a racially integrated church with the help of a retired minister. Eventually,

Sonny is brought to justice, but not until he has made a positive impact on his new community. Particularly notable are Sonny's conversations with God, as he seeks to discern his course of action.

Franco, L. J., and C. Gordon (producers) and J. Johnston (director). *October Sky*. United States: Universal Pictures, 1999. Growing up in a small town in West Virginia, Homer Hickum Jr. (played by Jake Gyllenhal) seems destined for the same life as his coal-miner father. But after seeing Sputnik fly over his town one night, Homer is inspired. With the help of friends, Homer builds his own rockets in hopes of winning the national science fair, attending college, and breaking free of his small-town fate. An uplifting tale based on a true story, *October Sky* engages the pursuit of one's passions, even in the face of adversity. His father's good intentions to discourage Homer from this pursuit as well as the encouragement he receives from his physics teacher illustrate the role of mentorship.

Ghia, F., and G. Puttnam (producers) and R. Joffe (director). *The Mission*. United States: Warner Bros. Pictures, 1986. Inspired by historical events, *The Mission* has deep relevance for purpose exploration. In the 1750s, Spanish Jesuits enter the jungles of South America to convert the Guarani Native Americans. Father Gabriel (played by Jeremy Irons) establishes a peaceful community, which the converts embrace as their home. Father Gabriel is later joined by Rodrigo Mendoza (played by Robert DeNiro), a former slave trader who becomes a Jesuit himself. When a papal emissary, for political and economic reasons, decrees that Father Gabriel's mission must close and abandon its residents, the missionaries refuse to leave and allow the Guarani to be sold into slavery. Mendoza takes up arms to defend the mission, while Father Gabriel rejects violence. The film fosters discussion of faith, community, pacifism, resistance, and injustice.

Haft, S., P. J. Witt, and T. Thomas (producers) and P. Weir (director). *Dead Poets Society*. United States: Touchstone Pictures, 1989. John Keating (played by Robin Williams) is an unconventional English teacher who accepts an appointment at his alma mater, a prestigious male boarding school in Vermont. More than expose students to classic literature and poetry, Keating encourages students to know themselves and pursue their dreams, to the chagrin of the administration and parents. Inspired by their teacher, students embark on a quest to be true to themselves, their interests, and their passions, ruffling many feathers in the process. In addition to speeches by John Keating on finding joy in life, *Dead Poets Society* illustrates the power of mentorship and the role of tradition, authority, and expectations in individual hopes and dreams.

Hugo, J. (producer), and C. T. Dreyer (director). *The Passion of Joan of Arc*. France: Société générale des films, 1928. *The Passion of Joan of Arc* is the haunting story of a resolutely purposeful young woman. Based on transcripts of Joan's trials, the film depicts the nineteen-year-old woman's encounter with the English government and corrupt French clergy, who accuse her of heresy, torture her, and eventually kill her. Years later, she is found innocent of her crimes, declared a martyr, and eventually canonized as a saint in the Catholic Church.

Keiser, E. (producer), and J. Duigan (director). *Romero*. United States: Paulist Pictures, 1989. Depicting the final three years of the life of Óscar Romero, archbishop of El Salvador from 1977 to 1980, *Romero* is a film with powerful implications. Initially perceived as a potential ally for the wealthy and oppressive military, Romero disappoints the El Salvadoran ruling class. Indeed, as Romero discovers the brutal treatment of the poor and incessant violence, he becomes an outspoken advocate for social justice in the country, despite considerable danger to himself.

Keiser, E. (producer), and M. C. Rhodes (director). *Entertaining Angels: The Dorothy Day Story*. United States: Paulist Pictures, 1996. *Entertaining Angels* tells the story of Catholic activist Dorothy Day as she discovers and then serves the disenfranchised of the United States. Living as a bohemian journalist in New York City, Day embarks on a journey that leads to her conversion and ultimately her cofounding of the Catholic Worker Movement and becoming an advocate for the poor and homeless. Despite personal, religious, and political obstacles, Day remained true to her faith and sense of purpose.

Kilik, J., T. Robbins, and R. Simmons (producers) and T. Robbins (director). *Dead Man Walking*. United States: Havoc, 1995. Inspired by true events, *Dead Man Walking* recounts the complicated relationship between a Catholic religious sister, Helen Prejean (played by Susan Sarandon), and a death row inmate, Matthew Poncelet (played by Sean Penn). When Poncelet asks her to assist in his legal appeal and serve as his spiritual adviser, Sister Helen agrees, to the outrage of many, who question how she can show mercy to a man capable of a brutal rape and murder of a teenage couple. While this film explores the morality of capital punishment, it also conveys Sister Helen's resolute purpose to demonstrate love for the world, even in the face of evil.

Morrissey, J. (producer), and T. Kaye (director). *American History X*. United States: New Line Cinema, 1998. Growing up in Venice Beach, California, brothers Derek and Danny Vinyard are exposed to the racism of their father. When their father is murdered by a black drug dealer, Derek embraces white supremacism. His rhetoric gains him a leadership position in a skinhead organization, and his violence lands him in jail. During his prison term, Derek is transformed by friendship with a black prisoner and the counsel of a former high school teacher. Upon his release from prison, Derek embarks on a mission to convert his younger brother from the trap of racism and save him from a similar fate.

Overview of Programmatic Tools

Exploration programs typically deployed multiple and overlapping tools to accomplish their goals, but some focused on one or two tools. A brief description of these tools, their target participants, and variations in implementation follows.

Programmatic Tool: Retreats

Whether a flagship program or a supplemental tool, retreats were popular vehicles for purpose exploration. Retreats remove distraction, facilitate reflection, and nurture discussion.

- *Participation:* Student retreats ranged from general, offered to any interested party, to specific, such as programs for sophomores only or women discerning a call to ordained ministry. They were held under the auspices of campus ministry or as culminating experiences for classes, internships, or semesters abroad. Faculty retreats typically explored purpose and vocation in relation to academic professions, institutional missions, and liberal arts education. Faculty especially appreciated the cross-disciplinary camaraderie and intellectual engagement they fostered. Participation was sometimes restricted to newly hired faculty or specific academic programs, and sometimes required application. Attractive retreat sites and stipends helped launch these programs on religiously heterogeneous campuses. Staff retreats disclosed fuller identities and united staff as vocation stories were shared. Staff particularly appreciated retreat validation of their work with students. Some programs invited students, alumni, faculty, and staff to a common retreat. These retreats offered reflection, discussion, and presentations, tapping alumni and employees as leaders and launching mentoring relationships.
- *Implementation:* Shared reading assignments were a frequent starting point. Autobiographies, classical literature, and religious texts engaged the construction of a meaningful life, with writing assignments and small-group discussion follow-up. Guest speakers who shared their religious and professional journeys were common. Devotional activities, keyed to institutional heritage (prayer, meditation, religious services, etc.), often played a large role. And personality tests developed by positive psychologists were sometimes used to discuss gifts, talents, and passions.

Programmatic Tool: Internships

Internships provided students with opportunities to investigate career interests firsthand. Supplemented with reflective opportunities and mentorship, internships lend themselves to purpose exploration.

- *Participation:* Typically juniors or seniors, sometimes restricted to fellowship or scholarship recipients.
- *Implementation:* Some internship programs were open to all career fields; some were restricted to nonprofit organization or ministry fields only. They were often coordinated by a staff member and sometimes by a faculty adviser. A reflective component, be it individual or in a group setting, was standard. Links to alumni mentors were also common. Stipends for needy students or to support internships in nonprofit organizations were sometimes offered. Nonprofit and volunteer service fairs often overlapped with internship programs.

Programmatic Tool: Courses

Coursework was the most direct avenue for introduction of purpose exploration texts. This ranged from enhancements to preexisting courses to restructurings of core curriculum.

- *Participants:* Students enrolled in elective courses, meeting academic program requirements, or campus-wide requirements, taught by faculty volunteers, new faculty hires, or staff adjuncts.
- *Implementation:* Some campuses infused exploration themes into first-year writing seminars; others into senior capstones; and still others into certificate programs, fellowship programs, or academic minors. Individual academic departments sometimes infused exploration throughout their programs, as did some campuses with undeclared majors. Service-learning was a frequent and natural link to course-based purpose exploration. Assignments included writing, journaling, blogs, website creation, and video projects.

Programmatic Tool: Themed Residence Halls

A themed residence hall concentrated exploration programming among a select group of participants. Intentional community, academic connections, extracurricular activities, and spiritual reflection were common components.

- *Participants:* Students generally self-select into such programs through an application process, which may include essays, recommendations, and interviews. Invitations to participate based on recommendations from staff or faculty can be extended as well. Hall alumni can return as resident advisers or student chaplains. Faculty and staff can be called upon as instructors, mentors, or guest speakers to guide students in exploration, and they may receive training (via seminars, workshops, or retreats) as a precursor to their involvement.
- *Implementation:* An entire dorm building can be devoted to purpose exploration, or a single floor can host a select group of participants. Exploration can be focused around a specific vocation (e.g., clergy) or notable person, such as a saint or heroic figure whose life exemplified vocation. Residents can be assigned mentors (alumni, faculty, or staff) with whom students meet to review their exploration process, career plans, service activities, or internship experiences. Residents can be required to read and discuss assigned texts, attend presentations and lectures, view and analyze exploration-themed films, and discuss these in small groups or with mentors. Community-building activities, such as service trips or retreats, can foster communication and cohesion among residents. Residents can enroll in exploration-related courses together, taught by allied faculty or staff, creating a living-learning-exploring community.

Programmatic Tool: Employee Development

Faculty development keyed to purpose exploration could result in deep and systematic impact, as participants shared what they learned with others and infused it into their teaching and scholarship. Development programs for staff, separately or jointly with faculty, were also influential. Such programs varied widely, and were made available to employees in general or restricted to specific subpopulations.

- *Participation:* Institutions with a small faculty pool could opt to involve all faculty members in development activities, introducing the program in waves. Alternatively, participants could self-select into the program, by application or nomination. Newly hired faculty members could be invited or required to participate in exploration programming as part of their employee orientation. Staff members in direct contact with students, residence life employees, and career services officers were often keenly interested in purpose exploration programming. Given the busyness of campus workplaces, employees frequently voiced appreciation for the camaraderie and time to reflect. Stipends or teaching releases encouraged wide involvement.
- *Implementation:* Exploration could be introduced via retreat, seminar, or workshop. Topics could include faith and learning, liberal arts and student formation, the institutional mission, religious heritage of the college or university, or discussion of teaching and scholarship. Exploration readings, sampling from literature, philosophy, and theology, were common, as were discussions of implications for scholarship, student development, and institutional mission. Participants often shared their vocation stories, detailing the influences, decisions, and experiences that led them to pursue a life in higher education. These programs could serve as gateway activities to further exploration-related resources, such as curriculum development resources or special project minigrants.

Programmatic Tool: Personality Testing and Advising

A common strategy for fostering exploration was personality tests with post-test advising or workshops. The most popular tool was Gallup's *StrengthsFinder,* which identifies test takers' top-five character strengths, and promotes capitalizing on one's inherent talents and tendencies rather than addressing deficiencies. A few campuses made these campus-wide initiatives, with employees posting their own results outside their office doors, and new students being tested and advised during the orientation process, generating a language about strengths and purpose exploration. Other campuses used these tests during a larger program, such as a retreat, course, or seminar.

Programmatic Tool: Service-Learning

Actively engaging the world via service was frequently understood as a core component of purpose exploration. Embedding service within a course, academic program, or fellowship program, and especially service that required higher-level skills and specialized knowledge, reaped pedagogical, individual, and program-level rewards. Some service-learning activities were mandatory, campus-wide events. Most were local, but many involved interstate and even international travel, and the latter often fostered long-term relationships between site organizations and the campus. Alternative spring breaks were another popular structure. As with all service-learning, a reflective component was essential to individual and collective learning.

Programmatic Tool: Scholarships and Fellowships

Scholarship programs deployed a wide variety of tools among select participants. This concentration of effort had high potential to profoundly impact students, and the presence of a small group of deeply engaged students could invigorate others on campus. Such programs were usually organized around a particular career field or academic discipline, and featured broad involvement by faculty or staff advisers. Student participants completed a series of courses, service requirements, or off-campus activities. A few programs focused on scholarly research activity and careers. Minigrants for student fellows were common, as were stipends for faculty or staff mentors.

Programmatic Tool: Seminary Semesters

The opportunity to spend time living and learning in a seminary or school of divinity can be invaluable to undergraduate students considering graduate theological education. Outstanding students can be invited to apply, or this opportunity can be announced openly. In either case, requisite academic ability and personal dedication must be sufficient for a successful graduate school experience. Follow-up projects, internships, or reflection exercises were common. A frequent variation was enrollment in a three- to six-week summer or winter seminary course.

Programmatic Tool: Campus-Wide Events

Events vary widely in type, intended audience, and specific topic. Events may focus on: spirituality and higher learning, meaning and work, student formation, or denomination-specific theology. While events can stand alone, they are often combined into a "series" or designed to augment related activities. Guest lectures — by religious or humanitarian leaders, authors of exploration texts, or respected members of the campus community — can relay stories, research findings, or religious insights into the construction of a meaningful life. Local, regional, or national conferences allow participants to learn from keynote speakers, workshops, and panel discussions. Networking possibilities afforded are additional benefits. Chapel services can be devoted to purpose exploration topics, career fairs can feature nonprofit organizations and service opportunities, and film or performance series can engage exploration themes.

Programmatic Tool: Formal Mentorship

Formalized mentorship programs offer purpose exploration through one-on-one or small-group academic, professional, and spiritual conversations. Relationships can be launched via these programs, or existing relationships can be enhanced. Mentors may receive stipends, and mentorship can be guided by a common structure or simply facilitated by common access to resources — such as reimbursement for meals, texts, or travel.

Programmatic Tool: Student Chaplaincies

Chaplaincy programs offered an innovative way to foster purpose exploration among students. Undergraduate or graduate students were assigned to residence halls to supplement residence life staff. Providing spiritual support, religious activities, and counsel, student chaplains foster exploration among students while themselves considering ministry callings directly. Student chaplains were typically selected, trained, and supervised by campus chaplains.

Selected Bibliography of Theological Works

Alviar, J. J. *Klesis: The Theology of the Christian Vocation According to Origen*. Dublin: Four Courts Press, 1993.

Bennethum, D. M. *Listen! God Is Calling! Luther Speaks of Vocation, Faith, and Work*. Minneapolis: Augsburg Fortress, 2003.

Bezzerides, A. M., ed. *Christ at Work: Orthodox Christian Perspectives on Vocation*. Brookline, MA: Holy Cross Orthodox Press, 2006.

Bolles, R. N. *How to Find Your Mission in Life*. New York: Ten Speed Press, 2005.

Brennfleck, K., and K. M. Brennfleck. *Living Your Calling: A Practical Guide to Finding and Fulfilling Your Mission in Life*. San Francisco: Jossey-Bass, 2004.

Buechner, F. *Now and Then: A Memoir of Vocation*. New York: HarperOne, 1991.

Chatham, J. O. *Is It I, Lord?* Louisville: Westminster John Knox, 2002.

Clapper, G. S. *Living Your Heart's Desire: God's Call and Your Vocation*. Nashville: Upper Room, 2005.

Coombs, M. T., and F. K. Nemeck. *Called by God: A Theology of Vocation and Lifelong Commitment*. Eugene, OR: Wipf and Stock Publishers, 1992.

Cross, T. L. *Answering the Call in the Spirit: Pentecostal Reflections on a Theology of Vocation, Work and Life*. Cleveland, TN: Lee University Press, 2007.

Duffy, M. F. *The Skeptical, Passionate Christian: Tools for Living Faithfully in an Uncertain World*. Louisville: Westminster John Knox, 2006.

Dunaway, J. M., ed. *Gladly Learn, Gladly Teach: Living Out One's Calling in the Twenty-First Century Academy*. Macon, GA: Mercer University Press, 2005.

Dunnam, M. D., and S. G. W. Malone, eds. *Living Life on Purpose: The Joy of Discovering and Following God's Call*. Franklin, TN: Providence House Publishers, 2005.

Fowler, J. *Becoming Adults, Becoming Christian: Adult Development and Christian Faith*. San Francisco: Jossey-Bass, 1999.

Grisez, G., and R. Shaw. *Personal Vocation: God Calls Everyone by Name*. Huntington, IN: Our Sunday Visitor, 2003.

Guinness, O. *The Long Journey Home: A Guide to Your Search for the Meaning of Life*. Colorado Springs, CO: Waterbrook Multnomah, 2001.

Haughey, J. C., ed. *Revisiting the Idea of Vocation: Theological Explorations*. Washington, DC: Catholic University of America Press, 2004.

Henry, D. V., and B. R. Agee, eds. *Faithful Learning and the Christian Scholarly Vocation*. Grand Rapids, MI: Eerdmans, 2003.

Herring, B. *The Rabbinate as Calling and Vocation: Models of Rabbinic Leadership*. Lanham, MD: Jason Aronson Publishers, 1991.

Holderness, G. W., and F. Palmer. *Career and Calling: A Guide for Counselors, Youth and Young Adults*. Louisville: Westminster John Knox, 2001.

Hughes, R. T. *The Vocation of the Christian Scholar: How Christian Faith Can Sustain the Life of the Mind*. Rev. ed. Grand Rapids, MI: Eerdmans, 2005.

Hunter, V. L. *Desert Hearts, Healing Fountains: Gaining Pastoral Vocational Clarity*. Atlanta: Chalice Press, 2003.

Jensen, D. H. *Responsive Labor: A Theology of Work*. Louisville: Westminster John Knox, 2006.

John Paul II. *The Meaning of Vocation*. New York: Scepter Publishers, 1998.

Kath, R. R. *Called to Ecumenism: A Sense of Vocation at Luther College*. Minneapolis: Kirk House Publishers, 2006.

Landy, T. M., ed. *As Leaven in the World: Catholic Perspectives on Faith, Vocation, and the Intellectual Life*. Lanham, MD: Sheed and Ward, 2001.

LaReau, R. M. *Getting a Life: How to Find Your True Vocation*. Maryknoll, NY: Orbis Books, 2003.

Leider, R. J., and D. A. Shapiro. *Whistle while You Work: Heeding Your Life's Calling*. San Francisco: Berrett-Koehler Publishers, 2001.

Levoy, G. M. *Callings: Finding and Following an Authentic Life*. New York: Three Rivers Press, 1998.

McSwain, L. L., and K. W. Shurden. *Call Waiting: God's Invitation to Youth*. Valley Forge, PA: Judson Press, 2005.

Meilander, G. C. *The Freedom of a Christian: Grace, Vocation, and the Meaning of Our Humanity*. Ada, MI: Brazos Press, 2006.

Miksch, J. A. *Fantastic Vocation!* Bloomington, IN: Xlibris Book Publishing, 2010.

Miller, M. R. *Doing More with Life: Connecting Christian Higher Education to a Call for Service*. Waco, TX: Baylor University Press, 2007.

Myers, W. H. *God's Yes Was Louder Than My No: Rethinking the African-American Call to Ministry*. Grand Rapids, MI: Eerdmans, 1994.

Parks, S. D. *Big Questions, Worthy Dreams: Mentoring Young Adults in Their Search for Meaning, Purpose and Faith*. San Francisco: Jossey-Bass, 2000.

Peterson, E. H. *Under the Unpredictable Plant: An Exploration in Vocational Holiness*. Grand Rapids, MI: Eerdmans, 1994.

Portaro, S. *Crossing the Jordan: Meditations on Vocation*. Lanham, MD: Cowley Publications, 1999.

Portaro, S. *Transforming Vocation*. Edited by J. Lemler. Harrisburg, PA: Church Publishing, 2008.

Proctor, M. *Do You Heart What I Hear? Religious Calling, the Priesthood, and My Father*. New York: Viking Adult, 2005.

Rulla, L. M. *Anthropology of the Christian Vocation*. Vol. 1, *Interdisciplinary Bases*. Rome, Italy: Gregorian University Press, 1989.

Rulla, L. M., J. Ridick, and F. Imoda. *Anthropology of the Christian Vocation*. Vol. 2, *Existential Confirmation*. Rome, Italy: Gregorian University Press, 1989.

Schultze, Q. J. *Here I Am: Now What on Earth Should I Be Doing?* Ada, MI: Baker Books, 2005.

Schuster, J. P. *Answering Your Call: A Guide to Living Your Deepest Purpose*. San Francisco: Berrett-Koehler Publishers, 2003.

Schuurman, D. J. *Vocation: Discerning Our Callings in Life*. Grand Rapids, MI: Eerdmans, 2004.

Schwehn, M. R. *Exiles from Eden: Religion and the Academic Vocation in America*. New York: Oxford University Press USA, 2005.

Sheldrake, P. *Befriending Our Desires*. Notre Dame, IN: Ave Maria Press, 1994.

Svennungsen, A., and M. Wiginton, eds. *Awakened to a Calling: Reflections on the Vocation of Ministry*. Nashville: Abingdon Press, 2005.

Veith, G. E., Jr. *God at Work: Your Christian Vocation in All of Life*. Wheaton, IL: Crossway Books, 2002.

Volf, M. *Work in the Spirit: Toward a Theology of Work*. Eugene, OR: Wipf and Stock Publishers, 2001.

Warren, R. *The Purpose Driven Life*. Grand Rapids, MI: Zondervan, 2002.

Williams, R. *Ray of Darkness*. Lanham, MD: Cowley Publications, 1995.

Wingren, G. *Luther on Vocation*. Eugene, OR: Wipf and Stock Publishers, 2004.

Preface

1. Richard Arum and Josipa Roksa, *Aspiring Adults Adrift: Tentative Transitions of College Graduates* (Chicago: University of Chicago Press, 2014); Richard Arum and Josipa Roksa, *Academically Adrift: Limited Learning on College Campuses* (Chicago: University of Chicago Press, 2010); and Christian Smith with Kari Christoffersen, Hilary Davidson, and Patricia Snell Herzog, *Lost in Transition: The Dark Side of Emerging Adulthood* (New York: Oxford University Press, 2011).

2. Indeed, there are academics actively discouraging students from pursuing PhDs in the humanities. The best example of this is Thomas H. Benton, "Graduate School in the Humanities: Just Don't Go," *Chronicle of Higher Education*, January 30, 2009. And there was plenty of evidence in the years that immediately followed the Great Recession of a sharp rise in graduate school applications. For example, Daniel Luzer, "Economic Meltdown Causes Surge in Grad School Applications," *Washington Monthly*, January 10, 2010.

3. Melissa Korn, "Colleges Try Cutting Tuition — and Aid Packages," *Wall Street Journal*, October 11, 2013, accessed March 25, 2014, http://online.wsj.com /news/articles/SB10001424052702303643304579107683540651404; Karen Farkas, "Ohio Northern University Will Reduce Tuition Next Year," *(Cleveland) Plain Dealer*, October 10, 2013, accessed April 30, 2014, http://www.cleveland .com/metro/index.ssf/2013/10/ohio_northern_university_will.html; and

Roberts Wesleyan College in Rochester, NY, offers "free rooms for freshmen" as of March 2014 (https://www.roberts.edu/home/free-room.aspx).

4. Andrew Delbanco, *College: What It Was, Is, and Should Be* (Princeton, NJ: Princeton University Press, 2012), 177.

5. Robert J. Nash and Michele C. Murray, *Helping College Students Find Purpose: The Campus Guide to Meaning-Making* (San Francisco: Jossey-Bass, 2010).

Chapter 1

1. Shirley M. Tilghman, "Commencement 2009: In Pursuit of Purpose and Meaning," *Princeton Alumni Weekly*, July 15, 2009, 2.

2. Dismantling the privileges that restricted higher education to white males from moneyed backgrounds was extraordinarily important in democratizing higher education. Unfortunately, there was a widespread sense that higher education was a formative experience, and that its recipients possessed important social obligations, that disappeared from all but the rhetoric of higher education.

3. Among my favorites in this genre are Andrew Delbanco, *College: What It Was, Is, and Should Be* (Princeton, NJ: Princeton University Press, 2012); Anthony T. Kronman, *Education's End: Why Our Colleges and Universities Have Given Up on the Meaning of Life* (New Haven, CT: Yale University Press, 2007); Harry R. Lewis, *Excellence without a Soul: How a Great University Forgot Education* (New York: PublicAffairs/Perseus Book Group, 2006); Derek Bok, *Our Underachieving Colleges* (Princeton, NJ: Princeton University Press, 2006); Derek Bok, *Universities in the Marketplace: The Commercialization of Higher Education* (Princeton, NJ: Princeton University Press, 2004); Robert Zemsky, Gregory R. Wegner, and William F. Massy, *Remaking the American University: Market-Smart and Mission-Centered* (New Brunswick, NJ: Rutgers University Press, 2006); William H. Willimon and Thomas H. Naylor, *The Abandoned Generation: Rethinking Higher Education* (Grand Rapids, MI: Eerdmans, 1995); Harold T. Shapiro, *A Larger Sense of Purpose: Higher Education and Society* (Princeton, NJ: Princeton University Press, 2005); Adrianna J. Kezar, Tony C. Chambers, John C. Burkhardt, and Associates, *Higher Education for the Public Good: Emerging Voices from a National Movement* (San Francisco: Jossey-Bass, 2005); Parker J. Palmer and Arthur Zajonc, *The Heart of Higher Education: A Call to Renewal* (San Francisco: Jossey-Bass, 2010); and Robert J. Nash and Michele C. Murray, *Helping College Students Find Purpose: The Campus Guide to Meaning-Making* (San Francisco: Jossey-Bass, 2010).

4. According to the National Study of Youth and Religion, conducted in 2002–3, 52 percent of US teens attend religious services regularly: 12 percent attend two to three times per month, 24 percent attend once a week, and 16 percent attend more than once a week. We also know that 45 percent of teens attend with both parents, 21 percent with one parent, and 10 percent attend without their parents (with only 24 percent never attending). See Christian Smith with Melinda Lundquist Denton, *Soul Searching: The Religious and Spiritual Lives of American Teenagers* (New York: Oxford University Press, 2005), table 6, p. 37.

5. In my first book, *The First Year Out: Understanding American Teens after High School* (Chicago: University of Chicago Press, 2007), I described how most American teens view

religion as akin to vegetables: as something good for you, but not anything to get excited about. Thus, religion is easily trumped by more exciting offerings on life's buffet. Smith with Denton, *Soul Searching*, make a similar point.

6. See Arlie Hochschild with Anne Machung, *The Second Shift: Working Parents and the Revolution at Home* (New York: Avon Books, 1989).

7. Salary data are available from the American Association of University Professors (American Association of University Professors, *AAUP Contingent Faculty Index 2006*, accessed April 30, 2014, http://www.aaup.org/reports-publications/publications/see-all /aaup-contingent-faculty-index-2006 and http://www.aaup.org/sites/default/files/files /AAUPContingentFacultyIndex2006.pdf) Student entrance exam statistics, as well as student body characteristics, can be found in numerous places, including the *Princeton Review* (http://www.princetonreview.com/college-education.aspx), *U.S. News & World Report* (http://www.usnews.com/rankings), and national university associations: American Association of State Colleges and Universities (http://www.aascu.org/), American Council on Education (http://www.acenet.edu/Pages/default.aspx), Association of American Colleges and Universities (http://www.aacu.org/), Association of American Universities (http://www.aau.edu/), Association of Catholic Colleges and Universities (http://www .accunet.org/i4a/pages/index.cfm?pageid=1), Association of Jesuit Colleges and Universities (http://www.ajcunet.edu/), Council for Christian Colleges and Universities (http:// www.cccu.org/), Council of Independent Colleges (http://www.cic.edu/Pages/default .aspx), and National Association of Independent Colleges and Universities (http://www .naicu.edu/).

8. For general information about private, nonprofit colleges, see National Association of Independent Colleges and Universities, *Independent Colleges and Universities: A National Profile*, 2011, accessed April 30, 2014, http://www.naicu.edu/data_research/detail/private _colleges_factfile.

9. For an engaging account of Dr. Paul Farmer's work, see Tracy Kidder, *Mountains beyond Mountains: The Quest of Dr. Paul Farmer, a Man Who Would Cure the World* (New York: Random House, 2003).

10. Navigational charts need not be religious, of course. In *Helping College Students Find Purpose*, education scholars Robert Nash and Michele Murray describe therapeutic metanarratives that have been successfully used to support college students' search for meaning and purpose.

11. Results are from the Spirituality Project at the University of California–Los Angeles's Higher Education Research Institute, as released to Elizabeth Redden of the *Chronicle of Higher Education*, and published in her article "More Spiritual, but Not in Church," *Chronicle of Higher Education*, December 18, 2007.

12. The first two figures come from Astin, Astin, and Lindholm's longitudinal panel research of 14,527 college students enrolled at 136 four-year colleges and universities. See Alexander W. Astin, Helen S. Astin, and Jennifer A. Lindholm, *Cultivating the Spirit: How College Can Enhance Students' Inner Lives* (San Francisco: Jossey-Bass, 2010). For earlier findings and related findings among faculty, visit the Spirituality in Higher Education project at the University of California–Los Angeles's Higher Education Research Institute, http://www.spirituality.ucla.edu/). Their figure on spirituality is a statistically significant

8 percentage point increase from these students' first year of college, while following religious teachings is a constant figure from first year to junior year of college. From the Pew Research Center's February 2010 report, we learn that 68 percent of Americans between the ages of eighteen and twenty-nine identify as Christians. See *Religion among the Millennials*, Pew Research Center, 2010, accessed April 30, 2014, http://www.pewforum.org /2010/02/17/religion-among-the-millennials/.

13. The problem may well be that fewer than one-third of college faculty believe that colleges or universities should be concerned with students' spiritual development. These statistics and much more can be found in *Spirituality and the Professoriate: A National Study of Faculty Beliefs, Attitudes, and Behaviors*, Higher Education Research Institute, University of California, Los Angeles, 2006, accessed April 30, 2014, http://spirituality.ucla .edu/docs/results/faculty/spirit_professoriate.pdf. See also Astin, Astin, and Lindholm, *Cultivating the Spirit*.

14. The current president of Harvard University, for example, wrote an op-ed for the *New York Times* claiming a prophetic place for higher education in society, and citing specifically the university's role in producing citizens who ask challenging questions of society. See Drew Giplin Faust's "The University's Crisis of Purpose," *New York Times*, September 1, 2009. Her predecessor, the prolific scholar of American higher education Derek Bok, made a similar case in the *Chronicle of Higher Education*: see his "College and the Well-Lived Life" in the January 31, 2010, issue.

15. Richard P. Keeling and Richard H. Hersh, *We're Losing Our Minds: Rethinking American Higher Education* (New York: Palgrave Macmillan, 2011), 5–6.

16. See Delbanco, *College*; Nash and Murray, *Helping College Students Find Purpose*; Palmer and Zajonc, *Heart of Higher Education*; Lewis, *Excellence without a Soul*; Kronman, *Education's End*; and Stephen T. Asma, "Soul Talk," *Chronicle Review*, May 2, 2010.

17. Richard Arum and Josipa Roksa, *Academically Adrift: Limited Learning on College Campuses* (Chicago: University of Chicago Press, 2010). Ernest T. Pascarella and Patrick T. Terenzini's replication of Arum and Roksa's findings, using the Wabash National Study of Liberal Arts Education, is reported by Dan Barrett, "What Spurs Students to Stay in College and Learn? Good Teaching Practices and Diversity," *Chronicle of Higher Education*, November 6, 2011. See also Keeling and Hersh's *We're Losing Our Minds*.

Chapter 2

1. From my web survey of Ignatius University, $N = 230$; in-house surveys by IU report similar figures. See app. 2, "Methodology," for more information.

2. This was fortunate for IU. Those programs that hired PhDs whose (secret) personal goals were finding a path into the professoriate often discovered that the central student development piece of this initiative got placed on a back burner, while secondary projects involving scholarship, course creation, and instruction preoccupied the director. Not all directors with PhDs and without faculty appointments had such goals, but several did— and it was deadly for their programs' impact. See chapter 6 for a fuller discussion.

3. This happened because the Campus Center realized that some faculty could not be released from their teaching and others did not want such a release. It also saved money.

4. Beckie Supiano, "More Top Students Answer the Ministry's Call," *Chronicle of Higher Education*, July 4, 2008.

5. The numerator of 414 proposals is based on 37 first-round and 50 second-round invitations, all of whose recipients applied (would any college not apply for $2 million?), plus 326 applications received during the open third round (and one grandfathered invitation to a pilot program that preceded the first round and is not counted above). The 900 denominator figure is a commonly cited estimate of religiously affiliated colleges and universities in America, based on the US Department of Education, National Center for Education Statistics, Higher Education General Information Survey (HEGIS), "Fall Enrollments in Institutions of Higher Education" and "Institutional Characteristics" surveys, and Integrated Postsecondary Education Data Systems (IPEDS), "Fall Enrollment" and "Institutional Characteristics" surveys (see http://nces.ed.gov/; see also http://www.cccu.org/filefolder/Profile_US_Post-Secondary_Education-updated2010.pdf, accessed July 15, 2010). See also the appendix of Merrimon Cuninggim's *Uneasy Partners: The College and the Church* (Nashville: Abingdon Press, 1994) for a useful typology of these colleges and universities. Note that not all 900 religiously affiliated colleges were eligible to apply, as the Lilly Endowment restricted awards to Christian-affiliated colleges only, eliminating more than 100 colleges and universities and giving an actual application rate in excess of 50 percent.

6. Craig Dykstra, "Plenary Conference Address: The Theological Exploration of Vocation," lecture, Programs for the Theological Exploration of Vocation 2003 Conference, accessed 9 June 2014, http://www.ptev.org/hints.aspx?iid=22.

7. Paul Brest and Hal Harvey, *Money Well Spent: A Strategic Plan for Smart Philanthropy* (New York: Bloomberg Press, 2008), 83.

8. That book has the working title *The First Year Out of College: Driven, Dazed, or Disillusioned.*

9. Three applied sociologists did propose a "solution-centered" sociology that proactively tackled social problems. See Stephen F. Steele, AnneMarie Scarisbrick-Hauser, and William J. Hauser, *Solution-Centered Sociology: Addressing Problems through Applied Sociology* (Thousand Oaks, CA: Sage Publications, 1999). And Robert A. Stebbins, sociologist of leisure, recently proposed a positive sociology focused on how individuals fulfill social obligations and use free time to find fulfillment. See Stebbins's *Personal Decisions in the Public Square: Beyond Problem Solving into a Positive Sociology* (New Brunswick, NJ: Transaction, 2009). But neither effort attracted the follow-up necessary to generate momentum around the idea of positive sociology.

10. William Damon, *The Path to Purpose: Helping Our Children Find Their Calling in Life* (New York: Free Press, 2008), 7.

11. See Daniel Goleman, *Emotional Intelligence: Why It Can Matter More Than IQ* (London: Bloomsbury, 1996), xii, 79–80.

12. For an introduction to this voluminous literature, I would recommend the following: Howard Gardner, Mihaly Csikszentmihalyi, and William Damon's *Good Work: When Excellence and Ethics Meet* (New York: Basic Books, 2001); Christopher Peterson and Martin Seligman's *Character Strengths and Virtues: A Handbook and Classification* (New York: Oxford University Press, 2004); C. R. Snyder and Shane J. Lopez's *Oxford*

Handbook of Positive Psychology, 2nd ed. (New York: Oxford University Press, 2009); and Martin Seligman's *Authentic Happiness: Using the New Positive Psychology to Realize Your Potential for Lasting Fulfillment* (New York: Free Press, 2002).

13. In other words, four out of five full-time students spend fewer than thirty hours weekly in class *and study*, effectively making college into a convenient part-time job.

14. See the American Association of University Professors' *AAUP Contingent Faculty Index 2006*, based on US Department of Education surveys of 2,617 institutions of higher education in 2005, accessed April 30, 2014, http://www.aaup.org/reports-publications/publications/see-all/aaup-contingent-faculty-index-2006 and http://www.aaup.org/sites/default/files/files/AAUPContingentFacultyIndex2006.pdf. See also the American Association of University Professors' *Trends in Faculty Employment Status: 1975–2011*, 2014, accessed April 30, 2014, http://www.aaup.org/sites/default/files/Faculty_Trends_0.pdf.

15. Pressures to publish and to staff committees have meant a decline in full-time faculty hours spent advising students, despite a steady uptick in student numbers. For example, the National Study of Postsecondary Faculty (NSOPF), conducted in 1998–99 and 2003–4 by the US Department of Education, reveals across-the-board declines (with just a couple of exceptions) in "weekly hours spent with advisees" for all instructors. Ditto for "hours spent on unpaid tasks," using all three waves of the NSOPF (1992–93, 1998–99, and 2003–4). Author's analysis using the National Center for Education Statistics, DAS-T Online Version 5.0 software, on July 22, 2010.

16. The analogy of higher education to the newspaper industry comes courtesy of Kevin Carey's "College for $99 a Month," *Washington Monthly*, September–October 2009.

17. Mary Grigsby, *College Life through the Eyes of Students* (Albany, NY: SUNY Press, 2009).

18. Anthony Giddens, *Modernity and Self-Identity: Self and Society in the Late Modern Age* (Stanford, CA: Stanford University Press, 1991).

19. Zygmunt Baumann, *The Individualized Society* (Cambridge: Polity Press, 2001).

20. Robert N. Bellah, Richard N. Madsen, William M. Sullivan, Ann Swidler, and Steven M. Tipton, *Habits of the Heart: Individualism and Commitment in American Life* (Berkeley and Los Angeles: University of California Press, 1985).

21. Robert Putnam, *Bowling Alone: The Collapse and Revival of American Community* (New York: Simon and Schuster, 2000).

22. Robert Wuthnow, *Loose Connections: Joining Together in America's Fragmented Communities* (Cambridge, MA: Harvard University Press, 1998).

23. The figure-illustrated drop in the public's confidence in "education" and the "scientific community" from 49.5 percent and 50.5 percent, respectively, in 1974 to 29.5 percent and 40.4 percent in 2008 is in keeping with the following findings: 59 percent of a nationally representative survey agree that "many young people are just wasting their time and money in college because they don't know what else to do with their lives," 44 percent agree that "faculty and administrators should do more to help [increase access to higher education] by teaching more classes and cutting costs," and 28 percent agree that colleges and universities "are failing to teach [students] the important things they need to know." See John Immerwahr, *The Price of Admission: The Growing Importance of Higher Education*, a report of the National Center for Public Policy and Higher Education, Spring 1998,

accessed April 30, 2014, http://publicagendaarchives.org/pages/the-price-admission-the-growing-importance-higher-education. A survey of business leaders in 1999 found the following: 83 percent agreed that "business and government have had to become leaner and more efficient—higher education must now do the same," and only 30 percent agreed that "since society benefits from having a large number of college graduates, taxpayers should pay more of the cost of a college education." One might expect the latter from business leaders, who have often been critical of higher education. What is even more surprising, then, is that when deans and professors were asked the same question, fewer than half of these educators agreed. See John Immerwahr, *Taking Responsibility: Leaders' Expectations of Higher Education*, conducted and reported by Public Agenda for the National Center for Public Policy and Higher Education, January 1999, accessed April 30, 2014, http://www.highereducation.org/reports/responsibility/responsibility.shtml.

24. John Immerwahr and Jean Johnson, *Squeeze Play 2010: Continued Public Anxiety on Cost, Harsher Judgments on How Colleges Are Run*, Washington, DC, Public Agenda, February 2010, accessed April 30, 2014, http://www.publicagenda.org/media/squeeze-play-2010.

25. Derek Bok, "Reclaiming the Public Trust," *Change*, July–August 1992, 13–21.

26. See Harry R. Lewis, *Excellence without a Soul: How a Great University Forgot Education* (New York: PublicAffairs/Perseus Book Group, 2006); Anthony T. Kronman, *Education's End: Why Our Colleges and Universities Have Given Up on the Meaning of Life* (New Haven, CT: Yale University Press, 2007); Harold T. Shapiro, *A Larger Sense of Purpose: Higher Education and Society* (Princeton, NJ: Princeton University Press, 2005); and Derek Bok, *Our Underachieving Colleges* (Princeton, NJ: Princeton University Press, 2006).

27. See Arthur W. Chickering, Jon C. Dalton, and Liesa Stamm, *Encouraging Authenticity and Spirituality in Higher Education* (San Francisco: Jossey-Bass, 2006); George D. Kuh and Robert M. Gonyea, "Spirituality, Liberal Learning, and College Student Engagement," *Liberal Education* (Winter 2006): 40–47; Sharon Daloz Parks, *Big Questions, Worthy Dreams* (San Francisco: Jossey-Bass, 2000); Parker J. Palmer, *Let Your Life Speak: Listening for the Voice of Vocation* (San Francisco: Jossey-Bass, 1999); Robert J. Nash and Michele C. Murray, *Helping College Students Find Purpose: The Campus Guide to Meaning-Making* (San Francisco: Jossey-Bass, 2010); Parker J. Palmer and Arthur Zajonc, *The Heart of Higher Education: A Call to Renewal* (San Francisco: Jossey-Bass, 2010); and Alexander W. Astin, Helen S. Astin, and Jennifer A. Lindholm, *Cultivating the Spirit: How College Can Enhance Students' Inner Lives* (San Francisco: Jossey-Bass, 2010).

28. Steve Stewart-Williams, *Darwin, God, and the Meaning of Life: How Evolutionary Theory Undermines Everything You Know* (New York: Cambridge University Press, 2010).

Chapter 3

1. Huffington did depart Phi Beta more than a decade later, but its programs continued without missing a beat under the energetic leadership of a new Meaningful Work Initiative director, who was an alum of another campus that had received a PTEV grant.

2. There are about 300 religiously homogeneous colleges and universities in the United States. Some 182 are affiliated with the evangelical Council for Christian Colleges and Universities (a nonprofit organization in Washington, DC; see http://cccu.org/

members_and_affiliates), and another 94 are affiliated with the evangelical Association for Biblical Higher Education (see http://www.abhe.org/pages/NAV-Directory.html). There are also 224 colleges and universities in the United States affiliated with the Roman Catholic Church, of which 21 are proudly profiled in a guidebook by the conservative Cardinal Newman Society for their "faithfulness to Catholic teaching." See Cardinal Newman Society, *The Newman Guide to Choosing a Catholic College*, 2014 ed. (Manassas, VA: Cardinal Newman Society, 2014). For a more comprehensive discussion of church-related colleges, along with helpful appendixes listing and variously grouping 784 religiously affiliated institutions of higher education, see Merrimon Cuninggim's *Uneasy Partners: The College and the Church* (Nashville: Abingdon Press, 1994).

3. See chapter 2's discussion of the third reason for the Rebound retreats' success, and my book *The First Year Out: Understanding American Teens after High School* (Chicago: University of Chicago Press, 2007).

4. The continuous story is, to be sure, one of several types of life stories. See Mary Catherine Bateson, *Composing a Life* (New York: Grove Press, 2001).

5. From my web survey of 257 students and alumni of Pullman College.

6. I base that estimate on a figure of two-thirds to three-quarters that Pullman's chaplain gave me. He cited Cooperative Institutional Research Program (CIRP), National Study of Student Engagement (NSSE), and internal survey results, as well as his anecdotal experience, to support that figure. He may be right, but social desirability is also operative, so I take his lower figure and halve it.

7. There were only twenty-eight responses to my web survey at CDD. The chaplain, a delightful and energetic woman, was weak administratively and with technology. Thus, the web survey invitation received neither the breadth of distribution nor the follow-up reminders that netted more participants on other campuses.

8. I cannot cite the evaluation report due to my confidentiality agreements with Richboro. But I can say that it administered well-known and externally validated psychological measures of maturity to a stratified random sample of Richboro students in general, for which it had a response rate of over 50 percent, and to the entire population of PEH, for which it had a response rate of nearly 90 percent. It repeated this result across several cohorts of PEH participants, and the results consistently showed: (1) significant gains in maturity from entrance into the PEH program to exit from the program; (2) higher maturity scores by PEH participants than by Richboro sophomores in general, but only modestly so at PEH entrance and considerably so at PEH exit; and (3) PEH exit maturity scores equivalent to those of graduating Richboro seniors.

9. See Christian Smith with Kari Christoffersen, Hilary Davidson, and Patricia Snell Herzog, *Lost in Transition: The Dark Side of Emerging Adulthood* (New York: Oxford University Press, 2011.

10. I have been privileged to consult with the Woodrow Wilson National Fellowship Foundation for over twenty years, evaluating several of its grant programs designed to increase diversity in academia. Mentorship is extraordinarily important for scholarly and professional success, but always difficult for a grant program to externally foster. See Charles V. Willie, Michael K. Grady, and Richard O. Hope's *African Americans and the Doctoral Experience: Implications for Policy* (New York: Teachers College Press, 1991).

11. See chap. 2, n. 15, which cites results from the National Study of Postsecondary Faculty (NSOPF).

12. See the business best seller that started this mini-industry for Gallup: Marcus Buckingham and Donald O. Clifton, *Now, Discover Your Strengths* (New York: Free Press, 2001).

13. I am grateful to have one of the country's foremost experts on persuasion, Gary Woodward, as my colleague. His textbook on persuasion, used nationwide, is up to its sixth edition: Gary C. Woodward and Robert E. Denton Jr., *Persuasion and Influence in American Life*, 6th ed. (Long Grove, IL: Waveland Press, 2008).

Chapter 4

1. I obtained permission from "Danny" and "Danielle" to include this description of them from my course. They were happy, in fact, at the prospect of being included in my book.

2. I wrote about this at length in *The First Year Out: Understanding American Teens after High School* (Chicago: University of Chicago Press, 2007). See also Rebekah Nathan's *My Freshman Year: What a Professor Learned by Becoming a Student* (Ithaca, NY: Cornell University Press, 2005) and Mary Grigsby's *College Life through the Eyes of Students* (Albany, NY: SUNY Press, 2009).

3. In developing this typology, I drew from my work in *First Year Out*, where I identified 80 percent of students as "Practical Credentialists," and 20 percent as a hodgepodge of types who refused to use the "identity lockbox"—including the "Future Intelligentsia," which I use again here. Other helpful typologies have been provided by Mary Grigsby (*College Life*, 92) and Helen Lefkowitz Horowitz, *Campus Life: Undergraduate Cultures from the End of the Eighteenth Century to the Present* (New York: Knopf, 1987).

4. Such students abound in preprofessional programs, and according to columnist David Brooks, in the Ivy League. See Brooks's "The Organization Kid," *Atlantic Monthly* 287, no. 4 (2001): 40 ff. And the guru of academic integrity is Donald McCabe, who helped to found the Center for Academic Integrity at Clemson University (http://www.academicintegrity.org/icai/home.php), and whose scholarly review documents the wide extent of cheating on college and university campuses: Donald L. McCabe, Linda Klebe Trevino, and Kenneth D. Butterfield, "Cheating in Academic Institutions: A Decade of Research," *Ethics and Behavior* 11, no. 3 (2001): 219–32.

5. As Murray Sperber so aptly worded it in his book *Beer and Circus: How Big-Time College Sports Is Crippling Undergraduate Education* (New York: Henry Holt, 2000).

6. From the ACT's 2010 *What Works in Student Retention?* survey. Twenty-five percent of students enrolled at private four-year colleges or universities fail to return for their sophomore year, and just 57 percent of students starting at these colleges graduate within six years. That means 18 percent of entering students fall through the cracks starting in their sophomore year. See *What Works in Student Retention?*, ACT Research and Policy Issues, 2010, accessed April 20, 2014, http://www.act.org/research/policymakers/reports/retain.html.

7. The Integrated Postsecondary Education Data System (IPEDS) is a service of the US Department of Education's Office of Educational Research and Improvement's

National Center for Education Statistics, and is available online (http://nces.ed.gov /ipeds/). Using the IPEDS Data Center, I downloaded a spreadsheet containing enrollment counts and six-year graduation rates for all 88 PTEV campuses, along with 672 additional not-for-profit, private-sector, four-year or higher degree-granting institutions from the same thirty states as PTEV campuses. I alphabetized the 672 campuses to create a sampling frame, set my sampling interval to select 88 campuses, and rolled dice to choose the first campus.

8. "Hawthorne effect": *Dictionary of the Social Sciences*, ed. Craig Calhoun (New York: Oxford University Press, 2002), *Oxford Reference Online* (New York: Oxford University Press), accessed May 18, 2011, http://www.oxfordreference.com/views/ENTRY.html ?subview=Main&entry=t104.e741.

9. As judged by minimal postaward program continuation. See app. 4.

10. It is also possible that vocational programs led some students to exit their campuses — as talk of "God's calling" alienated them. One female student told me that participation in her campus's vocational program had led her "to a room of questions more than answers," and that this was increasing her anxiety rather than lessening it. I urged her to make an appointment with her college's counseling center, and urged that campus's program director to ensure that students knew about these resources if overwhelmed by anxiety as a result of vocational reflection. Deep questions will unsettle a person, and this is regarded as a good thing when it moves individuals to more considered answers. With increasing numbers of young adults struggling with anxiety, however, staff should be sure appropriate psychological supports are in place to help those whose unsettling turns into anxiety.

11. The 2009 College Senior Survey (CSS) of the Higher Education Research Institute at the University of California–Los Angeles reports a 49 percent satisfaction rate with "career and academic counseling," and a 63 percent satisfaction rate with "academic advising." So on the narrow question of academic advising — degree requirements, course selection, and so forth — most students are satisfied. When broadened to the larger matter of *career and* academics, however, most students are dissatisfied — except for those students on nine PTEV campuses who responded to my web survey. See Ray Franke, Sylvia Ruiz, Jessica Sharkness, Linda DeAngelo, and John Pryor, *Findings from the 2009 Administration of the College Senior Survey (CSS): National Aggregates*, Higher Education Research Institute, Graduate School of Education and Information Studies, University of California, Los Angeles, February 2010, accessed April 30, 2014, http://www.heri.ucla.edu/PDFs /pubs/Reports/2009_CSS_Report.pdf.

12. See Wesley R. Habley, ed., *The Status of Academic Advising: Findings from the ACT Sixth National Survey*, National Academic Advising Association Monograph Series no. 10 (Manhattan, KS: National Academic Advising Association, 2004), 86.

13. Meg Jay, *The Defining Decade: Why Your Twenties Matter — and How to Make the Most of Them Now* (New York: Twelve, 2012).

14. Clydesdale, *First Year Out*; Nathan, *My Freshman Year*; and Grigsby, *College Life*.

15. Tracy Kidder, *Mountains beyond Mountains: The Quest of Dr. Paul Farmer, a Man Who Would Cure the World* (New York: Random House, 2003); and Bruce Olson, *Bruchko* (Lake Mary, FL: Charisma House, 2006).

16. While no student should be "yelled at," I note this respondent revealed that he was

a free rider. That is, he voluntarily applied to participate in his university's vocation program, accepted the program's considerable benefits, but then sought to opt out of required program activities.

17. See Christian Smith with Patricia Snell's *Souls in Transition: The Religious and Spiritual Lives of Emerging Adults* (New York: Oxford University Press, 2009) and Jeffrey Jensen Arnett's *Emerging Adulthood: The Winding Road from the Late Teens through the Twenties* (New York: Oxford University Press, 2004).

18. For insightful discussions of this phenomenon, see Barbara Ehrenreich's *Fear of Falling: The Inner Life of the Middle Class* (New York: Harper Perennial, 1990) and Katherine S. Newman's *Falling from Grace: Downward Mobility in the Age of Affluence* (Oakland: University of California Press, 1999).

19. This statistic is widely quoted, and occasionally attributed to the Bureau of Labor Statistics (BLS) of the US Department of Labor. But the common inference is inaccurate. The BLS reports 4.4 as the median number of years that wage and salary workers have been with their employers as of September 2010. See US Bureau of Labor Statistics, "Employee Tenure Summary," economic news release, September 18, 2012, accessed April 30, 2014, http://www.bls.gov/news.release/tenure.nr0.htm. Projecting a lifetime employment of thirty-five years, workers would, on average, change employers about eight times—which is not the same as changing careers. We do not have individual, longitudinal datasets that have tracked workers for thirty-five years. The closest we have is the Bureau of Labor Statistics' National Longitudinal Survey of Youth 1979 (NLSY79), which reports that younger baby boomers held an average of 10.8 jobs from ages eighteen to forty-two, with more jobs held during the teen and early twenties years than during later twenties and up. See US Bureau of Labor Statistics, "Number of Jobs Held, Labor Market Activity, and Earnings Growth among the Youngest Baby Boomers: Results from a Longitudinal Survey," news release, July 24, 2012, accessed April 30, 2014, http://www.bls.gov/news.release/pdf/nlsoy.pdf. None of the foregoing should be construed as altering the basic idea that the workplace is shifting profoundly, and with it, career definitions—making a broad education and the ability to learn and acquire skills independently the most essential traits for career success.

20. John H. Pryor, *The American Freshman: National Norms Fall, 2010* (Los Angeles: Higher Education Research Institute, 2010).

21. See Robert P. Gallagher, *National Survey of Counseling Center Directors, 2010*, American College Counseling Association, International Association of Counseling Services Monograph Series 8S, accessed April 30, 2014, http://www.iacsinc.org/NSCCD%20 2010.pdf, as well as previous annual reports produced by the American College Counseling Association. The *New York Times* put an article about the increased seriousness of college student mental health issues on its December 19, 2010, front page: "Mental Health Needs Seen Growing at College" by Trip Gabriel. The *Chronicle of Higher Education* highlighted this matter years earlier: "More College Students Report Diagnoses of Depression" by Eric Hoover and "The Mental Health Crisis: What Colleges Must Do" by Richard D. Kadison, both published on December 10, 2004. See also Richard Kadison and Theresa Foy DiGeronimo's *College of the Overwhelmed: The Campus Mental Health Crisis and What to Do about It* (San Francisco: Jossey-Bass, 2004).

22. Pryor, *American Freshman*.

23. I am grateful to William Sullivan for connecting me to this literature. He saw these studies cited in Peter Turchin's *War and Peace and War: The Rise and Fall of Empires* (Saint Paul: Pi Press, 2005), 119, and Turchin cites Austrian economist Ernst Fehr of the University of Zurich, Switzerland. Fehr collaborates with various coauthors, and there are a substantial number of journal articles that evaluate his theories and replicate his public-good experiments. See Ernst Fehr and Klaus M. Schmidt, "A Theory of Fairness, Competition, and Cooperation," *Quarterly Journal of Economics* 114, no. 3 (August 1999): 817–68; Ernst Fehr and Simon Gachter, "Cooperation and Punishment in Public Goods Experiments," *American Economic Review* 90, no. 4 (September 2000): 980–94; and Ernst Fehr and Urs Fischbacher, "Why Social Preferences Matter: The Impact of Non-selfish Motives on Competition, Cooperation, and Incentives," *Economic Journal* 112, no. 478, Conference Papers (March 2002): C1–C33.

24. Jonathon Kahn with Paul MacDonald, Ian Oliver, and Sam Speers, "Secularity and the Liberal Arts: Reconceiving the Secular and the Practice of the Liberal Arts," posted November 24, 2010, to the Social Science Research Council's Immanent Frame: Secularism, Religion, and the Public Sphere website, accessed April 30, 2014, http://blogs.ssrc .org/tif/2010/11/24/reconceiving-the-secular-and-the-practice-of-the-liberal-arts/. See also my response to Kahn et al., "Secularity and the Liberal Arts: Yearning, Yawning, and Resisting," posted December 8, 2010, in the same forum (http://blogs.ssrc.org/tif/2010 /12/08/yearning-yawning-resisting/).

25. The term, of course, is famously Max Weber's, from his opus *Economy and Society: An Outline of Interpretive Sociology*, ed. Guenther Roth and Claus Wittich (1913; repr., Berkeley: University of California Press, 1978).

26. Ann Braude, *Women and American Religion*, Religion in American Life (New York: Oxford University Press, 2000).

27. Gar Kellom and Miles Groth, eds., *Engaging College Men: Discovering What Works and Why* (Harriman, TN: Men's Studies Press, 2010).

28. Neil Howe and William Strauss, *Millennials Rising: The Next Great Generation* (New York: Vintage, 2000).

29. Here is how I identified this striking difference in life satisfaction: During our follow-up interviews, we asked each graduate to tell us about six broad areas of his or her life. We would ask, "Are you satisfied with _____?" and then name one of the six areas. Since these were open-ended questions, we would listen carefully, ask for further information, and probe for significant changes. By this point in our interview, respondents knew we wanted them to elaborate on their answers and give examples, which they did quite thoughtfully. I realized, however, that I could code these responses quantitatively, assigning 1 point for positive and mature responses, −1 point for negative and immature responses, and 0 for ambivalent and mixed responses. For example, the former trumpet major who enlisted in the marines to hone her performance skills in its drum and bugle corps, who carefully described the "pros" and "cons" of military life and concluded that the pros outweighed the cons, received a score of 1 for work life satisfaction; the college graduate who was "not at all satisfied" with his love life because he "had not met enough members of the Swedish bikini team" received a score of −1 for love life satisfac-

tion; and the young humanitarian who said he struggled with having no friends during his year of international service, but who had recently returned to the United States and was reconnecting with old friends, received a 0 for social life satisfaction. I summed each interviewee's scores across all six items, generating a general life satisfaction index that ranged from −5 to 6 across my 123 interviewees, but skewed toward high satisfaction, with a median of 4. This meant that most interviewees — 82 percent, in fact — expressed more satisfaction than dissatisfaction with their lives (i.e., had positive scores), and 1 in 4 reported satisfaction across all six areas.

While it is typical to use only positive integers in index construction, I wanted this index to be intuitively meaningful. Coding positive and mature responses compared to negative and immature responses is inherently normative, but it is impossible to define maturity without a normative base. A couple of more examples should help clarify my coding schema. One interviewee, for example, would have preferred to be in a long-term romantic relationship — but she was not at the time of our interview and she knew she could not start one given her departure in six weeks for a two-year international service assignment in a remote village. Since she was "OK with that," I coded her love life response as positive and mature. Another interviewee was frustrated with the status of his personal finances — because "months of medical treatment" after graduating from college had left him unable to work, he had only recently recovered and begun working full-time, and had not yet accomplished his long-standing goal of financial independence from his parents. I regarded his drive and efforts to become financially independent, although not fully realized, as positive and indicative of financial maturity. My guiding principle in coding was the Socratic notion of living "an examined life." Interviewees who revealed self- and social awareness as they evaluated different areas of their life thus showed maturity. Those offering scant evidence of self- or social awareness, by contrast, showed immaturity. Like US Supreme Court justice Potter Stewart, who said of pornography, "I know it when I see it," I found that maturity and immaturity could take diverse forms, but believe most readers would concur with the overwhelming majority of my coding decisions.

30. Conversion of this project's qualitative panel interviews into quantitative data made multivariate analysis possible, but its results are not comparable to those gathered from a deductive, quantitative dataset generated from probability-based samples. I sincerely hope that future researchers will replicate my suggestive, nonprobability results using probability-based samples, and inform me of their results. (For further methodological discussion, see app. 2.)

31. I approximated socioeconomic status using two dichotomous indicators: one for those respondents whose parent(s) had completed graduate degrees (41 percent of interviewees), and one for respondents whose parent(s) had a nonsupervisory occupation (22 percent of interviewees). Asking Americans to self-report their social class is notoriously unreliable, since so many idealize being "middle-class." It is also difficult to get children — even young adult offspring — to provide accurate occupational descriptions of their parent(s). Often, one hears "She does something in business." But young adults are quite certain about the educational attainments of their parent(s), and also know if their parent(s) supervise other employees.

32. Those who attended religious services at least monthly were deemed regular attenders, those who attended at least a couple of times a year were deemed occasional attenders, and the rest were deemed nonattenders.

33. For an overview, see Mark D. Regnerus, "Religion and Positive Adolescent Outcomes: A Review of Research and Theory," *Review of Religious Research* 44, no. 4 (2003): 394–413. For the most current research, see Christian Smith with Melinda Lundquist Denton, *Soul Searching: The Religious and Spiritual Lives of American Teenagers* (New York: Oxford University Press, 2005); Smith with Snell, *Souls in Transition*; Lisa D. Pearce and Melinda Lundquist Denton, *A Faith of Their Own: Stability and Change in the Religiosity of America's Adolescents* (New York: Oxford University Press, 2001); Mark Regnerus, *Forbidden Fruit: Sex and Religion in the Lives of American Teenagers* (New York: Oxford University Press, 2007); and Mark Regnerus and Jeremy Uecker, *Premarital Sex in America: How Young Americans Meet, Mate, and Think about Marrying* (New York: Oxford University Press, 2011).

34. I know statistically oriented readers prefer this information in tabular format — I do, too. But designing and publishing multivariate analysis tables drives up book costs, so bear with me as I describe these results in paragraph form. Using my Life Satisfaction Index (mean = 3.11, standard deviation = 2.63) as dependent variable, I fit two linear regression models. With 123 valid cases included, the first model evaluated six predictors: five dichotomous indicators (for PTEV/not, female/not, nonwhite/not, parent with graduate degree/not, parent job nonsupervisory/not) and one continuous indicator (date of birth). Only my PTEV indicator was significant, with a standardized beta of .556, and a model adjusted R-square = .273. The second model added to the foregoing religious service attendance, a three-level ordinal scale with 0 = nonattender, 1 = occasional attender, and 2 = regular attender. The model adjusted R-square rose to .433, with only two significant predictors: PTEV, with a standardized beta of .388, and religious service attendance, with a standardized beta of .432. For all three significant predictors, $p < .001$.

35. For a more complete discussion of multiple regression in an evaluation context, see Laura Irwin Langbein and Claire L. Felbinger, *Public Program Evaluation: A Statistical Guide* (Armonk, NY: M. E. Sharpe, 2006), 141.

36. There were a few interviewees who described congregational surrogates that reinforced their efforts to explore questions of calling and purpose. Most commonly, these surrogates emerged from the shared housing that full-time service programs (like Teach for America or AmeriCorps) arranged for recent graduates who joined their efforts. But there was one young man who formed a "Tuesday dinner club" for himself and four other "sexual minorities," where they could talk freely about spirituality and living intentionally. He actually called this his "congregation," his way of recreating the "inclusivist Masses" of his undergraduate experience.

37. There were 383 cases (out of 409 alumni web respondents) with complete data for all variables. Dependent variable was the five-level ordinal item "Since graduating from college, I have drawn upon vocational discernment and reflection to guide my decisions," with "strongly disagree" coded as 1 and "strongly agree" coded as 5. I fitted one model that simultaneously included all items, which had a significant model chi-square of 33.4

($p < .001$), a pseudo-R-square of .091 (Negelkerke), and two significant and positive predictors: months since graduation ($p < .05$) and religious service attendance ($p < .001$). Neither gender, race, field of study, nor grade point average was a significant predictor.

38. To evaluate this, I compared each program's sustainability proposal description with the program elements still in place in 2011, which was two to four years following the award's expiration. In two cases, program frugality and other extenuating circumstances meant the grant had not yet expired; those two cases are not included in the calculations above.

39. Fifty-eight of the original 88 PTEV campuses (or 66 percent) have paid to join the Council of Independent Colleges' NetVUE, according to the membership listing accessed May 24, 2011, at http://www.cic.edu/Programs-and-Services/Programs/NetVUE/Pages/default.aspx. Despite CIC's efforts to the contrary, NetVUE primarily draws CIC members: 141 of its 153 members (or 92 percent) are CIC members, with 10 of the 12 non-CIC members of NetVUE being former PTEV campuses. Or, to put it another way, 3 out of 4 joint PTEV/CIC members joined NetVUE, while only 1 out of 3 PTEV/non-CIC members joined (data courtesy of NetVUE). According to the coordinator of NetVUE, Shirley Roels, a former PTEV program director who spoke with staff on many former PTEV campuses, the reasons PTEV campuses did not join varied: some did not join because they wanted to narrow their focus to their particular theological tradition or their particular geographical region rather than join an ecumenical and national organization; some were "embarrassed" by their weaker performances in PTEV; and some very much wanted to join, but campus budget constraints or new senior administrators unfamiliar with PTEV kept them from doing so.

40. See Robert Wuthnow, *After the Baby Boomers: How Twenty- and Thirty-Somethings Are Shaping the Future of American Religion* (Princeton, NJ: Princeton University Press, 2007); Christian Smith with Kari Christoffersen, Hilary Davidson, and Patricia Snell Herzog, *Lost in Transition: The Dark Side of Emerging Adulthood* (New York: Oxford University Press, 2011); and Alexandra Robbins and Abby Wilner, *Quarterlife Crisis: The Unique Challenges of Life in Your Twenties* (New York: Tarcher, 2001).

Chapter 5

1. That figure of 790 unique faculty or staff respondents is an absolute minimum, as it presumes that 100 percent of the 79 faculty or staff participants in my field interviews on eight campuses also completed the web survey. One can reasonably assume that 20 percent or more of this "elite" target sample did not complete my web survey, having already shared their views with my evaluation team directly, pushing the number of unique faculty or staff respondents solidly into the 800s. See also app. 2, "Methodology," for further discussion of the web survey design and administration.

2. Mark R Schwehn, *Exiles from Eden: Religion and the Academic Vocation in America* (New York: Oxford University Press, 1993); and Richard Russo, *Straight Man: A Novel* (New York: Vintage, 1998).

3. Jonathon Kahn with Paul MacDonald, Ian Oliver, and Sam Speers, "Secularity and the Liberal Arts: Reconceiving the Secular and the Practice of the Liberal Arts," posted November 24, 2010, to the Social Science Research Council's Immanent Frame: Secular-

ism, Religion, and the Public Sphere website, accessed April 30, 2014, http://blogs.ssrc
.org/tif/2010/11/24/reconceiving-the-secular-and-the-practice-of-the-liberal-arts/.

4. Timothy Clydesdale, "Secularity and the Liberal Arts: Yearning, Yawning, and Resisting," posted December 8, 2010, to the Social Science Research Council's Immanent Frame: Secularism, Religion, and the Public Sphere website, accessed April 30, 2014, http://blogs.ssrc.org/tif/2010/12/08/yearning-yawning-resisting/.

5. Kahn et al., "Secularity and the Liberal Arts."

6. This does not imply that requiring instructors to welcome and respect the full range of students' religious or nonreligious perspectives would be improper; indeed, that is foundational.

7. This is an example of what counselors and conflict resolution experts call "I" language. Using it makes civil discussion possible. See Clydesdale, "Yearning, Yawning, and Resisting."

8. See Carolyn McNamara Barry and Stephanie Madsen's "Friends and Friendships among Emerging Adults," 2010, which appeared in the Who Are Emerging Adults? web forum, which I edited as part of the Changing Spirituality of Emerging Adults project, http://doc.wrlc.org/handle/2041/122313.

9. And three years later, a check of this school's website yielded terms such as *calling* and *vocation* included prominently in the school's mission, reinforced through a lecture series, and infused through the school's extensive community service programs.

10. See tables 12 and 13, "State Appropriations for Higher Education," in Sandy Baum, Jennifer Ma, and Kathleen Payea, *Analysis Brief: Trends in Public Higher Education: Enrollment, Prices, Student Aid, Revenues, and Expenditures*, 2012, accessed April 20, 2014, https://trends.collegeboard.org/sites/default/files/trends-2012-public-higher-education-expenditures-brief.pdf. Table 12 shows that state appropriations per full-time-equivalent student ranged between $8,300 and $9,300 from 1980 to 2006, then plunged to $7,200 in 2010–11 (of which $300 was a pass-through grant from the federal government); table 13 shows state and local appropriations as a percentage of net tuition and fee revenue dropping from 49 percent to 34 percent between 1998 and 2008 at public doctoral institutions, from 56 percent to 43 percent at public master's institutions during this same decade, from 56 percent to 42 percent at public bachelor's institutions, and 64 percent to 57 percent at public two-year institutions. See also National Conference for State Legislatures, Fiscal Affairs Program, "State Funding for Higher Education in FY 2009 and FY 2010," n.d., accessed April 30, 2014, http://www.ncsl.org/documents/fiscal/higheredfunding final.pdf; and John Aubrey Douglass, "Higher Education Budgets and the Global Recession: Tracking Varied National Responses and Their Consequences," Center for Studies in Higher Education, Research and Occasional Paper Series CSHE.4.10, University of California, Berkeley, 2010, accessed April 30, 2014, http://cshe.berkeley.edu/sites/default /files/shared/publications/docs/ROPS.5Douglass.HEGlobalRecession.3.13.10.pdf.

11. Ernst L. Boyer, *Scholarship Reconsidered: Priorities of the Professoriate* (Princeton, NJ: Carnegie Foundation for the Advancement of Teaching, 1990).

12. Elaine Howard Ecklund, *Science vs. Religion: What Scientists Really Think* (New York: Oxford University Press, 2010).

13. George Marsden, *The Soul of the American University: From Protestant Establishment to Established Nonbelief* (New York: Oxford University Press, 1994).

14. It is true that Pope John Paul II's *Ex corde ecclesiae* has been operationalized by the US bishops as requiring theology faculty to possess a *mandatum* (teaching authorization) from the Vatican. Very few Roman Catholic colleges or universities adhere to that requirement, however. It is also true that Roman Catholic colleges and universities have canceled some public speakers and events — but these occurrences are rare, attract disproportionate media attention, and have little connection to the academic freedom granted to campus faculty in general.

15. I recently chaired a faculty search at my own public institution — a search that required full participation of a nondepartmental faculty member on the search committee, as well as candidate interviews with the dean and provost. My institution requires this to make sure the wider interests of the college are represented during application review and candidate interviews. New hires learn that excellence in the classroom is essential, that general education is valued, that citizenship pertains as much to the college as it does to the department or discipline, and that active research programs — while important — may not trump one's commitment to undergraduate education.

16. See *Report: Survey of Faculty Interaction with Undergraduate Students*, West Campus Council Research and Evaluation Committee and Institutional Research and Planning, Cornell University, Fall 2004, accessed April 30, 2014, http://www.dpb.cornell.edu /documents/1000120.pdf.

17. This same Cornell study reports that "58% of faculty agreed that 'Cornell ignores or only minimally rewards faculty efforts at out-of-class interaction with undergraduates.'"

Chapter 6

1. Martin Seligman, *Flourish: A Visionary New Understanding of Happiness and Well-being* (New York: Free Press, 2011).

2. There are, of course, good and well-considered discussions about the definition of student development that regularly infuse graduate courses in higher education. But as with most things, the gap between theory and practice can be sizable, and hence there is a broad understanding of student development that informs how student life professionals engage a fraction of students, and an operating definition of student development that accepts student academic progress and lack of disciplinary issues as indicative of healthy development.

3. A significant claim, but we did not encounter a single student or employee whose participation in purpose exploration did not lead, in some form, to wider or better involvement with campus, regional, or global communities.

4. As evidenced by two best sellers: Gail Sheehy's *Passages: Predictable Crises of Adult Life* (New York: Dutton, 1976), and William Bridges's *Transitions: Making Sense of Life's Changes*, rev. 25th anniv. ed. (Cambridge, MA: Da Capo Press, 2004). It is also underscored by scholarly research into the life course, for which the *Handbook of the Life Course*, edited by Jeylan T. Mortimer and Michael J. Shanahan (Norwall, MA: Kluwer Academic/ Plenum Publishers, 2003), provides a good introduction, especially its chapter by Glen H.

Elder Jr., Monica Kirkpatrick Johnson, and Robert Crosnoe: "The Emergence and Development of Life Course Theory."

5. Jeffrey Jensen Arnett, *Emerging Adulthood: The Winding Road from the Late Teens through the Twenties* (New York: Oxford University Press, 2004).

6. The Institute for Intercultural Studies, founded by Margaret Mead and Gregory Bateson in 1944, used this quote as its motto until it closed in 2009. The institute was never able to identify a specific source for the quotation, but attributed it to an offhand statement by Mead that diffused orally before appearing in multiple written sources. See Institute for Intercultural Studies, "Frequently Asked Questions about Mead/Bateson," accessed December 29, 2011, http://www.interculturalstudies.org/faq.html#quote.

7. One of the support services that the initiative's coordination office provided was visits by members of the initiative's advisory board. These were generally academics who had training in student development and theological education, and aside from offering advice and recommendations during their visit, they wrote summary reports for the coordination office, site project director, and the religious division of the Lilly Endowment. I obtained all of these consultant reports as part of my general research into the initiative, and added these to the program dossiers I created for each campus that the evaluation studied. See app. 2, "Methodology," for more information.

8. I am indebted to Max Weber's work on charismatic authority, and with respect to his thinking conclude that these project directors were warm and dynamic individuals, but not charismatic figures with a capital C, like the prophets who found new religious sects. See Max Weber's *Economy and Society: An Outline of Interpretive Sociology*, ed. Guenther Roth and Claus Wittich (1913; repr., Berkeley: University of California Press, 1978).

9. Daniel Goleman, *Emotional Intelligence: Why It Can Matter More Than IQ* (London: Bloomsbury, 1996).

10. James Lang, "The Myth of First-Year Enlightenment," *Chronicle of Higher Education*, February 1, 2008.

11. The term *group* is often used loosely, but I use it sociologically to indicate a *primary group* that is self-sustaining; characterized by ongoing, face-to-face interaction; and possesses a shared sense of identity.

12. See, for example, the research on professor attractiveness and student evaluations: Daniel S. Hamermesh and A. M. Parker, "Beauty in the Classroom: Instructor's Pulchritude and Putative Pedagogical Productivity," *Economics of Education Review* 24, no. 4 (August 2005): 369–76; and Nalini Ambady and Robert Rosenthal, "Half a Minute: Predicting Teaching Evaluations from Thin Slices of Nonverbal Behavior and Physical Attractiveness," *Journal of Applied Social Psychology* 17 (1993): 108–26.

13. Dorothy C. Bass and Mark R. Schwehn's anthology, *Leading Lives That Matter: What We Should Do and Who We Should Be* (Grand Rapids, MI: Eerdmans, 2006), made this substantially easier, but its publication came during the sustainability period for most funded programs.

14. See NSSE discussion and notes in chap. 2.

15. I have no reason to think these are onetime opportunities, however; interested campuses continue to pursue them. See chap. 4's discussion of NetVUE.

16. Tim Clydesdale, "Wake Up and Smell the New Epistemology," *Chronicle Review*, January 23, 2009.

17. Malcolm Gladwell, *The Tipping Point: How Little Things Can Make a Big Difference* (Boston: Little, Brown, 2000).

18. For example, Neil Fairbairn, *A Brief History of Gardening* (New York: Rodale Books, 2001); and Anthony Huxley, *An Illustrated History of Gardening* (Guilford, CT: Lyons Press, 1998).

Chapter 7

1. Robin Marantz Henig, "What Is It about 20-somethings? Why Are So Many People in Their 20s Taking So Long to Grow Up?" *New York Times Magazine*, August 18, 2010.

2. See, for example, book 4 of Plato's *Republic* (Plato, *The Republic: The Influential Classic* [originally published ca. 380; repr., Padstow, Cornwall, UK: Wiley, 2012]) or chaps. 1–7 of the Bible's book of Proverbs.

3. Author's analysis of 1960 and 2010 US census data, extracted from the Integrated Public Use Microdata Series (IPUMS), Minnesota Population Center, University of Minnesota.

4. Reported by both Jeffrey Jensen Arnett, *Emerging Adulthood: The Winding Road from the Late Teens through the Twenties* (New York: Oxford University Press, 2004); and Frank F. Furstenberg Jr., Sheela Kennedy, Vonnie C. McLoyd, Rubén G. Rumbaut, and Richard A. Settersten, "Growing Up Is Harder to Do," *Contexts* 3, no. 3 (2004): 33–41.

5. See *National Assessment of Adult Literacy Report*, US Department of Education, 2003, accessed April 30, 2014, http://necs.ed.gov/NAAL/; *National Study of Student Engagement: Annual Reports*, 2000–2013, accessed April 30, 2014, http://nsse.iub.edu/html/annual_results.cfm and http://nsse.iub.edu/html/past_annual_results.cfm; and Richard Arum and Josipa Roksa, *Academically Adrift: Limited Learning on College Campuses* (Chicago: University of Chicago Press, 2010).

6. See Christine B. Whelan, *Generation WTF: From "What the #%$&?" to a Wise, Tenacious, and Fearless You* (West Conshohocken, PA: Templeton Press, 2011); Alexandra Robbins and Abby Wilner, *Quarterlife Crisis: The Unique Challenges of Life in Your Twenties* (New York: Tarcher, 2001); Richard Arum and Josipa Roksa, *Aspiring Adults Adrift: Tentative Transitions of College Graduates* (Chicago: University of Chicago Press, 2014); Christian Smith with Kari Christoffersen, Hilary Davidson, and Patricia Snell Herzog, *Lost in Transition: The Dark Side of Emerging Adulthood* (New York: Oxford University Press, 2011).

7. Steven Brint, "Schooling in the Developing World," in *Schools and Societies* (Thousand Oaks, CA: Sage Publications, 1998).

8. For example, Andrew Hacker and Claudia Dreifus, *Higher Education? How Colleges Are Wasting Our Money and Failing Our Kids—and What We Can Do about It* (New York: Times Books, 2010); Mark C. Taylor, "End the University as We Know It," *New York Times*, April 26, 2009; and Mark C. Taylor, *Crisis on Campus: A Bold Plan for Reforming Our Colleges and Universities* (New York: Knopf, 2010).

9. See Katherine S. Newman, *The Accordion Family: Boomerang Kids, Anxious Parents,*

and the Private Toll of Global Competition (Boston: Beacon Press, 2012); Jennifer Tanner, "Mental Health in Emerging Adulthood," *Who Are Emerging Adults?*, 2010, Changing
Spirituality of Emerging Adults Project, Catholic University of America, http://doc.wrlc
.org/handle/2041/122327. See also Arum and Roksa, *Aspiring Adults Adrift*; and Smith
et al., *Lost in Transition.*

10. A campus could, for example, require a closing course on career development in a
globally competitive era, which prepares students to (1) think like independent contrac-
tors regardless of their official status — continually developing skills and knowledge to
remain marketable, (2) keep track of industry changes and developments, and (3) be alert
to specific global phenomena that will shape career opportunities. I have not encountered
such a closing course, but such a course may well exist and, if not, would be fairly easy for
a career counselor and economist to create and coteach.

11. Katherine S. Newman, "Ties That Bind: Cultural Interpretations of Delayed Adulthood in Western Europe and Japan," *Sociological Forum* 23, no. 4 (December 2008):
645–69.

12. Sandy Baum, Jennifer Ma, and Kathleen Payea, *Education Pays 2010: The Benefits
of Higher Education for Individuals and Society*, Trends in Higher Education Series (New
York: College Board Advocacy and Policy Center, 2010), fig. 1.3, accessed April 30, 2014,
https://trends.collegeboard.org/sites/default/files/education-pays-2010-full-report.pdf.

13. Thomas Vander Ven, *Getting Wasted: Why College Students Drink Too Much and
Party So Hard* (New York: New York University Press, 2011); see also Smith et al., *Lost in
Transition.*

14. From author's review of the *National Study of Student Engagement: Annual Reports.*

15. Some may prefer to redouble efforts to draw in more lovers of the liberal arts;
on campuses where the liberal arts program is moribund, that might be useful. And Delbanco, like many before him, makes a compelling case for more attention to teaching,
which would also be useful. See Andrew Delbanco, *College: What It Was, Is, and Should Be*
(Princeton, NJ: Princeton University Press, 2012). But nationally, we have had a liberal
arts model in place for scores of years; if it were going to convert the majority of students
into idealists, it would have done so by now. Instead of fruitless efforts to turn everyone
into a lover of learning, we should work to turn everyone into a respecter of learning. For
a fuller discussion of this issue, see Tim Clydesdale, "Wake Up and Smell the New Epistemology," *Chronicle Review*, January 23, 2009.

16. "Leadership is a self-concept measure comprising the student's self-rating on six
traits that are often exhibited by persons in leadership roles: social self-confidence, understanding of others, cooperativeness, leadership ability, and public speaking ability." Alexander W. Astin, Helen S. Astin, and Jennifer A. Lindholm, *Cultivating the Spirit: How College
Can Enhance Students' Inner Lives* (San Francisco: Jossey-Bass, 2010), 122.

17. Astin, Astin, and Lindholm's study was drawn from students at 136 colleges and
universities, both public and private. The authors do not reveal the identities of their 136
participating institutions, so it is possible, then, that their sample included some of the 88
PTEV campuses, but it is highly unlikely that more than a few PTEV colleges or universities were included. Astin, Astin, and Lindholm's results, then, may be safely interpreted as
coming from campuses without purpose exploration programming.

18. Astin, Astin, and Lindholm, *Cultivating the Spirit*, 31.

19. The term *gracious* was deployed by one evangelical college to describe its engagement of a nonevangelical world without surrendering its particularist, and hence defining, worldview.

20. Eighty-one percent of current students who participated in purpose exploration, and 86 percent of alumni who participated, agreed that their participation "encouraged me to both see and serve the needs of others." Sixty-six percent of current students, and 59 percent of alumni, also indicated that they were "committed to making a positive contribution to the church both now and in the future." Data are from the evaluation's web survey of nine campus programs. See app. 2 for further information about the survey.

21. George D. Kuh and Robert M. Gonyea, "Spirituality, Liberal Learning, and College Student Engagement," *Liberal Education* (Winter 2006): 40–47.

22. Arthur W. Chickering, Jon C. Dalton, and Liesa Stamm, *Encouraging Authenticity and Spirituality in Higher Education* (San Francisco: Jossey-Bass, 2006).

23. Parker J. Palmer and Arthur Zajonc, *The Heart of Higher Education: A Call to Renewal* (San Francisco: Jossey-Bass, 2010).

24. Robert J. Nash and Michele C. Murray, *Helping College Students Find Purpose: The Campus Guide to Meaning-Making* (San Francisco: Jossey-Bass, 2010).

25. See Christian Smith with Melinda Lundquist Denton, *Soul Searching: The Religious and Spiritual Lives of American Teenagers* (New York: Oxford University Press, 2005); and Christian Smith with Patricia Snell, *Souls in Transition: The Religious and Spiritual Lives of Emerging Adults* (New York: Oxford University Press, 2009).

26. See Hilde de Ridder-Symoens, ed., *A History of the University in Europe*, vol. 1, *Universities in the Middle Ages* (New York: Cambridge University Press, 1992). See also George Marsden, *The Soul of the American University: From Protestant Establishment to Established Nonbelief* (New York: Oxford University Press, 1994).

27. See Astin, Astin, and Lindholm, *Cultivating the Spirit*.

28. See Linda DeAngelo, Sylvia Hurtado, John H. Pryor, Kimberly R. Kelly, José Luis Santos, and William S. Korn, *The American College Teacher: National Norms for the 2007–2008 HERI Faculty Survey* (Los Angeles: Higher Education Research Institute, 2009), 42.

29. See DeAngelo et al., *American College Teacher*.

30. See Anna Neumann's *Professing to Learn: Creating Tenured Lives and Careers in the American Research University* (Baltimore: Johns Hopkins University Press, 2009); see also the outpouring of discussion that followed publication of Robin Wilson's "Why Are Associate Professors So Unhappy?," in the June 3, 2012, issue of *Chronicle of Higher Education*.

31. There was clear variance by type of four-year institution in faculty views on students' spiritual development, with nearly two-thirds agreeing at private, religiously affiliated colleges, down to one-fifth at public universities. See DeAngelo et al., *American College Teacher*.

32. At least in second-tier programming. Since new educators and new students join academic communities each year, campuses that discern a need for implicit theology might be wise to maintain that in their first-tier programming and general campus communication.

33. See Network for Vocation in Undergraduate Education, "View the NETVUE

members," Council of Independent Colleges, http://www.cic.edu/Programs-and-Services/Programs/NetVUE/Pages/View-the-NetVUE-Members.aspx.

34. Grigsby estimates that the individualist trajectory guides slightly more than one out of two American college students, the traditionalist guides more than one out of three students, and together they comprise the default trajectories of nearly 90 percent of American college students. See Mary Grigsby, *College Life through the Eyes of Students* (Albany, NY: SUNY Press, 2009), 141 ff.

35. See Arum and Roksa, *Aspiring Adults Adrift*; Smith et al., *Lost in Transition*; Robbins and Wilner, *Quarterlife Crisis*; Tanner, "Mental Health in Emerging Adulthood"; Gina Oberto, "A Lost Generation," *Huffington Post*, June 8, 2012; and Sarah Shanfield, "What It Means to Be 25 Today," *Huffington Post*, June 15, 2012.

36. Although a graduating senior at my institution recently confided that he had been homeless for about a month during a previous semester, living out of his car and using the gym's locker rooms to shower. Upon my relaying this, a colleague shared several similar stories, suggesting that at least some fraction of students find themselves on the razor's edge of survival during their college years. This deserves closer attention by scholars of American higher education, and may well be a result of declining need-based support for students.

37. Tanner, "Mental Health in Emerging Adulthood."

38. Newman, *Accordion Family*.

39. Smith et al., *Lost in Transition*.

40. See Richard Settersten and Barbara Ray, *Not Quite Adults: Why 20-somethings Are Choosing a Slower Path to Adulthood, and Why It's Good for Everyone* (New York: Bantam Trade Paperbacks, 2010).

41. Tim Clydesdale, *The First Year Out: Understanding American Teens after High School* (Chicago: University of Chicago Press, 2007).

42. William Damon, *The Path to Purpose: Helping Our Children Find Their Calling in Life* (New York: Free Press, 2008).

43. See n. 35 for this chapter.

44. Angela L. Duckworth, Christopher Peterson, Michael D. Matthews, and Dennis R. Kelly, "Grit: Perseverance and Passion for Long-Term Goals," *Journal of Personality and Social Psychology* 92, no. 6 (2007): 1087–1101; and Martin Seligman, *Flourish: A Visionary New Understanding of Happiness and Well-being* (New York: Free Press, 2011).

45. See n. 42 for this chapter; and Richard Lerner, *The Good Teen* (New York: Three Rivers Press, 2007).

46. Diane Ravitch, *The Death and Life of the Great American School System* (New York: Basic Books, 2010).

47. See Clydesdale, "Wake Up and Smell the New Epistemology."

Appendix 2

1. Alexander W. Astin, Helen S. Astin, and Jennifer A. Lindholm, *Cultivating the Spirit: How College Can Enhance Students' Inner Lives* (San Francisco: Jossey-Bass, 2010), 31.

The letter *f* following a page number denotes a figure, and the letter *t* denotes a table. Names of colleges/universities in quotation marks are pseudonyms.

Fabric of This World, The (Hardy), 283
faculty: academic advising by, 51, 81, 102–3,
304n15, 308n11; academic counseling
by, 308n11; academic freedom of, 161,
205, 315n14; attractiveness and student
evaluations of, 316n12; campus good citizens (*see* campus good citizens); campus
stars, 136–37, 181; candidate search process for, 315n15; career counseling by, 62,
109, 308n11; challenges faced by, 55–56;
characteristics of effective, 83; on church-
affiliated campuses, 154–63; cocurricular activities of, 153; as cofacilitators at
retreats, 38; community-engaged learning grants for, 195–96; conversations on
meaning and purpose with, 174–75; curricular development grants for, 194–96;
daily work pattern of, 136–38, 209–10;
deadwood, 136t, 137, 181, 209; in design
process, 194; development programs for,
68, 81–82, 292–93; early adopters, 152,
212; effects of PTEV on, 212; employment status of, 51, 304n14; on ethnic and
evangelical campuses, 163–69; fellowships
for, to explore theology of vocation, 145;
flourishing, 172; in focus groups, 163, 233,
238–40, 245, 255–56; in future purpose
exploration programs, 195–96; garden
analogy for, 184, 194, 212; on goals of
undergraduate education, 217–18; identity
of, 174; incentives for participation of in
PTEV, 151–53; and incorporating meaning and purpose exploration in classroom,
226–27; institutional context for, 135–42;
institutional grumblers, 136t, 137, 181, 210;
institutional grunts, 136–37, 181, 209–10;
interviews with, 233, 238–41, 244–45,
266–67; junior, participation in research
by, 39; life course location of, 174; marginalizing, 179t, 183–84; minigrants for,
195–96; moral language use by, 71; new
epistemology and, 229–30; occupational
orientation of, 136–38, 209–10; positive
engagement by, 51, 195; in proexploration
communities, 153, 176, 196; promentorship culture of, 68, 70; on PTEV's impact, 132, 133t, 134, 313n1; receptivity to
purpose exploration of, 174; reflexivity

of, 212, 218; residential program, involvement with, 77, 194–95, 292; resocialization of, 135–36; retreats for, 290; sample
bias with, 240–41; in seminars on PTEV,
27–34, 40, 64–65, 302n3; for service-
learning projects, 64; on spiritual development during higher education, 76, 217,
302n13; strategic blunders related to, 181–
83; tenure-track (*see* tenure-track faculty); types of, 136–38, 181, 209–10; on
virtually unaffiliated campuses, 142–49,
162–63; web survey for, 248–50, 267,
270–73
Farmer, Paul, 16, 284, 301n9
Farnham, S. G., *Listening Hearts*, 283
Faust, Drew Giplin, 302n14
Fehr, Ernst, 310n23
fellowship programs, 64, 81, 294
Field of Dreams fallacy, 179t, 184–85
First Year Out, The (Clydesdale), 300–301n5
First Year Out of College, The (Clydesdale),
303n8
foundations, forced innovations by, 228–29
free riders, 37, 113, 128, 209, 308–9n16
freshman programs: at "College of Douglass
and DuBois," 70–73; at "Ignatius University," 39–40; internalizing purpose and
vocation through, 115; at "Pullman College," 67; resistance in, 173; strategic blunders related to, 181; visiting of exploration
residence halls in, 195
Freud, Sigmund, 283
Future Intelligentsia: conversations on meaning and purpose with, 175; description
of, 88; on educational performance continuum, 87f; engagement of, positive,
128–29; instrumental vs. idealistic orientation of, 87f, 209; life course location of,
174; life trajectory of, 110–12; new epistemology and, 229–30; prevalence of, on
campus, 174; in proexploration communities, 176; in purpose exploration programs,
89, 97, 128–29, 211; retention of, 97
Futures Project (2005), xxi

Gill, J. P., *Listening Hearts*, 283
"God squad," 90, 115
Goleman, Daniel, 50–51